BRAZIL
EMPIRE AND REPUBLIC
1822–1930

The complete *Cambridge History of Latin America* presents a large-scale authoritative survey of Latin America's unique historical experience from the first contact between Indians and Europeans at the end of the fifteenth century to the present day. *Brazil: Empire and Republic, 1822–1930* is a selection of five chapters from volumes III and V – three on the Empire (1822–89) and two on the First Republic (1889–1930) – brought together to provide a continuous history of Brazil from independence in 1822 to the Revolution of 1930. A chapter on the separation of Brazil from Portugal (1808–22) forms an introduction to the volume and a link with *Colonial Brazil*, a collection of chapters drawn from volumes I and II of the *Cambridge History of Latin America*. Bibliographical essays are included for all chapters. The book will be a valuable text for both teachers and students of Latin American history.

The following titles drawn from
The Cambridge History of Latin America edited by Leslie Bethell
are available in hardcovers and paperback:

Colonial Spanish America

Colonial Brazil

The Independence of Latin America

Spanish America after Independence, *c.* 1820–*c.* 1870

Brazil: Empire and Republic, 1822–1930

Latin America: Economy and Society, 1870–1930

BRAZIL
EMPIRE AND REPUBLIC
1822–1930

edited by

LESLIE BETHELL

Professor of Latin American History
University of London

CAMBRIDGE
UNIVERSITY PRESS

Published by the Press Syndicate of the University of Cambridge
The Pitt Building, Trumpington Street, Cambridge, CB2 1RP
40 West 20th Street, New York, NY 10011-4211, USA
10 Stamford Road, Oakleigh, Victoria 3166, Australia

The cintents of this book were previously published as part of
Volumes III and V of *The Cambridge History of Latin America*,
copyright © Cambridge University Press, 1985 and 1986

© Cambridge University Press 1989

First published in 1989
Reprinted 1993

British Library cataloguing in publication data
Brazil: empire and republic, 1822-1930
I. Brazil, 1822-1930
I. Bethell, Leslie II. The Cambridge history of Latin America
981.'04

Library of Congress cataloging in publication data
Brazil, empier and republic: 1822-1930 / edited by Leslie Bethell.
p. cm.
"Previously published as part of volume III and V of the
Cambridge history of Latin America ... 1985 and 1986" - T.p. verso.
Bibliography: p.
Includes index.
ISBN 0-521-36293-8 - ISBN 0-521-36837-5 (pbk.)
I. Brazil - History - 1822-1889. 2. Brazil - History - 1889-1930.
I. Bethell, Leslie.
F2535.B76 1989
981'.04-dc19 88 26736 CIP

ISBN 0-521-36293-8 hardback
ISBN 0-521-36837-5 paperback

Transferred to digital printing 1999

CONTENTS

MAPS

PREFACE

The Cambridge History of Latin America is a large scale, collaborative, multivolume history of Latin America during the five centuries since the first contacts between Europeans and the native peoples of the Americas in the late fifteenth and early sixteenth centuries.

Brazil: Empire and Republic, 1822–1930 brings together five chapters from volumes III and v of the *Cambridge History* – three on the Empire (1822–89) and two on the First Republic (1889–1930) – to provide in a single volume an economic, social and political history of Brazil from independence in 1822 to the Revolution of 1930. This, it is hoped, will be useful for both teachers and students of Latin American history. A chapter on the separation of Brazil from Portugal (1808–22) forms an introduction to the volume and a link with *Colonial Brazil*, a collection of seven chapters drawn from volumes I and II of *The Cambridge History of Latin America*. Each chapter is accompanied by a bibliographical essay.

Introduction

FROM COLONY TO EMPIRE

1

THE INDEPENDENCE OF BRAZIL

Portugal at the end of the eighteenth century was a small, economically backward, culturally isolated country on the edge of western Europe, with limited natural resources and only modest military and naval strength, but, at least on the face of it, with one great asset: a world-wide empire stretching across three continents which included the vast and potentially rich colony of Brazil. Portugal's overseas territories in Asia, Africa and America, and above all Brazil, were an important source of crown revenue; income over and above what was necessary to administer and maintain the empire was drawn from taxes on production, consumption and internal trade, from crown monopolies, from voluntary donations (some more voluntary than others) and from duties on imports and exports. Portugal maintained as far as possible a monopoly of trade within its empire and, as well as being the hubs of the trade in Portuguese goods, Lisbon and Oporto were the entrepôts for non-Portuguese goods exported to the colonies and colonial produce imported and re-exported to the rest of Europe. Brazilian re-exports in particular – in the late eighteenth century primarily sugar and cotton – were essential for Portugal's balance of trade. England was Portugal's principal trading partner, supplying Portugal and, indirectly, Brazil with manufactured goods (mainly textiles) in return for wine, olive oil and Brazilian cotton. (During the first three-quarters of the eighteenth century Brazilian gold had also been a major item in Anglo-Portuguese trade, legal and illegal.) Under treaties going back to the end of the fourteenth century England was also the guarantor of Portugal's independence and the territorial integrity of the Portuguese empire.

During the second half of the eighteenth century, that is to say, during the reigns of José I (1750–77), Maria I (1777–92) and from 1792, when Dona Maria was declared mentally incapable, the Prince Regent João, the future João VI, Portugal, like Spain under the late Bourbons, had taken stock of itself and its empire. Sebastião José de Carvalho e Melo, the Marquês de Pombal, who was in effect prime minister, virtually dictator, throughout the reign of Dom José I, and his successors, notably Martinho de Melo e Castro, Secretary of State for the Navy and Overseas Territories (1770–95), and Rodrigo de Sousa Coutinho, later Conde de Linhares, Secretary of State for the Navy and Overseas Territories (1796–1801) and President of the Royal Treasury (1801–3), were influenced by the 'enlightened' ideas of the time as well as by political and economic realities. They initiated and implemented a series of administrative and economic measures aimed at overcoming Portugal's economic and cultural backwardness and lessening her economic and political dependence on England. Portuguese agriculture was to be modernized; manufacturing, especially the textile industry, developed; education improved; colonial trade expanded; a greater proportion of the profits of empire retained; the balance of trade deficit reduced; and, above all, in a period of rising government expenditure, especially on defence, both in Portugal and in the empire, state revenues increased.

As far as Brazil was concerned this meant in the first place a tightening up, and to some extent a centralization, of administration. The Estado de Grão Pará e Maranhão, a separate state since 1621, was integrated into an enlarged Estado do Brasil in 1774 under a single viceroy (whose seat had been transferred in 1763 from Salvador to Rio de Janeiro). In practice, however, the viceroy had only limited powers outside the captaincy-general of Rio de Janeiro and its subordinate captaincies of Santa Catarina and Rio Grande do Sul. The governors-general and governors of the eight other captaincies-general – Grão Pará (which included the subordinate captaincy of Rio Negro), Maranhão (including Piauí), Pernambuco (including Ceará, Rio Grande do Norte and Paraíba) Bahia (including Sergipe and Espírito Santo), Minas Gerais, São Paulo, Mato Grosso, and Goiás – were for the most part directly responsible to Lisbon. The authority of the district (*comarca*) and county (*município*) crown judges (*ouvidores* and *juízes de fora*), who had administrative as well as judicial duties, was strengthened at the expense, for example, of the elected *senados da câmara* (town councils). And methods of tax collection in particular were improved. But there was nothing like the intendancy system introduced into Spanish America. Secondly, strictly within the framework of the mercantilist monopoly, colonial trade was somewhat liberalized. The *frota* (fleet) system between Portugal, Bahia and Rio de

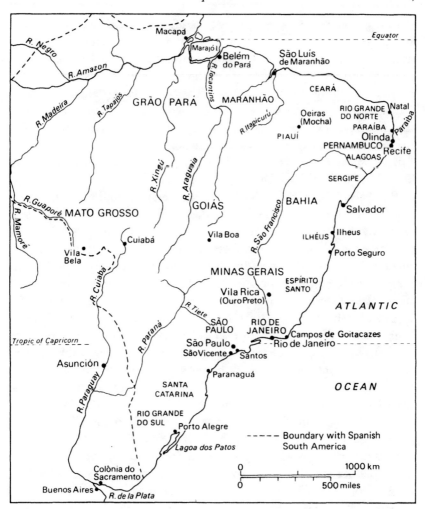

Map 1   Colonial Brazil, *c.* 1800

Janeiro was ended in 1766; the privileged companies created to trade with Grão Pará and Maranhão and with Pernambuco and Paraíba in 1755 and 1759 (and replacing the fleets to São Luís and Recife) were themselves wound up in 1778–9; some of the state monopolies were abolished. Thirdly, great efforts were made to stimulate production for export, which it was hoped would at the same time widen the market for Portuguese manufactures. (The restrictions on local manufacturing, particularly textiles, were considerably reinforced in, for example, 1785.)

This was a matter of some urgency since after more than a century and a half of growth and prosperity based primarily on plantation agriculture and, during the first half of the eighteenth century, gold and diamond mining, the third quarter of the eighteenth century was for Brazil a period of prolonged economic crisis. The North-East (Pernambuco and Bahia) had lost its virtual monopoly of world sugar production in the middle of the seventeenth century and, though sugar remained Brazil's major cash crop, exports had stagnated somewhat since the 1680s. The production and export of gold and diamonds from Minas Gerais, Goiás and Mato Grosso declined steeply after 1755.

Pombal and his successors failed to regenerate the mining industry of the interior, but by the 1780s, partly as a result of their efforts, coastal Brazil was beginning to experience an agricultural renaissance.[1] This was reinforced in the late eighteenth century by the steady expansion of the market for foodstuffs, including sugar, and raw materials, especially cotton, as a result of population growth, urbanization and the beginnings of industrialization in Western Europe. The French Revolution and its consequences, not least the bloody slave uprising in the French sugar island of Saint Domingue, crippled many of Brazil's competitors and raised world prices for primary produce. Moreover, unlike Spain, which from 1796 until the crisis of 1808 was virtually cut off from its colonies, Portugal until 1807 remained neutral in the wars which followed the French Revolution and the rise of Napoleon, and trade between Portugal and its colonies was not seriously disrupted. The main sugar producing captaincies-general, Bahia and Pernambuco, recovered, albeit temporarily, something like their former prosperity. Increasing quantities of sugar were also exported from the captaincy-general of Rio de Janeiro, where Campos de Goitacazes and the rural hinterland of the capital itself were the centres of production (exports of sugar from Rio doubled between 1790 and 1807), and from São Paulo. Cotton, which was primarily produced in the North (Maranhão and Ceará) and in Pernambuco but now also in Rio de Janeiro, strengthened its position as Brazil's second major export crop. Bahia continued to export tobacco as well as sugar. And in different parts of Brazil new exports emerged; for example, cacao in Pará, rice in Maranhão, Pará and Rio de Janeiro, wheat in Rio Grande do Sul. At the end of the 1790s significant quantities of coffee were for the first time exported from Rio de Janeiro. (Coffee

---

[1] For a discussion of the Brazilian economy in the second half of the eighteenth century, and especially the 'agricultural renaissance', see Dauril Alden, *CHLA* II, ch.15.

exports from Rio were to increase sevenfold between 1798 and 1807, signalling the modest beginning of the Brazilian economy's coffee cycle which was to last for more than a century.)

The growth of Brazil's agricultural exports in volume and in value during the last quarter of the eighteenth century, and most dramatically from the mid-1790s, was the biggest single factor behind Portugal's apparent prosperity in the early years of the nineteenth century. J. B. von Spix and C. F. P. von Martius, the German naturalists, described Lisbon as a scene of 'activity and opulence'; it was 'after London . . . the first commercial place in the world'.[2] Portugal's trade with the rest of the world was in surplus in all but two years during the period 1791–1807 and, even more remarkably, with England alone from 1798. Brazilian produce, mainly sugar and cotton, accounted for 80 per cent of the imports from Portugal's colonies and 60 per cent of Portugal's exports and re-exports.[3] As early as 1779 Martinho de Melo e Castro had recognized that 'without Brazil Portugal is an insignificant power'. Twenty-five years later Portugal's dependence on Brazil's resources was greater still. Brazil's economic growth 1780–1800, however, coincided with, and was partly the result of, the Industrial Revolution in Britain and, especially, the unprecedented growth of the British textile and iron and steel industries. The expanding Brazilian market was supplied not with Portuguese but with British manufactures, either as before through the British factory, the community of British merchants in Lisbon, or else on an increasing scale directly smuggled through Brazilian ports, especially Rio de Janeiro, despite all Portugal's efforts, supported by the British merchants resident in Portugal, to prevent unauthorized ships trading with Brazil. From the 1790s Portugal, an underdeveloped dependent metropolis, had an adverse balance of trade with its most important overseas territory. It might be added here that demographic as well as economic forces were also moving against Portugal. At the end of the eighteenth century the population of Brazil (not counting the Indians outside Portuguese control) was more than two million, albeit only 30 per cent white, and growing faster than that of Portugal. Some estimates put it as high as 3–3½ million which was in fact the population of Portugal at the time. Clearly the population of Brazil would soon surpass, if it had

[2] Quoted in Kenneth R. Maxwell, *Conflicts and conspiracies. Brazil and Portugal 1750–1808* (Cambridge, 1973), 234.

[3] For a discussion of Portugal's (and Brazil's) trade in the late eighteenth century, see Andrée Mansuy-Diniz Silva, *CHLA* I, ch.13, Dauril Alden, *CHLA*, II ch.15, and Fernando A. Novais, *Portugal e Brasil na crise do antigo sistema colonial (1777–1808)* (São Paulo, 1979).

not already surpassed, that of Portugal. 'So heavy a branch', wrote
Robert Southey in his *Journal of a Residence in Portugal 1800–1*, 'cannot long
remain upon so rotten a trunk.'[4]

Some historians have argued that the roots of Brazilian national self-
consciousness are to be found in the middle of the seventeenth century in
the victory in 1654 over the Dutch, who occupied the North-East for a
quarter of a century, or even before, in the exploration of the interior of
Brazil by the *bandeirantes* of São Paulo and the early conflicts with Spain in
the Río de la Plata. It was, however, during the second half of the
eighteenth century that there emerged in Brazil, as in the English and
Spanish colonies in the New World, a more acute and more generalized
sense of their separate identity among some sectors of the white,
American-born colonial oligarchy, which in Brazil consisted primarily of
senhores de engenho (sugar planters and millowners), cattle barons and other
poderosos da terra, and, to a lesser extent, mine-owners, merchants, judges
and bureaucrats. A minority, though a sizeable minority, of Brazilians
now travelled to Europe and were influenced, however indirectly, by the
new intellectual climate they encountered there; more Brazilians were
educated at Coimbra and other European universities like Montpellier,
Edinburgh and Paris; despite the efforts of the Board of Censorship in
Lisbon more books were imported into Brazil from Europe (and from
North America) and found their way to private libraries; some may even
have been read. As a result of the economic, demographic – and
intellectual – growth of Brazil in the late eighteenth century voices could
be heard for the first time on a significant scale criticizing, first, the
mercantilist system and the restrictions it imposed on colonial trade and
therefore on agricultural production, secondly, excessive taxation and,
thirdly, the limited availability and high price of imported manufactured
goods. And the demand for liberalization beyond the limited measures
implemented by Pombal and his successors was not confined to the
economic sphere. A few liberals – mostly intellectuals, lawyers, bureaucrats and priests, but some landowners and merchants – were prepared to
challenge Portuguese absolutism and demand at least a greater degree of
political autonomy and Brazilian participation in government.

There was thus in Brazil a growing awareness of conflicts of interest,
economic and political, real and potential, with the metropolis, and at the

---

[4] Robert Southey, *Journal of a residence in Portugal 1800–1 and a visit to France 1839*, ed. Adolfo Cabral
(Oxford, 1960), 137–9.

same time not only of Portugal's relative economic backwardness *vis-à-vis* its most important colony but also its political and military weakness. The Portuguese crown had a monopoly of political legitimacy and had an important bureaucratic function; it provided, above all, political and social stability. It had, however, little military power. As late as 1800 there were in Brazil only around 2,000 regular troops, *tropas da linha* or *tropa paga*, compared with more than 6,000 in New Spain, for example. Moreover, many of the officers were Brazilian-born, from prominent colonial landed or military families, and the rank and file were mostly recruited in the colony. No wholly European units were stationed in Rio until the 1760s and there were none in Bahia until 1818. Officers in the *milícia*, the reserve army in case of external attack or slave uprising, were mostly landowners and the rank and file theoretically were all the free men in a particular geographic area, except in the major towns where the organization of the militia was based on colour and occupation. The third line *corpos de ordenanças* (territorial units) responsible for internal order and recruitment for the regular army were also dominated by the Brazilian landed class.

Discontent with the economic and political control exercised from Lisbon and hostility between native-born Brazilians and the Portuguese in Brazil, who monopolized so many of the higher offices of state and who dominated the Atlantic trade, was undoubtedly becoming both more extensive and more intensive in the late eighteenth century. But it should not be exaggerated. Brazilians had much closer ties with the metropolis, and much less cause for dissatisfaction, than had the creoles in Spain's American colonies and for many different reasons.

In the first place, the Brazilian oligarchy was for the most part less firmly rooted; Portuguese settlement of Brazil had been a slow, gradual process (the population of the settled areas as late as 1700 was less than half a million) and although there were, of course, particularly in Bahia and Pernambuco, landed families which could trace their origins back to the *donatários* of the sixteenth century, many prominent Brazilian land-owners were only first generation Brazilians (or even Portuguese-born but already identifying with Brazil). Secondly, Portuguese colonial rule was by no means as oppressive or as exclusive as Spanish rule; Portugal was a weaker power with more limited financial, military – and human – resources; the Brazilian-born were to be found throughout the middle and lower ranks of the bureaucracy and they even penetrated the ranks of the crown magistrates and governors, not only in Brazil but in other parts of the Portuguese empire such as Goa and Angola and held senior administrative posts in Portugal itself. Much more than Spain, Portugal governed through the local dominant class which was directly involved in at least the implementation if not the formation of policy; entrenched colonial interests were rarely challenged. Thirdly, the family and personal ties which existed between members of the Brazilian and Portuguese elites were sustained and reinforced by their common intellectual formation – predominantly at the university of Coimbra. Unlike Spanish America, Brazil itself had no universities – nor even a printing press – in the colonial period. Fourthly, unlike colonial Spanish America (except Cuba) where native American Indians formed the bulk of the labour force, Brazil was a slave society. Slaves constituted a third or more of the total population and were a characteristic feature of both rural and urban society throughout Brazil. A further 30 per cent of the population was free mulatto or free black. In areas given over to single-crop, export oriented, plantation agriculture like the Mata of Pernambuco, the Recôncavo of Bahia, the coastal region of Maranhão and, increasingly towards the end of the eighteenth century, parts of Rio de Janeiro slaves probably formed the majority of the population. The white minority lived with the fear of social and racial upheaval and was prepared to compromise with the metropolis and accept colonial rule in the interests of social control. Fifthly, the economy of Brazil in the late eighteenth century was, as we have seen, overwhelmingly agricultural and pastoral and, moreover, export oriented. Unlike most Spanish American *hacendados*, *senhores de engenho* and other plantation owners in Brazil had close links with metropolitan merchants, the Atlantic trade and through the metropolitan entrepôts, Lisbon and Oporto, European markets. And the export economy based on agriculture was growing during the last quarter of the eighteenth century, booming even in the 1790s. The planter class was at the same time dependent on the transatlantic slave trade, a predominantly Portuguese enterprise, for their labour supply. And the producers of meat, cereals, hides, oxen and mules in the *sertão* of the North East or in Rio Grande do Sul were in turn heavily dependent on the plantation sector. Compared with colonial Spanish America the domestic economy and internal trade were modest in scale. And Brazil had few, and small, cities; in 1800 only Rio de Janeiro and Salvador had populations of 50,000. Sixthly, Portugal's commercial monopoly was less jealously guarded than Spain's; British manufactures made up the bulk of Portuguese exports to Brazil through Lisbon and, on an increasing scale, directly as well.

Finally, Portugal's reappraisal of its political and economic relations with its colonies and the imperial reorganization which occurred in the second half of the eighteenth century was less far-reaching than Spain's and amounted to less of a direct threat to the colonial status quo and the interests of the colonial elite. On the contrary, many Brazilians profited from the 'agricultural renaissance', the confiscation of Jesuit properties after the expulsion of the Jesuits in 1759 and the expansion of trade, and the growth of the bureaucracy – and the militia – opened up new opportunities for participation in public affairs. The fact is that although Portugal and Brazil did not entirely avoid the 'Democratic Revolution' and the 'crisis of the old colonial system' in the Atlantic world in the second half of the eighteenth century there were only two significant conspiracies (they hardly had time to develop into rebellions) against Portuguese rule in Brazil – the first in Minas Gerais in 1788–9 and the second in Bahia in 1798. (Two other conspiracies – in Rio de Janeiro (1794) and in Pernambuco (1801) – were stifled at birth.)

The *Inconfidência mineira* was by far the most serious of the anti-Portuguese movements of the late eighteenth century. Minas Gerais in the 1780s was one of Brazil's most important and populous captaincies, but one which was undergoing a serious recession as it adjusted to the decline of the mining industry since the mid-1750s and the transition to a mixed agricultural and pastoral economy. It was also a captaincy with a rich intellectual and cultural life. Some of the wealthiest and most influential men in the region – crown judges, *fazendeiros*, merchants, tax farmers, lawyers, priests, regular army officers – were involved in the conspiracy. Most were Brazilian-born, a few were Portuguese. The ideological justification for rebellion was provided by a brilliant generation of intellectuals and poets, many of whom had studied at Coimbra and in France. (An unusually high proportion of the Brazilians educated at Coimbra in the 1770s and 1780s were *mineiros*.) It began as a protest against increasingly oppressive, and clumsily imposed, taxation, especially the collection of arrears in the payment of the royal fifth on gold, the *derrama* (head tax), and a more efficient and less corrupt system of tax collection, but it soon became anti-colonial in character, aiming to end Portuguese rule in Minas Gerais – and Brazil. Its leaders, inspired by the American Revolution, dreamed of a 'republic as free and as prosperous as English America'. The conspiracy, however, failed; it was discovered and the principal conspirators were arrested, tried, banished and, in the case of Joaquim José da Silva Xavier (known as 'Tiradentes', the Toothpuller), hanged. And it is important to remember that the

Inconfidência mineira totally failed to inspire similar movements for political separation from Portugal in São Paulo or Rio de Janeiro, much less in Bahia or Pernambuco.

The conspiracy in Bahia ten years later was a predominantly urban and a much more radical movement aiming at an armed uprising of mulattos, free blacks and slaves. Its leaders were mainly artisans (especially tailors) and soldiers. A small number of young educated white Brazilians, notably Cipriano Barata de Almeida, were also involved. Here the influence of the French Revolution was predominant. The leaders of the rebellion wanted political independence from Portugal, democracy, republican government and free trade but also liberty, equality and fraternity and an end to slavery and all racial discrimination in a captaincy in which one-third of the population were slaves and two-thirds of African origin. (Indeed in the city of Salvador whites were outnumbered 5 to 1.) The dominant class in Bahia was, however, in no mood to listen to demands for political change. The insurrection of *affranchis* (free coloureds) and slaves in Saint Domingue had provided a grim warning to slaveholders throughout the Americas of the consequences of the propagation of ideas of liberalism, egalitarianism and the rights of man in slave societies – and of the challenge to metropolitan control by revolutionary elements among the white population. The sugar boom and overall economic prosperity of the 1790s, which incidentally further strengthened their attachment to slavery and the slave trade, was a further powerful incentive for the Bahia oligarchy to put up with the existing colonial relationship. The 'Tailors' Revolt' was heavily repressed with several dozen arrests and severe punishments; four of the leaders were hung, drawn and quartered; six more were exiled to non-Portuguese Africa.

This is not to say that criticism of the colonial system within the white elite of colonial Brazil had entirely subsided by the 1790s. The economic writings of the reforming bishop of Pernambuco, José Joaquim da Cunha de Azeredo Coutinho (1742–1821), for example, *Memoria sobre o preço do assucar* (1791), *Ensaio economico sobre o commercio de Portugal e suas colonias* (1794) and *Discurso sobre o estado actual das minas do Brasil* (1804) and the *Cartas economico-politicas sobre a agricultura e comercio da Bahia* of João Rodrigues de Brito (1807) serve as a reminder that there remained in Brazil considerable resentment not only at the high level of taxation but also at privileges and monopolies and restrictions on production and trade (especially the role of Portugal as entrepôt) in a period of expanding international markets and the beginnings of the Industrial Revolution.

Whatever the strength of the ties that bound Brazil and Portugal together a fundamental, and eventually irreconcilable, conflict of interest now existed between colony and metropolis. And there was always the danger for Portugal that the demand for a loosening of economic ties would one day lead to the demand for political separation as well.

At this critical juncture Portugal, unlike Spain, was fortunate not only in maintaining its neutrality in the European wars but also in the quality of its political leadership. The contrast between Manuel Godoy, Charles IV of Spain's corrupt and incompetent chief minister from 1792, and Dom Rodrigo de Sousa Coutinho, who came to power in Portugal in 1796, could hardly be sharper. Sousa Coutinho was a determined opponent of all that the French Revolution stood for – the conspiracy of 1798 in Bahia was, as we have seen, firmly repressed – but in, for example, his *Memoria sobre os melhoramentos dos dominios na America* (1798) he recognized the need for enlightened government and political and economic reform to secure the continued loyalty of the Brazilian oligarchy. England had already lost its American colonies; France was struggling to keep Saint Domingue; and there was evidence of growing resistance and revolt among the creoles in different parts of Spanish America. The Portuguese government therefore continued to introduce limited but important measures of economic liberalization (the salt and whaling monopolies were abolished in 1801) and to appoint Brazilians – Manuel Ferreira de Câmara and José Bonifácio de Andrada e Silva, for example – to high positions in the metropolitan and colonial administrations. At the same time Sousa Coutinho was sufficiently intelligent to realize that reform could only delay, and might even precipitate, the inevitable. Moreover, Portugal's future relations with Brazil were somewhat at the mercy of external factors. If Portugal were to be drawn into the war and, in particular, if Napoleon were to invade Portugal (and from 1801 there were hints that he might), Dom Rodrigo before his resignation at the end of 1803 recommended that rather than run the risk of losing Brazil as a result, either through internal revolution or seizure by a colonial rival, the Prince Regent Dom João could and should in the last resort abandon Portugal, move to Brazil and establish 'a great and powerful empire' in South America. Portugal was after all 'neither the best nor the most essential part of the monarchy'.[5]

The idea of transferring the Portuguese court to Brazil was not new. It

[5] See Mansuy-Diniz Silva, *CHLA* I, ch.13; Maxwell, *Conflicts and conspiracies*, 233–9; and K. R. Maxwell, 'The Generation of the 1790s and the idea of Luso-Brazilian Empire', in Dauril Alden (ed.), *Colonial roots of modern Brazil* (Berkeley, 1973).

had been canvassed on earlier occasions when the survival of the dynasty had been in danger, and even in less critical times: for example, in 1738 by the great eighteenth-century statesman Dom Luís da Cunha, on the grounds that Brazil's natural resources were greater than Portugal's and that Rio de Janeiro was better situated than Lisbon to be the metropolis of a great maritime and commercial empire. There was, of course, bitter opposition to Dom Rodrigo's proposals of 1803 from vested interests – mainly merchants in colonial and foreign trade and to a lesser extent manufacturers – in Lisbon. The British government, on the other hand, for a mixture of strategic and commercial reasons was in favour of such a Portuguese move to Brazil in the circumstances of a French invasion. As early as 1801 Lord Hawkesbury, the British Foreign Secretary, had instructed the British ambassador in Lisbon to let it be known that if a decision were made to go to Brazil Britain was ready 'to guarantee the expedition and to combine with [the Prince Regent] the most efficacious ways to extend and consolidate his dominions in South America'.[6]

It was after Tilsit (25 June 1807) that Napoleon finally determined to close the few remaining gaps in his continental system aimed at destroying Britain's trade with Europe. On 12 August 1807 he issued an ultimatum to António de Araújo de Azevedo, the Portuguese Foreign Minister: the Prince Regent must close his ports to English ships, imprison English residents in Portugal and confiscate their property, or face the consequences of a French invasion. In reply George Canning, the British Foreign Secretary, through Percy Clinton Sydney Smythe, the 6th Viscount Strangford, a young Irish peer in charge of the Lisbon legation at the time, threatened, on the one hand, to capture and destroy the Portuguese naval and merchant fleets in the Tagus (as he had already in September destroyed the Danish fleet at Copenhagen) and seize Portugal's colonies, including Brazil, if Dom João gave in to French threats, while promising, on the other hand, to renew Britain's existing obligations to defend the House of Braganza and its dominions against external attack if he stood firm. And by secret convention in October 1807 Canning offered British protection in the event of the Prince Regent's deciding to withdraw temporarily to Brazil. From Britain's point of view, this would be the most satisfactory outcome: not only would the Portuguese court, the Portuguese fleet and conceivably Brazil

---

[6] Quoted in Maxwell, *Conflicts and conspiracies*, 235.

for that matter be kept out of Napoleon's hands, but at a critical time for British trade when British goods were being excluded from Europe and were threatened with exclusion from North America, and British merchants had recently suffered what seemed a major setback on the Río de la Plata (the defeat of the British invasion of 1806–7), it might be expected that Brazil would be opened up to direct British trade. Brazil was itself an important market; it was also a convenient back door to Spanish America.

For a time Dom João tried to satisfy Napoleon by adopting some anti-British measures without totally antagonizing Britain and thus to avoid an agonizing choice. Early in November, however, he learned that General Junot had left Bayonne with 23,000 men and was marching on Portugal. On 16 November Britain tightened the screw when a British fleet under the command of Rear Admiral Sir Sidney Smith arrived off the Tagus. On 23 November news arrived that four days before the French army had actually crossed the Portuguese frontier with Spain and was now only four days' forced march from Lisbon. The next day Dom João took the decision to leave the kingdom he could not retain except as a vassal of France (indeed the survival of the House of Braganza was in serious doubt) and withdraw across the Atlantic to his most important colony. The decision to transfer the court to Brazil was regarded by the local population as a cowardly desertion, an ignominious and disorderly flight, a *sauve-qui-peut*. Certainly it was forced upon Dom João and there were elements of confusion, even farce. But, as we have seen, it was also an intelligent, political manoeuvre which had been long premeditated – and, in the interval between Napoleon's ultimatum and Junot's invasion, carefully planned. Between the morning of 25 November and the evening of 27 November some 10–15,000 people – the Prince Regent Dom João and a dozen members of the royal family (including his mother, the demented Queen Maria, his wife Princess Carlota Joaquina, the daughter of Charles IV of Spain, his sons Dom Pedro (aged nine) and Dom Miguel), the members of the council of state, ministers and advisers, justices of the High Court, officials of the Treasury, the upper echelons of the army and navy, the church hierarchy, members of the aristocracy, functionaries, professional and businessmen, several hundred courtiers, servants and hangers-on, a marine brigade of 1,600 and miscellaneous citizens who managed by various means to secure passage – embarked on the flagship *Principe Real*, eight other ships of the line, eight lesser warships and thirty Portuguese merchant vessels. Also packed on board were the contents of the royal treasury – silver plate, jewels, cash and all moveable assets – government files, indeed the entire paraphernalia of government, a printing press and several libraries including the Royal Library of Ajuda which was to form the basis for the Bibliotheca Publica, later Biblioteca Nacional, of Rio de Janeiro. As soon as the wind was favourable, on 29 November (the day before Junot arrived), the ships weighed anchor, sailed down the Tagus and set out across the Atlantic for Brazil – escorted by four British warships. The head of a European state along with his entire court and government was emigrating to one of his colonies; it was an event unique in the history of European colonialism. Although greatly exaggerating the role he and Admiral Sir Sidney Smith had played in persuading Dom João to leave (the Prince Regent had already embarked when British assistance was offered) Lord Strangford wrote, not entirely without reason, 'I have entitled England to establish with the Brazils the relation of sovereign and subject, and to require obedience to be paid as the price of protection'.[7]

It was a nightmare journey: a storm divided the fleet; the royal party suffered from overcrowding, lack of food and water, lice (the ladies had to cut off their hair) and disease; changes of clothing had to be improvised from sheets and blankets provided by the British navy. Nevertheless, the crossing was successfully accomplished and on 22 January 1808 the royal fugitives arrived in Bahia to a warm reception; it was the first time a reigning monarch had set foot in the New World. Dom João declined an offer to establish his residence in Salvador and after a month left for Rio de Janeiro, arriving on 7 March to another heartwarming welcome, it should be noted, from the local population.

Whatever conclusions are drawn about the political and economic condition of Brazil, its relations with the mother country and the prospects for its future independence before 1808, there is no disputing the profound impact the arrival of the Portuguese court had on Brazil and especially on Rio de Janeiro. The viceregal capital since 1763 and in the late eighteenth century increasingly important economically, Rio de Janeiro overnight became the capital of a worldwide empire stretching as far as Goa and Macao. Between April and October 1808 the major institutions of the absolutist Portuguese state were installed, including the Conselho de Estado, the Desembargo do Paço (the Supreme High

---

[7] Quoted in Alan K. Manchester, *British preeminence in Brazil. Its rise and decline* (Durham, N.C., 1933), 67.

Court), the Casa de Supplicação (Court of Appeal), the Erário Real (Royal Treasury), the Conselho da Real Fazenda (Council of the Royal Exchequer), the Junta do Comércio, Agricultura, Fábricas e Navigação and the Banco do Brazil. Brazil itself was now governed from Rio, not Lisbon, although the government was, of course, in the hands of the same people, all Portuguese: the Prince Regent, his ministers (notably Dom Rodrigo de Sousa Coutinho, Conde de Linhares, now Minister of Foreign Relations and War and by far the most influential minister until his death in 1812), the Council of State, the higher judiciary and bureaucracy. Significantly, no Brazilians were included. Provincial and local administration were left in the hands of the crown appointed governors of the captaincies and crown judges (many of whom were Brazilians), although the very presence in Rio de Janeiro of the Portuguese king and the Portuguese government in place of the viceroy ensured a degree of increased centralization of power.

The nineteenth-century Portuguese historian, J. P. Oliveira Martins, wrote of the events of 1807–8: 'Portugal was [now] the colony, Brazil the metropolis.' Modern Brazilian historians refer to the metropolitanization of the colony. Certainly, the relationship between mother country and colony had been decisively altered. Brazil was no longer strictly speaking a colony. But neither was it independent and in control of its own destiny. The transfer of the Portuguese court to Rio de Janeiro is nevertheless generally regarded as a major stage in the evolution of Brazil towards independence since it would prove impossible, as we shall see, to restore the *status quo ante*.

Of even greater significance perhaps than the establishment of the metropolitan government in Rio – because it would prove even more difficult to reverse – was the ending of the 300-year-old monopoly of colonial trade and the elimination of Lisbon as an entrepôt for Brazilian imports and exports. During his brief stay in Bahia – indeed within a week of his arrival – Dom João had by means of a *Carta Régia* (28 January 1808) opened Brazil's ports to direct trade with all friendly nations. In doing so, he had been advised by, among others, Rodrigo de Sousa Coutinho, Dom Fernando José de Portugal e Castro, the future Marquês de Aguiar, a councillor of state, who had only recently served as viceroy (1801–6) and who would become Minister of the Interior and Finance Minister in the new government in Rio, the Conde de Ponte, governor of the captaincy of Bahia who had only the year before conducted a survey of Bahian planters' views on the economy, and José de Silva Lisboa

(1756–1835), the future visconde de Cairú, a native of Bahia and graduate of Coimbra, a distinguished political economist and author of *Princípios de Economia Política* (1804) which had been greatly influenced by the writings of Adam Smith. The Prince Regent, however, had in fact little alternative – and there is some evidence that the opening of the ports was seen at the time as a temporary measure. The Bahian warehouses were full of sugar and tobacco which could not otherwise be exported; the Portuguese ports were closed as a result of the French occupation and the British blockade. Moreover, government finances were dependent on foreign trade and the duties imports in particular paid. To legalize the existing contraband trade would enable the Portuguese government to control – and tax – it. Britain in any case expected the Portuguese government to open Brazilian ports to direct British trade now that Portugal was occupied by the French. It was part of the secret convention of October 1807, the price of British protection.

Thus, almost accidentally, Dom João on his arrival in Brazil immediately identified with the interests of the big Brazilian landowners and conceded what critics of the old colonial system had most eagerly demanded. (In April he also revoked all the decrees prohibiting manufacturing, especially textile manufacturing, in the colony, exempted industrial raw materials from import duties, encouraged the invention or introduction of new machinery and offered direct subsidies to the cotton, wool, silk and iron industries.) The opening of the ports to foreign trade created a storm of opposition from Portuguese interests in Rio as well as Lisbon, and by decree on 11 June 1808 Dom João in response (but also to facilitate the administration of the customs houses) restricted foreign trade to five ports – Belém, São Luís, Recife, Bahia and Rio de Janeiro – and restricted the Brazilian coastal trade and trade with the rest of the Portuguese empire to Portuguese vessels. He also discriminated in favour of Portuguese shipping by reducing the general tariff on imported goods fixed in January at 24 per cent to 16 per cent in the case of goods brought in Portuguese ships. Nevertheless, the basic principle of open trade had been established.

In practice, at least until the end of the war, direct trade with all friendly nations meant trade with England. As Canning had anticipated Rio de Janeiro became 'an emporium for British manufactures destined for the consumption of the whole of South America'[8] – not only Brazil

<hr />

[8] Quoted in Manchester, *British preeminence*, 78.

itself but the Río de la Plata and the Pacific coast of Spanish America. As early as August 1808 between 150 and 200 merchants and commission agents formed a thriving English community in Rio de Janeiro. One merchant who arrived there in June – John Luccock, a partner in the firm of Lupton's of Leeds, who stayed for ten years and in 1820 published his *Notes on Rio de Janeiro and the southern parts of Brazil*, one of the first comprehensive descriptions of south-central Brazil and especially of the economic transformation which occurred in and around the capital during the years after 1808 – found the city 'heaped high with [British] cloth, ironmongery, clothing and earthenware'.[9] It has been estimated that the total value of all British goods exported to Brazil in 1808 amounted to over £2 million – a figure not equalled for ten years. The number of ships entering Rio in 1808 was more than four times higher than in 1807; most of them were British. Brazilian sugar, cotton and coffee exports which continued to grow after 1808 – and primary commodity prices were at an all-time high for the duration of the war – were also now mainly shipped to Europe in British vessels.

Britain was not satisfied, however, with an open door in Brazil. She wanted the kind of preferential rights she had enjoyed in Portugal for centuries. And Dom João could not refuse these, and other, demands: he was entirely dependent on British troops and arms in the war to defeat the French in Portugal and on the British navy for the defence of Brazil and the rest of Portugal's overseas empire. Lord Strangford, who as British minister had followed the Prince Regent to Rio, finally extracted from him in February 1810, after lengthy negotiations, a Treaty of Navigation and Commerce and a separate Treaty of Alliance and Friendship. The commercial treaty fixed a maximum tariff of 15 per cent ad valorem on British goods, mainly cottons, woollens, linens, hardware and earthenware, imported into Brazil. (A decree of 18 October 1810 lowered duties on Portuguese imports from 16 to 15 per cent, but this could do nothing to restore Portuguese trade with Brazil which collapsed in 1809–13 to some 30 per cent of its 1800–4 level. The only trade to Brazil still dominated by the Portuguese was the trade in slaves from Portuguese Africa. At the same time cheap British imports became even cheaper and to a considerable extent undermined the efforts being made after 1808 to establish Brazilian industries.) Needless to say, Britain did not reciprocate by lowering its virtually prohibitive duties on Brazilian sugar and

[9] See Herbert Heaton, 'A merchant adventurer in Brazil, 1808–1818', *Journal of Economic History*, 6 (1946).

coffee, though not cotton, entering the British market. The Prince Regent in 1810 also formally conceded to British merchants the right to reside in Brazil and to engage in the wholesale and retail trades. Moreover, the British government was given the right to appoint judges conservators, special magistrates responsible for dealing with cases involving British subjects in Brazil.

Under article 10 of the treaty of alliance, the Prince Regent entered into his first treaty engagement for the reduction and eventual abolition of the slave trade. In April 1807, within three weeks of its own abolition, Britain had appealed to Portugal to follow its lead – not surprisingly without success. The new circumstances of the Prince Regent's residence in Brazil presented Britain with a rare opportunity to extract concessions on this front, too. The Prince Regent was obliged as a first step to confine the Portuguese slave trade to his own dominions, that is not allow Portuguese traders to take over the trade from which the British were now obliged to withdraw, and to promise gradually to abolish it. British pressure for the fulfilment of that last commitment would henceforth be unrelenting.

The transfer of the Portuguese court to Rio de Janeiro in 1808 not only opened up Brazil economically but ended Brazil's cultural and intellectual isolation as well. There was an influx of new people and new ideas. In May 1808 a printing press was established in the capital for the first time (followed by new presses in Salvador in 1811 and Recife in 1817); and newspapers and books were published. Public libraries, literary, philosophical and scientific academies, schools and theatres were opened. Between 1808 and 1822, in addition to 24,000 Portuguese émigrés (including the families and retainers of those already there), Rio de Janeiro alone registered 4,234 foreign immigrants, not counting their wives, children and servants. 1,500 were Spanish, especially Spanish American, 1,000 French, 600 English, 100 German, the rest from other European countries and from North America.[10] They were mostly professional men and artisans: doctors, musicians, pharmacists; tailors, shoemakers, bakers, etc. During the period of Dom João's residency the population of the city of Rio de Janeiro doubled from 50,000 to 100,000.

The Portuguese government in Rio also welcomed and facilitated visits – the first since the Dutch occupation of North-East Brazil in the 1630s and 1640s – by distinguished foreign scientists, artists and

---

[10] Arquivo Nacional, *Registro de Estrangeiros 1808–1822*, pref. José Honório Rodrigues (Rio de Janeiro, 1960).

travellers. John Mawe, the English naturalist and mineralogist and author of the classic *Travels in the Interior of Brazil* (1812), was the first foreigner to be granted a licence to visit the mining areas of Minas Gerais, then very much in decline. Henry Koster who had been born in Portugal, the son of a Liverpool merchant, went to Pernambuco in 1809 for health reasons and apart from brief visits home remained there until his death in 1820; his *Travels in Brazil* (1816) is regarded as one of the most perceptive descriptions of the Brazilian *Nordeste*. In March 1816 a French artistic mission arrived in Rio. It included the architect Auguste-Henri-Victor Grandjean de Montigny, who designed the Academia de Belas-Artes and many other new and imposing buildings in the capital, and the painters Jean Baptiste Debret (1768–1848) and Nicolas-Antoine Taunay (1755–1838), whose drawings and watercolours are an important record of the landscapes and daily life of Rio in the early nineteenth century, as well as the composer Sigismund von Neukomm (1778–1858), a pupil of Haydn. Two other Frenchmen, Louis-François de Tollenare and the botanist Auguste de Saint-Hilaire, wrote outstanding accounts of their travels in different parts of Brazil between 1816 and 1822. Brazilian geography, natural resources, flora and fauna – and Brazilian Indians – were also studied by a number of remarkable German explorers and scientists – notably Baron von Eschwege, Georg Freyreiss, Frederik Sellow, Maximilian von Wied-Neuwied, Johann Baptist Pohl and the great partnership of Johann Baptist von Spix, zoologist, and Carl Frederick Philip von Martius, botanist – many of whom visited Brazil under the patronage of Princess Leopoldina of Habsburg, the daughter of the Austrian emperor who married Dom João's eldest son, Dom Pedro, in 1817. Princess Leopoldina also brought to Brazil the Austrian painter Thomas Ender (1793–1875). Another notable artist, Johann-Moritz Rugendas (1802–58), first came to Brazil in 1821 with the scientific mission to Mato Grosso and Pará led by Count Georg Heinrich von Langsdorff.

With the liberation of Portugal and the end of the war in Europe it had been generally expected that the Portuguese Prince Regent would return to Lisbon. In September 1814 Lord Castlereagh, the British Foreign Secretary, sent Rear Admiral Sir John Beresford to Rio de Janeiro with two ships of the line and a frigate to conduct Dom João home. On his arrival at the end of December 1814 Beresford put *HMS Achilles* at the Prince Regent's disposal for the return journey. But Dom João had enjoyed his residence in Brazil. Moreover, he was not simply a king in exile; he had brought with him the entire apparatus of the Portuguese state as well as several thousand members of the Portuguese governing class, many though by no means all of whom had put down roots in Brazil and were now reluctant to leave. In the face of conflicting advice Dom João was as usual indecisive. Finally, he listened to Araújo de Azevedo, Conde da Barca, his chief minister (1814–17), and decided to stay in Brazil. And on 16 December 1815 Brazil was raised to the status of kingdom – equal with Portugal. For some historians this, rather than the arrival of the Portuguese court in 1808, marks the end of Brazil's colonial status. Three months later, on the death of his mother, the Prince Regent became King João of Portugal, Brazil and the Algarves. The experiment of a Luso-Brazilian dual monarchy with its centre in the New World was, however, doomed to failure. Dom João was unable to commit himself wholly to Brazil. The Portuguese court and government remained close to the Portuguese community in Brazil and conscious of its interests as well as, ultimately, the interests of Portugal itself. At the same time the demographic and economic trends which so favoured Brazil at the expense of Portugal in the period before 1808 had been reinforced by the differences in their respective fortunes since 1808. The fundamental conflicts between Brazilians and Portuguese had not been and could not be resolved.

In one sense, it is true, the ties between the crown and the Brazilian landowning elite had been strengthened after 1808 as they found a coincidence of interest in open commerce. In particular, both Rio de Janeiro, indeed the centre-south region as a whole, and Bahia under the 'enlightened' governorship of the conde de Arcos (1810–18) had seen their exports of sugar, cotton and, in the case of Rio, coffee grow, although in the post-war period international prices especially of cotton (with the growth of United States production) and sugar (as Cuban production accelerated) began to fall. But royal economic policy was still not entirely free of irritating mercantilist monopolies and privileges as Dom João did what he could to protect the interests of Portuguese merchants resident in Brazil and in Portugal. Moreover, at the back of the Brazilian mind was the possibility of the restoration of Brazil's colonial status and the loss of all the gains since 1808 if Dom João were eventually to return to Lisbon.

On the political side, enlightened absolutism had proved reasonably tolerable to the Brazilian elite, since Dom João now ruled in harmony with their interests and promoted the growth and development of Brazil while at the same time guaranteeing political and social order. Unlike

Spanish America, where after the overthrow of the Spanish monarchy by Napoleon in 1808 there was no king to obey, there had been no crisis of political legitimacy in Brazil. And Brazil had, after all, achieved equal political status in 1815. Moreover, Dom João had made good use of his power to grant non-hereditary titles of nobility – barão, visconde, conde and marquês – and decorations at various levels in the five Orders of Christo, São Bento de Aviz, São Tiago, Tôrre e Espada and Nôssa Senhora da Conceição, to native Brazilians as well as to continental Portuguese (and foreigners), that is to say, offering enhanced social status in return for loyalty to the crown. Below the surface, however, there lurked political aspirations, both liberal and, more strongly, anti-Portuguese. With the absolutist Portuguese government in Rio metropolitan rule was more immediately felt. Avenues to some limited form of political power sharing had been closed; discrimination in favour of the Portuguese, now that there were so many more of them, was more pronounced. The fiscal burden was also greater since the Brazilians alone were obliged to support the court and a larger bureaucracy and military establishment. Moreover, Brazilians were called upon to pay for the dynastic ambitions of Dom João and his wife Carlota Joaquina (as well as the interests of the *estancieiros* of southern Brazil) in the Río de la Plata. The revolutions for independence in Spanish America, and especially the struggle between Artigas and Buenos Aires, had offered a great opportunity for Portugal to regain control of Colônia do Sacramento which had finally been ceded to Spain in 1778 after a century of conflict. As early as 1811 Portuguese troops had crossed the Spanish frontier, but then withdrew. In April 1815 Lord Strangford, who had played a restraining influence, left Rio for London. And soon after Portuguese troops released from the war in Europe began to arrive in Brazil. In June 1816 a Portuguese fleet and 3,500 men left Rio for the Río de la Plata, and in January 1817 General Lecor occupied Montevideo. (In July 1821 the entire Banda Oriental – present-day Uruguay – was incorporated into Brazil as the Cisplatine province.)

There were other examples of the government in Rio apparently sacrificing Brazilian interests to the interests of the Portuguese state, most obviously the Anglo-Portuguese commercial treaty but also the various treaties with England for the suppression of the transatlantic slave trade. For a time the British navy had mistakenly interpreted the treaty of 1810 restricting the Portuguese slave trade to Portuguese territories to mean that the trade was illegal north of the equator, and until 1813 when they were stopped from doing so British warships captured a number of Portuguese slavers. Traders exporting slaves to Bahia and Pernambuco suffered heavy losses and slave prices rose. Then at the Congress of Vienna Portugal did finally agree, by treaty in January 1815, to ban the trade north of the equator in return for a financial indemnity and reiterated its determination to bring about a gradual end to the trade which in February 1815 eight powers (including Portugal) declared 'repugnant to the principle of humanity and universal morality'. Worse was to come from the point of view of the Brazilian slaveholders. In July 1817 the Conde de Palmella, Portugal's minister in London, signed an additional convention to the 1815 treaty giving it teeth: the British navy was given the right to visit and search on the high seas Portuguese vessels suspected of illegal slaving north of the equator and Anglo-Portuguese mixed commissions were to be set up to adjudicate the captures and liberate the slaves. Again Portugal promised to introduce and enforce anti-slave trade legislation and to move towards the final abolition of the entire trade. Diplomatic pressure for further concessions was, however, resisted and the Brazilian slave trade, legal south of the equator, now illegal north, continued to supply the labour needs of Brazil. The trade grew from 15–20,000 per annum at the beginning of the nineteenth century to 30,000 per annum in the early 1820s. Yet for many Brazilians it seemed like the beginning of the end of the slave trade, and the Portuguese had, therefore, sold out a vital Brazilian interest.

Although it undoubtedly existed, and perhaps was growing, Brazilian disaffection from the Portuguese regime now apparently permanently installed in Rio de Janeiro should not be exaggerated. There was still no strong and certainly no widespread demand for political change. The most persistent criticism of Portuguese absolutism and the political system it imposed on Brazil came from Hipólito José da Costa who from June 1808 to 1822 published a highly influential liberal newspaper, the *Correio Brasiliense* – in London. There was only one open rebellion and this as much against political – and fiscal – subordination to Rio de Janeiro as against Portuguese rule as such. Nevertheless, in March 1817 a military revolt which was joined by a few planters and slaveholders facing lower returns from their sugar and cotton exports and higher slave prices, some wealthy merchants, crown judges and priests as well as *moradores* (small, dependent tenant farmers and squatters) and artisans, led to the proclamation of a republic in Pernambuco. The 'organic law' of the republic included religious toleration and 'equality of rights', but defended property and slavery. The revolt spread rapidly to Alagoas, Paraíba and Rio Grande do Norte. But then it faltered. It suffered a good deal of internal factionalism. Britain, having secured the opening of Brazilian ports, favoured the stability and unity of Brazil and refused to encourage it by granting recognition when agents were sent. Two converted merchant ships blockaded Recife from the sea. Finally, an army was gathered together from Bahia, which under governor Arcos remained loyal, and from Rio de Janeiro, and on 20 May 1817 the rebels surrendered. The republic of the north-east had lasted two and a half months. The rest of Brazil had remained quiet. Nevertheless, the revolution of 1817 had revealed the existence of liberal and nationalist ideas, not least within the military. Troops from Portugal were now brought in to garrison the principal cities, and within existing units, in Bahia for example, Portuguese were more often promoted over the heads of Brazilians. With the rapid progress of the revolutions for independence in both southern and northern Spanish South America as a warning, the Portuguese regime showed signs of becoming more repressive. Certainly Thomaz A. Villa Nova Portugal (1817–20) was the most reactionary and pro-Portuguese of all Dom João's chief ministers during his residence in Brazil.

The independence of Brazil was in the event precipitated by political developments in Portugal in 1820–1. On 24 August 1820 a liberal-nationalist revolt erupted in Oporto, followed by another in Lisbon on 15 October. Triggered by the military, they were supported by many sectors of Portuguese society, but especially the bourgeoisie, deeply dissatisfied with political and economic conditions in post-war Portugal. The absolutist King João VI remained in Rio de Janeiro, insensitive it seemed to the problems of Portugal; the roles of metropolis and colony had been reversed. Portugal was governed in the continued absence of Dom João by a Council of Regency presided over by an Englishman, Marshal Beresford, who after the war remained Commander in Chief of the Portuguese Army. Portuguese trade with Brazil had recovered somewhat in the period since the end of the war, but was still far below its pre-1808 level. Landowners, manufacturers, merchants, shippers, indeed most Portuguese, whose economic well-being, as we have seen, had been so heavily dependent before 1808 on Portugal's monopoly position in the trade to and from Brazil, and on the re-export trade in

Brazil's colonial staples, continued to suffer great economic difficulties (although Portugal's economic decline was not entirely due to the 'loss' of Brazil). Moreover, without revenue from Brazil and the Brazilian trade the Portuguese budget was in permanent deficit; civil functionaries and military personnel went unpaid. At the end of 1820 the liberals established a *Junta Provisória* to govern in the name of the king whose immediate return to Lisbon was demanded. João VI would be expected to adopt the Spanish liberal constitution of 1812 – in force again in Spain after the liberal Revolution there in January–March 1820 – pending the formulation of a new Portuguese constitution for which purpose a *Côrtes Gerais Extraordinárias e Constituintes* was hastily summoned. According to the instructions of 22 November, the Côrtes was to be elected – for the entire Portuguese world – on the basis of one deputy for every 30,000 free subjects. (Brazil was allocated some 70–75 seats in an assembly of over 200.) Provisional *juntas governativas* loyal to the Portuguese revolution were to be set up in the various Brazilian captaincies (now provinces) to supervise the elections to the Côrtes in Lisbon. Behind all these anti-absolutist, liberal measures, however, there lay also a Portuguese determination to restore Brazil to its colonial status before 1808.

News of the liberal constitutionalist revolution in Portugal produced minor disturbances in many Brazilian towns. But, as in Portugal, it was the military which made the first significant moves against absolutism in Brazil. On 1 January 1821 Portuguese troops in Belém rebelled and set up a liberal *junta governativa* for Pará to which Maranhão (3 April) and Piauí (24 May) later adhered; it immediately declared itself prepared to organize elections for the Côrtes in Lisbon. On 10 February in Bahia a similar military conspiracy by liberal troops against their absolutist officers led to the removal of the governor, the Conde de Palma, and the establishment of a provisional junta pledged to a liberal constitution for the United Kingdom of Portugal and Brazil; its members were mostly Portuguese but it was supported by many prominent Brazilians, if only to head off the more extreme liberals. In the capital Rio de Janeiro, too, on 24–26 February a pronunciamento in favour of the constitutionalist revolution and a gathering of Portuguese troops in the Largo de Rossio (now the Praça Tiradentes) forced a reorganization of the ministry and obliged the king himself to approve a future liberal constitution for Portugal and Brazil; he also decreed, in line with the instructions of the *junta provisória* in Lisbon, the establishment of governing provincial juntas where these did not already exist and the preparation of indirect elections for the Côrtes.

Serious political conflict arose, however, over the Côrtes' demand that
the king return to Lisbon. A Portuguese faction in Rio de Janeiro made
up of senior army officers, senior bureaucrats and merchants whose ties
were still essentially with Portugal, and who were anxious to recover
their monopoly status, naturally favoured the return, although many of
them were absolutist or anti-Brazilian more than liberal. On the other
hand a 'Brazilian' faction or party now emerged to oppose it. Its main
elements were big landowners throughout Brazil, but especially in the
captaincies closest to the capital, and Brazilian-born bureaucrats and
members of the judiciary. Not all members of the 'Brazilian' party were,
however, Brazilian-born. It included those Portuguese whose roots and
interests now lay in Brazil: Portuguese bureaucrats who had benefited
from the establishment of royal government in Rio, Portuguese merchants who had adjusted to the new economic circumstances of open
trade, particularly those in the retail trade in foreign goods and in the
internal trade, Portuguese who had invested in land and urban property
or who had married into Brazilian families, or who simply now preferred
Brazil to Portugal. Many 'Brazilians' though by no means revolutionary
and anti-colonialist and certainly not yet nationalist were in favour of a
constitution which would reduce the power of the king while at the same
time increasing their own power. And it was still not clear that the Côrtes
was profoundly anti-Brazilian. It was, however, in the interests of all
'Brazilians' to defend the status quo, to maintain the political equality
with the mother country and the economic freedom secured by Brazil
since 1808, which would be threatened were Dom João to leave.

The Brazilian dominant class was for the most part conservative, or at
most liberal–conservative. It wished to maintain colonial economic and
social structures based on the plantation system, slavery and exports of
tropical agricultural produce to the European market. But there were
liberals, even radical liberals, and some authentic revolutionaries in the
city of Rio de Janeiro and in São Paulo as well as in Salvador and Recife,
most of them in the professions – especially lawyers and journalists – or
artisans – tailors, barbers, mechanics – but also small retailers, soldiers
and priests. Most were white, but many were mulatto and free black.
They looked for profound changes in politics and society: popular
sovereignty, democracy, even a republic; social and racial equality, even
land reform and the abolition of slavery. They were ambivalent on the
question of whether Dom João should return to Portugal or remain in
Brazil.

Dom João faced a difficult dilemma: if he returned he would fall into the hands of the liberals and, possibly, risk the loss of Brazil; if he stayed he would undoubtedly lose Portugal. He considered sending his son Dom Pedro, now 22 years old, to Lisbon, but finally on 7 March 1821 he agreed to return. He had again come under pressure from the military and from the Conde de Palmella, a liberal constitutionalist who won the internal power struggle with Thomaz Villa Nova Portugal, the absolutist first minister, in the court. (Britain also threw its weight behind Dom João's return to Lisbon. Castlereagh hinted that while Britain was obliged to guarantee the Braganzas against external attack this did not extend to internal revolution.) Still Dom João vacillated as the political crisis in Rio de Janeiro deepened. On 21–22 April there were popular demonstrations in the Praça do Comércio demanding a governing junta like those in Pará and Bahia and elections for the Côrtes. Finally, on 26 April Dom João and around 4,000 Portuguese (together with the contents of the Treasury and the Banco do Brasil) set sail for Lisbon after a thirteen-year residence in Brazil, leaving the young Dom Pedro behind in Rio as Prince Regent.

The 'Brazilians' had no alternative now but to organize themselves for the defence of Brazilian interests in the Côrtes. Elections took place for the most part between May and September. They were notable for the fact that almost all those elected were Brazilian-born. And they included several prominent radicals who had participated in the revolution of 1817: for example, Cipriano Barata (Bahia), Muniz Tavares (Pernambuco), Antônio Carlos Ribeiro de Andrada Machado e Silva (São Paulo). The six deputies elected for São Paulo included, besides Antônio Carlos, three others who became distinguished liberal politicians after independence: Padre Diogo A. Feijó, Francisco de Paula Sousa e Melo and Dr Nicolau Pereira de Campos Vergueiro. The elections – and the instructions given to the elected deputies – were also notable for the fact that, apparently, independence for Brazil was not yet regarded as a serious political issue.

The Côrtes had met in Lisbon for the first time at the end of January 1821. The seven deputies from Pernambuco were the first of the Brazilians to arrive – on 29 August; the five from Rio arrived during September and October, those from Maranhão in November, from Bahia on 17 December and the Paulistas, the most formidable group, not until February to May 1822; some, the Mineiros, for example, never arrived. Long before the majority of the Brazilian deputies had taken their seats, however, the Portuguese Côrtes had made its fatal attempt to put back the clock and reduce Brazil to its former colonial status. The Portuguese bourgeoisie in its determination to re-establish its hegemony over Brazil and in particular to deny Britain direct access to Brazil totally failed to recognize the strain put upon the colonial pact by the political, economic and demographic development of Brazil, not least since 1808, and the economic, political and ideological changes which had taken place in Europe and in America which made it unlikely that Portugal alone of European powers would be able to keep its mainland American colonies.

In April 1821 with the news of the constitutional movements in Pará, Bahia and Rio de Janeiro and particularly after the return of Dom João (he arrived in Lisbon on 4 July) the Côrtes, without much success, began bypassing Rio de Janeiro, dealing directly with the different provincial governments in Brazil. An unsuccessful attempt was also made to revoke the trade agreements with Britain; the Portuguese wanted to direct British goods through the metropolis once more and to impose a much higher tariff. Furthermore, in August troop reinforcements were sent to Brazil. Then came what proved to be the decisive moves. On 29 September the Côrtes demonstrated that it intended to govern Brazil by ordering the dismantling of all government institutions established in Rio in 1808 and their transfer back to Lisbon. And on 1 October the appointment of military governors for each province with powers independent of the provincial juntas and directly subject to Lisbon was announced. Finally, on 18 October the Prince Regent himself was ordered to return home. As the Brazilian deputies began at last to arrive during the final months of 1821 and the first half of 1822 they were met – or so they claimed (it could perhaps be argued that they were over-sensitive to their dignity) – with ridicule, insults, threats and a good deal of open antagonism. In the famous words of Manoel Fernandes Thomaz, one of the leaders of the Portuguese liberal revolution, Brazil was a 'terra de macacos, de negrinhos apanhados na costa da Africa, e de bananas'. Not surprisingly, Brazilian demands, presented, for example, by Antô-nio Carlos in March 1822 in the *Apontamentos e Lembranças* of the São Paulo junta, for political and economic equality with Portugal and parallel organs of government with perhaps the seat of the monarchy alternating between Rio de Janeiro and Lisbon, met with little response. It was in any case too late. Events in Brazil were moving inexorably and swiftly towards a final break with Portugal. In October 1822 seven Brazilian deputies – four paulistas, including Antônio Carlos, and three baianos, including Cipriano Barata – illegally fled Lisbon, first to London, then to Brazil, rather than swear allegiance to the 1822 Constitution and become members of the Côrtes Ordinárias due to meet for the first time in December. And the other Brazilian deputies, many of them radicalized by their unfortunate experience in Lisbon, soon followed.

Brazil had progressed too far since 1808 for anything less than complete equality with the mother country to be acceptable. The decrees of late September and early October, news of which arrrived in Rio on 11 December 1821, were the final confirmation of Portuguese intransigence and determination to reverse all the changes in relations between Portugal and Brazil since 1808. There followed a major political realignment in Brazil. The 'Portuguese' faction (what was left of it after Dom João returned to Lisbon) and the 'Brazilian' faction finally – and permanently – split. The divergent forces within the 'Brazilian' party of the centre-south – Portuguese-born in Rio de Janeiro with interests in Brazil, Brazilian conservatives and moderate liberals, especially in São Paulo and Rio de Janeiro, Brazilian extreme liberals and radicals in Rio de Janeiro – closed ranks in united resistance to the Portuguese Côrtes. Since he clearly could not guarantee the continuation of the arrangement of 1808, the increasingly self-confident Brazilians finally withdrew their allegiance from King João VI and transferred it to the Prince Regent Dom Pedro. The battle to keep Dom João in Brazil had been lost in April 1821. The immediate key to the future autonomy of Brazil was now to persuade Dom Pedro to stay. There was intense political activity in Rio during the last weeks of 1821 and the first weeks of 1822 as politicians – and the press – brought pressure to bear on the Prince Regent who, after some hesitation, finally allowed himself to be won over. In response to a petition with 8,000 signatures presented by José Clemente Pereira, himself a Portuguese merchant long resident in Rio, a liberal and the president of the Senado da Câmara of Rio de Janeiro (which had largely been ignored by João VI during his residence there), Dom Pedro announced on 9 January 1822 that he would stay in Brazil. (This episode is known as *O Fico* from the Portuguese *ficar*, to remain.) The union with Portugal had not yet been broken, but this significant act of disobedience by the Prince Regent amounted to a formal rejection of Portuguese authority over Brazil. A few days later Portuguese troops who refused to swear allegiance to Dom Pedro were obliged by those who did so – and who thus formed the nucleus of a Brazilian regular army – to leave Rio de Janeiro (and fresh troops arriving from Portugal in February were not allowed to land). On 16 January José Bonifácio de Andrada e Silva (1763–1838), a member of a rich Santos family, educated in Coimbra and for 35 years (until 1819) employed in Portugal as a scientist and royal administrator, now at the age of 58 president of the São Paulo provisional junta, was appointed head of a new 'Brazilian' cabinet. All the other members of the cabinet were Portuguese, it is true, but the appointment was symbolic of the enormous shift which had now taken place in Brazilian politics.

There is some suggestion in the private correspondence between Dom João and Dom Pedro that the former anticipated this course of events when he left Brazil for Portugal and advised his son to throw in his lot with the Brazilians in order that both parts of the empire should at least remain in the hands of the Braganzas with the possibility that one day they might be reunited. For his part Dom Pedro had written bluntly to Dom João in Lisbon, 'Portugal is today a fourth-class state and needful, therefore dependent; Brazil is of the first class and independent.'[11] It may also be that given the threat posed by the Brazilian liberals Dom Pedro, whose political inclinations were decidedly authoritarian, chose to lead rather than be overwhelmed by a movement which was beginning to look more and more like a movement for independence. There is considerable debate among historians about the point at which total political separation from Portugal became the preferred goal of the Brazilians. Until the end of 1821, when the intentions of the Côrtes could no longer be doubted, independence had been the aim of only a radical minority. Even in 1822, it is argued, for some elements in the Brazilian dominant class and, for example, the Brazilian deputies, including the São Paulo group, in Lisbon who constantly emphasized their loyalty to the crown, independence, when it was mentioned at all, still meant autonomy within a dual monarchy and the continuation of some kind of union with Portugal.

At the beginning of 1822 José Bonifácio was unquestionably the dominant figure in the political process in Brazil. His views on social questions were remarkably progressive – he favoured the gradual abolition of the slave trade and even slavery, free European immigration and land reform – but, politically, he was conservative and profoundly hostile to democracy. Once the campaign to keep Dom Pedro in Brazil, which had temporarily and artificially united the Brazilian party, had

---

[11] Quoted by Manoel da Silveira Cardozo in A. J. R. Russell-Wood (ed.), *From colony to nation. Essays on the independence of Brazil* (Baltimore, 1975), 207.

succeeded, José Bonifácio immediately distanced himself not only from the extreme liberals and democrats ('anarquistas e demagogos' he called them), some of whom were republicans, but also many more moderate liberals and set about rallying support from conservative and liberal-conservative landowners, high ranking bureaucrats and judges (many of them Coimbra-trained) and merchants in Rio de Janeiro, São Paulo and now Minas Gerais for the establishment of an independent monarchy in Brazil. The monarchy he saw as the only means of maintaining political order and social stability – and, it was hoped, territorial unity – in the dangerous period of the transition to independence.

The conflict during the first half of 1822 between José Bonifácio and liberals and radicals like Joaquim Gonçalves Lêdo, Padre Januário da Cunha Barbosa, Domingos Alves Branco Muniz Barreto, José Clemente Pereira and Martim Francisco Ribeiro de Andrada (like Antônio Carlos, the leader of the paulista delegation in Lisbon, a younger brother of José Bonifácio) largely took the form of competition between their respective masonic lodges, the Apostolado and the Grande Oriente, for influence over the young, inexperienced Prince Regent. Insofar as the struggle for power had an ideological element it centred on the question of whether or not a Constituent Assembly should be summoned. On 16 February 1822 José Bonifácio, who was strongly opposed to popular representation in an elected national assembly, persuaded Dom Pedro that a *Conselho de Procuradores da Província* consisting of *homens bons* nominated by means of the traditional procedures was all that was required. It was installed on 2 June, but did not survive. On 3 June despite the opposition of José Bonifácio, Dom Pedro agreed to call a Constituent Assembly. The more extreme liberals then lost the initiative when on 19 June they failed in their efforts to secure direct popular elections for the Assembly. (It was to be elected indirectly on a strictly limited suffrage and in any case did not meet for the first time until 3 May 1823 by which time the leading radicals had been imprisoned or driven into exile.) In the meantime, it had been decided in May 1822 that no further decree of the Portuguese Côrtes would be implemented without the express approval of the Prince Regent. In July more Brazilians were included in José Bonifácio's cabinet. And August saw an increasing number of 'independent' acts by Dom Pedro and the Brazilian government. The final step was taken on 7 September 1822 on the banks of the River Ipiranga, not far from São Paulo. There Dom Pedro received the latest despatches from Lisbon revoking his decrees, charging his ministers with treason and once again demanding his return and the complete subordination of

Brazil to Portuguese rule. At the same time he was advised by José Bonifácio and his wife Princess Leopoldina to break with Portugal once and for all. According to one eye witness (a member of the royal party), in a typically impulsive gesture Dom Pedro grabbed the despatches from the messenger, crumpled them in his hands and ground them under his heel, remarking angrily to those around him, 'From today on our relations with them are finished. I want nothing more from the Portuguese government, and I proclaim Brazil forevermore separated from Portugal.' And then, drawing his sword with a flourish he shouted, 'Long live independence, liberty and the separation of Brazil.' On 12 October, his 24th birthday, Dom Pedro I was acclaimed Constitutional Emperor and Perpetual Defender of Brazil. He was crowned in Rio de Janeiro with, it should be said, much pomp and ceremony on 1 December 1822.

The Brazilian movement for independence from Portugal had drawn its strength from the most important provinces of the centre-south – Rio de Janeiro, São Paulo, Minas Gerais – and especially from the capital, Rio de Janeiro. Pernambuco, where the Brazilian dominant class was anti-Portuguese but remembered the revolution of 1817 and the attempt to establish a republic and where the military garrison, in any case relatively small, proved willing to transfer its allegiance to Dom Pedro, quickly recognized the authority of the independent Brazilian empire. The other provinces of the north-east and the north, where there was still a considerable Portuguese military presence, sizeable Portuguese merchant communities and a good deal of pro-Portuguese sentiment, at least in the coastal cities, remained loyal to the Côrtes in Lisbon. There were fanciful rumours that Portugal might send a punitive expedition and as a first stage of reconquest attempt to separate the north-east and the north, which were closer to Portugal geographically, which were not economically integrated with the centre-south and which in many respects historically had closer ties with Lisbon than with Rio de Janeiro, from the rest of Brazil. If the process of independence were to be completed and consolidated, a long drawn-out civil war avoided and the authority of the new emperor imposed over the whole of the former Portuguese colony, it was imperative to bring the north-east and north, and especially Bahia, by far the most important of the provinces still under Portuguese control, into line as quickly as possible.

At the beginning of 1823 Bahia was bitterly divided, broadly speaking between the Recôncavo and the city of Salvador. This division can be traced back to the appointment of Ignácio Luís Madeira de Mello, a conservative Portuguese colonel, as military governor of the province in February 1822 which was resisted by members of the governing junta, by Brazilian army officers, by the *senhores de engenho* of the Recôncavo and by urban radicals. The resistance was unsuccessful and Madeira de Mello had managed to establish himself in power. In March the Portuguese troops forced to leave Rio in January arrived in Salvador, and they were later further reinforced from Portugal. Madeira de Mello then had at his disposal in Salvador a garrison of 2,000 regular troops plus a militia of 1,500 – the greatest concentration of Portuguese military force in Brazil. But first at Santo Amaro on 22 June, and later at Cachoeira, the conservative sugar barons of the Recôncavo rose in rebellion against the Portuguese attempts to recolonize Brazil. They withdrew their allegiance from João VI and together with a number of Brazilian-born judges set up at Cachoeira an All Bahia Interim Council of Government loyal to Dom Pedro and the government in Rio de Janeiro. The conservative revolutionaries were thus able to head off the more radical opponents of Portuguese colonialism ('demagogues and anarchists', some of whom favoured a separate republic of Bahia) and at the same time guarantee social stability which was increasingly threatened by a series of slave uprisings in the Recôncavo and popular disturbances in the depressed southern areas of the province. The Brazilian military forces, inferior in number, equipment and command, were not, however, strong enough to expel the Portuguese army, although they did begin a seige of the city of Salvador. For his part, Madeira de Mello twice – on 8 November 1822 and 6 January 1823 – failed to break out from Salvador. It was stalemate.

In July 1822, Dom Pedro had appointed a French officer Pierre Labatut as commander of the anti-Portuguese forces in Bahia. Travelling overland from Recife on the final stages of his journey he did not arrive until the end of October, but then with a good deal of energy and professional expertise set about organizing an *Exército Pacificador*. Although Labatut himself was removed by a mutiny in May 1823 and replaced as commander by general José Joaquim de Lima e Silva, he had by the middle of 1823 mobilized a respectable army – at least in terms of numbers: 14,000 men (including 3,000 from Rio and Pernambuco). Madeira de Mello and his troops, nevertheless, still presented a formidable military force to be overcome. Moreover, a Portuguese naval squadron – 1 line of battle ship, 5 frigates, 5 corvettes, 1 brig and 1 schooner – stationed at Bahia gave the Portuguese complete command of the sea.

It was in these circumstances that Dom Pedro turned to Lord Cochrane, the future 10th Earl of Dundonald. Arrogant, ill-tempered, cantankerous, bellicose, Cochrane was one of the most daring and successful frontline frigate captains of his day. He had been struck off the Navy List following a Stock Exchange scandal in 1814, but a few years later began a new career as a mercenary, selling his services to the highest bidder – although usually, it is true, on the side of liberty and national independence. He had already, in 1818, organized the Chilean navy and, with San Martín, had played a major role in securing the independence of Chile and liberating at least the coastal areas of Peru from Spanish rule. Temporarily in semi-retirement on his estate at Quintera in Chile, he now received Dom Pedro's invitation to serve Brazil.

Once again flouting the British Foreign Enlistment Act of 1819, Cochrane accepted the invitation – although only after a certain amount of haggling over rank (he eventually settled for First Admiral and Commander-in-Chief) and emoluments (he indignantly rejected the offer of a Portuguese admiral's pay, which he dismissed as 'notoriously the worst in the world'). Cochrane arrived in Rio de Janeiro on 13 March 1823, bringing with him several other English officers who had served with him in the Pacific, and immediately set about organizing a small Brazilian naval squadron – 9 ships in all – for the blockade of Bahia – in part by encouraging British seamen in Rio at the time to desert their ships. Apart from the flagship, the 74-gun double-decked *Pedro Primeiro* (formerly the *Martim Freitas* and one of the ships which had left Lisbon in November 1807), it was, however, a miserable force. Nevertheless, more out of fear of Cochrane's reputation than the actual force at his command, his arrival persuaded the Portuguese to evacuate Bahia and on 2 July 1823 General Lima e Silva, at the head of a Brazilian army, marched into the city – 'without any disturbance or acts of cruelty or oppression by either party', reported Vice Admiral Sir Thomas Hardy, commander-in-chief of the British South American squadron who, in anticipation of a threat to British lives and property, had moved his flagship *Creole* to Bahia the previous September. In local terms it was essentially a victory for the landowners of the Recôncavo – another conservative revolution.

Once the Portuguese convoy – 13 warships and about 70 transports and merchant vessels carrying 5,000 troops, vast quantities of military stores and a number of leading Portuguese families – had cleared the harbour, Cochrane pursued it relentlessly as far as the Canaries, night after night picking off ships from the rear until less than a quarter remained. Furthermore, the Brazilian frigate *Nitheroy*, commanded by another Englishman, John Taylor, who had served with Nelson at Trafalgar and who had deserted his ship in Rio to join Cochrane earlier in the year, followed the rump of the Portuguese convoy to the mouth of the Tagus and burned another four vessels under the very guns of the *Dom João VI*, the pride of the Portuguese navy.

Cochrane meanwhile had turned his attention to the northern province of Maranhão and on 26 July, largely by bluff, persuaded the small Portuguese garrison at São Luís to surrender. Two days later Maranhão (together with the former sub-captaincy of Piauí) was formally incorporated into the Brazilian empire. On 13 August Cochrane's second-in-command, Captain John Pascoe Grenfell, on board the *Maranhão* (formerly the Portuguese brig *Dom Miguel*), successfully secured the submission of loyalist elements at Belém, again more by the demonstration than the use of force, and the province of Pará (together with the former sub-captaincy of Rio Negro), that is, the whole of Amazonia, became part of the empire. The last Portuguese troops to leave Brazil left Montevideo in March 1824 after the Cisplatine province had also joined the independent Brazilian empire. After his exploits in the north Cochrane had returned to Rio de Janeiro where he was received by Dom Pedro on 9 November 1823 and, among other rewards and decorations, awarded the title Marquês de Maranhão. Though no doubt somewhat exaggerated in British accounts based on his own *Narrative of Services in the Liberation of Chili, Peru and Brazil* (1859) Cochrane and other British naval officers, entirely unofficially, had made a not inconsiderable contribution to the cause of Brazilian independence and, more important, Brazilian unity.[12]

---

[12] Of those who served with Cochrane, Grenfell became an admiral in the Brazilian navy (he was supreme commander in the war against the Argentine dictator Rosas in 1851–2) and served as Brazilian consul in Liverpool (where he died in 1868). Taylor, who also became an admiral in the Brazilian navy, married a Brazilian and eventually retired to a coffee plantation near Rio de Janeiro. Cochrane's own relations with Brazil were less happy. Not satisfied with the rewards he believed that his services merited and, as always, at loggerheads with his masters – the story of his life – after he had helped put down the republican-separatist revolt in Pernambuco in 1824, Cochrane 'deserted' on board the frigate *Piranga* and sailed to Spithead (where, on 16 June 1825, the Brazilian flag was first saluted in British waters). He then refused to return to Brazil and was dismissed from the Brazilian navy. However, not only was he later reinstated in the British navy – he served, for instance, as commander-in-chief of the North American and West Indian station – but shortly before his death (in 1860) the government of Marquês de Olinda (1857–8), willing to let bygones be bygones, granted him a life pension equal to half the interest on the £100,000 he still claimed from the Brazilian government, and his descendants were eventually paid the sum of £40,000.

By the middle of 1823 Brazil had established her independence from Portugal beyond all doubt, while at the same time avoiding civil war and territorial disintegration. The new Brazilian government, however, was still anxious to secure international recognition of Brazil's *de facto* independence. There were two principal reasons for this: first, to forestall any last ditch attempt by Portugal, once more as a result of the Vilafrancada (May 1823) governed by an absolutist João VI, encouraged and possibly assisted by the reactionary Holy Alliance powers of Europe, to reassert its authority over Brazil in any way; secondly, and ultimately more important, to strengthen the emperor's own authority within Brazil against loyalist, separatist and republican elements. Clearly the attitude of Britain, whose navy commanded the Atlantic, who had emerged from the Napoleonic Wars pre-eminent not only in Europe but in the world at large, and who exercised so much influence in Lisbon, would be decisive. In July 1823 Felisberto Caldeira Brant Pontes (the future Marquês de Barbacena), Dom Pedro's agent in London since July 1821, wrote 'With England's friendship we can snap our fingers at the rest of the world . . . it will not be necessary to go begging for recognition from any other power for all will wish our friendship.'[13]

Although Britain had done nothing to promote it, George Canning, who as a result of Lord Castlereagh's suicide had returned to the Foreign Office only a week after the *Grito de Ipiranga* of 7 September 1822, had been eager to recognize Brazil's independence as quickly as possible: there were particularly strong reasons for doing so (and, incidentally, recognition of Brazil would facilitate the recognition of the new Spanish American republics, at least those whose *de facto* independence from Spain was beyond question and with whom Britain had close commercial ties). In the first place, Portugal was too weak, militarily and financially, to reimpose its rule; Brazil was *de facto* independent, Canning believed, notwithstanding the Portuguese hold on areas of the north-east and the north, from the moment it declared its separation from Portugal. Secondly, Britain already had established relations with Brazil as a result of the Portuguese court's residence there. And Brazil was now Britain's third largest foreign market. By proffering the hand of friendship in her hour of need Britain would consolidate its political and economic ascendancy over Brazil. Thirdly, unlike Spanish America Brazil had retained the monarchy, and Canning was anxious to preserve it as an

---

[13] Quoted in Manchester, *British preeminence*, 193.

antidote to the 'evils of universal democracy' on the continent and as a valuable link between the Old and New Worlds. Any undue delay in recognizing the Brazilian empire might endanger the country's political institutions and undermine its precarious unity. (In March 1824 an armed revolt originating in Pernambuco did, in fact, lead to the establishment of an independent republic, the Confederation of the Equator, in the north-east, but it was defeated after six months.) Finally, Brazil's declaration of independence presented Britain with a unique opportunity to make significant progress on the slave trade question.

In normal circumstances it might have been thought impossible to persuade a newly independent Brazil, one of the greatest importers of African slaves in the New World – 'the very child and champion of the slave trade, nay the slave trade personified' in Wilberforce's eyes – to abolish the trade. But just as Britain had wrung concessions, however limited, from a reluctant Portugal as the price for British support during the war and immediate post-war years so, Canning was quick to realize, Brazil's anxiety for British recognition 'put [her] at our mercy as to the continuation of the slave trade'. In November 1822 Canning and Brant, the Brazilian agent, who had been instructed by Dom Pedro as early as 12 August to negotiate for recognition, discussed unofficially the question of the immediate abolition of the slave trade by Brazil in return for immediate recognition by Britain. Once Brazil's independence had been recognized, and Brazil had abolished the slave trade, Portugal's own excuse for not fulfilling its treaty engagements with Britain to abolish at some future date its trade south as well as north of the equator – the interests of its foremost colony, Brazil – would collapse. In any case, the transportation of slaves to territories outside the Portuguese empire had been prohibited by Portuguese legislation as far back as 1761 as well as by recent Anglo-Portuguese treaties. In the event Canning was restrained from any over-hasty action with respect to Brazil by the ultra Tory members of the Cabinet and by King George IV. Despite the preservation of the monarchy the Brazilian regime was, after all, revolutionary and the crowning of Dom Pedro as emperor had popular, Napoleonic overtones. (In fact the title sprang more from the liberal masonic tradition and in José Bonifácio's eyes it was simply a reflection of the size of Brazil.) Moreover, Britain had to take account of its traditional economic and strategic interests in Portugal. For his part Brant could not deliver the *immediate* abolition of the slave trade. Although Dom Pedro and José Bonifácio both personally abhorred the slave trade – and many

members of the Constituent Assembly which met in May 1823 opposed it
– they dared not alienate the great Brazilian landowners, the main
supporters of the independent Brazilian monarchy, who had no alternative source of labour. The political – and economic – dangers arising
from premature abolition were greater than those that might arise from
non-recognition. The most they could offer, therefore, was gradual
abolition over four or five years in return for immediate British recognition. In the meantime they promised to observe the Anglo-Portuguese
treaties of 1815 and 1817 for the suppression of the trade north of the
equator. Canning, however, was firmly committed to the policy that no
state in the New World would be recognized unless it had already
abolished the slave trade. 'Recognition', he had told the Duke of
Wellington, Britain's representative at the Congress of Verona, 'can only
be purchased by a frank surrender of the slave trade.' He agreed with
Wilberforce that Brazil 'must be purged of its impurity before we take it
into our embraces'.[14]

In September 1823 Portugal requested Britain's good offices in its
relations with Brazil, and Canning agreed. He made it clear, however,
that he was not prepared to wait indefinitely for an acknowledgement by
Portugal of Brazilian independence: to do so would endanger Britain's
commercial interests and its political influence in Brazil. He had in mind
in particular the fact that the Anglo-Portuguese commercial treaty of
1810, which had been accepted by the new Brazilian government, came
up for renewal in 1825 at which time direct negotiations with Brazil
could no longer be avoided. The longer international recognition was
delayed the more difficult it would become to secure from a grateful
Brazil in return not only the continuation of Britain's commercial
privileges in Brazil but also abolition of the Brazilian slave trade. Talks in
London between Brazil and Portugal sponsored by both Britain and
Austria opened in July 1824, were suspended in November and finally
broke down in February 1825. Canning now decided it was time for
Britain to act alone. Sir Charles Stuart, former British minister in Lisbon
during the Peninsular War and ambassador in Paris since 1815, was sent
on a special mission to Rio de Janeiro to negotiate an Anglo-Brazilian
commercial treaty. En route he was successful in persuading a new and
more flexible Portuguese government to accept the inevitable; he was
empowered to negotiate on behalf of Portugal as well.

[14] Quoted in Leslie Bethell, *The abolition of the Brazilian slave trade* (Cambridge, 1970), 31.

Stuart arrived in Rio on 18 July and on 29 August signed the treaty by which Portugal recognized the independence of Brazil.[15] In return Brazil agreed to pay Portugal compensation amounting to £2 million. Dom Pedro also pledged himself to defend the territorial integrity of the rest of the Portuguese empire and never to permit any other Portuguese colony – for example, Luanda and Benguela in Portuguese Africa which historically had close ties with Brazil – to unite with the Brazilian empire. (As early as February 1823 José Bonifácio had already told the British chargé in Rio, 'with regard to colonies on the coast of Africa, we want none, nor anywhere else; Brazil is quite large enough and productive enough for us, and we are content with what Providence has given us'.)[16] On the other hand, Dom Pedro retained the right to succeed to the Portuguese throne – leaving open the possibility, as Canning intended, that one day Brazil and Portugal might be peacefully reunited under the House of Braganza.

There was a price to pay for services rendered by Britain in securing Brazil its independence – and for future British friendship and support. In the first place, Britain had throughout all the negotiations since 1822 demanded the abolition of the slave trade in return for the recognition of Brazilian independence, and after a treaty negotiated by Stuart at the time of Portuguese recognition had been rejected by Canning a treaty was finally signed in November 1826 under which the entire Brazilian slave trade would become illegal three years after the ratification of the treaty (i.e. in March 1830). Secondly, an Anglo-Brazilian commercial treaty signed in August 1827 included the continuation of the 15 per cent maximum tariff on British goods imported into Brazil and the right to appoint judges conservators to deal with cases involving British merchants resident in Brazil. The process begun in 1808 whereby Britain successfully transferred its highly privileged economic position from Portugal to Brazil was thus completed.

The separation of Brazil from Portugal, like that of the North American colonies from England and Spanish America from Spain, can to some extent be explained in terms of a general crisis – economic, political and

---

[15] *De facto* recognition by Britain followed in January 1826 when Manuel Rodrigues Gameiro Pessôa was received as Brazilian minister in London. Robert Gordon was sent to Rio de Janeiro as British minister later in the year. The United States, on 26 May 1824, had, in fact, been the first to recognize Brazil. See Stanley E. Hilton, 'The United States and Brazilian independence', in Russell-Wood (ed.), *From colony to nation*.

[16] Quoted in Bethell, *Abolition*, 49–50.

ideological – of the old colonial system throughout the Atlantic world in the late eighteenth and early nineteenth centuries. The independence of Brazil, even more than Spanish American independence, was also the outcome of a chance combination of political and military developments in Europe during the first quarter of the nineteenth century and their repercussions in the New World. The half-century before independence certainly witnessed a growth in colonial self-consciousness and some demand for economic and political self-determination, but for a variety of reasons – the nature of Portuguese colonial rule, the nature of the colonial economy, the overwhelming predominance of slavery, the close ties between the metropolitan and colonial elites – less so in Brazil than in Spanish America. Napoleon's invasion of Portugal and the transfer of the Portuguese court from Lisbon to Rio de Janeiro in 1807–8 can be seen as merely postponing the final confrontation between colony and metropolis which the overthrow of the Spanish monarchy by Napoleon triggered off in Spanish America, but it also brought the Portuguese crown and the Brazilian oligarchy closer together and to a large extent satisfied Brazilian economic and even political grievances. Brazil can be regarded as moving gradually and inevitably towards independence from 1808, but it also has to be recognized that as late as 1820 there was in Brazil no widespread desire for total separation from Portugal. It was the Portuguese revolutions of 1820, the return of the Portuguese court to Lisbon in 1821 and Portugal's determination to reverse the political and economic gains since 1808 which forced the Brazilian dominant class (which included many Portuguese-born) along the road to independence. And in this José Bonifácio de Andrada e Silva, who had spent most of his adult life in Portugal, played a crucial role.

Once decided upon, Brazilian independence was relatively quickly and peacefully established, in contrast to Spanish America where the struggle for independence was for the most part long drawn out and violent. There was little loyalist sympathy and in the last analysis Portugal did not have the financial and military resources to resist it. Moreover, Brazil, unlike Spanish America, did not fragment into a number of separate states. There was no great sense of national identity in Brazil. The centre-south, the north-east and the north were to a large extent different worlds, with their own integrated economies, separated by huge distances and poor communications, though no great geographical barriers. Rio de Janeiro and São Paulo took the lead in the movement for independence, but the other provincial and regional elites whose political, economic and social interests broadly coincided gave their support to the new state with its capital in Rio. Here the availability in Brazil of a prince of the House of Braganza willing to assume the leadership of the independence movement was decisive. Dom Pedro was a symbol of legitimate authority and a powerful instrument of political and social stability and of national unity. The country was also held together by its highly centralized bureaucratic and judicial system. The 'War of Independence' to expel from the north-east and the north the troops which remained loyal to Portugal was short and virtually bloodless, and provided little opportunity for the assertion of separatist tendencies or for that matter the mobilization of popular forces. The Brazilian empire was also fortunate in securing early international recognition of its independence.

The transition from colony to independent empire was characterized by an extraordinary degree of political, economic and social continuity. Pedro I and the Brazilian dominant class took over the existing Portuguese state apparatus which, in fact, never ceased to function. The economy suffered no major dislocation: patterns of trade and investment changed (in particular Britain became Brazil's major trading partner and source of capital), but both the 'colonial' mode of production and Brazil's role in the international division of labour were largely unaffected. There was no major social upheaval: the popular forces which were in any case weak – and divided by class, colour and legal status – were successfully contained; no significant concessions were made to the underprivileged groups in society; above all, the institution of slavery survived (although the slave trade was now under threat). A conservative revolution had been effected. Insofar as the extreme liberalism (and republicanism) of 1789, 1798, 1817, 1821–3 and 1824 had been confronted and defeated it was a counter-revolution.

Part One

EMPIRE (1822–1889)

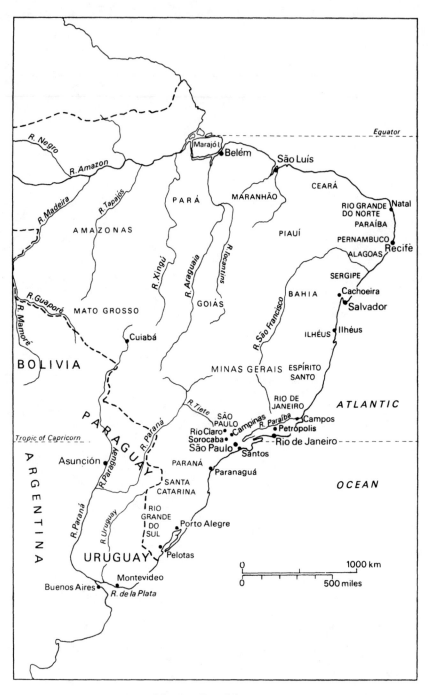

Map 2   Brazil in 1830

2

1822–1850

At the time of its independence from Portugal in 1822 Brazil had a population of between 4 and 5 million (if the Brazilian Indians numbering perhaps as many as 800,000 are included). This relatively small population was scattered over a vast territory of over 3 million square miles, but remained heavily concentrated in an area within 200 miles of the Atlantic coast from the provinces of the north-east (with 40–45 per cent of the total population) to Rio de Janeiro, São Paulo and the south. The only inland province with a significant population was Minas Gerais which had been the focus of the gold rush in the first half of the eighteenth century and which still accounted for 20 per cent of Brazil's population, though most of it was located in the south of the province adjoining Rio. Some provinces of the interior like Mato Grosso had populations of less than 40,000. It was an overwhelmingly rural population. The largest city was the capital, Rio de Janeiro, with around 100,000 inhabitants; the second largest city, Salvador (Bahia), the former capital, had only 60,000, and half of the provincial capitals no more than 10,000 each. Conditions of health were very poor and average life expectancy low. The general level of education was also low. Education had never been a priority of Portuguese colonial policy. As late as 1872, when the first official figures became available, only a fifth of the free population was even literate.

In 1822 less than a third of Brazil's population was white. The great majority was black or mulatto. At least 30 per cent were slaves. The best estimate of the total number of slaves is probably 1,147,515 in 1823.[1] Three-quarters of the slaves were concentrated in only five of the

---

[1] 'Memória Estatística do Império', date and author unknown, published in *Revista do Instituto Histórico e Geográfico Brasileiro*, LVIII, 1 (1959), 91–9. The total population, according to this source, was 3,960,866.

eighteen provinces – Maranhão, Pernambuco, Bahia, Minas Gerais and
Rio de Janeiro – where in many areas they constituted the majority of the
population. Besides supplying Brazil's additional labour needs in periods
of economic expansion, the transatlantic slave trade from Africa was
essential, as it always had been, to replenish the existing slave population,
which did not reproduce itself. Annual imports of slaves into Brazil had
risen from 15,000–20,000 at the beginning of the century to 30,000 in the
early 1820s.

Slaves were to be found throughout rural Brazil in stockraising, in
cereal production, in the cultivation of basic staples for local consumption and in subsistence agriculture. Minas Gerais, with an economy
largely given over to cattle ranching and *pequena lavoura* since the end of
the gold cycle in the middle of the eighteenth century, had the largest
slave population of any single province: 170,000 in 1819. Slaves were also
widely employed as domestic servants in the city of Rio, in Salvador and
Recife, indeed in every town from Belém and São Luís in the north to
Porto Alegre and Pelotas in the south. Urban *escravos de ganho* worked, for
example, as stevedores and porters in the docks, as water and refuse
carriers, as transporters of people, as masons and carpenters, prostitutes,
even as beggars. Religious houses and hospitals owned slaves; the state
owned, and hired, slaves for building and maintaining public works.
Until the slave trade from Africa to Brazil became illegal in 1830 and the
first serious efforts were made to end it slaves were both available and
cheap. The existence in Brazil of an 'open frontier' with an almost
limitless supply of free or cheap land together with an overall *falta de
braços* (shortage of labour) also helps explain why slavery was so essential
and characteristic a feature of economic and social life, rural and urban.
However, as in every slave society throughout the Americas, the majority of slaves in Brazil were concentrated in single-crop, export-oriented
plantation agriculture (*grande lavoura*).

Brazil had lost its near monopoly of the world's sugar supply in the
middle of the seventeenth century, but sugar remained Brazil's major
cash crop throughout the colonial period. The economic disruptions
caused by the French Revolution and the Napoleonic Wars had given a
fresh impetus to sugar planting in Brazil not only in the north-east, in the
Zona de Mata of Pernambuco and the Recôncavo of Bahia where sugar
had been produced since the 1530s, but also in the Campos region of Rio
de Janeiro province and, most recently, in the province of São Paulo. At
the time of independence sugar accounted for 40 per cent of Brazil's

export earnings. Cotton, mainly grown in Maranhão and to a lesser extent in Pernambuco, came next with 20 per cent, although Brazil's share of British raw cotton imports was by now in decline. And coffee exports from Rio province which had increased from 160 *arrobas* in 1792 to 318,032 in 1817 and 539,000 in 1820, made up almost another 20 per cent of the value of Brazil's exports. The rest consisted mainly of hides, tobacco and cacao.

Since the arrival of the Portuguese court and the opening of the ports in 1808 Brazil's foreign trade, exports as well as imports, had been in the hands of foreign, especially British, but also French, German and American, as well as Portuguese merchants. Britain was now Brazil's main trading partner. The system of colonial preference effectively excluded sugar and coffee though not cotton from the British market. Nevertheless, British merchants shipped a large proportion of Brazilian produce to the European market. And Britain supplied the bulk of the manufactured goods, especially cottons, woollens, linens and hardware, imported into Brazil. The Portuguese were for the most part confined to the retail trade in foreign goods and the internal trade in Brazilian goods. Thus, whereas the productive sector of the Brazilian economy was almost completely in the hands of Brazilians, foreigners controlled the commercial sector.

In the areas of export agriculture – the north-east, Rio de Janeiro and parts of São Paulo – there had developed rural oligarchies based on plantations and slave labour. This was particularly true of older export centres like the Mata of Pernambuco, the Recôncavo of Bahia and the river valleys around São Luís in Maranhão. Here, if anywhere, was to be found the classic society of masters and slaves. Elsewhere society was more complex. The free population of Brazil was, after all, twice as large as the slave population and only a small minority of the free were planters or *estancieiros*. In the vast cattle raising areas of the interior of the north-east, from northern Minas Gerais to southern Maranhão, in Rio Grande do Sul, in the frontier areas of south and west, and in the periphery of the plantation zones throughout Brazil there existed a large intermediate stratum of small landowners and cattle ranchers, tenant farmers and squatters of varying degrees of independence. In Minas there was a substantial number of slaves, but they were not concentrated on plantations, as we have seen; and in 1823 there were already as many free blacks and mulattos as slaves. In some northern provinces, such as Ceará and Piauí (as in Santa Catarina in the south), slaves represented no more than 10 per cent of the population. In Pará 30 per cent were slaves, but there was also a large Indian population and no well-established landowning or commercial class. In the cities social stratification was, of course, even more complex. A large number of small merchants, petty officials, artisans, clerks and journeymen filled the space between the high-level bureaucrats, big merchants and capitalists on the one hand and the slaves on the other. And within the urban slave population, as we have seen, there was extraordinary occupational diversity.

The centre-south of Brazil (Minas Gerais, Espírito Santo, Rio de Janeiro, São Paulo, Santa Catarina, Rio Grande do Sul) had been somewhat integrated economically since the gold boom of the first half of the eighteenth century. The growth of the port of Rio and the expansion of sugar and coffee production in the area during the last decade of the eighteenth and the first two decades of the nineteenth century had further strengthened Rio's economic ties with Minas Gerais and the southern provinces. Minas Gerais supplied the Rio market with meat, beans and dairy produce. Rio Grande do Sul exported wheat and *charque* (dried meat) to feed the slaves and the free poor. And there was a profitable trade in mules and cattle from Rio Grande to São Paulo, Minas Gerais and Rio de Janeiro via the famous fair at Sorocaba in São Paulo. Bahia and its satellite Sergipe, Pernambuco and the neighbouring provinces of Alagoas, Paraíba, Rio Grande do Norte and Ceará and the north (Maranhão, Piauí and Pará, which then included present-day Amazonas) were mostly worlds apart from each other and from the centre-south. They had their own integrated export and subsistence economies. They were not, however, totally isolated. There was an inter-regional trade, for example the cattle trade between Bahia and the centre-south and the trade in *charque* from Rio Grande do Sul as far north as Bahia and Pernambuco. But land communications by primitive roads and by cattle and mule trails were extremely precarious. Communications between provinces were mostly by sea and by some major rivers, such as the São Francisco which linked Minas Gerais to the north-east, the Amazon crossing the northern rain forests and the Paraná on the south-west frontier. Before steam navigation it took less time to travel from Maranhão to Lisbon than to Rio de Janeiro. It could even take three weeks by sea from Recife to Rio – with a favourable wind.

Brazil in 1822 had no economic unity. Nor was there in Brazil any strong sense of national identity. The unity maintained in the transition from Portuguese colony to independent empire was political – and precarious. It would be seriously threatened when, a decade later, the alliance of forces which had brought about Brazil's independence from Portugal finally disintegrated.

The independence Brazil achieved in 1822 was incomplete. The presence of a Portuguese prince willing to assume the leadership of the movement for independence from Portugal was a crucial factor in ensuring a smooth transition to independence, political – and social – stability and national unity.[2] At the same time many leading Brazilian politicians had serious doubts about the strength of the emperor's commitment to constitutionalism and, even more serious, his willingness to sever all family and dynastic ties with the former colonial power. Although distinct these two concerns were interconnected and reinforced each other, since Pedro I's suspected absolutist convictions were easily linked by Brazilian elite and populace alike to the protection of Portugal's remaining interests in Brazil and, indeed, the fear of recolonization. The reign of Pedro I was a period of constant political tension and conflict which culminated in his abdication in April 1831.

The Constituent Assembly was the scene of the first clashes between the Brazilian political elite and Pedro I, less than a year after the declaration of independence but before, it should be remembered, Portuguese troops had been removed from Bahia, the north and the Cisplatine province. The assembly had first been summoned by the Prince Regent on 3 June 1822 but was not officially inaugurated until 3 May 1823. There the future organization of the new Brazilian state was vigorously, at times violently, debated. Even though many of the most outspoken critics of the 1822 arrangement, like Joaquim Gonçalves Lêdo who fled to Buenos Aires and Cipriano Barata who was imprisoned until shortly before the abdication of Pedro I, had been excluded, liberals, both 'moderate' and 'extreme', attempted to curb the powers of the young emperor, especially his powers to veto legislation and dissolve the legislature. For a while José Bonifácio de Andrada e Silva, the patriarch of Brazilian independence who continued to serve as Dom Pedro's adviser and first minister after independence, sided with the emperor in the interests of strong government. At the same time he tried to prevent Dom Pedro from going over completely to the 'Portuguese' faction at a time when absolutism in France, Spain and Portugal itself, where the liberal experiment was brought to an end in May 1823, was

[2] On the independence of Brazil, see Ch. 1 above.

clearly resurgent. The resignation of José Bonifácio on 16 July 1823 is, therefore, an important episode in the political polarization which occurred in Brazil immediately after independence.

During the second half of 1823 opposition to the emperor both in the Constituent Assembly and in the press became increasingly bitter. Finally, on 12 November 1823 the assembly was forcibly dissolved and, among others, José Bonifácio and his more liberal younger brothers, Antônio Carlos Ribeiro de Andrada Machado e Silva and Martim Francisco Ribeiro de Andrada, were arrested and banished to France.[3] Dom Pedro himself immediately set up a Council of State which quickly drafted a constitution. It included a Senate (50 members) as well as a Chamber of Deputies (100 members). Senators were selected by the emperor from lists of three elected in the provinces and served for life. Deputies were to be elected – indirectly elected, first by voters, then by electors, on a limited suffrage – for four years. To be a voter it was necessary to have an annual net income from property or employment of 100 milréis (about £10 in 1830); electors had a minimum income of 200 milréis. (Deputies were required to have an income of 400 milréis, senators 800 milréis.) The constitution confirmed the Council of State, the ten members of which were chosen by the emperor and also served for life. The emperor had veto powers over legislation. He nominated both ministers, who were responsible to him, and high court judges, and his 'moderating power', based on Benjamin Constant's *pouvoir royal* for resolving conflicts between executive, legislature and judiciary, specifically enabled him to dissolve the Chamber and to call elections. There was, finally, a high degree of political centralization: the emperor appointed provincial presidents, and the *Conselhos Gerais de Província* and the *câmaras municipais*, although elected (the *Conselhos* by indirect and the *câmaras* by direct vote), had only limited powers. The decisions of the *Conselhos Gerais* had to be approved by the Chamber of Deputies. Finally, the Catholic religion was declared the religion of the state and the emperor, as head of state, appointed bishops and dispensed ecclesiastical benefices.

The arbitrary dissolution of the Constituent Assembly in November 1823 followed by the promulgation of a new constitution in March 1824 brought to an abrupt end the honeymoon period in the relations between

---

[3] José Bonifácio returned to Brazil in July 1829 but, after serving as deputy for Bahia and after the abdication of Pedro I in 1831 as tutor to the young Dom Pedro, he was arrested in 1833 and confined to the island of Paquetá in Guanabara Bay. He died in Niterói in 1838.

Dom Pedro and important sections of the Brazilian dominant class, not only in the centre-south where the movement for independence had originated but also in the north-east. When news of the dissolution reached Bahia, on 12 December 1823, there were anti-Portuguese disturbances and threats of secession. Then in March 1824 came an armed revolt in Pernambuco led by a radical priest, Frei Caneca, and Manuel Carvalho Paes de Andrade. It was supported by Rio Grande do Norte, Paraíba and Ceará, attracted sympathy throughout the north-east, including Bahia, and led to the proclamation of an independent republic, the Confederation of the Equator. For Caneca Dom Pedro I's constitution did not define 'positively and exclusively the territory of the empire and because of this it leaves open the possibility for any future aspirations to union with Portugal'; 'it was not liberal, but totally contrary to the principles of liberty, independence and the rights of Brazil, apart from which it has been presented to us by someone who does not have the power to do so'; the Senate would become 'a new aristocracy and oppressor of the people'; the moderating power, 'a Machiavellian invention', was 'the master key to the oppression of the Brazilian nation and effectively strangles the freedom of the people'; and, finally, the constitution's centralism was particularly prejudicial to the political freedom of Brazil since it deprived the provinces of their autonomy and isolated them, each totally dependent on the central executive, subject to a type of 'Asiatic despotism'.[4] The rebellion of 1824 was put down by imperial troops after six months. The harshness with which the rebels were treated after their defeat – by specially created and unconstitutional military courts – only served to increase the gap between the emperor and the liberal opposition, moderate and radical. Frei Caneca himself, like many others throughout the north-east, and some in Rio de Janeiro, paid for his convictions with his life; he was executed by firing squad in Recife on 13 January 1825.

In addition to his autocratic methods of government and his scandalous private life (in which before and after the death of his wife Leopoldina in December 1826 his mistress Domitila de Castro Canto, the Marquêsa de Santos, figured prominently), Pedro I's close association with the Portuguese community in Rio – Portuguese bureaucrats who had come to Rio with the court in 1808, married into local landed and commercial families, acquired property themselves and chosen to stay in 1821, as well as Portuguese merchants – and his 'Portuguese' cabinets

[4] Frei Caneca, *Ensaios políticos* (Rio de Janeiro, 1976), 67–75.

were by now a matter of growing concern. Particularly resented was the influence exerted by a 'secret cabinet' of his Portuguese friends among whom was his notorious drinking companion, Francisco Gomes de Silva, o Chalaça. It is not without significance that 50 per cent of the ministers were bureaucrats, civil or military, and more ministers were linked to commercial activities in the *primeiro reinado* than at any time during the empire.[5]

The negotiations over the recognition of Brazil's independence by Portugal reinforced the view that Dom Pedro was inclined to put dynastic considerations before Brazil's national interests. Under the treaty of 29 August 1825 which Sir Charles Stuart, the head of a special British mission to Brazil, negotiated on behalf of Portugal, Brazil agreed to pay Portugal compensation of £2 million, £1.4 million of which was earmarked to repay a Portuguese loan floated in London in 1823 to cover the cost of the campaign to restore Portuguese authority in Brazil. Moreover, the treaty deliberately left open the question of the succession. Pedro I did not expressly abdicate his rights of succession to the Portuguese throne, giving to many Brazilians the impression of a family deal and justifying the fear that on Dom João's death Dom Pedro would become king of Portugal. Brazil and Portugal would thus automatically be reunited – with Brazil possibly reduced to its former colonial status.[6]

Brazil had to pay a price for British help in securing early Portuguese – and international – recognition of its independence, but Dom Pedro was strongly criticized for paying too high a price, although it could be argued he had little choice in the matter. Brazil had, in particular, clear if unwritten obligations to come to some agreement with Britain on the slave trade question. Throughout all the diplomatic negotiations since 1822 a bargain had been implied: abolition for recognition. In any case, once Brazil and Portugal were formally separated the bulk of the slave trade to Brazil became illegal, or so George Canning, the British Foreign Secretary, argued. Portugal, whose African territories south of the equator, principally Angola, supplied the Brazilian market with an

---

[5] José Murilo de Carvalho, *A Construção da Ordem; a elite política imperial* (Rio de Janeiro, 1980), 87.
[6] João VI died in March 1826 and Dom Pedro did become enmeshed in the problems of the dynastic succession in Portugal. On 2 May he reluctantly abdicated the Portuguese throne in favour of his seven-year-old daughter. Maria da Glória married her uncle, Pedro I's younger brother, Dom Miguel, who was appointed Regent. When in 1828 Miguel dissolved the Côrtes and re-established absolutist government with himself as king, Pedro became almost obsessed with the idea of defending his daughter's right to the Portuguese throne. In 1828 Maria da Glória joined her father in Brazil. And after Dom Pedro's abdication of the Brazilian throne in April 1831 they returned together to Portugal where Dom Pedro achieved his goal just before his death in September 1834.

increasing proportion of its slaves, was bound by treaties which Britain had every intention of enforcing (by force, if necessary) not to export slaves to non-Portuguese territories across the Atlantic. After some tough negotiations conducted on the British side first by Stuart, then by Robert Gordon, Britain's minister in Rio, whom Dom Pedro was to refer to as 'that ill-mannered and obstinate Scot', a treaty was signed on 23 November 1826 under which the entire Brazil slave trade became illegal three years after its ratification. (The treaty was immediately ratified by the emperor on board a Brazilian warship sailing out of Rio harbour bound for Rio Grande do Sul, and by Britain on 13 March 1827).

Despite Canning's efforts to make it appear that the abolition of the slave trade within three years was a necessary corollary of independence arising out of obligations under existing Portuguese treaties which Brazil had no alternative but to accept – 'a positive engagement rather than . . . a demand on our part and an unconditional surrender on his [the emperor's]' – most Brazilians saw the treaty as a major sacrifice of Brazil's national interests at the insistence of a powerful foreign nation. Robert Gordon had no doubt that it had been 'ceded at our request in opposition to the views and wishes of the whole empire' and was 'in the highest degree unpopular'.[7] Moreover, the emperor had been persuaded to ignore the opinion of the Chamber of Deputies which met for the first time in May 1826 and debated two bills for the *gradual* abolition of the slave trade, one from José Clemente Pereira (Rio de Janeiro) for abolition by 31 December 1840, the other from Nicolau Pereira de Campos Vergueiro (São Paulo) for abolition after six years. When the Chamber met again in May 1827 abolition was a *fait accompli* but few deputies, even those of enlightened views, believed that it would be anything other than a disaster, above all for Brazilian agriculture but also for commerce, shipping and government revenue. Until Brazil was able to recruit free European immigrants in large numbers – 'the poor, the wretched, the industrious of Europe', José Bonifácio had called them – Brazilian agriculture, especially large-scale plantation agriculture, had no alternative to slave labour. The few attempts to promote European, mainly German and Swiss, immigration since 1808 had been rather disappointing, and strategic and military considerations continued to be more important than economic. Of the 10,000 or so Europeans who arrived in Brazil between 1823 and 1830 more than 6,000 ended up in the southern frontier province of Rio Grande do Sul.

[7] Quotations in Leslie Bethell, *The abolition of the Brazilian slave trade* (Cambridge, 1970), 54–5, 62.

To the growing list of what many Brazilians regarded as Dom Pedro's failures should be added his unpopular, expensive and ultimately unsuccessful policy in the Río de la Plata. The Banda Oriental, the source of more than a hundred years of conflict between Spain and Portugal, had been occupied by Portuguese troops in 1817 in the struggle against Artigas during the Spanish American wars of independence and incorporated into Brazil in 1821 as the Cisplatine Province. The government in Buenos Aires, which had inherited Spanish claims to the territory, was determined to reconquer it. Taking advantage of a rebellion led by Lavalleja which found broad support outside Montevideo at least, the Congress in Buenos Aires on 25 October 1825 announced the incorporation of the Banda Oriental into the United Provinces of the Río de la Plata. It amounted to a declaration of war and six weeks later the emperor felt obliged to follow suit. The war went disastrously for Brazil; the imperial troops were consistently defeated. The war at sea was notable for the fact that both fleets had a British commander – Admiral Brown on the Argentine side, Admiral Norton on the Brazilian – and most of the seamen were English. In the end, largely as a result of British diplomatic mediation, the Banda Oriental was recognized in October 1828 by both Argentina and Brazil as the independent buffer state of Uruguay.

The war effort had been substantial and had placed an extra burden on the already strained national finances. It also led to a great increase in military recruitment, possibly the most hated government measure in nineteenth-century Brazil. In fact, the measure was so unpopular that the emperor decided to hire foreign troops to complement the national draft. The decision proved disastrous since not only did it fail to prevent defeat in the war, but it also resulted in the mutiny of several thousand Irish and German mercenaries in Rio in June 1828. For two days the city was at the mercy of the troops and the government had to go through the humiliation of asking for the help of British and French naval units. A last negative consequence of the war was the disruption it caused to the supply of mules and cattle from Rio Grande do Sul to São Paulo, Minas Gerais and Rio de Janeiro. The sharp rise in mule and cattle prices in the final years of the decade had an adverse effect on the economies of all three provinces.[8] For their part the ranchers of Rio Grande do Sul were

---

[8] The number of mules and cattle passing through the Sorocaba fair in São Paulo fell from 30,474 in 1822 to 21,817 in 1829, and the price of mules went up from 14$000 in 1820 to 60$000 in 1829. Maria Theresa Schorer Petrone, *O Barão de Iguape* (São Paulo, 1976), 21–8.

unhappy about the lack of adequate compensation for their efforts during the war and would add this to their list of grievances in 1835 to justify their rebellion against the central government.

It would be wrong to suggest that Dom Pedro had no support outside a narrow 'Portuguese' circle. The monarchy as an institution had great popular appeal and was still considered by most of the national elite as a powerful instrument of national unity and social stability. And Pedro I, who as the hero of independence could still draw on some goodwill, was the only member of the house of Braganza in a position to govern Brazil. It was not the case that the entire national elite had turned against the emperor: many were co-opted as ministers, senators, councillors of state; some were bought with honorific titles. During 1825–6 Pedro granted 104 titles of nobility (mostly *barão* and *visconde*), more than two-thirds of all the titles awarded during the *primeiro reinado*.⁹ Among Pedro's Brazilian supporters there were diehard absolutists, and many hesitated to oppose him in case the monarchical system itself should thus be threatened. Nevertheless, there is no doubt that in the late twenties the rift between Dom Pedro and the majority of his subjects was widening. The alienation from power of the dominant groups in Minas Gerais and São Paulo and some elements in Rio de Janeiro combined with popular hatred of the Portuguese and military disaffection eventually brought him down.

Economic and financial difficulties also played their part. Coffee exports from Rio more than tripled between 1822 and 1831, it is true, but the prices of most of the country's major exports – cotton, hides, cacao, tobacco, as well as coffee – fell steadily throughout the 1820s. A small increase of 1.7 per cent in the price of sugar which still accounted for between 30 and 40 per cent of Brazil's exports was not enough to compensate.¹⁰ The Anglo-Brazilian commercial treaty of August 1827 – the second of Britain's bills for services rendered at the time of independence – confirmed all the privileges conferred on British trade in 1810 including the 15 per cent maximum tariff on imported British goods and Britain's right to appoint judges conservators to deal with cases involving British merchants in Brazil, but offered no reciprocity. To protect West Indian produce Britain imposed duties amounting to 180 per cent ad valorem on Brazilian sugar and 300 per cent on Brazilian coffee.

---

⁹ R. J. Barman, 'A New-World nobility: the role of titles in imperial Brazil', *University of British Columbia Hispanic Studies* (1974), 43.

¹⁰ Carlos Manuel Pelaez and Wilson Suzigan, *História monetária do Brasil: análise da política, comportamento e instituições monetárias* (Rio de Janeiro, 1976), 51.

The limit on tariffs on British goods to 15 per cent ad valorem (extended in 1828 to all imported goods), besides obstructing the growth of manufacturing in Brazil, imposed a ceiling on revenue and exacerbated the problems the Brazilian government had in organizing state finances on a sound basis. Two years after independence Brazil had floated its first loan, for £3 million, in London to pay the Portuguese indemnity. It was followed by a second of £400,000 in 1829 to cover the servicing of the first. While the 1824 loan was negotiated at 80 per cent, the second was at 52 per cent, a clear indication of the low standing of the country's economy in the eyes of British merchant bankers. The Bank of Brazil, created by Dom João in 1808, had been in difficulties since 1821 when the king drained it of metals and the crown jewels before returning to Portugal. Dom Pedro resorted to a policy of issuing great amounts of copper coins, which contributed to the growth of inflation and opened the way for widespread counterfeiting. From 1822 to 1829 the money supply increased by 10 per cent a year, pushing up the cost of living, particularly in the major cities. The invasion of counterfeit copper coins, especially in Bahia, brought chaos to the money market and forced the government to try to substitute bills for coins in 1827. But both the bills of the Bank of Brazil and the treasury bills were not well received outside Rio and were submitted to discount rates (*ágios*) that reached 43 per cent in São Paulo in 1829.[11] The Bank was finally closed in 1829. The exchange value of the milreis also suffered a decline of almost 8 per cent a year in relation to the pound sterling between 1822 and 1830. Although beneficial to the export sector, this devaluation was responsible for an increase in the price of imported goods.[12]

Urban popular discontent added a new, explosive element to the deepening political crisis in Brazil. Independence had brought expectations of improvements, however vague they may have been. When these expectations failed to materialize, when instead living conditions deteriorated, frustration mounted. In the circumstances, this frustration found an easy target in the Portuguese, particularly those who controlled the commercial sector, and also in the emperor who still seemed not to have separated himself from his former compatriots. There were repeated demands both in Rio and other coastal cities for the expulsion of the Portuguese from the country.

A contributory factor in the transition from opposition to open

---

[11] See Petrone, *O Barão de Iguape*, 16.
[12] For the financial history of this period, see Pelaez and Suzigan, *História monetária*, 47–57.

rebellion was the crisis of the absolute monarchy in France. The July (1830) Revolution and the fall of Charles X had profound repercussions in Brazil and was the subject of discussions even in the Council of State. Dom Pedro himself at the end of a visit to Minas Gerais, on 22 February 1831, issued a proclamation against the *partido desorganizador* which was attacking his person and his government, taking advantage of what had happened in France. Upon the emperor's return to Rio in the middle of March there was an explosion of street clashes lasting five consecutive days and nights between his supporters, mostly Portuguese, and his opponents, in what became known as the *Noites das Garrafadas* (Nights of Bottle Throwing). Dom Pedro tried to assemble a group of ministers to form a liberal 'Brazilian' cabinet, but on 5 April, exercising his powers under the Constitution, he abruptly replaced it with another more to his liking, more reactionary, more 'Portuguese'. This decision was the immediate cause of what proved to be the final crisis of the First Empire.

On the morning of 6 April people started gathering in several public places in the capital and by late afternoon between three and four thousand people were concentrated at the Campo de Sant'Anna, a traditional meeting place since the turbulent political events of 1821–2. A delegation of justices of the peace was sent to the emperor to urge him to reinstate the former 'Brazilian' cabinet, which he refused to do. More than twenty deputies had now joined the crowd and around 9 o'clock in the evening General Francisco de Lima e Silva, commander of the Rio garrison, agreed to try to convince the monarch to make concessions. By this time two artillery corps and one battalion of grenadiers had joined the populace and shortly after the emperor's own battalion, under the command of a brother of Lima e Silva, did the same. Although Brazilian officers, with very few exceptions, had no sympathy with radical ideas, they were willing to join the movement against the emperor, not least because they wanted the dismissal of Portuguese officers. As for the rank and file, mostly mulattos, they shared the frustrations, discontents – and nativist prejudices – of the lowest sectors of the urban population from which they were largely drawn. Indeed, their condition was often worse because they also suffered frequent delays in pay and the harsh discipline of the barracks.

In the early hours of 7 April, finding himself without military support, unwilling to yield to popular pressure ('I will do everything for the people, but nothing by the people', he is reported to have remarked) and perhaps more concerned with securing the Portuguese throne for his daughter, Dom Pedro impulsively abdicated the Brazilian throne in favour of his five-year-old son, Pedro. The news was received at the Campo de Sant'Anna amidst intense jubilation and Pedro II was immediately acclaimed emperor by the crowd. The legislature, although not officially in session, acted quickly and elected a provisional three-man regency, composed of General Francisco de Lima e Silva, Nicolau Pereira de Campos Vergueiro, a liberal senator from São Paulo, and José Joaquim Carneiro de Campos, the Marquês de Caravelas, a conservative politician and former Minister of Justice.[13] On the day of his abdication, Dom Pedro I, his family, including the twelve-year old Queen of Portugal, and his entourage boarded HMS *Warspite* at anchor in Rio bay. (The British navy was always on hand, it seems, when there was any question of transporting Portuguese or Brazilian royalty across the Atlantic.) On 13 April the *Warspite* departed for Europe.

The events of 5–7 April 1831 in which only one person had died, and then by accident, had changed the political life of the country. In a short unofficial speech on board the *Warspite*, referring to his decision to leave Brazil, Dom Pedro is reported by an English naval officer to have said: 'The Brazilians do not like me; they look upon me as a Portuguese.' He was undoubtedly right. The abdication of Dom Pedro I, the Portuguese prince who led Brazil to independence in 1822, in favour of his son, who had been born in Brazil, constituted a *nacionalização do trono* and represented the completion of the process of independence. Only in 1831 did Brazil sever her last remaining ties with Portugal. Henceforth Brazil belonged to the Brazilians – or at least to the Brazilian dominant class.

The abdication of Dom Pedro sent shock waves throughout the empire. As news of events in the capital arrived in the provinces – and in the case of the more distant provinces such as Goiás it could take up to three months for news from Rio to reach the provincial capital and even longer to reach the interior – a series of popular disturbances and military uprisings erupted. They were for the most part urban and, insofar as they had an ideological element, radical or at least nativist, but not republican. A few were restorationist. They had largely subsided – or been repressed – by the middle of 1832. One rebellion, however, in the wake of the abdication, the War of the Cabanos in Pernambuco, was rural, restorationist and lasted until 1835.

---

[13] The last two were replaced on 17 June by deputy José da Costa Carvalho (the future Marquês de Monte Alegre) and deputy João Bráulio Muniz.

In Rio itself the abdication crisis was followed by a series of five uprisings. Except for the last (in April 1832), which was restorationist, they were all essentially anti-Portuguese, initiated by troops, with the populace frequently joining in. One after the other, an army battalion, the police corps, the Navy artillery and two fortresses took up arms led by some radical agitators such as Major Frias de Vasconcelos and the permanent revolutionary, Cipriano Barata. In July 1831, almost the whole Rio garrison rose in arms and congregated in the Campo de Sant'Anna as they had on 6 April, where they were again joined by the populace. For ten days they kept the city in fear. The demands were almost exclusively of an anti-Portuguese nature: the deportation of 89 Portuguese, the dismissal of scores of others from public jobs and a ban on the immigration of Portuguese nationals for ten years. In Salvador, Brazil's second city, popular demonstrations had begun as early as 4 April when news of the *Noites das Garrafadas* arrived. During the next two years at least six uprisings by *tropa e povo* were registered. The most common demands were for the dismissal of the authorities, usually the military commander, and the deportation of Portuguese merchants and officials. An additional demand in Bahia was the introduction of a federal political structure, an indication of the resentment felt in the former capital at the concentration of power in Rio. In Recife, the third major city, things were not very different. One day after the arrival of the news of the abdication, troops and people organized demonstrations, picking as their main targets the absolutist society *Coluna do Trono e do Altar*, whose members and sympathizers had been in control of the government since the defeat of the 1824 revolt. The demonstrators demanded the dismissal of the military commander, of judges and several officers whose loyalty to the national cause was considered suspect. In September 1831 a more serious riot broke out. This time some slaves also joined in, apparently interpreting the news of the abdication as meaning the advent of freedom for them. Here was a good example, typical of the period, of a popular explosion without clearly defined leadership and demands. The crowd shouted *viva* Pedro II and *viva* Brazil, and *fora* (out with) the *Colunas*, the *marinheiros* (Portuguese) and the military commander. The city was completely taken over and around 42 shops and 25 taverns were looted. Many rebels got drunk and spent the night in the red light district where later on most of the looted goods were found. The government was forced to appeal to the militia and to arm civilians to put down the insurrection. Students of the Olinda law school also volunteered to help.

In the end about a hundred rebels and thirty loyal soldiers and civilians had been killed; more than a thousand arrests had been made. In November another uprising produced a list of Portuguese to be deported to which was added the demand that all single Portuguese, except artisans and capitalists, be expelled from the country and all Portuguese disarmed.

In April 1832 there was a restorationist rebellion in Recife as there was in Rio. It was led by a militia battalion made up almost exclusively of Portuguese troops. It was easily defeated, but there followed the most intriguing popular uprising of the early thirties. Known as the War of the Cabanos it was the first to take place outside the cities, reaching much deeper into the foundations of society. The war lasted from 1832 until 1835 and involved small landowners, peasants, Indians, slaves and, particularly at the beginning, some *senhores de engenho*. It took place between the southern periphery of the rich sugar-producing Mata of Pernambuco and the north of the neighbouring province of Alagoas. The main leader, Vincente Ferreira de Paula, the son of a priest, was a sergeant before he deserted the army. He gave himself the title of General Commander of the Restorationist Force. Supported by Portuguese merchants in Recife and by politicians in Rio, all advocates of the restoration of Pedro I, the *cabanos* fought a guerrilla war for three years, hiding from the government troops in the thick forests of the region. At the end, the government realized that other means besides force were necessary to defeat them and the bishop of Olinda was called upon to help. He managed to convince many *cabanos* that Pedro I had already died (which he had in September 1834), that Pedro II was the legitimate emperor and that they were living a sinful life. Many turned themselves in, but the last ones, mostly slaves, were hunted down in the forest 'like deer', one by one. The leader managed to escape and organized a community of former supporters where he lived until he was arrested in 1850. In a report to the governor of Alagoas (7 July 1834), the commander of the government troops, Colonel Joaquim de Sousa, registered his shock at the physical and psychological conditions under which the rebels had lived. After the government troops were ordered to destroy all the rebels' manioc plantations and presses, the rebels had been reduced to eating wild fruits, lizards, snakes, insects and honey. The *cabanos* had hesitated in turning themselves in for fear of being tortured and skinned alive by the irreligious constitutionalists, or of being killed by their own leaders. Unable to articulate the true nature of their plight, these heroic guerrillas fought for their religion, the emperor and against what they called the *carbunários jacubinos*. Ironically, they were defeated in the end by the same person who had proclaimed the Confederation of the Equator in 1824 and was now president of the province, Manuel Carvalho Paes de Andrade.

The War of the Cabanos in Pernambuco, however, was an exceptional reaction to the abdication of Pedro I. In almost all other provinces – and of the eighteen provinces only Piauí and Santa Catarina avoided disturbances of some kind – popular demonstrations were urban and anti-Portuguese similar to those in Rio and varying in intensity according to the size of the city and the strength of Portuguese presence in government and in commerce. In general, public order was least affected in Minas and in the southern provinces of São Paulo, Santa Catarina and Rio Grande do Sul which lacked important urban centres and ports.

The First Empire was brought to an end in 1831 by a heterogeneous coalition of political and social forces. The main beneficiaries of the abdication of Dom Pedro I, and his successors in the exercise of political power under the three-man Regency, were those sectors of the Brazilian dominant class which had supported independence from Portugal in 1822, but which had increasingly opposed absolutism, extreme centralization of power – and the emperor's pro-Portuguese policies and predilections – in the decade after independence. These Brazilian liberals called themselves *moderados* to distinguish themselves from the extreme liberals or radicals (*exaltados* or *farroupilhas*), some of whom like Cipriano Barata and Borges da Fonseca were republicans. Drawing on the masonic tradition of social and political organization so influential at the time of independence, a *Sociedade Defensora da Liberdade e Independência Nacional* was established first in São Paulo and then, in May 1831, in Rio to which most liberal politicians and their more influential supporters affiliated, and *Defensoras* soon spread to other provinces throughout the country. (Somewhat less cohesive were the *Sociedades Federais* organized by the radicals in a number of provinces at the end of 1831. The *Sociedade Conservadora da Constituição Brasileira*, later *Sociedade Militar*, was set up in 1832 by absolutists and restorationists (*caramurus*) in the bureaucracy, the army and commerce, many though by no means all of Portuguese origin.) Among the *moderados* there was a high proportion from Minas Gerais, São Paulo and Rio. There was also a significant presence of priests among them and some graduates of Coimbra. In social terms, most were landowners and slave-owners. The most prominent leaders of the group at the time were Bernardo Pereira de Vasconcelos, a Mineiro magistrate trained at Coimbra; Diogo Feijó, a priest from São Paulo; and Evaristo da Veiga, a printer and bookseller from Rio de Janeiro and since 1827 publisher of the *Aurora Fluminense*, the most influential liberal paper. Influenced by French and American ideas, they all stood for liberal changes in the constitution in the direction of greater decentralization, but always within the monarchical framework. Some were attracted to American-style federalism. However, since most of them were linked to Rio or to the Rio economy, it was in their interest to defend national unity and to reform the existing political system to permit their participation, indeed domination, rather than destroy it. Moreover, elite consensus on the need to maintain the institution of slavery in Brazil imposed, as it always had, severe limitations on Brazilian liberalism. On the question of the slave trade no attempt was made by the liberals to reverse the Anglo-Brazilian treaty of 1826. On the contrary, taking advantage of the fact that the Brazilian slave trade was virtually at a standstill as a result of a glut on the slave market following several years of unusually heavy imports (in anticipation of the end of the trade) and uncertainty in trading circles as to what measures the British and Brazilian governments might now adopt, a law of 7 November 1831 imposed severe penalties on those found guilty of illegally importing slaves into Brazil and declared all slaves entering Brazil legally free. Few, however, believed it would actually be enforced when the demand for slaves revived (which it did in the mid-thirties): it was *uma lei para inglês ver*. Among some members of long-established rural oligarchies, pro-slavery but without strong economic ties to Rio, like, for example, the Cavalcantis of Pernambuco, who had a representative, Holanda Cavalcanti de Albuquerque, in the 'Brazilian' cabinet dismissed by Dom Pedro on 5 April, liberalism was almost identical with local rule. Holanda was an advocate of splitting up the Empire into two or three different countries, a proposal he made in 1832 and again in 1835. The fight for provincial power represented by the Cavalcantis and the fight against absolute government, best represented by urban liberals like Evaristo da Veiga and the Mineiro Teófilo Ottoni, together constituted the major drive behind the liberal reforms that were implemented between 1831 and 1835.

It came as a disappointment to committed liberals like Teófilo Ottoni that the first measures taken under the regency were not directed against the absolutist elements in society but against former allies of the 7 April, particularly soldiers. Liberals had always disliked the army: it was seen as an instrument of absolutism. In fact, the Paulistas had already suggested in 1830 the creation of a National Guard to take over its internal security duties. After the abdication liberals came to dislike the army even more, but for the opposite reason; it had apparently become an instrument of popular radicalism. A bill creating the National Guard was now rushed through the legislature in 1831 as a way of dealing with both military and popular unrest. While the bill was being discussed, the regency drafted electors (persons with a minimum income of 200 milreis a year) in Rio de Janeiro into municipal guards to whom it entrusted the policing of the city. The minister of justice, Diogo Feijó, also distributed arms to some 3,000 electors. The *Sociedade Defensora* of Rio offered its services to help patrol the city. After the popular–military revolt in Rio in July 1831, the *Sociedade Defensora* of São Paulo quickly gathered almost two thousand volunteers to come to the rescue of the central government if necessary. From Minas Gerais came also guarantees of support. After the revolt had been put down a proclamation of the regency told the people of Rio to keep calm; the government had taken measures against the 'anarchists': 'the arms are in the hands of citizens who have an interest in public order'.

Given its importance at the time and the role it played during the whole of the period of the empire, the creation of the National Guard deserves some comment. The Brazilian law of August 1831 was a copy of the French law of the same year, which had as its basic philosophy the bourgeois idea of entrusting the defence of the country to its propertied citizens. In Brazil it was at the same time a way of wresting the means of coercion from the control of the government and also a protection against the 'dangerous classes'. However, since officers were to be elected, with relatively low income requirements (200 milréis in the four major cities and 100 milréis in the rest of the country) and with no racial discrimination, the Brazilian Guard still represented an important democratic advance in relation to the colonial militias and *ordenanças* which it replaced. Moreover, it was put under the jurisdiction of the minister of justice, not the minister of war, at the national level and locally under the justices of the peace. The tasks of the Guard, which were defined in the first article of the law as being 'to defend the Constitution, the Liberty, Independence and Integrity of the Empire', were in practice the police duties of patrolling the streets, protecting public buildings, transporting prisoners and keeping order in general. In special cases, it could be taken outside the *município* as a militarized unit under army command to fight rebellions or even to help in the protection of Brazil's frontiers. Hailed by liberals as the citizens' militia, the National Guard played an important role in its initial years as a counterweight to, and substitute for, a regular army disrupted by the indiscipline and open revolt of the rank and file, and deliberately reduced by Feijó to a token force of 6,000 men. (The Rio garrison, for instance, had been completely disbanded by 1832, and the officers concentrated in one battalion.) The transformations that profoundly changed the nature of the Guard will be examined later.

A less ambiguous liberal move was the attack on the old (predominantly Portuguese) magistracy, considered, together with the army, a major pillar of the old system and frequently accused of arbitrariness and corruption. Liberal changes in the judicial structure had already begun during the reign of Dom Pedro I. In 1827 justices of the peace (*juízes de paz*), elected local magistrates, were introduced into each parish (*freguesia*) and given many administrative, judicial and police functions (at the expense of the centrally appointed and controlled *juízes de fora*). In 1830 a liberal Criminal Code strongly influenced by Benthamite utilitarianism, among other things, aimed at protecting political opposition from the arbitrary measures of government, in particular such devices as the military courts which had prosecuted the Pernambuco rebels after 1824. But only after the abdication did these liberal measures come to full fruition with the enactment, in 1832, of the Code of Criminal Procedures which strengthened the police and judicial powers of the justices of the peace; they now had the power both to arrest and to pass judgment on minor offenders. They also proposed to the municipal *câmaras* names of citizens they wished to be appointed as block inspectors (*inspetores de quarteirão*), and together with the local priest and the president of the *câmara*, made up the list of jurors. In addition, the Code created a new category of professional county judge (*juiz municipal*) who was appointed by the provincial president but from a list prepared by the local *câmara*. Finally, the Code introduced the jury system and habeas corpus, copied from American and British practices and legislation. As in the case of the National Guard, liberals had great hopes that the elected justice of the peace and the jury in particular would prove important instruments for the protection of individual liberties.

A third attack was made on those parts of the 1824 constitution considered incompatible with a liberal system. The law of the regency (1831) had already stripped the regents of several of the constitutional powers of the emperor, especially those relating to the exercise of the moderating power. The regents could not dissolve the Chamber of Deputies, grant an amnesty, bestow honorific titles, suspend guarantees for individual liberties or declare war. Except for the power to appoint ministers, senators and provincial presidents, the regents were almost completely dependent on parliament. Certainly there was no other period in the Brazilian history in which the elected legislature was so influential. However, great difficulties emerged when the constitution itself became the target of the reform movement. Most controversial were the attacks on the moderating power, the council of state and the appointment of senators for life, and the attempt to increase the powers of provincial institutions. The Senate objected strongly to most of these reforms and was locked in battle with the Chamber of Deputies for almost three years. Finally, a compromise bill was agreed which resulted in the Additional Act of August 1834. The moderating power remained intact (though not exercised under the regency) and, as could be expected, so did the Senate. But the Council of State was abolished. And although provincial presidents continued to be appointed, newly created provincial assemblies were given much greater powers than the old *Conselhos Gerais*. Moreover, a revenue-sharing system between the central government and the provinces was agreed (and implemented for the first time in the fiscal year 1836–7). In a further effort to republicanize the country, the Act introduced a popularly elected regency to replace the permanent three-man regency established in 1831. The liberal Paulista priest and minister of justice, Diogo Feijó, was elected regent in April and took office in October 1835.

A succession of liberal cabinets, in which Antônio Paulino Limpo de Abreu, Manuel Alves Branco and Holanda Cavalcanti were prominent, governed Brazil during the next two years (1835–7). With the Additional Act of August 1834 and the election of Feijó as regent in April 1835, however, the major thrust of the liberal reform movement could be said to have come to an end. Both aspects of the liberal struggle – anti-absolutism and anti-centralization – had been partly satisfied. The more radical demands for a republican government and for federalism had been defeated. It was an almost complete victory for the moderate liberals over both radicals and absolutists. This victory had been reinforced in September 1834 with the death of Pedro I in Portugal, which eliminated the *raison d'être* of the restorationist party. The divisions of political forces into *moderados, caramurus* and *farroupilhas* was coming to an end. And new political alignments were emerging, in part as a consequence of the implementation of the liberal reforms.

The transplantation of liberal ideas and institutions in Brazil did not bear the expected fruit. The reforms of 1831–4 had scarcely been implemented before disappointment and disillusion set in. The judgement of the former regent, Senator Vergueiro of São Paulo, who had been a strong supporter of the liberal reforms ('we set our political organization ahead of our social organization')[14] reflects the feelings of perhaps a majority of the Brazilian political class, especially those who had assumed power at the national level after the fall of Dom Pedro I.

If before 1831 the instruments of law and order were in the oppressive hands of the central government, they now fell into the oppressive hands of the locally powerful. In the rural areas, the elected justices of the peace were dependent on the local bosses and were themselves mostly members of the local dominant families. In major cities, less socially prominent elements were elected, but they still depended on the powerful for support in furthering their careers. It was well known, for example, that justices of the peace protected money counterfeiters and slave traders. Their ignorance of the law was a further obstacle to the proper discharge of their duties. In his famous comedy, *O Juiz de Paz na Roça*, written in 1833, Martins Pena pictures a guardsman appealing to his constitutional rights against an illegal threat of arrest, to which the justice of the peace retorts by declaring the constitution abolished. Moreover, justices of the peace were continuously involved in conflicts with professional magistrates, commanders of the national guard, priests and even the municipal *câmaras*. They could not serve as brokers in conflicts among local bosses, or between the bosses and the central government; they belonged to local factions and, since they were also able to influence the electoral process, they became a further element in local strife. rather than local peace. As for the jury, although the rich themselves usually avoided serving, those who did so seldom recommended harsh sentences for fear of reprisals. Even more than the justices of the peace, the jury was responsible for the enormous increase in impunity, a fact recognized by liberals and conservatives alike. This was not only true of criminal offences (including involvement in the now illegal slave trade) but also of political crimes, such as rebellions, conspiracies, seditions, whose leaders were frequently acquitted or received light sentences. It was true not only when the powerful were brought to court (a rare enough occurrence) but also the less powerful, who seldom lacked connections with the powerful. Crimes against slaves – and women –

---

[14] Speech in the Senate, 12 July 1841. Quoted in Visconde do Uruguai, *Ensaio sobre o Direito Administrativo* (Rio de Janeiro, 1960) 504.

were everywhere regarded for the most part as a private matter.

The National Guard was relatively democratic when it was founded, as we have seen. There was even some reluctance among landowners to join the organization for fear of a defeat in the elections for the higher posts by a social inferior. Without them, however, the preservation of order, the Guard's major task, could not be achieved. Within a year, by a decree in October 1832, the government doubled the income requirement for officers, raising it to 400 milréis in the major cities and to 200 milréis elsewhere. Later the Guard came under the influence of the new provincial assemblies. They chose to interpret the Additional Act (1834) as giving them power over senior positions in the Guard. It was then tempting to use this power as a political resource, as an instrument of patronage. Almost all provincial assemblies ended up tampering with the law and introducing some sort of control over the appointment of officers. In São Paulo, for example, elections had disappeared by 1836. The notion of a citizens' militia could not work in a highly unequal and stratified society, and the National Guard had soon adapted itself to the social reality.

Some of the greatest problems emerged from the Additional Act itself. It was, as has been said, a compromise measure. More radical proposals, such as the right of provincial assemblies to elect provincial presidents and to impose import duties, had been defeated. The author of the project, Bernardo Vasconcelos, then a liberal, had already warned that to push federalism as far as the United States had done would lead to anarchy and be disastrous for the unity of the country. But, moderate as it was, the Act did give the assemblies control over provincial and municipal matters. More importantly, it gave them power over the appointment of public officials. Given the obscurity of the wording of the Act, this power became a bone of contention between the assemblies and the central government. As it turned out, they started exercising authority over almost all public employees within the provincial territory, including the *juízes de direito* – district (*comarca*) judges – who had clearly remained under central control. Some assemblies also created and appointed local mayors, transferring to them the powers of the justices of the peace. The only officials they did not interfere with were the appeal court judges (*desembargadores*), army and navy personnel, and the provincial presidents themselves. They could, however, nominate the vice-presidents who had frequent opportunities to exercise power, since the presidents were often absent in Rio serving in the national parliament.

The measures adopted by the liberals, who came to power in 1831, and the political decentralization effected after 1834, encouraged and facilitated an intensification of the struggle for power between factions within the provincial rural oligarchies. And this opened the way for social conflicts wider, deeper and more dangerous to the established order than any which had occurred in the immediate aftermath of the 1831 crisis. At the same time the fragile political unity of the empire was seriously threatened. In 1835 provincial revolts broke out in the extreme north and the extreme south of the country, Pará and Rio Grande do Sul. They were followed by revolts in Bahia (in 1837) and Maranhão (in 1838). The most radical and violent rebellions in Brazilian history, before or since, these four were merely the most serious of a series of provincial disturbances which, although their roots went deeper, significantly followed the implementation of the liberal reforms and especially the Additional Act of 1834. Their differences reflected the different conflicts and tensions within a variety of provincial social (and racial) structures. All, however, were federalist, and several, including the most serious and prolonged, were frankly secessionist or at least had distinct separatist overtones.

Pará was the scene of the first of these major provincial revolts of the 1830s. It became known as the *Cabanagem* (from *cabanos*, as the rebels, like those in Pernambuco earlier (see above), were called). The province had a little less than 150,000 people, 30 per cent of whom were slaves. There was also a large free Indian and *mestizo* population, called *tapuios*, most of them living along the great rivers of the Amazon basin. Pará had no well-established landed oligarchy and in general a much looser social structure than, for example, the provinces of the north-east. The capital, Belém, was a small city of about 12,000, but it was a commercial centre and important for its location at the mouth of the Amazon. It was the major outlet for the province's modest production of tobacco, cacao, rubber and rice. It had a substantial presence of Portuguese merchants, as well as a few British and French. Since the abdication province and capital had been plagued by conflicts between liberal Brazilian and restorationist Portuguese factions. In 1833 the provincial council refused to accept a new president appointed by the regency, arguing that he was pro-*caramuru*. Later in the same year a conflict broke out between the two factions which resulted in about 95 casualties. Many Portuguese were killed and others left the province. A new liberal president managed to maintain a semblance of government until January 1835 when a radical element among the liberals killed both the president and the military commander and started a revolt. The leadership of the rebels included justices of the peace, officers of the national guard and of the army, priests, and a *seringueiro* (rubber gatherer). One of the leaders was made president and the independence of Pará was proclaimed.

The new president appointed by the regents in Rio de Janeiro, an octogenarian marshal born in Portugal, took sixty days to arrive and did so with only 120 men whom he had collected in Maranhão. He was eventually allowed to take over the presidency, and the rebel president withdrew. But the truce was shortlived. In August 1835 a rebel army, in which the majority of the rank and file were blacks and *tapuios*, attacked the city. After nine days of house-to-house fighting, in which about 180 whites were said to have been killed, not even the support of British and Portuguese vessels stationed in the port could save the president. He decided to abandon Belém and took refuge in a Brazilian warship. He was followed by about 5,000 people, Portuguese and Brazilians, most of them 'proprietors, merchants, first class citizens', as the president described them.

The rebel president had been killed in the battle. He was replaced by Eduardo Angelim, a 21-year-old Cearense, one of the most extraordinary popular leaders of the period. Angelim tried to organize the new government, creating new military units and appointing new officers (usually promoted from the ranks). A priest served as the president's secretary, one of the few among the rebels who was able to write with any fluency. The war spread to the interior of the province and up the Amazon river. The rebels raided cities and farms for food, weapons and valuables, retreating afterwards into the forest. Few cities were able to keep them at a distance.

A naval blockade of the mouth of the Amazon and the total disorganization of production throughout the province soon weakened the rebels' position in the capital. When the new official president, General Andreia, arrived in April 1836 with fresh troops, ammunition and vessels, Angelim decided to abandon the city with 5,000 followers, leaving behind a population almost exclusively of women and, astonishingly, 95,000 milréis from the provincial treasury in the hands of the bishop. General Andreia proceeded with a ruthless campaign of repression. He arrested the rebels *en masse*, gave orders to shoot on sight those who resisted, militarized the whole province through the creation of auxiliary corps and rounded up all those over ten years of age who had no property or occupation into 'worker corps', forcing them to work either for private employers for a small wage or in public works. Violence and cruelty were widespread on both sides. Some people were seen proudly wearing rosaries made from the ears of dead *cabanos*. Around 4,000 *cabanos* died in prisons, ships and hospitals alone. In October 1836 Angelim was arrested, without resistance, by the same officer who had defeated the *cabanos* of Pernambuco the year before. Colonel Joaquim de Sousa was impressed by the poverty, dignity and honesty of the rebel leader. The last *cabanos*, many of them armed with bows and arrows, turned themselves in when a general amnesty was granted in 1840. The death toll in the rebellion has been calculated at 30,000, that is to say, 20 per cent of the total population of the province, more or less evenly divided between rebels and non-rebels. The capital Belém was almost totally destroyed. The economy had been devastated.

The *cabanos* never presented a systematic set of demands, nor did they organize any programme of government. They simply shouted slogans and war cries against foreigners, Portuguese, masons, and in favour of the Catholic religion, Pedro II, Brazilians, Pará and liberty. The secession of the province, proclaimed again in 1836, was not a central demand. A puzzling aspect is the fact that, despite the existence of a substantial number of slaves among the *cabanos*, slavery was not abolished; an insurrection of slaves was put down by Angelim. The *Cabanagem* was an explosion of the Indian and *caboclo* (*mestizo*) population's long-repressed hatred of the colonial power and its representatives and of the white, rich and powerful in general, released by the political mobilization of the regency period and triggered off by conflicts among sectors of the higher strata of the population. It was a popular movement, but not of the people the liberals had in mind. Evaristo da Veiga referred to the *cabanos* in the most derogatory terms – *gentalha, crápula, massas brutas* – and observed that Pará looked more like part of Spanish America than of Brazil.[15]

The second rebellion, chronologically, was quite different in nature. It became known as the *Farroupilha*, a name used to characterize the radicals after the abdication of Pedro I, and took place in the southern province of Rio Grande do Sul. The province had over 100,000 inhabitants, and the capital, Porto Alegre, had, in 1830, a population of between 12,000 and 15,000. As in Pará, slaves composed more or less 30 per cent of the total population. But Rio Grande do Sul had a very

[15] *Aurora Fluminense*, 1 January, 11 November 1835.

different social structure from the rest of Brazil. The historical circumstances of the formation of the province had led to a fusion of military status and landownership, and the militarized dominant class exercised almost total control over the subordinate groups in society. Moreover, the province had gone through an important economic transformation in the second decade of the century, moving from agriculture to livestock production. A *charque* industry also developed along the coast. The occupation of the Banda Oriental in 1817 had given a tremendous boost to the *estancieiros*. They not only bought land in what became the Cisplatine Province but also transferred vast numbers of cattle to Brazil. The loss of the Banda Oriental in 1828 had been a severe blow, although it did not stop the regular smuggling of cattle across the frontier. In fact, economic and political relations among the *estancieiros* of Rio Grande do Sul, Uruguay and the Argentine provinces of Entre Ríos and Corrientes were an important factor in the rebellion of 1835. They formed a powerful group of caudillos in search of a political organization that could best suit their interests.

The beginning of the revolt was not very different from that of the *Cabanagem*, in the sense that it, too, turned on the reaction of local liberals against the formation of a *Sociedade Militar* by *caramurus* in 1833 and against a president appointed by the regency. The president, who suspected secessionist plans among the local leaders, was overthrown in September 1835. Under the next president, himself a rich *estancieiro*, factions coalesced and in February 1836 open war broke out. In September 1836 the *farroupilhas* proclaimed the independence of the province under a republican government, although they were not able to keep control of the capital. In 1839 with the help of a small naval task force organized by the Italian revolutionary, Giuseppe Garibaldi, they invaded the neighbouring province of Santa Catarina, where a shortlived republic was also proclaimed. The fight dragged on for ten years until an armistice was agreed in March 1845.

It was a war in which a good proportion of the *estancieiros*, particularly those who had their power base and their *estâncias* in the region bordering Argentina and Uruguay, fought against the forces of the central government. But the *charque* industrialists stayed with the government as did a section of the *estancieiros*. Without going here into the classic debate as to whether or not the *farroupilhas* seriously wanted to secede from Brazil, it is important to point out those factors which favoured and those which were against secession. First of all, there were some differences between *estancieiros* and *charqueadores*. The latter depended on the Brazilian market to sell their product; the former could do without it as long as they could count on Uruguayan *charqueadas*. On the other hand, the Rio Grande *charqueadores* depended on the *estancieiros* for their raw material. From the point of view of the central government it was essential for Brazil to have both *estancieiros* and *charqueadores*. And in view of the constant threat posed by Argentina the province of Rio Grande do Sul had great strategic importance. Here was a complex network of economic and political interests, involving taxation of *charque* and its related products, both for the internal and the external markets; taxation of cattle across international borders; the price of feeding the slave population in other provinces; and strategic considerations. It seems that secession was a workable plan for the *estancieiros*, as long as they could secure an arrangement, possibly a political merger, with Uruguay together with, perhaps, some Argentinian provinces. The leader of the rebellion, Colonel Bento Gonçalves, an *estancieiro* and a mason, seemed to have definite plans for a federation with Uruguay and Argentina through his contacts with Lavalleja and Rosas. But this was a risky project, given the volatile nature of politics in the Río de la Plata area. The second most important leader of the *farroupilhas*, Bento Manuel, another colonel and *estancieiro*, changed sides three times during the struggle, starting with the rebels, going over to the government, then back to the rebels and ending the campaign with the government again. In the end it was to pay the *estancieiros* to stay with a government which would give special protection to *charque* and related products so that Rio Grande do Sul could compete successfully with Argentina and Uruguay.

These ambiguities and some concessions made by the central government, such as 25 per cent import duties on foreign *charque* introduced in 1840, together with the exhaustion of the people and the decline of the cattle industry caused by the protracted war, finally brought the struggle to an end in 1845. The failure of rebellions in other provinces – Pará, Bahia, and by this time Minas Gerais and São Paulo (see below) – prevented the *gaúchos* from extracting even the introduction of a Brazilian federation.

The third major rebellion took place in Bahia and was called the *Sabinada* from the name of its leader, Dr Sabino Barroso. It was a repetition on a larger scale of the urban upheavals of the first part of the decade, with the added dimension of a strong federalist, if not secessionist, tendency. Several of its leaders had participated in the previous rebellions. The revolt started in the army barracks of Salvador on 6 November 1837 and gained the immediate support of almost the whole garrison of the capital. Only the national guard and the navy remained loyal, but they were no match for the army and police forces which, apart from the officers, joined the rebellion *en masse*. The next day the city was taken and the provincial president fled without a shot being fired. The municipal *câmara* was summoned and proclaimed Bahia to be a 'free and independent state'.

What followed was an almost perfect replica of the war of independence: the capital was put under siege by the sugar barons of the Recôncavo, helped at sea by the imperial navy. The interior of the province outside of the Recôncavo remained quiet, frustrating the hopes of the rebels to extend the fight to the rural areas as had happened in Pará. Completely surrounded, the defeat of the rebels was only a matter of time. On 13 March 1838 a final three-day battle took place inside the capital, fought, as in Belém, from house to house. The 5,000-strong rebel army was defeated by a more experienced 4,000-strong legal force. In all, about 1,200 rebels and 600 loyalists were killed. The amnesty of 1840 saved the life of seven leaders who had been sentenced to death.

The support of some important elements among the business community and the intellectuals of Salvador gave the Sabinada a larger base of support than earlier, more purely popular upheavals in Bahia. Sabino Barroso was a journalist and a professor at the prestigious School of Medicine, one of only two in the empire. But besides the federal and republican tendencies, there is not much more information on the plans of the rebels. The initial separation from Rio seemed to have alienated some support, since this decision was later qualified: the secession was restricted to the duration of the regency. The revolution also did not take advantage of the revolutionary potential of the slave population, a legacy perhaps of the panic caused by the Bahian slave revolt of 1835 (see below). In 1837–8 a battalion of blacks was organized, but there was no general mobilization of slaves, and slavery was not abolished. The anti-Portuguese sentiment, so prominent in previous movements, had by now subsided and was barely voiced. The landed and commercial elites were afraid to join popular elements and urban intellectuals in separating the province from the rest of Brazil, much as the idea might have appealed to some of them. The resistance to the rebellion was organized by the chief of police of Salvador, who was also the scion of a powerful family of *senhores de engenho* of the Recôncavo.

The last revolt to erupt in this period was similar to the Cabanagem, although it lacked its depth and violence. Its battlefield was the southern part of the province of Maranhão, close to the border with Piauí. The area was settled by small farmers and small cattle ranchers for the most part. To the north it bordered the rich valleys of the Mearim, Itapicuru and Pindaré rivers dominated by a strong oligarchy of planters and slave-owners engaged in the production of rice and cotton. The population of the province was at the time over 200,000, of which more than 50 per cent were slaves, the highest percentage in Brazil. São Luís, the capital, was a city of over 30,000 with a strong Portuguese business sector. The revolt in Maranhão became known as the *Balaiada* because one of its leaders was nicknamed *balaio* (the basket-maker). It was the one most directly linked to the liberal reforms, particularly to the Additional Act of 1834. Two factions fought for local supremacy, much in the same style as in other provinces: the liberals, called *bentevis*, after the name of a liberal newspaper, and the conservatives, called *cabanos*. The conservative president, taking advantage of the new powers given to the provincial assemblies by the Additional Act, had a new law passed creating *prefeitos* (mayors) at the municipal level and transferring to them most of the powers of the justices of the peace. Another provincial law enabled him to appoint officers of the national guard. These measures meant the dislodgement of the *bentevis* from the positions of power they enjoyed, and it was no surprise that they mounted a vicious campaign against the president and the new laws in their newspapers in the capital. Emotions were running high when a trivial incident triggered off the rebellion. A *cafuso* (mixed Indian and black) cowboy, Raimundo Gomes, in the service of a *bentevi* priest, who was also a rich planter, attacked a local jail to free Gomes's brother and some of his hands, unjustifiedly arrested by the sub-*prefeito*, a *cabano* enemy of the priest. Supporters poured in from several quarters and in December 1838 Gomes found himself the leader of a rebellion. Balaio joined the rebellion later. His motive was to revenge the honour of his daughter who had been raped by a police captain. A third leader Cosme, a black, self-styled Dom Cosme, Tutor and Emperor of the Bentevi Freedoms, fought a parallel revolt at the head of 3,000 runaway slaves.

The *balaios* managed to mobilize some 11,000 men and in August 1839 occupied Caxias, the second most important city of the province, which was also a liberal stronghold. There a provisional government was organized and a set of demands, including the repeal of the two provincial laws and the expulsion of the Portuguese from the province, was formulated. The central government sent a total of 8,000 troops, gathered from several provinces, under the command of Colonel Luís Alves de Lima. The back of the movement was quickly broken, not least by internal divisions between free and slave *balaios*. Colonel Lima played one against the other to good effect: Cosme arrested Gomes and was then opposed by other *balaio* leaders. By mid-1840 the rebellion had been put down. An amnesty followed, except for Dom Cosme, who was hanged in 1842. Luís Alves de Lima earned the first of a long series of titles of nobility: barão de Caxias.

The demands of the *balaios* remained very much inside the limits of the struggle between *bentevis* and *cabanos*: revocation of the law of the *prefeitos* and of the changes in the national guard; to this they added traditional anti-Portuguese measures, amnesty and pay for the rebel troops. The proclamation of one *balaio* leader, a semi-literate, ended with *vivas* for the Catholic religion, the constitution, Pedro II, the justices of the peace and the 'Holy Cause of Freedom'. Nothing of a social or economic nature was included. Despite the popular nature of most of its leadership and rank and file, the *Balaiada* could not escape from the ideological and political trappings of upper and middle sector conflict. It was perhaps more articulate than the *Cabanagem*. But it was also the product of a less polarized social structure. Many *balaois* were small farmers, cowboys and artisans; some were rich landowners. One of the proclamations mentioned the need to save 'our families and properties'. This was probably one of the reasons why there was never a good relationship between the free and slave *balaios*. But the rebels remained also isolated from the urban liberals who had created the atmosphere for the revolt. The *bentevis* of São Luís, either fearing a conservative backlash, or fearing the violence of the popular elements in the rebellion, retreated as soon as the action started. Only in Pará did urban and rural radicalisms join together. The division amongst the underdogs, slaves and free, rural poor and urban poor, was the strength of the ruling groups and frequently saved them from their own divisions.

The disappointment at the way the liberal reforms of 1831–4 had worked out in practice and the wave of rebellions that swept the country, either as a direct or indirect consequence of the Additional Act of 1834 in particular, bringing instability and threatening both internal order and the unity of the country, opened the way for the development of a new alignment of political forces and to the formation of the two parties – Conservative and Liberal – that would dominate politics during the Second Empire.

It should be remembered that at the beginning the conservative reaction was quite general among members of the national elite. As early as 1835 Evaristo da Veiga's *Aurora Fluminense* as well as Vasconcelos's *O Sete de Abril* began to criticize the liberal reforms. Still allies at the time, they would later disagree about exactly how far and how deep the reaction, the return (*regresso*) to order, authority and a stronger central executive, should go. While Vasconcelos's position became more radically conservative, Evaristo remained in the middle ground, fighting for adjustments to the liberal laws rather than major changes. The rapid transition from absolutism to freedom, Evaristo argued, had loosened social networks and 'we see anarchy all over the empire'. Brazil was in danger of being plunged into the kind of political instability endemic in the former Spanish colonies, and this could possibly lead to political fragmentation. He conceded that the excesses of the progressive measures had caused a reaction in public opinion, and claimed that Vasconcelos had been quick – too quick – to notice this change and had decided to become the champion of reaction. Many would certainly support a 'short and rational *regresso*', but Vasconcelos, he felt, had 'exaggerated beyond limits a just idea.'[16]

Pessimism had also begun to affect the recently elected regent, Diogo Feijó, one of the bulwarks of the *moderado* faction. He was convinced that the secession of Rio Grande do Sul was inevitable and that maybe Pernambuco would soon follow. In the *Fala do Throno* (speech from the throne) in 1836, he referred to widespread and growing disregard for the authorities and warned that the country's basic institutions were threatened. A growing uneasiness was even more noticeable within the legislature which had passed the Additional Act of 1834. Under the leadership of Vasconcelos there emerged a strong opposition group that soon became a majority and constituted the nucleus of the future Conservative party. In 1837 the death of Evaristo da Veiga left Feijó without his major supporter in parliament and in the press. Unable to deal with the congressional opposition, not least because of his own authoritarian character, and under pressure for not dealing with sufficient energy with the *farroupilhas* in Rio Grande do Sul, among whose leadership there was one of his cousins, in September 1837 Feijó

[16] *Aurora Fluminense*, 6 April, 12 August, 4 September 1835.

resigned, handing the government over to the recently appointed minister of the empire (internal affairs) Pedro de Araújo Lima (the future Marquês de Olinda), a conservative senator, former president of the Chamber, and a *senhor de engenho* in Pernambuco. A new election for regent was held and the results indicated that the new conservative trend was nationwide. Araújo Lima carried fifteen of the eighteen provinces, including Minas Gerais, São Paulo and Rio Grande do Sul, and won around 45 per cent of the total vote. (In contrast, Feijó in 1835 had secured only 30 per cent of the vote and carried only eight provinces.) The elections for the new legislature had already pointed in the same direction: all the leaders of the opposition to Feijó were re-elected. Significantly, the number of magistrates in the legislature, more inclined to conservatism, rose from 24 per cent to 39 per cent, while the number of priests, most of them liberals, fell from 23 per cent to 12 per cent.[17]

Araújo Lima's opponent in the elections for regent in 1838 was Holanda Cavalcanti. (He had also stood against Feijó in 1835.) Both Araújo Lima and Holanda Cavalcanti were members of the Pernambucan sugar oligarchy. But Araújo Lima was Coimbra-educated and had been involved in national politics since independence. He had travelled to several European countries and attended a law course in France. Holanda had no higher education and often preferred to tend to the affairs of his *engenho* than to stay in Rio. Their positions regarding the political organization of the country were quite different. While Holanda was known for his advocacy of maximum decentralization, and even of secessionism, Lima, a convinced centralist, had voted against the Additional Act and had been a staunch supporter of the *regresso* from the beginning.

The *moderado* group had split. The bulk of the magistrates and bureaucrats and part of the landowning class, particularly the landed interest of Rio de Janeiro, Bahia and Pernambuco, had moved steadily to the right, leaving behind as the nucleus of what would become the Liberal party the more urban-oriented elements, a few priests, and many landowners from less traditional areas, particularly São Paulo, Minas Gerais and Rio Grande do Sul. The splinter *regressionista* group was joined by what was left of the *caramurus*, many of them entrenched in the bureaucracy and in the Senate, and the *caramurus'* traditional supporters, the Portuguese merchants of the major cities. In the government organized by Araújo Lima in 1838, reflecting the conservative majority in the

[17] Carvalho, *A Construção*, 83

Chamber, Vasconcelos, himself a Coimbra-educated magistrate, a Mineiro without landed connections, was given two portfolios (empire and justice) and was recognized as the leader of the cabinet. He was joined by Miguel Calmon do Pin e Almeida (the future Marquês de Abrantes), a *senhor de engenho* from Bahia, also educated at Coimbra; Rego Barros, an army officer trained in Germany, and Maciel Monteiro, a doctor trained in England, both linked to the Pernambucan oligarchy; José da Costa Carvalho (the future Marquês de Monte Alegre), the former regent; and Joaquim José Rodrigues Tôrres (the future Visconde de Itaboraí), educated at Coimbra and linked to the coffee planters of Rio de Janeiro. It was an alliance of magistrates and sugar and coffee planters, well educated (for the most part in Europe, above all in Coimbra), and with considerable experience in government.

The rationale for the new alliance was provided by Vasconcelos and Paulino José Soares de Sousa (the future Visconde do Uruguai), another magistrate who had started his training at Coimbra and who had family ties with Rodrigues Tôrres (their wives were sisters). Vasconcelos and Paulino were also the main drafters of the legislation that finally reformed the earlier liberal laws. Their basic premise was that the country was not ready for the advanced liberal measures adopted after 1831. Events were proving that social order and national unity could not be maintained without a strengthening of the central government. But while Paulino always stressed the political and administrative aspects of the nation's problems, Vasconcelos went deeper. *O Sete de Abril*, known to be published under his influence, discussed the need for a government supported by the *classe conservadora*, defined as an alliance of landowners, capitalists, merchants, industrialists and those in the arts and sciences, people who 'in sudden changes have everything to lose and nothing to gain'.[18] This class, according to the *Sete*, was interested in progress but with order. *O Chronista*, the journal of the talented mulatto journalist and protégé of Vasconcelos, Justiniano José da Rocha, agreed with this idea and equated it with Guizot's concept of the 'legal country'.[19] The *Aurora*, revived under a new publisher in 1838, counter-attacked, but forgot that Evaristo himself had written in 1835 that the *moderado* party represented 'progress in order'. In a long and perceptive analysis of Vasconcelos's political philosophy the *Aurora* described him as a follower of Bentham-

---

[18] *O Sete de Abril*, 19 November 1838. Capitalists (*capitalistas*) in the vocabulary of the day were financiers or big urban property owners.

[19] Quoted in *O Sete de Abril*, 7 December 1838.

ite utilitarianism, a believer only in the morality of interests, in the principle that the only motor of human action was material interests, and that the only constraint was the fear of those interests being damaged.[20] Here the *Aurora* probably came close to putting its finger on Vasconcelos's purpose: to find solid material interests on which to base the monarchy and the entire political system.

The difficulty in the late thirties and early forties was that the conservative classes in general had no consensus on what would be the best institutional framework to suit their interests, in part because these interests did not totally coincide, in part because many of their members, landowners more than merchants, were not prepared to think in terms of rule through the mediation of the state. In 1843, J. J. da Rocha was still arguing that the monarchy had no solid roots in Brazil. It was a product of reason, of the perception of its importance in maintaining order. It was still necessary to convince landowners and merchants, the aristocracy of land and wealth, that it was in their best interests to support it and be supported by it.[21] Owing to the lack of a unified perception on the part of the dominant groups, the *regresso* was far from unanimously supported in the late thirties and early forties. Besides the sugar planters of the northeast, especially Bahia, the conservative coalition relied heavily at the beginning on a group of magistrates and bureaucrats and on the coffee planters of Rio de Janeiro. The coincidence of a new economic boom based on coffee with the geographical area in which the political and administrative centre of the country was located was, as we shall see, a basic factor in the eventual success of the process of political recentralization.

The first regressionist law was the *interpretação* of the Additional Act in May 1840. It was presented as an 'interpretation', but in fact as far as the appointment and removal of public employees and the definition of their jurisdiction were concerned it substantially reduced the power of provincial assemblies. At this juncture, as a last resort, the liberal minority in the Chamber decided to promote, prematurely, the *maioridade* of the emperor in order to prevent further regressionist measures. The coming of age of the emperor was a widely accepted idea, which had been mentioned several times since 1835 as a way of bolstering the legitimacy of the central government. Although always more likely to be a conservative measure, political opportunism led the liberals to bring it forward. The

---

[20] *Aurora Fluminense*, 23 July, 17 October, 1838.
[21] *O Brasil*, 19, 21, 23, 26 September, 1843.

'parliamentary *coup d'état*' of 23 July 1840, which ended the regency of Araújo Lima and initiated the Second Empire, was supported by liberals, bureaucrats, the army and the National Guard, the people of Rio and, last but not least, the 15-year-old emperor himself. The liberal *gabinete da maioridade* which was immediately formed included two Andrada brothers (Antônio Carlos and Martim Francisco), two Cavalcanti de Albuquerque brothers (Holanda and Francisco de Paula), Antônio Paulino Limpo de Abreu, the future Visconde de Abaeté, a mineiro liberal, and Aureliano Coutinho, a courtier with a strong personal influence over the young emperor. Given the inexperience and lack of leadership of Pedro II, conflict soon broke out inside the cabinet and it collapsed at the end of March 1841. The new *gabinete conservador* kept the influential Aureliano and introduced Paulino Soares de Sousa as Minister of Justice, Miguel Calmon, a *senhor de engenho* from Bahia, Araújo Viana, the tutor of Pedro II, Vilela Barbosa, an army officer, and José Clemente Pereira, a Portuguese-born magistrate, the last two well-known former supporters of Pedro I. (The cabinet of January 1843–February 1844 included, as well as Paulino, Rodrigues Tôrres and Honório Hermeto Carneiro Leão (the future Marquês de Paraná), a young Coimbra-trained magistrate and politician from Minas Gerais who was, like Rodrigues Tôrres, a Rio *fazendeiro*.) With the help of Vasconcelos in the Senate, Paulino rushed through parliament a law re-establishing the Council of State (November 1841) and the reform of the Code of Criminal Procedures (December 1841).

The reform of the Code was the central achievement of the *regresso*. It re-established in the hands of the central government total control over the administrative and judicial structure of the empire. All judges from *desembargador* (high court judge) and *juiz de direito* (district judge) to *juiz municipal* (county judge) were to be appointed by the minister of justice. The district judges, in particular, had their powers reinforced. Only local *juízes de paz* remained independent of the central power. But this also was taken care of: the new law created *chefes de polícia* in all provincial capitals – to be appointed by the minister of justice. At the *município* and parish level, the police chiefs were represented by *delegados* and *subdelegados* who were civilians appointed by the provincial presidents on their recommendation. Most of the judicial and police attributes of the justices of the peace were transferred to the *delegados* and *subdelegados*, reducing to powerlessness the elected justices, who also lost to these 'sheriffs' the task of organizing the list of jurors and of appointing block inspectors.

The electoral boards alone remained their responsibility. Through the police chiefs, the minister could even control the appointment of jail guards throughout the country, and it was he who decided their salaries. Furthermore, the requirements for jurors were stiffened: they had to be literate and to earn 400 milréis in the major cities and 200 milréis elsewhere, which doubled the previous income requirement. Significantly, if the income came from industry or commerce, it had to be doubled again, to 800 and 400 milréis, a further indication that landowners and bureaucrats were the most favoured elements. A further centralizing measure was the appointment of provincial vice-presidents by the minister of the empire. Previously they were nominated in lists of six names by the provincial assemblies, the central government limiting itself to establishing the order in which they should serve. As a last indication of the sweeping nature of the *regresso*, the new Code required every person travelling within the empire who wanted to avoid interrogation and possible expulsion from a *município* by the local *delgado* to carry a passport. Only the National Guard survived this onslaught on the liberal measures of 1831–4, even though its loyalty when the central government had attempted, and in the case of Rio Grande do Sul was still attempting, to crush provincial rebellions had often been uncertain. It was, however, only a temporary respite, as we shall see. And the government did now begin to increase once more the size of the army.

This package of measures aiming to recentralize political power included the restoration of the exercise of the 'moderating power' which had been suspended under the regency. In a decisive move on 1 May 1842 the conservative government then dissolved the legislature elected in October 1840 during the short liberal interregnum before it had even convened, and called new elections. The liberals feared that the conservative party, taking advantage of the youth of the emperor and of the recent legislation, which had vastly expanded government patronage and control, would entrench itself in power to their permanent exclusion. Two years earlier they had recourse to the *maioridade*. Now they only had open rebellion. In May 1842, São Paulo rose up in arms, followed by Minas Gerais in June, and the rebellion spread to parts of the Paraíba valley in the province of Rio de Janeiro. The most important liberal leaders of São Paulo and Minas Gerais, including Feijó and Vergueiro in the former, Limpo de Abreu and Teófilo Ottoni in the latter, were involved. The men appointed revolutionary presidents – Tobias de Aguiar in São Paulo and Pinto Coelho in Minas Gerais – were among the richest in their provinces. Aguiar had become rich for his participation in the mule trade of Sorocaba, the focus of the rebellion, where his family had also drawn great profits from tax farming during the colonial period and the early years of the empire; he was also a colonel in the National Guard and had been president of the province under the liberal government of 1840. Pinto Coelho had made his fortune in gold mining and had recently sold a mining concern to the British for £112,500. In Rio de Janeiro, the leader of the rebels, Joaquim José de Sousa Breves, was undoubtedly the richest man in the province. He is said to have owned more than 6,000 slaves and over 30 *fazendas*, from which he harvested 100–200,000 *arrobas* of coffee a year. He was also well known for his direct involvement in the illegal slave trade. He had long been at odds with the conservative presidents of the province, especially Paulino Soares de Sousa, because of their periodic attempts to put an end to coffee tax evasions and slave trading.

In terms of leadership, the revolts of 1842 were similar to the *farroupilha* rebellion which continued in Rio Grande do Sul, but the reasons behind them were different. Paulistas and Mineiros fought mostly against the new laws of the *regresso* and against the conservative cabinet in Rio. São Paulo was also protesting against a government act early in 1842 which had prohibited the trade in mules with the gaúcho rebels, but this does not seem to have been a major cause of the rebellion, although it might have been the reason why Tobias de Aguiar joined it. Secession was mentioned in São Paulo, but the idea did not seem to have had great appeal. For one thing, the north-east of the province formed part of the Paraíba valley and its coffee economy was closely linked to the port of Rio. Moreover, the fighting spirit and capacity of the *bandeirantes* seemed to have disappeared; unlike the militarized gaúcho *estancieiros*, the paulista *fazendeiros* were easily defeated by the rather weak troops of the central government. In Minas Gerais whose Zona da Mata was also part of Brazil's coffee economy there was no talk of secession at all. And as far as Breves was concerned, the idea made no sense, since his *fazendas* were in the very heart of the Rio coffee area.

The liberal rebellions of 1842 indicate the diversity of perception within the landed class at the time regarding the political organization of the country. Landowners in all three provinces joined in, but by no means unanimously. There were landowners on both sides of the conflict (and the National Guard was also split). In São Paulo, Vergueiro, for instance, was a revolutionary, and Costa Carvalho was the loyalist president of the province. In the Paraíba valley, Breves was opposed by other coffee planters who supported the central government. The president of Rio de Janeiro province at the time was Honório Hermeto, himself a coffee *fazendeiro* in the province, who, the following year, as we have seen, would join a much strengthened conservative cabinet. Minas Gerais, which did not have as strong an export sector as Rio or São Paulo, did have quite an important network of small towns developed at the time of the gold rush. Here was the source of a more authentic form of bourgeois liberalism, best represented by Teófilo Ottoni. But even these towns, like the landowners of the province, were divided during the revolt.

The rebellion lasted a month in São Paulo and two months in Minas Gerais before it was finally crushed. Throughout the following decades, until the fall of the empire in 1889, the liberal party drew its main strength from São Paulo and Minas Gerais together with Rio Grande do Sul. São Paulo and Minas Gerais having no strong reasons to secede and Rio Grande do Sul having failed to secede they accepted the unity of the country established at the time of independence and maintained despite the turmoil of the thirties. They were not able to dispute the supremacy in national politics of Rio de Janeiro. The most liberals in São Paulo and Minas Gerais could now do perhaps was to prevent the centralization of power from going too far.

Visiting Brazil in 1842 and 1843, the Comte de Suzannet observed that Rio Grande do Sul had already seceded, that São Paulo would soon follow and that 'the unity of Brazil is only apparent. All the provinces look forward to independence. A United States style republic, this is the dream they strive to realise.'[22] Three years after the beginning of the Second Empire, this was the impression the country gave to a visitor, unsympathetic as he was. In the event, the count's predictions were proved wrong. Political as well as economic factors accounted for a different outcome. On the political side, the continued influence of Aureliano over the emperor helped to bring about another change of government. At the beginning of 1844 the liberals returned to power. Amnesty was granted to Paulista and Mineiro rebels who were soon back in the Chamber and in ministerial posts. The fear of a permanent monopoly of power by the conservatives was thus eliminated, and a system in which power rotated periodically between the two parties or coalitions began to take shape. Even more important, once in power, the liberals found it useful to retain the regressionist laws of 1840–1 – to

[22] Comte de Suzannet, *O Brasil em 1845* (Rio de Janeiro, 1957), 87.

enforce law and order, to exercise patronage and to win elections. Before the first legislative elections promoted by the new government they removed almost half of the *juízes de direito* in the country and several commanders of the National Guard. From 1844 to 1848, the *quinqüênio liberal*, Brazil was governed by a succession of liberal cabinets – of which the most prominent members were once more Alves Branco, Limpo de Abreu and Holanda Cavalcanti, together with José Carlos Pereira de Almeida Tôrres (visconde de Macaé) and Francisco de Paula Sousa e Melo. No serious attempt was made to undo the work of the *regresso*, to the disappointment of more consistent liberals such as Teófilo Ottoni. In disgust, the Mineiro revolutionary abandoned national politics and returned to Minas, after first securing from the liberal government a forty-year licence to promote navigation on the Mucuri river.

At the same time, the political unity and stability of the empire was underpinned by the rapid growth of the coffee sector centred on Rio during the 1830s and 1840s. This not only consolidated the political authority of the Rio coffee *fazendeiros* who together with the bureaucrats and magistrates formed the backbone of the conservative party, but particularly after the 1844 tariff reform considerably strengthened the finances of the Brazilian state. The conservative cabinet led by the Visconde de Olinda (Araújo Lima) which took power in September 1848, like the cabinets of 1841 and 1843, included three out of six senior ministers linked to coffee interests in the province of Rio de Janeiro. After surviving one last liberal provincial rebellion – the *Praieira* in Pernambuco – it went on to complete the work of political centralization and even found the authority to tackle one of Brazil's most complex, intractable and pressing problems – the slave trade and relations with Britain.

During the 1830s and 1840s three products – sugar, cotton and coffee – continued to account for 75–80 per cent of Brazil's exports. It was coffee, however, which for the first time was largely responsible for Brazil's modest but steady overall economic growth. The dramatic expansion of coffee production and export was the most striking feature of Brazil's economic history in this period. Responding to the growth of demand in western Europe and the United States where the taste for coffee developed in the expanding urban centres, especially among the urban middle classes, coffee spread across the virgin highlands of the valley of the river Paraíba, which runs parallel to the coast some seventy miles inland from

Rio de Janeiro, for the most part in Rio province but also including the southeast of the province of Minas Gerais and the northeast region of São Paulo province. Soil, altitude and climate proved exceptionally favourable to the cultivation of the coffee bush in the Paraíba valley. Land values soared, landholdings were consolidated and the pattern of large plantations (*fazendas*), already so familiar in areas of sugar cultivation, was reproduced in the new and expanding coffee region of south-east Brazil.

At the time of independence coffee had already established itself as Brazil's third most important cash crop. During the five-year period 1831–5 it outstripped not only cotton but sugar to become the country's principal export accounting for 40 per cent of Brazil's total export earnings by the end of the decade and almost half by 1850 (see below Table 1). A new export cycle which was to last for more than a century begun. In this first stage almost all the coffee was grown in the Paraíba valley (80 per cent in the province of Rio de Janeiro) and exported in increasing quantities from the port of Rio (see below, Table 2). By the late forties, however, coffee was already spreading into the Paulista west, from Campinas to Rio Claro, displacing sugar and at the same time, despite the difficulties of transportation over the Serra do Mar, turning Santos into a major port. In 1836/7 Campinas, for example, was exporting through Santos 153,000 *arrobas* of sugar and only 5,000 *arrobas* of coffee. In 1850–1, for the first time, Campinas exported more coffee than sugar. And in 1854/5 313,000 *arrobas* of coffee and only 12,000 *arrobas* of sugar were exported.[23]

Brazil's share of world coffee output rose from a little under 20 per cent in the 1820s to 30 per cent in the 1830s and over 40 per cent in the 1840s, by which time Brazil was by far the world's largest producer. Most of Brazil's coffee was exported to Europe, especially Germany, the Low Countries and Scandinavia, and to the United States, the largest single market. Britain, which, in any case, preferred tea, imported coffee from its colonies in the Caribbean, Central America and South Asia and preferential duties in favour of colonial produce virtually excluded Brazilian coffee from the British market. Coffee exports were largely responsible for the steady growth in Brazil's export earnings from an average of £3.8m per annum in 1822–31 to £5.4m per annum in 1832–41. And, despite falling international coffee prices, increased production was

23 Maria Theresa Schorer Petrone, *A lavoura canavieira em São Paulo: expansão e declínio, 1765–1861* (São Paulo, 1968), 166.

Table 1 *Value of the Major Brazilian Exports in Relation to Total Exports,*
1821–1850 (%)

	Sugar (1)	Cotton (2)	Coffee (3)	(1)+(2) +(3)	Hides (4)	Others*
1821–30	30.1	20.6	18.4	69.1	13.6	17.3
1831–40	24.0	10.8	43.8	78.6	7.9	13.5
1841–50	26.7	7.5	41.4	75.6	8.5	15.9

* Tobacco, cacao, rubber, maté, etc.
Source: *Anuário Estatístico do Brasil* (Rio de Janeiro, 1939/40), 1380.

Table 2 *Exports of Coffee from Rio de Janeiro*
(in *arrobas*)

1792	160	1835	3,237,190
1817	318,032	1840–1	4,982,221
1820	539,000	1845–6	6,720,221
1826	1,304,450	1849–50	5,706,833
1830	1,958,925	1851–2	9,673,842

Source: Stanley J. Stein, *Vassouras, a Brazilian coffee county, 1850–1900* (Cambridge, Mass., 1957), 53.

sufficient to earn Brazil more than £1m more in the 1840s than the 1830s (see Table 3). Total export earnings rose to an average of £5.9m per annum in 1842–51 (and, more dramatically, to £10.9m per annum in 1852–61).[24] In view of the growth of Brazil's population during this period (it reached over 7 million by 1850), this was not yet enough to produce a more than modest increase in per capita incomes even in the south-east. In the north-east, where, except for sugar in the late 1840s, export sectors grew more slowly, stagnated or actually declined, per capita incomes probably fell.

The Brazilian sugar boom which followed the disruption of the world market caused by the French Revolution and the Napoleonic Wars, and particularly the abrupt end to Saint Domingue's reign as the world's greatest sugar producer, was short-lived. From the mid-1820s to the mid-1840s production of sugar continued to increase, albeit relatively slowly, in both the traditional sugar regions of the north-east, Bahia and Pernambuco, and in São Paulo and around Campos in Rio de Janeiro province. Overall production during the decade 1831–40 was up 50 per cent compared with 1821–30. However, like most commodity prices,

[24] Nathaniel H. Leff, *Underdevelopment and development in Brazil* (2 vols., London, 1982), I, 80.

Table 3 *Brazilian Coffee Exports, 1821–50*

Year	Thousand of 60 kg sacks	Thousands of £ sterling	Value per sack (£ sterling)	Coffee exports as percentage of total exports
1821	129	704	5.50	16.3
1822	186	789	4.24	19.6
1823	226	878	3.89	20.1
1824	274	704	2.57	18.3
1825	224	623	2.78	13.5
1826	318	690	2.17	20.8
1827	430	774	1.80	21.1
1828	452	659	1.46	15.9
1829	459	705	1.54	20.9
1830	480	663	1.38	19.8
Decade	3,178	7,189	2.26	18.4
1831	549	964	1.76	28.6
1832	717	1,832	2.56	39.2
1833	560	1,383	2.47	42.4
1833/34	1,121	2,775	2.47	49.3
1834/35	970	2,435	2.51	45.7
1835/36	1,052	2,555	2.43	37.7
1836/37	910	2,237	2.46	40.9
1837/38	1,149	2,197	1.91	53.2
1838/39	1,333	2,494	1.87	51.3
1839/40	1,383	2,657	1.92	46.7
Decade	9,744	21,529	2.21	43.8
1840/41	1,239	2,300	1.86	42.7
1841/42	1,363	2,311	1.69	46.8
1842/43	1,444	1,909	1.32	41.6
1843/44	1,541	1,933	1.25	41.0
1844/45	1,525	1,838	1.20	37.2
1845/46	1,723	2,259	1.31	39.7
1846/47	2,387	2,465	1.03	41.9
1847/48	2,340	2,936	1.25	43.4
1848/49	2,106	2,242	1.06	38.2
1849/50	1,453	2,462	1.69	41.5
Decade	17,121	22,655	1.32	41.4

Source: Affonso de E. Taunay, *Pequena História do café no Brasil* (Rio de Janeiro, 1945), 547.

international sugar prices were falling in this period and increased production was insufficient to maintain the existing level of export earnings. With coffee export buoyant, sugar's share of total exports fell from 30.1 per cent in 1821–30 to 24 per cent in 1831–40; it then rose a little to 26.7 per cent in the following decade (see Table 1 above).

Brazil remained, after the British West Indies and Cuba, the third leading exporter of sugar with 10–15 per cent of world output in the 1830s. But at a time of rapidly expanding world demand Brazil faced increasing competition from Cuban sugar cane (exported primarily to the United States where Louisiana expanded its own production) and from European sugar beet, and gradually lost ground in the international market. The Brazilian industry, based on cheap land and cheap labour, was technically backward and capital for modernization was in limited supply. Also transportation costs, within Brazil and across the Atlantic, were relatively high. As in the case of coffee, Brazilian sugar was virtually excluded from Britain, one of the biggest markets, by colonial preference; until duties were gradually equalized after 1846 Brazilian sugar was subject to a duty of 63*s*. per cwt compared with 24*s*. per cwt on sugar from the British West Indies, East Indies and Mauritius. Continental Europe was the main market for Brazilian sugar (much of it carried in British ships directly to European ports or to London for re-export).

As for cotton, for the first time since the initial boom during the last quarter of the eighteenth century, its production and export suffered during the 1830s and 1840s an absolute decline (from which it would recover only during the American Civil War). The main foreign market was, of course, Britain. There was no colonial preference in the case of cotton but a preference for cheaper United States cotton was responsible for a decline in Brazil's share of British raw cotton imports from 20 per cent in 1801–10 to 13 per cent in 1821–30 and only 3 per cent in 1841–50. As a result cotton's share of total Brazilian export earnings fell from 20.6 per cent in 1821–30 to 10.8 per cent in 1831–40 and 7.5 per cent in 1841–50 (see Table 1 above).

'We are not so absurd as to think of becoming manufacturers yet', José Bonifácio told Henry Chamberlain, the British consul-general, in November 1822; 'we will therefore buy your manufactures and sell you our produce.'[25] In the period after independence, Britain, as we have seen, was a less important market for Brazilian produce than continental Europe. As early as 1838 the United States too was almost as important an export market as Britain. In that year, however, Britain supplied 41 per cent of Brazilian imports compared with 8 per cent from the United States. By the late forties almost half Brazil's imports came from Britain (compared with approximately 10 per cent from France, 10 per cent from the United States and 10 per cent from Portugal). Cotton goods consti-

[25] Quoted in C. K. Webster (ed.), *Britain and the independence of Latin America, 1812–30. Select documents from the Foreign Office archives* (2 vols., London, 1938), I, 215.

tuted over half the imports from Britain and cottons, woollens and linens together accounted for 75 per cent of the total. The remaining 25 per cent was made up of a whole range of consumer goods from hardware, earthenware and glass to hats, umbrellas and musical instruments. Prices of manufactured goods fell even faster than commodity prices during the 1830s and 1840s. Thus, the real value of Brazilian exports (expanding anyway thanks mainly to coffee) in terms of Brazil's capacity to import increased. Trade figures are notoriously difficult to assess in this period, but it has been estimated that except for three years (1831, 1837 and 1842) the Brazilian market was worth between £2m and £3m per annum to British manufacturers during these two decades, rising to £3.5m in 1851. In most years British exports to Brazil were only slightly lower, and in some years higher, than British exports to the whole of Spanish America.[26] Although importing only 5–7 per cent of total British exports and only a quarter of the value of exports to Europe and one-third of exports to the United States Brazil, after the United States and Germany, was Britain's third largest single market.

Under the Anglo-Brazilian commercial treaty of 1827, like the Anglo-Portuguese treaty of 1810, the maximum tariff on imported British goods, which were already cheap, was 15 per cent ad valorem. This was one important factor in Brazil's failure to develop its own manufacturing sector during Dom João's residence in Rio (1808–21) and in the period immediately after independence. Rio de Janeiro (which had a population of 200,000 by 1850) and other Brazilian cities were full of artisans' establishments making soap, candles, cotton thread, clothing, hats, snuff, cigars, furniture and ironware, but the textile and food-processing factories which were to form the basis of Brazil's early industrial growth did not appear until after 1840. Indeed there was no significant growth until the 1870s. Other factors, however, besides cheap British imports during the first half of the nineteenth century explain Brazil's late industrialization: the lack of industrial fuels, especially coal; poor transportation (no roads, canals or railways; only rivers and coastal shipping); limited amounts of capital, domestic or foreign, and a rudimentary banking system; outdated commercial legislation hindering the establishment of joint stock companies; a labour market dominated by slavery; low levels of education and the almost total absence of scientific or technical training; the small size of the market for manufactured goods in a society in which the majority were either slaves or free poor with only

[26] D. C. M. Platt, *Latin America and British trade 1806–1914* (London, 1972), 30.

limited purchasing power; the self-sufficiency of many plantations; the absence of a national market (only loosely articulated regional and local markets); the prevalence of *laissez-faire* ideas amongst both Brazilian landowners and the merchants of the coastal cities; and the failure of government in any way to encourage the growth of industry.

A more direct consequence of the 15 per cent maximum tariff on British imports (indeed *all* imports because of Brazil's most favoured nation treaties with her other trading partners) was the strict limit it imposed on Brazilian government revenues, 80 per cent of which by the 1840s came from customs duties. (See Table 4.) Government expenditure in this period – a period of external and internal wars – was on average 40 per cent above government revenue. The amount of paper money in circulation was therefore expanded. And further loans were raised in London in 1839 and 1843.

Thus the Anglo-Brazilian commercial treaty of 1827 which, like the anti-slave trade treaty of 1826, had been negotiated during the period of Brazil's weakness and dependence on Britain following her declaration of independence from Portugal and negotiations for its recognition, proved increasingly irksome to Brazilians. It irritated in particular the conservatives who were in power, as we have seen, during the years 1837–40 and 1841–4. In the first place, they resented the extra-territorial privileges it conferred on Britain, especially the right to appoint judges conservators, which they considered incompatible with Brazilian sovereignty. Secondly, the treaty was with justification held largely responsible for Brazil's not inconsiderable financial difficulties. And by the 1840s there were the first signs of an awareness in some circles that, by providing protection for home manufacturing, higher tariffs could be an instrument of economic change as well as a valuable source of revenue. Certainly the low duties on British goods contrasted most unfavourably with the virtually prohibitive duties on Brazilian produce entering the British market. Unless Britain modified its commercial policy and lowered duties on Brazilian sugar and coffee, permitting a more balanced trade between Britain and Brazil, there was every reason for Brazil to seek to raise duties on British manufactured goods. An early attempt to revise the 1827 treaty and put Anglo-Brazilian commercial relations on a more equal footing – the Barbacena mission to London in 1836 – had failed. The treaty, however, was due to expire in November 1842, fifteen years after its ratification, or so it seemed. (In the event Britain invoked an article of the treaty under which it could continue in force until

Table 4 *Customs Duties and total Government Revenues, 1830–50*

Years	Rio's customs as % of total customs	Total customs as % of total revenues
1830/31	44	47
1831/32	54	42
1832/33	55	57
1833/34	55	59
1834/35	53	50
1835/36	53	59
1836/37	53	77
1837/38	54	74
1838/39	55	78
1839/40	57	78
1840/41	58	84
1841/42	60	82
1842/43	56	80
1843/44	54	79
1844/45	50	78
1845/46	51	80
1846/47	49	78
1847/48	49	78
1848/49	54	79
1849/50	49	81
1850/51	50	82

Source: Amaro Cavalcanti, *Resenha financeira do ex-Império do Brasil em 1889* (Rio de Janeiro, 1900), 330.

November 1844.) There was widespread feeling throughout Brazil that it should not be renewed without radical revision.

In Britain there was at this time growing pressure for free trade and, in particular, for lower duties on imported foodstuffs. In the case of sugar there was one complicating factor: slavery. Brazilian (and Cuban) sugar was slave-grown. The West India interest could defend colonial preference on more respectable grounds than economic self-interest. The abandonment of fiscal discrimination against slave-grown sugar would, besides ruining the West Indies, stimulate production, and therefore the demand for slaves, in Brazil and Cuba and undermine Britain's efforts to bring about the abolition of the slave trade and slavery throughout the world. At the end of 1841 the British government decided to submit proposals for a new Anglo-Brazilian commercial treaty similar to the one in existence (with its favourable tariffs on British manufactures) but with important and striking additions: Britain would reduce import duties on

Brazilian sugar; in return Brazil as well as fulfilling existing treaty commitments to suppress the slave trade would declare free all children born of slave mothers at an early date (to be determined by negotiation) and consider the emancipation of all slaves at the earliest possible moment.

A special mission to Brazil in 1842 led by Henry Ellis found both the press and public opinion in Rio 'absurdly violent and impertinent' in their opposition to 'enslaving Brazil with treaties'. It did not take Ellis long to realize that his principal objective – to persuade the Brazilian government to take the steps necessary to make the abolition of slavery in Brazil certain 'at no distant period' – was 'quite out of the question'.[27] Without a Brazilian concession on slavery there could be no British concession on sugar. And without the latter there could be no renewal of the existing commercial treaty. When he consulted British merchants in Rio Ellis found to his surprise that they no longer attached much importance either to their judicial privileges in Brazil or to the 15 per cent preferential tariff; these had been useful in the past when Britain was establishing its position in the Brazilian market but, provided there was no positive discrimination against British goods, Britain's economic superiority over its nearest rivals would ensure the continuation of Britain's pre-eminence in Brazil. Ellis, however, could not even secure a treaty which simply guaranteed that British merchants and their goods would be treated on a par with those of other nations. In return for most favoured nation status for British manufactures, the Brazilian negotiators demanded that Brazilian sugar, coffee, tobacco and other agricultural produce should enter Britain at duties no more than 10 per cent higher than those levied on colonial produce and where possible on equal terms. As for the abolition of slavery, Honório Hermeto Carneiro Leão, conservative Foreign Minister at the time, made it absolutely clear that this was 'a question for the future and not for the present'. Negotiations broke down in March 1843, having generated in Brazil a fresh wave of ill-feeling against Britain. They were renewed in London later in the year, but again without success. At the insistence of Brazil the 1827 treaty was thus terminated in November 1844.

There was a certain amount of apprehension in British manufacturing and commercial circles about the consequences for British trade of the failure to replace the 1827 treaty with at least a most favoured nation treaty. In December 1843, anticipating the ending of the treaty, the

---

[27] Quotations in Bethell, *Abolition*, 232.

conservative government in Brazil appointed a Tariff Commission to prepare new tariffs on imported goods and gave it instructions that revealed a new concern for the protection of national industries against foreign competition. The highest tariffs (60 per cent) were to be imposed on articles that were or could be produced inside the country. Machines for the infant textile industry, on the other hand, were to be free of all duties. (Decree of 17 May 1843.) Then, in February 1844, the liberals returned to power. The new tariffs announced by the Minister of Finance, Manuel Alves Branco, in August 1844 were somewhat less protectionist. Only tobacco and related products were taxed at 60 per cent. Cotton cloth and thread were taxed at only 20 per cent, which had little or no adverse effect on British imports. (Decree of 12 August 1844.) National industries, however, continued to be favoured with free imports of machines and raw materials, and with exemption from military service for their employees. (Decree of 8 August 1846.) And towards the end of the decade in a further effort to diversify the economy, the government began to lend money to industrialists such as Irineu E. de Sousa, the future barão de Mauá, who was to become the most dynamic businessman of the empire. (Decree of 2 October 1848.) Limited as they were, these measures indicate a broadening of state action and an attempt to diversify and expand economic activity in Brazil. Nevertheless, the main purpose of the increase in most tariffs from 15 per cent to 20 per cent or 30 per cent in 1844 was fiscal rather than protectionist. Government revenues increased 33 per cent from 1842/3 to 1844/5. And by 1852/3 they were double what they had been in 1842/3.[28]

For the Conservative government in Britain the ending of the 1827 treaty in 1844 had one positive advantage. The treaty had guaranteed to Brazilian sugar the benefit of any reduction in the duties on foreign sugar entering the British market. Sir Robert Peel, who had already in two stages reduced the duties on coffee from 15*d.* per lb foreign and 6*d.* per lb colonial to 6*d.* foreign and 4*d.* colonial (an example of British inconsistency – if coffee, why not sugar?), now lowered the duty on *free-grown* foreign sugar (from Java, for example) to 34*s.* per cwt while leaving that on slave-grown sugar at 63*s.* And a year later the duty on colonial sugar was reduced to 14*s.* per cwt and that on foreign free-grown sugar to 23*s.* per cwt. In 1846, however, following the repeal of the Corn Laws and the fall of Peel's government, the Whig Prime Minister Lord John Russell proposed the reduction of the differentials in favour of colonial sugar

[28] Amaro Cavalcanti, *Resenha financeira do ex-Império do Brasil em 1889* (Rio de Janeiro, 1900), 328.

over five years (later amended to eight years) until the final equalization of the duties on sugar 'of all sorts, of whatever growth and whencesoever imported'. (The duties on coffee were also to be equalized by 1851.) British discrimination against Brazilian sugar – and coffee – was thus gradually ended in the years after 1846. The Sugar Duties Act undoubtedly stimulated the sugar industry in Brazil, mainly in the north-east. Production in Pernambuco, for example, rose from 42,000 tons in 1844/5 to 51,000 tons in 1846/7 and 73,000 tons in 1848/9.[29] Sugar's share of total exports rose from 22 per cent in 1841–5 to 28 per cent in 1846–50. Exports of coffee also continued to rise; they were 40 per cent higher in 1846–50 than in 1841–5, but in the case of coffee the lowering of British import duties had only a marginal impact on Brazilian production. As some British abolitionists had feared, the demand for slaves in Brazil intensified during the late 1840s, although there were many reasons for this besides the ending of discriminatory duties on slave-grown produce entering the British market. And the Whig government in which Lord Palmerston was Foreign Secretary having, as they put it, abandoned the policy of 'fiscal coercion' had not the slightest intention of giving up the struggle to end the slave trade by means of 'physical coercion'.

The question of the Brazilian slave trade which continued long after it had been declared illegal by treaty with Britain in 1826 (effective from March 1830) and by Brazilian legislation (November 1831) dominated relations between Brazil and Britain during the 1830s and 1840s. In 1831, and several years after, very few slaves were in fact imported into Brazil, largely because, in anticipation of the abolition of the trade, 175,000 had been imported during the three years 1827–30. (For slave imports into Brazil after 1831, see Table 5.) There was a temporary falling off in demand which was reflected in low prices. The end of the legal slave trade coincided, however, with the rapid expansion of coffee throughout the Paraíba valley. From the outset coffee *fazendas* were worked by slaves, most of them imported from Africa. Slaves cleared the forests, planted the bushes, harvested and processed the beans, maintained the plantation and served in the Big House. Moreover, even when a slave labour force was established, the rate of slave mortality in Brazil was so high that it required regular replenishment from across the Atlantic. 'America', wrote the French émigré, Charles Auguste Taunay, in his

[29] David Albert Denslow, Jr, 'Sugar production in Northeastern Brazil and Cuba, 1858–1908' (unpublished Ph.D. thesis, Yale University, 1974), 9.

Table 5 *Slave Imports into Brazil,*
1831–1855

Years	Slaves	Years	Slaves
1831	138	1844	22,849
1832	116	1845	19,453
1833	1,233	1846	50,324
1834	749	1847	56,172
1835	745	1848	60,000
1836	4,966	1849	54,061
1837	35,209	1850	22,856
1838	40,256	1851	3,287
1839	42,182	1852	800
1840	20,796	1853	—
1841	13,804	1854	—
1842	17,435	1855	90
1843	19,095		

Source: Foreign Office memorandum, 4 August
1864, in Leslie Bethell, *The abolition of the Brazilian
slave trade* (Cambridge, 1970) 388–93, Appendix:
estimate of slaves imported into Brazil, 1831–55.

Manual do Agricultor Brazileiro (1839), 'devours the blacks. If continued
importation were not supplying them, the race would shortly disappear
from our midst.'[30] The demand for slaves in Brazil, therefore, especially
in the coffee regions of the centre-south, soon revived, prices rose and
the Brazilian slave trade was gradually reorganized after 1830 on an
illegal – and highly profitable – basis.

Successive Brazilian governments under the regency proved unwilling or unable to enforce the 1831 anti-slave trade law. They were for the
most part weak and short-lived, lacking adequate financial, military or
naval resources and preoccupied with political and constitutional issues
and the various provincial revolts which threatened to destroy the unity
and stability of the country. Law enforcement at the local level was in any
case in the hands of elected justices of the peace and officers of the
National Guard, few of whom were above accepting bribes and most of
whom were themselves landowners or closely linked by family and
interest to the landed class which had a stake in the revival and expansion
of the illegal slave trade. With rare exceptions they connived at illegal
slave landings. When a slave trader was apprehended he was brought

[30] Quoted in Stanley J. Stein, *Vassouras. A Brazilian coffee county, 1850–1900* (Cambridge, Mass.,
1957), 227.

before a local jury and invariably acquitted. Once clear of the coast illegally imported slaves were beyond the reach of the law; *fazendeiros de café* and *senhores de engenho* exercised virtually supreme authority on their own estates.

For one short period only, in 1835, was there a discernible reaction against the slave trade. This followed the major insurrection of the Malês (African Muslims) – the most serious urban slave uprising of the nineteenth century – in Bahia on 24/25 January 1835. It was in the event easily repressed, though with great violence. Around 40 blacks, slaves and freedmen, were killed. Hundreds were prosecuted and punished. Eighteen were sentenced to death, of whom 5 were actually executed. Other sentences included deportation to Africa, forced labour and physical punishment: some slaves were punished with up to 1,000 lashes. As a direct consequence of events in Bahia a drastic measure was introduced in 1835: all slaves who killed or gravely injured their masters or overseers would be punished by death. The requirement under the Criminal Code that where the sentence was death the verdicts of juries should be unanimous was changed; a two-thirds majority was sufficient and the sentence was to be carried out immediately, without appeal. Thus, internal security and white domination were quickly reinforced. Even so, the Bahia slave revolt, combined with threats of similiar revolts elsewhere, served to remind white Brazilians of the dangers inherent in the annual importation, legal or illegal, of thousands of African slaves. In the opinion of the liberal editor Evaristo da Veiga each new slave introduced into the country was another barrel of gunpowder added to the Brazilian mine.[31] And even when the fear of slave rebellion receded, the fear of 'Africanization' remained.

Nevertheless, the illegal slave trade gradually established itself during the mid-1830s with little or no interference from the Brazilian local authorities along the coast, until it eventually reached and passed its pre–1826 level. By the end of 1836 slave prices were falling for the first time in five years. The conservative government of September 1837 headed by Bernardo Pereira de Vasconcelos, a vociferous campaigner against the 1826 treaty and the law of 1831, resisted the growing demand from *municípios* in Rio de Janeiro, Minas Gerais and São Paulo for the repeal of anti-slave trade legislation, but made no effort to enforce it. And most of the limited anti-slave trade measures adopted by previous liberal governments were abandoned. Even ministers known to oppose the trade could

[31] *Aurora Fluminense*, 20, 27 March, 4 April 1835.

see little point in instituting proceedings against those involved in it since, as the Brazilian Foreign Minister told the British chargé d'affaires in February 1838, 'it may be safely predicted from experience, that no court of justice will be found to give sentence against them'.[32] During the three years 1837–9 at least 35,000 and probably as many as 45,000 slaves per annum were illegally imported into Brazil, mainly from the Congo, Angola and Mozambique. 80–90 per cent of them were landed along the coast to the north and south of Rio de Janeiro between Campos and Santos and in the capital itself, the majority clearly destined for the coffee *fazendas* of the Paraíba valley.

Brazilian governments before and after 1837 not only resisted persistent pressure from the British legation in Rio (which virtually assumed the role of an abolitionist society in Brazil) to introduce and enforce more effective anti-slave trade legislation, but also refused to concede to Britain the powers it needed if the British navy, particularly the West African squadron, were to suppress the trade on the high seas. In 1831 Brazil had agreed that the Anglo-Portuguese treaty of 1817, under which British naval vessels had the right to visit, search and, when their suspicions were confirmed, detain ships illegally trading in slaves between Africa and Brazil (at that time north of the equator only), should be extended to cover the entire Brazilian slave trade now that it was illegal south of the equator as well and should continue in force for fifteen years from March 1830. Captured Brazilian ships were to be sent for adjudication before Anglo-Brazilian mixed commissions in Sierra Leone or Rio de Janeiro. The treaty of 1817, however, lacked 'equipment' and 'break up' clauses, which were vital to the effectiveness of the West African squadron; that is to say, ships equipped for the slave trade but without slaves actually on board could not be visited, searched and captured, and slave vessels condemned by the mixed commission could not be destroyed to prevent their returning to the trade. All negotiations with Brazil for the strengthening of the treaty – and they were carried on year after year – ended in failure. Yet, even if they had been successful and if as a result the anti-slave trade operations of British warships had been less circumscribed, the West African squadron in the 1830s lacked the necessary numbers – and, it should be said, the speed – to prevent the growth of the Brazilian trade. At the same time a stronger maritime police force would have been similarly frustrated.

In 1839 the Whig government in Britain, and more particularly the

32 Quoted in Bethell, *Abolition*, 84.

Foreign Secretary Lord Palmerston, adopted tougher measures to curb
the Brazilian slave trade which was now growing at an alarming rate.
These included: the so-called Palmerston Act which unilaterally extended the powers of the British navy to intercept slavers flying the
Portuguese flag, with or without slaves on board, and to send them to
British vice-admiralty courts for condemnation; confirmation of the
ruling by British mixed commissioners in both Rio and Freetown that
the treaty of 1817 as it stood, taken in conjunction with the treaty of 1826,
permitted British cruisers to search and seize Brazilian vessels intending
to trade in slaves; the strengthening of the West African and Cape
squadrons which still had the primary responsibility for the suppression
of the slave trade; the decision to allow British warships on anti-slave
trade patrol to cruise inshore, to enter African waters and rivers and to
blockade key points on the African coast. (The South American squadron also became more active at this time, but there were relatively few
ships available to patrol the Brazilian coast and they had to be careful to
avoid unnecessary interference with legitimate coastal trade and to show
some token respect for Brazilian sovereignty in Brazilian territorial
waters. Even so clashes with the local Brazilian authorities were not
always avoided.) Partly as a result of these British initiatives – and a
marked increase in the number of slave ships captured by the British navy
– slave imports into Brazil during the three years from the middle of 1839
to the middle of 1842 fell to less than half their recent level (see Table 5
above). The somewhat more determined effort to restrict the slave trade
which some Brazilian authorities made during the liberal interregnum
(July 1840–March 1841) may have contributed to its relative decline.
More significant was the temporary glut on the market following the
huge imports of the late thirties.

It was against this background of reduced slave imports in the early
forties and the recognition by some, at least, that the slave trade, indeed
slavery itself, was in the long run doomed that the conservative government of March 1841 (a government, as we have seen, closely tied to coffee
interests in Rio province) began to concern itself with alternative sources
of labour. The budget allocation for European immigration had been
terminated in 1830, and during the regency almost nothing had been
done to foster immigration. Even fewer immigrants arrived in the 1830s
– none in fact during the first half of the decade – than in the 1820s. (See
Table 6.) Those who did come did not choose to travel thousands of
miles in order to work alongside African slaves on sugar or coffee

Table 6 *European Immigrants entering*
Brazil, 1820–55

Year	Immigrants	Year	Immigrants
1820	1,790	1838	396
1821	0	1839	389
1822	0	1840	269
1823	0	1841	555
1824	468	1842	5,568
1825	909	1843	694
1826	828	1844	0
1827	1,088	1845	2,364
1828	2,060	1846	435
1829	2,412	1847	2,350
1830	117	1848	28
1831	0	1849	40
1832	0	1850	2,072
1833	0	1851	4,425
1834	0	1852	2,731
1835	0	1853	10,935
1836	1,280	1854	18,646
1837	604	1855	11,798

Source: Computed from several sources in George P.
Browne, 'Government immigration policy in
imperial Brazil, 1822–1870', unpublished Ph.D.
thesis, Catholic University of America, 1972, 328.

plantations. A budget allocation for immigration was reintroduced for
1841–2. But this was not enough. The fundamental problem was how to
keep such free, immigrant labour as could be enticed to Brazil on coffee
plantations organized for slave labour when, in the first place, vast
expanses of public land were freely available (i.e. how to prevent an
immigrant from becoming a landowner by the simple process of occupying public land), and, secondly, there was competition from the periphery of the coffee region for scarce labour.

In August 1842 a project drafted by Vasconcelos and modelled on E.
G. Wakefield's plans for the colonization of Australia, first published in
A Letter from Sydney (1829), was put before the Council of State. Its
purpose was twofold. First, landownership would be regulated and
regularized. The system of *sesmarias* (royal grants of public land) had
been terminated in 1822–3 and not replaced. As a result, private land
titles, always confused, were now in a state of chaos, which undermined
the authority of the central government and promoted local conflict and

violence. *Sesmarias* (most of which had expanded beyond their original legal boundaries) would be revalidated and *posses* (the landholdings, large and small, of squatters) would be legalized. Properties would be measured, registered and sometimes reduced in size, all at the cost of the owners. Secondly, Vasconcelos's project aimed to promote the immigration of 'trabalhadores pobres, moços e robustos' and at the same time tie them to the coffee plantations. Public land would in future only be sold and at prices deliberately set above the market value. If land had to be bought and was made expensive, so the argument went, immigrants (who already had to repay part of the cost of their transportation) would be forced to work a few years before they could buy their own plot. And the income from the sale of public land together with an annual land tax would generate the funds necessary to subsidize the importation of free labour.

A bill along these lines was introduced into the Chamber by Rodrigues Tôrres in June 1843. 'We want', he said, 'to keep free workers, who come to us from other parts of the world, from being able to arrive in Brazil and, instead of working for the landowners for some time at least . . . finding crown lands immediately.'[33] The bill was strongly supported by the representatives of the coffee growers of the Paraíba valley, the main beneficiaries. But deputies from other provinces were not convinced of the urgency of the need for European immigrants and were reluctant to pay the price the initiative, largely for the benefit of Rio province, would cost. Reaction was particularly strong among mineiro and paulista deputies. In Minas Gerais and São Paulo there were many *posseiros*, owners of vast and non-legalized tracts of land. They objected to the land registration – and its cost. And the land tax caused an uproar. Some deputies predicted civil war if the bill were passed. On 16 September 1843 it was nevertheless approved with minor amendments by the Chamber in which the conservatives had a large majority and was sent to the Senate. But there it remained throughout the *quinqüênio liberal* until at the end of the decade another conservative cabinet, which included Rodrigues Tôrres, managed to pass it into law, although only after introducing important modifications.

In the meantime the slave trade had already begun to revive once again after several years of reduced activity. And in March 1845, on the advice first of the foreign affairs sub-committee of the Council of State (consist-

---

[33] Quoted in Warren Dean, 'Latifundia and land policy in nineteenth-century Brazil', *Hispanic American Historical Review*, 51 (November, 1971), 614.

ing of three leading conservatives, the Marquês de Monte Alegre (José da Costa Carvalho), Vasconcelos and Honório) and then of a full meeting of the Council presided over by the young emperor, the Brazilian government fifteen years after 1830 chose to terminate the anti-slave trade treaty of 1817 under which the British navy exercised the right of search and the Anglo-Brazilian mixed commissions adjudicated on captured Brazilian vessels. It was not simply a question of freeing the slave trade from British interference in the interest of the Brazilian coffee planter. (The Brazilians insisted not very convincingly – that left to themselves they could and would suppress the trade.) In pursuing the slave traders the British had acted arrogantly and at times violently. The continuation of the trade was now linked in the public mind with national sovereignty as well as economic survival. The treaty – and any attempt to negotiate a new treaty – was extremely unpopular. As early as October 1842 Justiniano José da Rocha had written in *O Brasil*: 'If there is today a generalized and highly popular idea in the country it is that England is our most treacherous and persistent enemy.'[34]

The Conservative government in London was in no mood to abandon the struggle against the Brazilian slave trade. The Prime Minister Peel and the Foreign Secretary Lord Aberdeen were already under attack from Palmerston for allowing the trade to recover after 1842. And having failed to renew or replace the commercial treaty of 1827 (see above) they could not afford a second retreat in the face of pressure from Brazil, a weak and formerly dependent state, particularly since by placing it 'beyond the reach of the only means of repression which have hitherto been found effective', it was bound to lead to a further increase in the slave trade. On the other hand, an opportunity to discard the treaty of 1817 which had always been less than satisfactory and had given rise to interminable wrangles was not entirely unwelcome – provided it was possible to find an equal, and preferably more effective, alternative. Now the treaty of 1826 remained in full force but lacked any specific provision for search and seizure. Under its first article, however, the Brazilian slave trade was to be 'deemed and treated as piracy'. And it was in the word piracy that the British found what they needed. In August 1845 the Slave Trade (Brazil) Act, known in Brazil as *o bill Aberdeen*, authorized the British navy to treat Brazilian slave ships as pirate vessels and send them for condemnation in British vice-admiralty courts.

The Aberdeen Act was based upon an interpretation of the 1826 treaty

[34] *O Brasil*, 1 October 1842.

which was and remained controversial even in England. (In his *Explorations of the Highlands of the Brazil* (1869) Richard Burton called it 'one of the greatest insults which a strong ever offered to a weak people'.) News of the passage of the Act inevitably produced in Rio, the British minister reported, '(an) excited state of public feeling . . . argument, virulence, invective in the public press'.[35] Palmerston who returned to the Foreign Office in June 1846 was not known for his sensitivity to foreign opinion. The Aberdeen Act was in his view a less drastic measure than the circumstances justified. He was, moreover, sensitive to the charge made by critics of the government at home that the Sugar Duties Act which the Whigs had introduced would undo all the good work of the Aberdeen Act. If the Brazilian slave trade continued to grow, he warned, Britain would resort to 'still sharper measures of coercion'.[36]

The five years 1845–50 were the most successful the West African and Cape squadrons had ever known. Over 400 ships engaged in the Brazilian slave trade alone were captured and sent to vice-admiralty courts (half of them to St Helena, the rest to Sierra Leone and the Cape of Good Hope). Yet the slave trade grew. Indeed, during the late forties, with demand and therefore prices high, it exceeded all previous levels: at least 50–60,000 slaves per annum were imported into Brazil, 1846–9. (See Table 5 above.) Two-thirds were landed along the 200-mile stretch of coast north and south of Rio, the rest in the capital itself, where it was still possible openly to visit auctions of newly imported slaves, in Bahia and Pernambuco, and, a new development, south of Santos, especially near Paranaguá. The trade was more highly organized than ever. For the first time steamships were employed – their engines 'the best England could manufacture'. The trade had become big business and traders like Manuel Pinto da Fonseca and José Bernardino de Sá who ten years earlier had served in small provision stores now commanded impressive financial resources and wielded considerable political influence. 'They are the nabobs of the Brazils', a British naval officer wrote. 'They form the dazzling class of the parvenus millionaires.'[37] In January 1847 barão de Cairú, the Brazilian Foreign Minister, is reported by James Hudson, the British minister, to have said: '[Fonseca] and scores of minor slave dealers go to the Court – sit at the tables of the wealthiest and most respectable citizens – have seats in the Chamber as our Representatives and have a voice even in the Council of State. They are increasing in vigilance, perseverance, audacity – those whom they dare not put out of

---

[35] Quoted in Bethell, *Abolition*, 265. [36] *Ibid.* 295. [37] *Ibid.* 289.

the way, they buy . . . with such men to deal with, what am I to do, what can I do?'[38]

No liberal government in Brazil between 1844 and 1848 was sufficiently strong nor in power long enough to conceive, much less secure parliamentary support for, and execute, new anti-slave trade measures. The more far-sighted political leaders were disturbed by the proportions the trade had now reached, even if in some cases they were primarily concerned at the consequences for Brazilian society of the continued importation of 'milhares de defensores das instituições de Haiti'. They were also conscious that a country whose flag was not respected on the high seas and some of whose laws were enforced by foreign agents could hardly regard itself as fully independent and sovereign. The majority of Brazilian politicians in the Council of State, the Senate and the Chamber, however, positively favoured the slave trade (and in some cases as planters and slave-owners themselves were indirectly engaged in it) or else, in view of its importance to the Brazilian economy, preferred to leave well alone. In 1848 the last of the liberal administrations led by Francisco de Paula Sousa e Melo finally came round to the idea of introducing new legislation into the Chamber, but discussion of a bill to replace the law of 1831 was deferred until the following session not due to begin until January 1850. It was left to the conservative government which took power in September 1848 to grasp this, the most prickly of all Brazilian nettles.

In Britain during the late forties there was mounting opposition, principally among northern manufacturers and merchants and Free Traders, but also among the abolitionists themselves, to Britain's self-appointed role as the world's anti-slave trade policeman. The suppression system was expensive; it had an adverse effect on political relations, and therefore commercial relations, with, for example, Brazil; and it had failed. Britain in the words of William Hutt, M.P. for Gateshead, should 'leave to a higher authority . . . the moral government of the world'. Even *The Times* in October 1849 questioned whether 'the difference between what the slave trade is and what it would be if our squadron were withdrawn is worth what it costs us to keep the squadron where it is'.[39] The leaders of both Whigs and Peelites – Palmerston, Peel, Aberdeen, Russell – were, however, determined to resist any attempt to weaken much less dismantle the system for the suppression of the slave trade based on British naval power. What the 'coercionists' badly needed

[38] *Ibid.* 290.   [39] *The Times*, 24 October 1849.

was a signal success and what better than the final suppression of the Brazilian slave trade. There were rumours in 1849 that Palmerston was preparing to take more extreme measures and for the first time on the Brazilian side of the Atlantic. The decade ended without a solution to the slave trade question, but it was becoming increasingly clear, both in Brazil and in Britain, that a solution would not be long delayed.

In September 1848, after four and a half years of Liberal rule, the Emperor Dom Pedro II invited Pedro de Araújo Lima, Visconde de Olinda, the former regent (1837–40), to form a Conservative cabinet. Almost immediately on their return to power the Conservatives were faced with a liberal armed revolt in the provinces, as they had been in 1841–2. This time the trouble arose not in São Paulo and Minas Gerais, now firmly tied to the central government in Rio, but in Pernambuco. What proved to be the last major provincial uprising of the period erupted there towards the end of 1848. Known as the *Praieira* from Rua da Praia, where a liberal newspaper was published, it presented some features which were common to earlier provincial rebellions, but also some that were specific to Pernambuco.

At first sight, the socio-economic structure of Pernambuco was not very different from that of Bahia, for instance. In both cases, a large urban centre was surrounded by a sugar belt controlled by a rich oligarchy of planters. On the periphery of this belt – and beyond it – a rich variety of lesser planters, farmers and *estancieiros* could be found. The tradition of political struggle in the two provinces, however, was quite different. In Bahia, the conservative Recôncavo was always able to keep in check the urban radicalism of the capital, while the vast interior remained quiet. In Pernambuco, ever since the rebellions of 1817 and 1824, both urban radicals and the planter class as a whole had been involved in provincial politics. Even the rural poor of the periphery had been mobilized in the War of the Cabanos (1832–5). The division of political forces between liberals and conservatives in the late 1830s and early 1840s resulted in complicated alliances in Pernambuco. The sugar oligarchy of the Zona da Mata split, with the prominent Cavalcanti clan forming the liberal wing and being joined by urban journalists and agitators and by landowners in the periphery of the Mata.

With the fall of the conservative government in Rio in 1844, the liberal Praia rose to power in Pernambuco. Making use of the legislation introduced by the conservatives, Praia presidents made sweeping changes in the police and National Guard, substituting their supporters for the conservatives. When a further shift in national politics – the formation of the conservative cabinet of Araújo Lima, himself pernambucano – brought the conservatives back to power in Pernambuco in 1848, they tried to dismantle the political base built by the *praieiros*. It was this which sparked off liberal armed rebellion in November 1848, although the situation had been tense since June (when anti-Portuguese riots had broken out in Recife leaving five Portuguese dead and another forty wounded). The struggle took place mostly in the southern periphery of the Mata, and in the so-called Dry Mata to the north of Recife. Twenty sugar *engenhos* were the basis for the recruitment and provisioning of the liberal troops. In February 1849 the northern and southern armies of the rebels – some 2,500 troops – joined forces to attack Recife. But they failed to gain the support of the urban populace and were defeated, leaving 500 dead in the streets. The fight continued in the interior for some time and guerrilla bands survived until early 1850 under the protection of planters, but without posing a serious threat to the government.

The most radical of the rebels' demands – federalism, abolition of the moderating power, the expulsion of the Portuguese and nationalization of the retail trade and, a novelty, universal franchise – were formulated by urban leaders, particularly Borges da Fonseca, Pedro I's old republican opponent. However, despite the considerable impact made by the French revolution of 1848, a republican government was not included in the demands. And, once again, slavery remained untouched. Despite the intense urban agitation, the struggle ended up being mostly limited to a dispute among sectors of the landowning class. The reasons for this division are not entirely clear. Certainly, there was resentment against the small group of families that controlled the fertile lands of the humid Mata, although the Cavalcantis themselves controlled one-third of the *engenhos* in this area. The British Sugar Duties Act (1846) may also have played a part. While as a direct consequence of the Act sugar production in Pernambuco increased by 70 per cent between 1844/5 and 1848/9, as we have seen, prices went down from US $78 per ton to US $64. The richer and long-established sugar producers were certainly better prepared to face the difficulties of overproduction. Smaller producers, and those who had abandoned cotton or cattle for sugar attracted by the initial increase in prices, were bound to be the ones most hurt. Also the expansion in sugar production led to encroachment by the big landowners on the land of smaller planters, squatters and free peasants, turning their sympathies toward the *praieiros*.

The defeat of the liberal *Praieira* in 1848–9, together perhaps with the defeat of liberals all over Europe during these years, reinforced the conservative government in Rio de Janeiro and consolidated conservative power throughout Brazil. The result of the elections for the Chamber of Deputies in 1849 was virtually a clean sweep for the conservatives; the liberals won only one seat. And in 1850 the conservatives put the final touch to the process of political centralization they had initiated in 1837: the National Guard was brought under tighter central government control. The elective principle established in 1831 was eliminated. Officers were now to be appointed either by provincial presidents or directly by the central government, and they in turn appointed their non-commissioned officers.[40] Moreover, officers were required to have the income of electors (which was now 400 milréis, about £46), and had to pay for their commissions a sum equal to one month's salary of the equivalent rank in the army. This in practice limited access to the officer corps to a minority among the guardsmen. At first sight, this measure could be interpreted as a move against local bosses. But it would be more accurate to see it, like other centralizing laws, as a compromise between the central government and the landowners. It indicated, on the one hand, that the government was not able to maintain order in the interior without the help of the landowners; on the other hand, it revealed the incapacity of the latter to solve their disputes without the arbitration of the government. The reform represented a further move to co-opt the ruling sectors into the political system in exchange for the recognition and legitimation of their social power.

The Brazilian government which came to power in September 1848, especially after October 1849 when the Marquês de Monte Alegre replaced Olinda as president of the Council of Ministers, proved to be by far the strongest since independence. Like the conservative governments of 1837–40 and, more especially 1841–4, it represented an alliance between, on the one hand, state bureaucrats and magistrates and, on the other, landowners, above all coffee *fazendeiros* in Rio de Janeiro province. Its dominant figures were Paulino Soares de Sousa (Foreign

---

[40] At the same time a decree of 6 September 1850 regulated promotion in the army on the basis of merit and length of service. According to John Schulz, 'The Brazilian army in politics, 1850–1894' (unpublished Ph.D. dissertation, Princeton University, 1973), 53–8, in eliminating promotion by personal influence and status, this was a crucial step in the professionalization of the army.

Affairs) and Joaquim José Rodrigues Tôrres (Finance) together with
Eusébio de Queiroz Coutinho Matoso da Câmara (Justice), who had
been born in Angola, the son of a judge, and who had married into a rich
'capitalist' family in Rio. In the Council of State the government had the
powerful support of, among others, Bernardo Pereira de Vasconcelos
(until his death from yellow fever in May 1850) and Honório Hermeto
Carneiro Leão.

All these men, except Eusébio, had been prominent members of
previous conservative governments which in defiance of Britain had
permitted the illegal slave trade to flourish. Yet this government, like to
some extent the last liberal government, seemed ready to get to grips
with this most intractable of problems. Apart from Spain and its colony
Cuba, Brazil was now isolated internationally on this question. Before
long Brazilian agriculture would have to adapt itself to the end of the
slave trade. And if the Brazilians did not want Britain to put a stop to the
trade – and there was every evidence that Britain remained more
determined than ever to do so, even if it meant transferring its anti-slave
trade naval operations to the Brazilian coast – they would one day have to
suppress it themselves. Moreover, no self-respecting Brazilian government with any claim to authority could permit the continuation of such
widespread contempt for the law. There was one further consideration:
Brazil was increasingly anxious about the situation in the strategically
sensitive Río de la Plata region where the independence of Uruguay and
the territorial integrity of the empire itself were believed to be threatened
by Juan Manuel de Rosas. In the event of war with Buenos Aires – and
the ground was being prepared for an alliance with the anti-Rosas faction
in Uruguay and General Urquiza in Entre Ríos – Brazil would require at
least the benevolent neutrality of Britain and that could only be secured
by a settlement of the slave trade question. Thus, in a number of respects
the larger interests of the Brazilian state were beginning to demand that
some action be taken against the Brazilian slave trade. Towards the end
of 1849 the Minister of Justice advised the Rio police chief that new
measures to end the slave trade were being prepared and would be
introduced into the Chamber the following year.

At about the same time a number of British ships of the South
American squadron were transferred from the Río de la Plata to the coast
of Brazil specifically for anti-slave trade duties. In terms of the number of
slaves captured, January 1850 was the most successful month the British
navy had ever had on the Brazilian side of the Atlantic. Before the

Brazilian government was able to take any action – in May in his *Relatório* to the Chamber Eusébio de Queiroz promised to bring forward a bill – Britain itself then took what proved to be a decisive step leading to the final suppression of the Brazilian slave trade. On 22 April 1850, a month after 154 members of the House of Commons – almost twice as many as in a similar debate in 1848 – had voted against the continuation of Britain's efforts to suppress the foreign slave trade by force, the Foreign Office advised the Admiralty that under the Aberdeen Act of 1845 British warships need not confine their anti-slave trade operations to the high seas: they could enter Brazilian territorial waters and even Brazilian ports. On 22 June Rear Admiral Reynolds, commander of the South American squadron, instructed his ships accordingly. There followed a series of incidents up and down the Brazilian coast of which the most serious was an exchange of shots between HMS *Cormorant* (Captain Schomberg) and the fort at Paranaguá.

When news of the incident at Paranaguá reached Rio it provoked a major political crisis. There was some talk of war. But Brazil had no moral or material means to resist this blatant violation of its sovereignty. Moreover British 'hostilities' if continued and extended would paralyse trade, damage the economy, undermine state finances, inflame the slave population, threaten internal stability and unity and weaken Brazil's position in the coming confrontation with Rosas. (The scale of the recent naval action and the degree of deliberate planning which lay behind it was exaggerated.) On 11 July a meeting of the Council of State decided that the Brazilian government had no choice but to push through its own plans to curb the slave trade even though they would appear, as indeed to a large extent they were, a capitulation to British aggression. It was too late now for spontaneous action. On 12 July Eusébio finally introduced into the Chamber his bill to strengthen the 1831 law, in particular by establishing special maritime courts to deal with cases of slave trading which was declared to be equivalent to piracy. It passed quickly through the Chamber and the Senate, and became law on 4 September 1850. The emperor, now 25 years old and beginning to play a more decisive role in government, resisted a last-minute bid by conservative diehards to force a change of ministry.

The Brazilian government's task was made somewhat easier by the fact that the slave trade was in a considerably weakened state in the second half of 1850, thanks partly to the efforts of both the West African and South American squadrons, but more particularly because of another glut after years of heavy imports. Between January and June only 8,000 slaves had in fact been imported along the coast from Campos to Santos, the lowest figure for more than five years. The coffee planters' apparently insatiable demand for slaves was, however temporarily, satisfied. Eusébio de Queiroz, the minister responsible for the law of 1850, pointed out that many landowners had become deeply indebted to, and in many cases had mortgaged their properties to, the most prominent slave dealers. The latter, the majority of whom were foreign and, worse still, Portuguese, were also by now resented for their ostentatious wealth and their political influence. The 1850 law was deliberately directed at those who shipped, imported and sold rather than those who illegally purchased slaves. And it was speedily and effectively enforced by the provincial presidents, provincial chiefs of police and county *delegados*, district and county judges, the National Guard, the army, the navy and the special courts. There were only nine successful landings of slaves in Brazil (a total of 3,287 slaves) during 1851 and only two of these – both in Bahia – occurred during the last four months of the year. There were to be only three further known landings (two in 1852 and one in 1855). The Brazilian slave trade had been brought to a complete standstill. (See Table 5 above.)

More impressive still, the trade was not allowed to revive, as it had in the 1830s, when the excess of imports had been absorbed, the market recovered and prices began to rise once more, offering the prospect of enormous profits to the slave traders. The price of slaves in the coffee *municípios* of Rio de Janeiro almost doubled between 1852 and 1854, but all attempts to re-establish the trade, one as late as 1856, failed. Of course, the British claimed that just as the British navy had been primarily responsible for ending the trade in the first place – 'the achievement which I look back on with the greatest and the purest pleasure was forcing the Brazilians to give up their slave trade, by bringing into operation the Aberdeen Act of 1845', wrote Palmerston in 1864[41] – the permanent threat of a resumption of naval hostilities in Brazilian waters was what kept it closed. (The Aberdeen Act, the 'Sword of Damocles', was not actually repealed until 1869.) More significant perhaps was the fact that for the first time since independence a government in Rio de Janeiro had the authority and the necessary muscle to enforce its will throughout the country.

The problem of the future supply of labour to the Brazilian coffee

[41] Quoted in Bethell, *Abolition*, 360.

plantations posed by the ending of the transatlantic slave trade was partly
solved in the short run by the internal slave trade and ultimately by
European immigration. Already in 1847, encouraged by the liberal
government at the time, Nicolau Vergueiro had been the first Brazilian
landowner to experiment with the *parceria* system (a form of
sharecropping), importing first German and later Portuguese *colonos*
(contract labourers, virtually indentured servants) to work on his plantations, recently converted from sugar to coffee, at Limeira (São Paulo). In
August 1850 the conservative government revived the 1843 land (and
immigration) bill which had been opposed by the Mineiros and Paulistas
and blocked in the Senate during the period of liberal rule. This time it
was quickly approved in both houses and became law on 18 September
1850 – two weeks after the passage of the new anti-slave trade law.
Changes were introduced to eliminate some of its more controversial
aspects and to adapt it to new circumstances. The land tax, for example,
was dropped. The bill was still viewed by some deputies as highly
detrimental to the landowning class; one mineiro deputy was even able to
find communist overtones in it. In the event the new law proved virtually
unenforceable; its major purpose, the regularization of land titles by
means of demarcation and registration, was to a great extent frustrated.
Nevertheless, the law indicates the growing concern of the government
with the long-term problem of labour supply. And the number of
European immigrants arriving in Brazil did increase, albeit slowly, after
1850. (See Table 6 above.)

The conservative government also turned its attention to Brazil's
future economic development. Brazil, the provincial president of Rio de
Janeiro, Manuel de Jesus Valdetaro, had written to the Minister of the
Empire in May 1848, had paid in full its 'tribute of blood on the fields of
civil discord', and now, 'weary of struggling and chasing after political
reforms, [the country] seems to be concentrating the lion's share of its
vitality on the exploitation of the abundant resources of its soil and in the
development of its material interests'.[42] In June 1850 Brazil was given its
first Commercial Code, which integrated and updated a variety of laws
and regulations dating back to the colonial period. Of particular importance in the Code was the definition of the different types of business
company and the regulation of their operations. The timing was oppor-
tune since within a few months substantial amounts of capital were
released from the slave trade. The country experienced for the first time a
fever of business activity and speculation, particularly in Rio de Janeiro.

[42] Quoted in Thomas Flory, *Judge and jury in Imperial Brazil 1808–1871* (Austin, Texas, 1981), 181.

While in the previous twenty years only seventeen enterprises had been authorized by the government, in the next ten years this number jumped to 155 and included banks, industries, steam navigation companies, railways, colonization companies, mining enterprises, urban transportation companies.[43] Despite the speculative nature of many of these initiatives, they do indicate a new mood in the country, a move from a dominant concern with political matters towards economic endeavours. The end of the slave traffic, the land and immigration law, the Commercial Code, these were all moves in the direction of capitalist modernization, in so far as they were all attempts to introduce and organize a market for the mobilization of labour, land and capital. Soon British capital would also be brought in to be invested in railways and urban transport, and British banks would be established forging new links with external capitalist economies.

At the beginning of the 1850s, nearly thirty years after independence, Brazil enjoyed political stability, internal peace from north to south and a certain prosperity based primarily on exports of coffee. Externally, Britain had been given satisfaction on the slave trade question and Rosas was defeated in February 1852. A state, or at least a working system of political domination, had been built. The dominant class had reached relative agreement on fundamental issues; during the next ten years liberals and conservatives served together in the same administrations (a period known as the *conciliação*). National unity had been maintained through difficult times. But had a nation also been forged? The answer must be qualified.

In a total population of seven and a half million, including the Brazilian Indians,[44] 25–30 per cent were still slaves and a much larger percentage, indeed the overwhelming majority, were, to use an expression of the time, non-active citizens, that is, Brazilians without

---

[43] Liberato de Castro Carreira, *História financeira e orçamentária do império do Brasil* (Rio de Janeiro, 1889), 378–9.

[44] Near the coast most Indian tribes lived in poverty and near extinction. On the Amazon and its main tributaries, especially the Rio Negro, a period of economic decline during the first half of the nineteenth century had provided a respite for the surviving tribes, many of whom had been contacted in the eighteenth century and were now less harassed. Two recently pacified tribes were, however, involved in the Cabanagem, the provincial revolt which erupted in Pará in 1835: the Mura on the side of the rebels, the Mundurucú on the side of the authorities. In the Tocantins–Araguaia basin and the interior of Maranhão and Piauí this was a period of frontier expansion. A number of Gê-speaking tribes accepted peaceful contact: Appinagé, Cherente and Krahô on the Tocantins; eastern Timbira in Maranhão; and some groups of northern Kayapó on the lower Araguaia. The Chavante retreated westwards and became increasingly hostile, and there were attacks in Goiás by the elusive Canoeiros. Some groups of the Bororo of central Mato Grosso fought settlers, but other tribes were generally peaceful – for example, Terena and Guató of the

either the legal rights, or the level of literacy and education, or the socio-economic conditions, which would enable them to participate in a meaningful way in the political life of the country. Ironically, the factors that had probably contributed most to the development of a sense of national identity were anti-Portuguese and anti-British feelings. The former permeated most of the social and political protests of the regency and was still prominent during the Praieira rebellion; the latter became predominant after 1839 as Britain stepped up its international crusade to suppress the slave trade. When the Comte de Suzannet visited Rio de Janeiro in the early forties, he was struck by the generalized hatred of foreigners, particularly the Portuguese and the British, and by the ease with which all the troubles of the country were blamed on them. Another Frenchman who settled as a businessman in Rio de Janeiro in the early fifties, Charles Expilly, made a similar observation. Immediately upon his arrival, he was advised by a German who had been living in the city for some time only to praise what he found there to avoid being considered an enemy of the country. 'Ce sentiment d'un inintelligent patriotisme est poussé à l'excès au Brésil', he concluded.[45] But it was still mostly a negative feeling, limited to certain sectors of the population. Even leaving aside the regional differences and the deep social and racial divisions, there was still in Brazil too little communication between the provinces, too little economic integration, too little sharing in the government of the country for a positive sense of national identity yet to have developed.

Paraguay, Apiaká of the Arinos, the surviving southern Kayapó and Guaran of south Brazil, Karajá of the Araguaia near Bananal. The laws authorizing the enslavement of the so-called Botocudo of Espírito Santo and eastern Minas Gerais and the Kaingang were repealed in October 1831. But many of these Indians continued to resist. Others responded to good treatment by the former French officer, Guy de Marlière, on the Rio Doce.

Missionary 'catechism' was again seen as the answer to the Indian problem, after the disastrous failure of Pombal's lay directors in the late eighteenth century. Generally speaking, however, the Italian Capuchin missionaries who arrived in the 1840s, especially after the Indian legislation of 1845, were a pathetic failure, unable to cope with the rigours of central Brazil and Amazônia and worse at communicating with Indians than their Jesuit and Franciscan predecessors had been in the colonial era.

It was in this period that Brazilian Indians were seen for the first time by non-Portuguese European naturalists and scientists. The most important were: Johann Baptist von Spix and Carl Friedrich Philip von Martius, who laid the foundations of Brazilian anthropology; Georg Heinrich von Langsdorff, accompanied by Hércules Florence, in Mato Grosso, 1825–9; the Austrian Johann Natterer who made ethnographic collections on the Amazon and upper Rio Negro, 1828–35; Prince Adalbert of Prussia (accompanied by Count Bismarck) on the Xingu, 1842–3; Francis, Comte de Castelnau on the Araguaia-Tocantins and upper Amazon in the 1840s; Henry Walter Bates and Alfred Russell Wallace who arrived on the Amazon in 1848; and Richard Spruce who arrived in 1849.

The authors are grateful to Dr John Hemming for the information on which this note is based.
[45] Charles Expilly, *Le Brésil tel qu'il est* (Paris, 1862), 34.

3

1850–1870

In the early 1850s Brazil's population numbered a little over seven and a half million. It was concentrated, as it always had been, along the eastern seaboard. Forty per cent lived in three south-eastern provinces – Rio de Janeiro, Minas Gerais and São Paulo – and the capital city of Rio de Janeiro with its 180,000 residents. The north-east, the principal area of settlement in colonial times, still accounted for 44 per cent. Black and mulatto slaves probably numbered between two and two and a half million, that is, between a quarter and a third of the population. By 1872, at the time of the first national census, Brazil's total population had increased to ten million. The proportion in the north-east had declined to 40 per cent while the city of Rio had grown to 275,000. Twenty years after the end of the slave trade the number of slaves had fallen to one and a half million (15 per cent), and a larger proportion of the slave population was to be found in the provinces of Rio de Janeiro, São Paulo and Minas Gerais. The rapid growth of coffee exports in the south-east, along with a relative decline of sugar, explains the regional shift in population from 1850 to 1870. Rio de Janeiro's commercial class prospered as the coffee trade linked planters to the international economy. Labour, however, whether slave or free, rural or urban, received little of the increased wealth. And planters and merchants subtly combined outright force with benevolent protection to maintain worker dependency. The government of the empire, responsive to the class interests of planters and merchants, had become an instrument in their efforts to maintain political and social control. During these twenty years political leaders also succeeded in co-opting those who once opposed central authority, while moving, sometimes grudgingly, toward the middle ground between conservatism and reform. A stable polity resulted, but loyalties to particular regions, defined by export crops, remained strong.

Sugar continued to have an important place in the Brazilian economy in
the early 1850s and sugar exports, though lagging behind coffee, easily
surpassed in value cotton, hides, tobacco and other products. Sugar
exports increased by 50 per cent from 1841–5 to 1871–5 (see Table 1). But
world production meanwhile quadrupled, and Brazil's share of the world
market fell from approximately ten to five per cent. All regions of Brazil
produced sugar for domestic consumption but, apart from a small centre
around Campos in the province of Rio de Janeiro, almost all the sugar
Brazil exported came from the narrow strip, 50 to 100 miles deep, along
the coast of the provinces of the north-east, especially Bahia and
Pernambuco. Contemporaries often attributed the relative stagnation of
sugar production in the north-east to technological backwardness.
Certainly sugar production in Brazil seemed primitive by the international standards of the day. Every two to three years slaves used hoes
to dig up the old cane and plant fresh shoots in the deep clay soil.
Eventually planters set them to work on new lands and abandoned the
old; with an abundance of land it made little sense to fertilize the soil.
Once a year slaves slashed the ripened cane and piled it into bundles to be
carried to the mill on oxcarts or mules. At the mill, metal or metal-
covered rollers crushed the cane to extract the juice. In 1854 80 per cent of
the mills in the province of Pernambuco relied upon oxen or horses,
while 19 per cent used waterwheels and only 1 per cent were steam
driven; by contrast, in 1860 70 per cent of Cuban mills operated with
steam power. The cane juice was then boiled in a succession of huge
cauldrons to remove the water. Heat came from burning wood, thus
contributing to deforestation. When the sugar began to crystallize,
workers poured the syrup into conical clay moulds from which the dark
brown molasses drained, leaving a damp raw sugar. Further refining
took place principally in Europe and North America.

The failure to adopt the latest technology, however, sprang from
experience and solid judgement. Milling improvements could not overcome the advantage of proximity to markets enjoyed by Cuban cane and
European beet producers. Some millowners in Bahia who did take steps
to modernize their mills – most notably João Maurício Wanderley, later
barão de Cotegipe – found it nearly impossible to secure encouraging
financial returns. For others the abundance of land and forest resources
discouraged investment in agricultural development: when cane fields
could be so readily extended into virgin lands it made sense to neglect the

Table 1 *Major Exports of Brazil (by decade), 1841–80*

Product	1841–50		1851–60		1861–70		1871–80	
	Value (in £1000)	%	Value (in £1000)	%	Value (in £1000)	%	Value (in £1000)	%
Coffee	22,655	46.99	49,741	53.67	68,004	50.38	112,954	59.49
Sugar	14,576	30.23	21,638	23.35	18,308	13.56	23,540	12.40
Cotton	4,103	8.51	6,350	6.85	27,293	20.22	19,070	10.04
Hides	4,679	9.70	7,368	7.95	8,958	6.64	11,106	5.85
Tobacco	974	2.02	2,679	2.89	4,567	3.38	6,870	3.61
Rubber	214	0.44	2,282	2.46	4,649	3.44	10,957	5.77
Cacao	537	1.11	1,033	1.11	1,388	1.03	2,438	1.28
Maté	477	0.99	1,583	1.71	1,817	1.35	2,945	1.55
Totals of Leading Exports	48,215	99.99	92,674	99.99	134,984	100.00	189,880	99.99

Source: Brazil, Instituto Brasileiro de Geografia e Estatística, *Anuário Estatístico do Brasil*, Ano 5 (1939–40), 1381.

fertilization of older fields. Loan capital sought less risky opportunities elsewhere, raising the cost of money. Furthermore, traditional practices brought in a reassuringly substantial income to the few largest planters, who thus maintained a comfortable social and political dominance.

As in colonial days, Brazilian sugar planters could be divided into two main categories: those who owned mills as well as land and those who merely owned land. The former, the *senhores de engenho*, towered over the cane farmers (*lavradores*) in economic and social importance, but managed to persuade the latter to share their outlook in opposition to that of tenants, free wage workers and slaves. The cane farmers supplied cane to the millowners either on contract, being paid for their cane in cash, or in exchange for half the sugar produced. Often the cane farmers, having borrowed excessively from the millowners, lost their land and found themselves reduced to tenantry. Among the *senhores de engenho* themselves sharp divisions separated a few into a virtual oligarchy. For one *município* (county) in the province of Pernambuco, it has been calculated that 15 per cent of the millowners accounted for 70 per cent of all plantation land. Just nine inter-related families owned almost all the properties. Henrique Marques Lins and his sons or sons-in-law owned thirty plantations and he and his clan not surprisingly occupied the most powerful political positions locally. In 1863 a journalist claimed the *município* was Lins's 'fief' and all the other families just 'so many slaves'.[1]

During the 1830s coffee had overtaken sugar as Brazil's leading export and by 1850 coffee accounted for nearly half of all Brazilian export earnings (see Table 1 above). Coffee cultivation had spread throughout the Paraíba valley, and by the middle of the century it had displaced sugar west of the city of São Paulo. Coffee exports grew from 9.7 million sacks (132 pounds each) in the 1830s, to 26.3 million sacks in the 1850s and 28.8 million in the following decade. It is important, however, to remember that there were commodities exported from other tropical or sub-tropical regions which were significantly more valuable than coffee: the cotton exported from the south of the United States in the 1850s, for example, brought in five times as much revenue as Brazilian coffee.

The sons of the original pioneers who had carved their estates out of the virgin forest of the Paraíba valley continued energetically to direct the process of deforestation either on inherited estates or in newer areas. Although some historians have stressed how they prized status and power over profit, newer evidence suggests the bulk of these planters were sound businessmen who carefully weighed the risks and advantages of each investment. By 1870 the careful observer could note the first signs of stagnation in the Paraíba valley: an ageing slave population, old coffee bushes not being replaced and a preference for investing capital elsewhere rather than in fertilizing the worn-out soils. From the middle of the century many had been attracted to the centre-west of São Paulo province. The hills there were not as steep, and yet a gently rolling terrain insured good drainage and slanting sunlight on the bushes. Still using the same agricultural methods, planters found the reddish soils of São Paulo even more fertile than that of the Paraíba valley. Land seemed to stretch endlessly westward. Although at first the costs of transportation across the escarpment to the sea ate up the profits of those located beyond a certain distance from the coast, planters confidently believed that railroad builders would eventually overcome that barrier – which they did in 1868. Nevertheless, before 1870 the major source of coffee remained the Paraíba valley, that is to say, the province of Rio de Janeiro and the north-east of São Paulo province.

At the centre of a coffee *fazenda*, the master's house faced slave quarters and processing sheds. These adobe and timbered structures

---

[1] Quoted by Peter L. Eisenberg, *The sugar industry in Pernambuco: modernization without change, 1840–1910* (Berkeley, 1974), 138–9.

stood solidly around large beaten-earth or bricked coffee-drying patios. At harvest time (July–November) slaves gathered the cherry-like fruit of the coffee bushes into large baskets for carrying down the hillsides to these patios. There they spread out the berries to be dried by the sun, raking them together at dusk to protect them from the dew. When the fruit blackened, a water-driven wooden mortar removed the dry shells and hulled the green coffee beans. Using laborious hand methods slaves then separated out the dirt and imperfect beans and sacked the coffee for shipment.

The public domain here, as in other settled areas, had long been alienated through royal land grants dating from colonial times or through legal and customary rights of squatters large and small. But with the spread of export agriculture, subsistence farmers quickly found their claims disputed by the more powerful and wealthy planters or yielded to attractive financial offers and moved elsewhere. Even the royal grants had often overlapped. Neither public officials nor private owners carried out systematic surveys or registered their properties. The land law of 1850, calling for the sale (rather than gift) of all public lands in the future and systematic surveys of existing holdings to be paid for by all who wished their titles confirmed promised to end a chaotic situation. But although many landowners did make formal initial depositions as called for by the law, their claims consisted of listing the names of their bordering neighbours; they made no measurements, did not resolve their conflicting claims and soon forgot further provisions of the law. Even today titles remain confused.

In addition to coffee and sugar, only cotton among Brazil's other export crops was important in this period. Although long-staple cotton – native to Brazil – had figured significantly in Brazil's exports at the turn of the century, its exportation declined steadily after the invention of the cotton gin made possible the use of the shorter staple variety so abundantly grown in the south of the United States. Most Brazilian cotton was produced in the less humid, slightly higher regions of the north-east, back from the coast thirty to one hundred miles. In 1863–4 Pernambuco led in cotton exports with 30 per cent of the total, and Maranhão followed next with 21 per cent. Other provinces of the north-east – especially Alagoas and Paraíba – supplied 45 per cent. As a result of the Civil War in the United States, Brazil enjoyed a sudden if ephemeral surge in cotton exports (see Table 1 above). From 21 million pounds exported in 1860–1, exports rose to 92 million pounds five years later, reaching somewhat higher levels in the early 1870s. Even some coffee areas of São Paulo province switched briefly to short-staple cotton.

At the end of the Civil War a number of southerners migrated to Brazil hoping to recreate slave-worked cotton plantations. But in Brazil cotton was predominantly produced by small proprietors; it required less capital investment for its processing before export than did coffee or sugar. In São Paulo they planted it in the less fertile areas, often along with beans and corn in the same field. Following practices used in the north-east, they burned off the bush before planting to kill off the pests and return nutrients to the soil rapidly, if wastefully. Although larger planters used ploughs and other agricultural machinery, most continued to rely on hoes as they did for food crops and coffee. Cultivation or weeding also proceeded laboriously with hoes rather than with horse-drawn tools and was, therefore, done less frequently than recommended by agricultural experts. When prices began to weaken many marginal producers abandoned the crop. Meanwhile, however, the growth of Brazilian textile manufacturing provided a new, domestic market for cotton.

Tobacco, in contrast to its prominent role in colonial times, accounted for only 3 per cent of Brazil's export earnings in the period 1850–70. It predominated in the region of Cachoeira, across the bay from Salvador. Like cotton, tobacco was raised on relatively small tracts and family farms with few slaves. The leaves were picked, one by one, as they ripened and hung to dry on outdoor racks. In Salvador factory workers made cigars, and there and in Rio de Janeiro they prepared snuff. Tobacco grown in Minas Gerais, usually twisted into ropes, could be bought by the foot for use in the preparation of hand-rolled cigarettes.

In the Amazon region Indians and their mixed-race descendants, collectively called *caboclos*, gathered cacao from trees that grew wild in the forest and sold it to small entrepreneurs. By the 1860s landowners using slave labour experimented with it in southern Bahia. Workers broke open the soft shells of the ripened large yellow or green fruit and drained the brown seeds of their surrounding thick white liquor, allowing them to dry either in the sun or in raised drying sheds. The manufacture of chocolate took place in Europe.

Brazilian rubber began to attract increasing attention following the discovery of the vulcanization process in 1839. Exports rose from 388 tons in 1840 to 1,447 tons ten years later, 2,673 tons in 1860, and 5,602 tons in 1870, just before the real 'rubber rush' began. In the Amazon rainforest *caboclos* tapped the wild rubber trees and stiffened the latex over a wood fire forming it into large balls. Itinerant peddlers traded implements and food for this rubber, often on credit at onerous rates. Landowners, who needed settled labourers for their agricultural enterprises, resented the mobility rubber-gathering allowed, not yet sensing the opportunities for wealth the trade would later bring.

In the southern provinces of Paraná, Santa Catarina, and Rio Grande do Sul *caboclos* also gathered maté from wild bushes. They cropped the leaves and tender shoots, toasted them in baskets over slow-burning fires, and then used primitive wooden mortars to crush the leaves into a coarse powder. After being bagged, maté was exported to the neighbouring countries to the south. Some maté, marketed within Brazil, was not toasted but merely dried and sold as leaves to be brewed as tea. Despite the rising exports of maté, cacao and rubber, these crops together accounted for less than 6 per cent of Brazil's exports between 1851 and 1870.

Cattle were raised in Brazil both for hides (largely exported) and for meat (principally consumed within the country). Foreign observers described three distinct cattle regions, each with a specific culture. In the arid *sertão* of the north-east, away from the humid coastal strip and westward even of the cotton areas, cattle raising had been a major occupation since the sixteenth century. Although the region has a sufficient average amount of rain, it tends to fall in torrential downpours, leaving the land most of the time with insufficient moisture for regular agriculture except on a small scale. Occasional droughts sear the land making it inhospitable even to cattle. The *mestizo* population, relatively nomadic, dressed in a characteristic style of leather chaps, hats, and jackets to protect themselves from the cactus and other prickly growth. The region supplied cattle to the sugar zone, both for fresh meat and as oxen to drive the mills or pull the heavy carts laden with cane or chests of sugar.

Another region, the rolling *cerrados* of Minas Gerais, had cattle as the mainstay of its economy. This land of grass and scattered gnarled trees had, in the eighteenth century, supplied meat to the gold and diamond panners and to the turbulently rich cities that sprang up in the mining region. In the nineteenth century cattlemen turned their attention to supplying fresh meat to Rio de Janeiro, a city rapidly growing in size and wealth because of rising coffee exports. Cattle drives down the escarpment to the fattening pastures in the lowlands became a common sight along the roads leading to the city.

It was in the province of Rio Grande do Sul, however, that cattlemen emerged as the most prosperous in nineteenth-century Brazil. The south's grassy plains especially favoured such activity although the province's resources could not match the even more luxurious pampas of Uruguay and Argentina. After some early experimentation with wheat growing, the early settlers (in contrast to more recently arrived European immigrants) had turned to cattle. By 1863–4 Rio Grande do Sul exported nearly seven-tenths of Brazil's hides. It also produced jerked (or salted) beef, sold for consumption on coffee and sugar plantations to the north. In *saladeros* slaves soaked the meat in brine and dried it in the sun. It would then last for months or even years.

Besides eating meat, Brazilians derived their proteins from a mixture of beans and rice or beans and maize. Coarse manioc meal made from the cassava root also supplied daily calories. Bacon occasionally enriched the diet. Except for dried beef from Rio Grande do Sul and imported wheat flour and codfish, a local population drew supplies from nearby producers. Planters doubtless used surplus labour during non-harvest seasons to produce food, and small owners and peasants sold their surplus to planters or city residents. Participants in the expanding coffee economy, both rural and urban, drew much of their food from farming regions of Minas Gerais. Immigrant settlements in Rio Grande do Sul also produced enough beans and corn to ship out of the province. Brazil increasingly imported some food to meet the demands of urban centres and even plantation needs. Generally, however, local self-sufficiency was the rule. Certainly many more Brazilians laboured at producing food for domestic consumption than at raising export crops.

Although every kind of agricultural activity in all regions of Brazil counted on some slave labour, as did stock raising, cereal production, even rubber and maté gathering – and, of course, slaves worked as artisans and domestics – it was the major cash crops of sugar and coffee that accounted for Brazil's heavy reliance on black slaves. Everywhere, the central question for the slaveowner was how best to make the slave do the master's will. Because the answer to that question varied, slavery comprised a number of working relationships. The bulk of field slaves laboured in regimented gangs under the watchful eye of an overseer who did not hesitate to use the whip, the stocks, or other punishments, to get sixteen or even eighteen hours of work per day out of those he drove. The centuries-long experiences with exceedingly cheap slaves led most planters to pay insufficient attention to slave welfare in food, clothing and housing. Other slave-owners, however, whether out of charitable impulse or good business sense, perceived that fullest control could be exerted through a combination of harsh discipline for the recalcitrant and paternalistic benefits for the docile and compliant. The Paraíba planter, Francisco Peixoto de Lacerda Werneck, barão do Patí do Alferes, for instance, included elaborate instructions on the proper care of slaves in his *Memória* (1847) on how to set up a coffee estate. The guiding purpose of a planter's solicitude, he implied, was to ensure a slave's willing obedience. When such techniques failed, however, he did not hesitate to 'lay bare the flesh'.[2] Benevolence acquired purpose only insofar as it sprang from the master's ability to exert maximum force.

Slaves in other activities encountered similar juxtapositions of controlling devices. For, even among plantation slaves, by no means all were engaged in raising and harvesting coffee and sugar or in processing these crops. They also worked at the myriad other artisan jobs demanded by the operation of a large estate. Towns were few and distances between them great, so a large planter with extensive holdings often preferred to maintain skilled slaves of his own to repair equipment, construct his warehouses, manufacture slaves' clothes, or even decorate his plantation house. Smaller landowners came to the plantation to rent the labour of these skilled slaves. Slaves also rendered domestic service and, as planters' wealth from exports increased, did so in greater numbers. An imposing house, frequently filled with guests and the centre of social and political life, required numerous servants. On the other hand, a declining export economy, as in the province of Minas Gerais, for example, also released a substantial number of slaves for domestic service as well as food production. House slaves and artisans enjoyed more comfortable living conditions than did the field slaves: better clothes, perhaps even shoes, and often the same food as that of the master. They might also acquire a certain conversational polish, even occasionally learn to read, and stood a greater chance of being freed for exceptionally loyal service than field hands. Their proximity to the master, however, lessened the space they could call their own and made their every move readily observed. It has even been argued that violence did more to recognize the humanity of a slave than did that all-enveloping paternalism.

Planters differed on how best to provide food for their slaves and this

---

[2] Francisco Peixoto de Lacerda, barão do Paty do Alferes, *Memoria sobre a fundação de uma fazenda na provincia do Rio de Janeiro, sua administração, e épochas em que devem fazer as plantações, suas colheitas, etc. etc.* (Rio de Janeiro, 1847); ibid. to Bernardo Ribeiro de Carvalho, Fazenda Monte Alegre, 31 March 1856, Werneck Papers, Arquivo Nacional (Rio de Janeiro), Seção de Arquivos Particulares, Códice 112, Vol.3, Copiador 1, fl.352.

difference had implications for the relations between master and slave. Some preferred to feed their slaves directly, while others allowed them provision grounds on which to raise foodstuffs. The former believed it better to keep slaves steadily at work on the main task – producing coffee and sugar – and to buy supplies from small landowners and squatters operating in the interstices of the plantation system or from free retainers working on the planters' land. Coffee *fazendeiros* in the Paraíba valley often had slaves produce foodstuffs in relatively new groves where beans and maize, planted between the rows of coffee bushes, benefited from the frequent cultivation while receiving plenty of sunlight. Others, especially those with mature coffee groves, chose to rid themselves of the responsibility of feeding their slaves and probably noticed that slaves worked for them more willingly six days a week if on the seventh they provided for themselves and their families. From the slaves' point of view we may guess some preferred the security of being fed by the master, while others enjoyed the relative freedom of their own plots, despite the unceasing toil and greater uncertainty and anxiety.

Efforts to control slaves – whether through force or benevolence – did not meet with uniform success. The very multiplicity of techniques directed to this end bears witness to the difficulty of making one man's will determine another's action. The slaves' response to those efforts consisted not only or even principally in rebellious behaviour, but in the failure to carry out instructions, in 'laziness' and sloppy work. Even obedience could be accompanied by a demeanour that made clear the existence of another will. The *jongos* or slave ditties remembered by ex-slaves reveal a clear consciousness of their plight.[3] And the murder of a master occurred with sufficient frequency to make slave-owners fear it. Flight could be another response. Advertisements for runaway slaves filled many columns of the daily newspapers in cities like Rio de Janeiro, Salvador and Recife. Often the runaways joined forces in the forest to form small *quilombos* or maroon communities where up to twenty or more fugitives planted manioc and corn, surviving for months, even years. They raided plantations for additional supplies and sometimes displayed considerable political acumen in selecting their targets.

Slaves also found it possible to create their own families and forge other social ties to both slave and free while shaping a pattern of shared understandings to be passed on to the next generation. Many documents

---

[3] See Stanley J. Stein, *Vassouras. A Brazilian coffee county, 1850–1900* (Cambridge, Mass., 1957), 208–9.

reveal the purchase of freedom for a slave by a father, mother, husband or lover. Wills left by freedmen bespeak their close emotional connections to former fellows in slavery. Isolated letters between slaves at distant plantations poignantly capture both the anguish of forced separation and the steadfastness of affection. Slaves passed on their culture not only in everyday family life, but also by practising traditional rituals (however modified they may have been). In special holiday dances or *batuques* participants learned the secrets of skilful drumming (and drum making) along with a set of inherited beliefs. The vitality in Brazil today of religious practices that derive from memories of Africa suggests a continuing effort to create and safeguard a cultural patrimony.

Not only did bondsmen find some opportunities for independence, the boundary between them and free workers was not always clearcut. Some historians have even seen in provision grounds elements of a peasant economy. Certainly slaves sometimes sold their excess production, by rights to the master but sometimes to the owner of a country store who did not hesitate to purchase small amounts of 'stolen' coffee as well. Thus, chattel slaves themselves came to own some property and exchange it for cash. Indeed, some planters used cash as an incentive for extra work, paying a monetary reward, for instance, for any basket of coffee harvested beyond a certain minimum. In this way the distinction between slave labour and wage labour tended to blur. Moreover, there was a real possibility that the individual slave might move from slavery to freedom. By which means, incidentally, the culture of slaves became the culture of the free poor.

The frequency with which Brazilian slave-owners granted freedom to individual slaves surprised foreign visitors in the nineteenth century. High interest rates combined with the long delay in recovering the cost of rearing slave children to working age had long encouraged the freeing of children at birth, especially girls who would not fetch a high price even once reared. The need for free workers to fill certain labour requirements, such as that of supervising slaves, further encouraged the practice. Perhaps most importantly, manumission, even of adult men, served as one more tool by which good behaviour could be encouraged through the example of a few whose exceptional loyalty and obedience had been thus rewarded. The hope of possible freedom may also have lessened the number of those slaves who ran away, killed their masters, or, out of despair, committed suicide. Sometimes owners granted freedom on the condition of continued faithful service for a specified number of years.

Society valued manumission and rewarded with praise the generosity of the planter who granted freedom. It was often argued with some basis in law that a slave who could pay his purchase price should be freed by right. The freed black did not threaten the social order for he or she could easily be absorbed into one of the many layers at the lower end of the social structure. Free blacks and mulattos accounted for 74 per cent of all blacks and mulattos by 1872, 44 per cent of the total population. There is some evidence, however, that the frequency of manumissions declined once no more slaves could be purchased in Africa.

The long established custom of occasional manumission did not undermine the institution of slavery as long as more slaves could be purchased. During the 1830s and 1840s slaves had been imported from Africa, albeit illegally, at an unprecedented rate, most of them destined for the coffee *fazendas* of the Paraíba valley. The transatlantic slave trade had finally been ended in 1850–1, but it was followed by the growth of the internal slave trade. The deportation in 1850 of the most notorious Portuguese slave traders merely opened the way for other slave merchants in the cities of Rio and Santos to continue as middlemen, selling slaves brought from the north-east. North-eastern sugar planters, with a declining share of the world market, began to sell slaves southward to the thriving coffee regions. During the ten years from 1852 the number of slaves arriving annually from other provinces at Rio de Janeiro port averaged 3,370.[4] Others were supplied overland. Although numbers are small compared to the yearly average of 41,400 imported from Africa between 1845 and 1850, they helped feed the still insatiable demand for workers on coffee plantations. Between 1864 and 1874 the number of slaves in the north-eastern, mainly sugar-producing, region declined from 774,000 (45 per cent of all Brazilian slaves) to 435,687 (28 per cent) while the coffee regions increased their slave population from 645,000 (43 per cent) to 809,575 (56 per cent) and São Paulo province more than doubled its slaves from 80,000 to 174,622.

The institution, nevertheless, did enter its long period of decline in the 1850s. With the end of the transatlantic slave trade, the number of slaves overall could not be maintained. The earlier reliance on levies from Africa had produced a sharply unbalanced sex ratio among slaves: only

---

[4] Estimates of their number differ. Cf. Robert Conrad, *The destruction of Brazilian slavery, 1850–1888* (Berkeley, 1972), 289, with Sebastião Ferreira Soares, *Notas estatísticas sobre a produção agrícola e carestia dos gêneros alimentícios no império do Brasil*, facsim. ed. (Rio de Janeiro, 1977), 135–6, Eisenberg, *Sugar Industry*, 156 n., and Herbert S. Klein, *The middle passage: comparative studies in the Atlantic slave trade* (Princeton, 1978), 97.

one-third of those transported to Brazil were females. In part because of the preference for freeing girls, the number of child-bearing women among slaves born in Brazil remained relatively low as well. The high interest rates that encouraged manumission of children also discouraged the care of pregnant women or new-born infants. Harsh working and living conditions no doubt also meant high mortality for men and women. Poor clothing, inadequate housing and insufficient food (most of it of poor quality), as well as overwork, accounted for a good part of the decline in the slave population. Epidemics of yellow fever, smallpox and cholera that marked the decade of the 1850s especially ravaged already debilitated slaves. No reliable count exists for slaves in 1850, but these have been estimated to have numbered between two and two and a half million. By 1864 Agostinho Marques Perdigão Malheiro, a careful student of slavery, put their number at only 1,715,000 and the official census of 1872 (which did not include children born after September 1871) at 1,510,806.

Meanwhile, as slaves became more regionally concentrated, Brazilian elites began to divide on the issue of slavery. The percentage of slaves among agricultural workers in the sugar counties of Pernambuco reached only 14 per cent by 1872, whereas in the coffee counties of Rio de Janeiro province it held at 46 per cent. Landowners in the north-east became steadily less wedded to the institution of slavery as they sold off their bondsmen and turned increasingly to free, though dependent, labour. Meanwhile, by the late 1860s, as the railway over the escarpment in São Paulo neared completion and wealthy coffee *fazendeiros* acquired western lands and organized railway companies to link them to the trunk line, they clearly saw that unless a new labour system were adopted, their hopes for the future would be frustrated. Finally, although the salt-meat factories in southern Brazil used slaves, the region as a whole and especially the cattlemen were not particularly tied to slavery. In the province of Rio de Janeiro, however, as well as in the older section of São Paulo province along the upper reaches of the Paraíba and in parts of the province of Minas Gerais there was still a firm commitment to slavery and a determination to see it continue as the dominant labour system in Brazil. Slaves, however, became more restive now that a larger proportion of them were Brazilian-born, often mulattos, and the promise of manumission seemed to decline.

Even before the end of the slave trade from Africa an attempt had been made to substitute slaves with indentured servants from Europe.

Nicolau Pereira de Campos Vergueiro (1778–1859) had drawn a good bit of his fortune from a slave-importing business in Santos during the 1830s and 1840s. He had also invested in several plantations in the *paulista* highlands and had distributed imported slaves to his neighbours as well as using them on his own properties. In 1847 he persuaded the imperial and provincial governments to issue interest-free loans with which he funded recruiters to travel through the Germanies and Switzerland then being ravaged by the potato famine. The first indentured servants went to his own plantation where he installed them in wattle-and-daub shacks and assigned them coffee bushes to plant, cultivate and harvest on a share-cropping basis. Soon neighbouring planters began to engage immigrant workers through his firm. And other Santos merchants successfully followed his example. Within a few years, however, the experiment was abandoned. Immigrant workers who found their correspondence censored, their egress from the plantation blocked and their debts mounting as a result of the planters' book-keeping manipulations proved unwilling to submit to such slave-like discipline. In 1856 a group of Swiss workers on one of Vergueiro's estates, frightened by threats to the life of their spokesman, Thomas Davatz, armed themselves while awaiting an official investigation into charges that Vergueiro had defrauded them; he, however, claimed they plotted a rebellion with the help of slaves, receiving direction from a Swiss 'communist' living in São Paulo city.[5] The incident exemplifies the difficulty of exerting control over free Europeans in ways inherited from slavery. The continuing ease of buying slaves from the north-east and the availability of more tractable free Brazilians served to discourage similar efforts and to postpone serious attempts to attract European agricultural workers for another thirty years.

The relationship between rural employers and Brazilian-born free workers bore a strong resemblance to slavery. Among the free, for instance, was a social type known as the *agregado* – a kind of retainer – commonly to be found in the sugar zone of the north-east as well as in the coffee regions of Rio de Janeiro and São Paulo. An *agregado* depended upon someone else, especially for housing or at least a space in which to live. He or she could be a family member, even a respected parent, sister, or brother who lacked an independent source of income; more often, however, the *agregado* was a poverty-stricken agricultural worker, or

---

[5] Quoted in Warren Dean, *Rio Claro. A Brazilian plantation system, 1820–1920* (Stanford, 1976), 102. Also see advertisement for a 'runaway settler' in *Correio Mercantil*, 10 Dec. 1857, 3.

single mother, sometimes a freed slave, to whom the landowner granted the right to raise subsistence crops on some outlying patch of the large estate. In exchange the *agregado* proffered occasional services, but especially loyalty. For men, that could frequently mean armed struggle in electoral disputes or against neighbouring and rival landowners. The *agregados'* claim upon security remained tenuous, and landowners could eject them without hesitation. In turn *agregados* too were free to move if they could find another protector, and landowners sometimes complained of how *agregados* would abandon one patron for another 'without the least apology'.[6] In the city the *agregado's* contribution to the family economy customarily resembled that of an apprentice or domestic servant. Whether in the city or in the country, the patron's care on the one hand and loyalty and service on the other dominated the relationship. The occasional cash payment for labour or surplus crops and the uncertainty of the tie to a particular landowner nevertheless suggests the partial penetration of monetary considerations and increasingly fluid social relations.

In the cotton- and food-producing area of the north-east, between sugar-producing coast and cattle-raising interior, the landlords – owning smaller tracts than on the coast – frequently peopled their estates almost entirely with *agregados* and relied on them for labour rather than on slaves. When, in late 1874, significant numbers of peasants rose up briefly in an apparently leaderless revolt called the Quebra Quilos against the payment of new taxes on the grain and vegetables they brought to market and against the local merchants who took advantage of the introduction of the metric system to alter prices, these interior landowners acquiesced as long as the notarial offices containing land records were not disturbed. In contrast, *agregados* from the coastal sugar region marched in under the leadership of mill owners to put down the revolt. The psychological weight of dependence varied markedly from region to region.

Whether as *agregados* or hired hands who worked for cash, agricultural labourers received minimum compensation for their work. Rural wages in this period have not been systematically studied, but evidence suggests they barely exceeded subsistence. Most of the free lived outside the market economy, in abject poverty, barefoot, unhealthy and undernourished. Small landowners – some of whom also worked part-time for cash – fared little better. Securing land became significantly more difficult after the passage of the 1850 land law which attempted to end the practice

---

[6] See quotation in Eisenberg, *Sugar Industry*, 148.

of squatting. Those who held land did so only insecurely and perched precariously between the estates of the wealthy. They had to forge alliances with the powerful and offer deference in exchange for security and protection.

A Brazilian planter relied on an astute combination of force and promised rewards or protection in order to manipulate both his workers, free or slave, and his dependent neighbours. Through careful attention to his honour and social status – sometimes requiring conspicuous consumption or displays of open-handed generosity – he attempted, on the whole successfully, to legitimize the deference he received from others lower down the social hierarchy. The efforts made by the planter to bolster and maintain his authority within the self-contained social system of the *fazenda* have sometimes misled observers into discounting his economic rationality. Most planters probably felt no tension between the roles of paternalistic seigneur and capitalist entrepreneur. They understood the complex internal structure of Brazil's export economy, and worried over their profit and loss accounts vis à vis Brazilian middlemen and foreign export houses. They were aware of Brazil's role in the international division of labour and kept a sharp eye on world commodity prices. They also made the Brazilian economy as a whole – the development of railways, the growth of the banking system, the level of imports as well as exports, even the beginnings of manufacturing – a vital part of their concern.

Before the railway, the most common means of transporting goods and people overland was by mule. Through the Paraíba valley muleteers contracted with the planters to carry the coffee to small coastal towns whence coffee was shipped to Rio de Janeiro on small sailing vessels. Or they led their muletrains into Rio directly, where the animals dirtied the already filthy streets. Two sacks of coffee, each weighing 60 kg, could be transported by one mule down the steep, winding trails to the coast. To get that far the mules had to overcome the obstacle of the escarpment, sometimes descending 2500 feet in the space of 5 miles. Heavy rainfall on the escarpment caused everyone to complain of the government's failure to improve mountain roads beyond laying a few large flat stones at the steepest curves. Mules often sank into the bogs, drenching the coffee, and delaying the descent for hours until the mules could be pulled out. Across the flatter terrain of the north-east slow-moving oxcarts, their fixed axles filling the air with a high-pitched moan, carried the heavy chests of sugar to the coast.

Muleteers, often independent small businessmen, bought the mules at a cattle fair in southern São Paulo province from drivers who herded them northward from Rio Grande do Sul. Besides transporting export crops, muleteers linked the interior towns northward, connecting coffee-rich São Paulo and Rio de Janeiro with sugar-producing Bahia and Pernambuco and, even beyond, with Piauí, Maranhão and Pará. Some bought land and became planters themselves. While ocean trade orien-ted port cities more toward Europe than toward each other, their hinterlands were woven together by a network of intersecting muletrain routes.

Coffee planters of the Paraíba valley took an active interest in road building, but could marshal only limited resources. The major mule tracks through the region had been cut by the pioneering planters and subsequently some large landowners took up subscriptions for improve-ments or sought government subsidies for the construction of bridges. Principally, however, they concerned themselves with assuring access from their own *fazenda* to the main routes. The first road for wheeled vehicles to cross the southern escarpment linked Rio de Janeiro to the summer retreat of the royal family in Petrópolis. In the 1850s a privately owned stagecoach company extended that route into the coffee region, opening its macadamized surface to use by horse-drawn wagons. A much less satisfactory road linked Santos to São Paulo where muletrains remained the rule until replaced by the railway.

Lack of capital proved the major obstacle to building railways in Brazil. Despite the prosperity of coffee producers, there was insufficient capital in this period to allow them either to finance construction themselves or even to attract foreign investors who remained more interested in expanding overland networks elsewhere, say, in the United States. Only in 1852, when the Brazilian government offered a guaran-teed return on capital, did investors find Brazilian prospects attractive. Even this benefit, however, did not draw overseas profit-seekers to the first project to connect the port of Rio across the escarpment to the Paraíba valley. Coffee planters launched the enterprise (the Dom Pedro II Railway) but relied on the public treasury for half the investment. The company foundered nevertheless, and the government assumed the entire bill for the line's construction. Its first section was completed in 1858 and the rails reached the Paraíba river in the early 1860s. The construction in 1868 of the São Paulo Railway, a highly profitable short line connecting the port of Santos to the plains beyond the coastal ridge in São Paulo, proved in the long run to be even more important for coffee exports. Relying on a series of inclined planes, this British-owned railway surmounted major technical difficulties and opened up the way for the spread of Brazilian railway lines across the emerging coffee-producing districts of the province of São Paulo. Also during the fifties and sixties British investors built other railways in the north-east, most notably the Recife and São Francisco, the Great Western of Brazil and the Bahia and São Francisco, unconsciously encouraging sugar planters to open up new lands rather than fertilize the old. Brazil delayed for a long time the construction of any kind of railway network that would connect major cities to each other rather than rural regions to a port. With their heavy investment in fixed routes railways tended to draw each region in upon itself economically, weakening those ties across the interior upon which muleteers had relied for their trade.

The Brazilian planter controlled production, but British and American businessmen predominated in the export trade, both of coffee from Rio de Janeiro and Santos and of sugar from Recife and Bahia. From the mid-forties to the late eighties, the twenty largest export firms in Rio de Janeiro – handling four-fifths of the coffee exports – were all foreign-owned. Phipps Brothers (British), Maxwell, Wright & Co. (American) and Edward Johnston & Co. (British) dominated coffee exports. The most important Brazilian and Portuguese houses trailed far behind. British export firms controlled the sugar trade even more fully, perhaps because the bulk of Brazil's sugar exports went to Great Britain.

Between the planter and the exporter stood a series of other middle-men, most of whom were Brazilians or, at least, Portuguese. In Rio de Janeiro city, for instance, one to two hundred coffee factors (*comissários*) linked the plantation to international trade. The factor stored coffee in his warehouse as soon as it arrived in town, whether on muleback or by rail. As the planter's agent, he sought the best price for the coffee, charging a percentage of the sale as his fee. Still acting as an agent, the factor purchased jerked beef, grains or manioc flour to feed plantation slaves, and iron implements, coffee-hulling equipment, or even bags for sacking coffee. As the coffee planter became more prosperous, the factors' bills also listed luxury goods, dresses and hats from Paris, wine and butter, crystal and china, pianos and books.

In all these activities, including the delivery of slaves, the factor derived his principal importance by channelling credit. Foreign manu-facturers and local merchants supplied him goods and slaves on credit which he then passed on to the planter. Or else the factor paid cash, in effect lending it to the planter. Planters hoped to replenish their accounts with their agents during the harvest season, but when production fell off they relied on him to carry them over until the next year. Sometimes factors extended short-term loans into mortgages. Factors were essential to planters' hopes for securing financing while they awaited the next crop, or over the long term.

Although coffee planters occasionally voiced complaints against the dealings of their agents, they rarely did so and for one simple reason: planter and factor were often relatives, even more frequently partners, and sometimes only a double role played by the same person. Earlier historians presumed a merchant–planter hostility, relying on isolated examples to verify it; but recent research has shown that at least a sixth of all partners in Rio factorage firms were interior coffee planters; and, furthermore, that numerous other merchants, though living in the city, owned plantations.[7] Still others married the daughters of planters, thus making their sons both planters and factors. Planters joined merchants, and even some foreigners, in the commercial associations of Recife, Bahia and Rio, lobbying together to protect their shared interests in the export trade. When factors did clash with planters it was more often with lesser ones than with the truly wealthy.

One example will serve to demonstrate the marriage of trade and land. Antonio Clemente Pinto (1795–1869) arrived from Portugal as a boy without a *real* to his name to begin life in Rio as an office boy. Through hard work, business acumen and luck he succeeded in the business world, first as a slave trader and then as a coffee factor. Next, he bought land and by 1850 could be counted among the largest landowners in the province of Rio de Janeiro, receiving the title of barão de Nova Friburgo in 1857. He lent money to other planters as well as investing in railways. His home in the then fashionable Catete district in the city of Rio, elaborately decorated by immigrant architects and designers, later became Brazil's presidential palace. Pinto's estate was appraised at nearly £800,000 (well over U.S.$3.5 million) at then current exchange rates. He left fourteen coffee *fazendas*, over two thousand slaves, his factorage firm and several town houses, one stocked with some fifteen hundred bottles of imported wine.

---

[7] Joseph E. Sweigart, *Coffee factorage and the emergence of a Brazilian capital market, 1850–1888* (New York, 1987), 66–98.

Only a short step separated factorage from banking. Capital derived from profits on coffee growing had long been lent by one planter to another: within the family, to trusted neighbours, or in the calculated hope of eventual foreclosure on desired properties. As partners in factorage firms which extended commercial credit, the planter had become accustomed to calculate risk and judge the vagaries of the money market. By the 1850s planters joined coffee factors as major investors in several banks. Investors deposited funds they would previously have loaned to slave traders. Almost all these banks concentrated on commercial loans, lending principally to factors who held planters' obligations as security. Some banks were also authorized to issue currency, especially from 1857 to 1860 when banking law was briefly liberalized. Financial opinion blamed either the lingering effect of this liberalization or its subsequent restriction for the financial crisis of 1864, which bankrupted several important banking firms. Three British banks set up in 1862 escaped the crisis and went on to prosper. Only in the next decade, when altered laws made it easier to recover on defaulted loans, did mortgage banks begin to lend money directly to planters. Always, however, the lack of firm land titles made slaves important as security; as slaves grew older and could not be replaced, planters found it ever harder to raise funds for long-term modernization or expansion. Not slavery, but the promised end of slavery seemed to threaten export prosperity.

Credit financed imports and most of those came from Great Britain. In the late 1840s Britain supplied half the goods imported into Brazil; the next most important supplier, the United States, accounted for only one-tenth. By 1875 the French had supplanted the Americans, but the British still led the way. Seventy per cent of the British imports from 1850 to 1870 consisted of textiles and half the remainder of other consumer goods. Capital goods and raw materials – hardware and other irongoods, coal, cement and machinery – accounted for only 15 per cent. Most imports arrived at Rio de Janeiro (54 per cent from 1845 to 1849), while Bahia (19 per cent) and Recife (14 per cent) trailed far behind. Foreigners, especially the British, owned most of the importing houses. Foreign firms sold either to Brazilian wholesalers or, more often, to retailers and, through the *comissários*, to the landowners themselves. They ensured that plantation slaves were dressed in British cottons and wielded British hoes.

Any measure to restrict imports – such as protective tariffs urged by some would-be industrialists – encountered the firm opposition of those policy-makers who wished to keep the price of imports low and thus diminish the cost of producing exports. On the other hand, planters and merchants shared a common interest in the effective performance of certain governmental functions which required revenue, preferring that this revenue come from import tariffs rather than from any other source. Taxes on imported goods accounted for approximately 60 per cent of governmental revenues in the third quarter of the nineteenth century, while only 16 per cent came from export taxes. In 1844 the government had found itself free at last from the limitation of the tariff to 15 per cent under the Anglo-Brazilian treaty of 1827. A new tariff raised the rates to 30 per cent in general, and in some cases to 60 per cent. Although principally fiscal in purpose, it had a moderately protective effect and for a while helped traditional craftsmen withstand a swelling flood of imported manufactures. However, the minister of finance in the new conservative administration which took office in 1848, Joaquim José Rodrigues Torres, the future visconde de Itaboraí (1802–72), himself a coffee planter, named a commission to study and revise the tariff. The report, published in 1853, enthusiastically urged the virtues of free trade. Citing a host of authorities, mostly British, its authors displayed a strong commitment to the principle that governments should not restrict international trade. Brazil should concentrate, they said, on what it did best: growing coffee. Nevertheless, the need for governmental revenue slowed steps toward free trade until the tariff of 1857 and the even more liberal tariff of 1860 significantly lowered duties. The costs of the Paraguayan War (1864–70), requiring additional revenues, brought a somewhat higher rate into effect, but without protectionist purpose.

In any case, most manufacturing consisted of craft shops. Skilled and unskilled workers in groups of 10 to 20 laboured in these small establishments making hats, shoes, saddles, bindings for books, rope, and furniture. They also worked in breweries and snuff factories and prepared vegetable oil or canned foodstuffs. Soap and candles were also manufactured locally. Brazilians or foreign entrepreneurs had established ten foundries in Rio by 1861, although their number decreased subsequently as it became easier to import machinery and spare parts. As transportation to the interior improved, textiles hand-loomed there became uneconomical in competition with imported cloth. Above all, the concentration of wealth in the hands of a few hampered economic development: the presence of slavery and the highly skewed distribution of wealth among the free considerably restricted the market for consumer goods.

Nevertheless, two Brazilian cotton mills established in the 1840s, protected by the tariff, prospered by mid-century. In 1850 one mill in the immediate hinterland of Rio de Janeiro, at the foot of the Orgão Mountains, had fifty looms, 2012 spindles and employed 116 workers. A mill in Bahia in 1861 used 4160 spindles and 135 looms. By 1866 a total of nine cotton mills, five of them in Bahia, produced a growing supply of textiles, requiring 800 workers on 350 looms and 14,000 spindles. Almost all depended on water power. By 1875 there were thirty mills, one-third of them in Bahia and the remainder in Rio de Janeiro, São Paulo, and Minas Gerais. Still, they produced a very small proportion of Brazil's consumption.

The Paraguayan War greatly stimulated industrial production in the late 1860s. Government procurement of war *matériel* did so directly, but two other factors contributed: the inflation caused by government deficits and the inadvertent protection provided by higher general tariffs to fund the war effort. Businessmen complained, nevertheless, that the government preferred to buy shoddy imported uniforms, for example, than to foster the expansion of Brazilian factories.

Before the war one entrepreneur particularly stood out by the variety of his concerns and the flamboyance of his business activity, if not by the success of his ventures. Irineu Evangelista de Sousa, barão, later visconde de Mauá (1813–89), born in Rio Grande do Sul, began work as an errand boy for a British importer in Rio de Janeiro at the age of thirteen. An uncle had secured him the position, but thereafter he seemed to rely principally on his own skills, both entrepreneurial and political. By the time he was twenty he was a partner in the firm and, at twenty-four, sole manager. Encouraged by the 1844 tariff and inspired by his earlier visit to England's industrial towns, he set up an iron foundry to supply the government with pipes for draining a swampy part of the city of Rio. By 1850 he employed 300 workers. Upon this establishment, Mauá built a business empire. Soon he successfully bid for the supply of gas to Rio and manufactured the necessary pipes and lamps. Next, he purchased and expanded a shipyard where he eventually constructed 72 small vessels, most of them steam. He then created a shipping company to ply the Amazon River and a tug-boat firm in Rio Grande do Sul. By 1857 he had more than doubled his workers to 667, including 85 slaves he owned outright, 75 more whom he rented and 300 foreigners.

The tariff reduction in 1857 forced Mauá to compete with foreign-made products and he then paid more attention to his banking activities and other investments. He had since 1840 been a partner in a Manchester commercial bank along with his British business partner. In 1851 he created his first bank in Brazil; a later Mauá bank had branches not only throughout southern Brazil but also in Uruguay and Argentina. He saw banks as allies of railways in which he also invested large sums. Indeed, he built the very first railway in Brazil (1854), although it was only fourteen kilometres long, really went nowhere, and, as he himself said, served only as a 'sample cloth' of what railways were and what they could do.[8] More important were Mauá's heavy investments in the São Paulo Railway and his recklessly large advances to its building contractor whose bankruptcy seriously undermined his own financial standing. The crisis that ruined several commercial banking firms in Rio in 1864 further drained Mauá's resources. His simultaneous involvement in Uruguayan politics as the chief financier of a shaky government brought him to his knees; the next financial crisis in Brazil (1875) forced him finally into an expected bankruptcy.

In all his activities Mauá was to some degree a client of the planter-dominated government and, like all clients, found his interests easily sacrificed when it suited the patron. The government's failure to extend credits to a beleaguered Mauá did not spring, however, from hostility to his commercial background on the part of a seigneurial planter class, as some have alleged, but from the planters' ability to use the system to defend their business interests with more acumen than he.

Economic decision-making increasingly centred in the port cities. Coffee factors and other merchants, bankers, fledgling industrialists, managers of insurance companies, agents of shipping lines and bureaucrats high and low, along with the accompanying shopkeepers, hoteliers, lawyers, doctors and teachers, filled the ranks of the urban upper and middle classes. Their employees or slaves – stevedores, maids, construction workers, water carriers, seamstresses, salesmen, accountants, and clerks – further extended the urban complex. By 1872 the city of Rio de Janeiro had a population of over a quarter of a million and both Recife and Salvador had over 100,000. Not big cities by international standards, they seemed enormous in contrast to other Brazilian cities or to themselves at earlier times.

[8] Quoted by Alberto de Faria, *Mauá – Ireneo Evangelista de Souza, barão e visconde de Mauá, 1813–1889* (2nd edn, São Paulo, 1933), 165.

Slaves supplied much of the labour in these expanding urban centres. Male slaves bore the curtained chairs on which fine ladies went about. At the port they loaded coffee sacks onto waiting ships. They also carried them through the streets to warehouses; and their heavy loads were said to cripple a man's hips and knees within ten years. Foreign travellers often commented on the widespread use of slaves in craft shops. A city such as Recife or Salvador, and much more so the metropolitan centre of Rio de Janeiro, demanded an almost endless range of work from silversmiths, carpenters, masons, painters, shoemakers and hatters, slave as well as free. Domestic slaves, principally women, were employed not only by the upper class but also by those of middling income, to carry water, fetch food from the marketplace, wash clothes at the public fountains, or empty the garbage and night-soil at the beach.

Two practices approximated urban slavery to wage labour. Slaves often did not work for their owner directly, but for someone else to whom they were rented. The practice lent a flexibility to slave labour often ignored by later theorists. The employer in this case had only a cash nexus to his worker and would prefer to find another labourer than to expend unusual effort or resources in exerting personal authority through force or favours. Some slaves hired themselves, returning to their master a fixed sum each month. These slaves found their own work, contracting out their skills or strength as best they could, but keeping for themselves any amount they earned over and above what the master demanded. They arranged for their own housing, took care of all their personal needs and sometimes even hired others – slave or free – to work for them in fulfilling contracts.

With the increasing demand for slaves in the expanding coffee sector, urban slaves decreased in number and in proportion to the urban population as a whole. Scores of city slave-owners tempted by the high prices paid by planters sold their slaves for work on the plantations, turning instead to free workers to supply their labour needs. Of the 30,000 female domestic servants of Rio de Janeiro in 1870 only 43 per cent were slave.[9] Slaves also gave way to wage-labourers in cotton manufacturing. Of the cotton-mill workers, a large proportion were free women and children, 'drawn', said one contemporary, 'from the poorest classes, a few from the direst misery'.[10] Simultaneously, immigrants

[9] Sandra Lauderdale Graham, *House and street: The domestic world of servants and masters in nineteenth-century Rio de Janeiro* (Cambridge, 1988), 8.
[10] Quoted in Stanley J. Stein, *The Brazilian cotton manufacture: textile enterprise in an underdeveloped area, 1850–1950* (Cambridge, Mass., 1957), 54.

Table 2 *Immigrants to Brazil, 1846–75*

Year	Portuguese	German	Italian	Other	Total
1846–50	256	2,143	5	2,399	4,925
1851–55	25,883	5,213		7,936	39,078
1856–60	43,112	13,707		25,813	82,669
1861–65	25,386	7,124	3,023	15,354	50,970
1866–70	24,776	5,648	1,900	13,689	46,601
1871–75	32,688	5,224	4,610	37,716	81,314
Total	152,101	39,058	9,533	102,907	305,557

Source. Imre Ferenczi, comp., *International Migrations*, ed. Walter F. Willcox (New York: National Bureau of Economic Research, 1929), 549–50.

pushed out of Portugal by unemployment, but unwilling to work in the coffee fields under harsh conditions identified with slavery, sought urban employment in Brazil. A little over 300,000 immigrants arrived during the 30-year period 1846–75 (an average of 10,000 per annum); half of them were Portuguese (see Table 2). By 1872 there were more Portuguese immigrants in Rio de Janeiro than there were slaves.

The city opened up opportunities lacking in the countryside not only for slaves but for the free. Cities allowed for some small increase in the impersonality of human relationships, more social mobility and a greater variety of acceptable behaviour. Blacks could more readily create and transmit their customs, language, music, family traditions, in short, their culture. Female domestic servants, although closely supervised, might enjoy stolen moments of liberty in their daily rounds; they certainly moved about the city with more familiarity and less restraint than did many of their mistresses hemmed in by the restrictive customs of a jealous male-dominated society. Relationships between workers and employers, nevertheless, hinged on favours provided in exchange for loyal service whether from slaves or free persons, Brazilian or Portuguese. Hierarchical social values permeated even urban life. City craft-shop owners or merchants, for example, lived in close proximity to their employees: typically, workers slept at the back of the shop and the employer and his family resided upstairs. Even the factory owner, like a paternalistic planter, supplied food, clothing and shelter, along with training. Employers wished to control the use of whatever free time remained to workers, watching over their coming and going, their casual relationships, in short, over every aspect of their behaviour. Free workers often received no wage at all but merely daily necessities and perhaps a cash bonus at the end of the year depending upon their good

behaviour (thus again closing the gap between slave and free). If in the
cities there was less overt violence against recalcitrant free workers than
against slaves, they could nevertheless be constantly threatened with
dismissal and a consequent loss not only of wages but of housing and
protection. The scarcity of alternative urban opportunities transformed
such threats into a disguised violence. Even as urban slavery declined,
cash wages only slowly displaced the obligations of dependence. And
while fewer and fewer urban dwellers felt committed to the maintenance
of slavery, slaves continued to be part of the urban scene until abolition in
1888.

Although with the growth of cities groups alien to, and even hostile
towards, landowners eventually emerged, in 1870 the latter still exercised
clear authority in most political decisions. Certainly, if the alleged
dichotomy between merchants and landowners is recognized as more an
historian's creation than a past reality and it is noticed that insofar as it
existed it only occasionally led to conflicting interests, landowners and
merchants together can be said to have played the dominant role in the
political system. Manufacturers before 1870 did not form an important
or independent political force and many of them were themselves
merchants engaged in the export and import trade. The non-propertied,
slave and free, although, of course, the vast majority, exercised little
influence upon the state except through the age-long processes of passive
resistance. Some historians have alleged that a bureaucratic-political
class or estate stood as a counterweight to the landowners, but most
politicians and bureaucrats at this time either held land themselves or
were connected to landowning interests through family ties. Others,
through their links to merchant and financial interests, had interests
essentially in harmony with those of the propertied class. Even those
landowners who did not feel they received a fair share of the system's
benefits were on the whole content to let the wealthiest sectors exercise
power in order to maintain social order, so essential for their own
continued control over slaves and the lower classes and for the political
stability that Brazilian publicists never tired of contrasting with the
disturbances allegedly endemic in Spanish America. The values that
justified the social hierarchy also reinforced the authority of the propertied within the political system.

A constitutional monarch reigned in Brazil. The cabinet was responsible both to him and to a parliament consisting of a Senate of a little over

fifty members and a Chamber of Deputies of around 120. The emperor, with advice from a Council of State, appointed Senators from among the three candidates who received the most votes in each province. Senators served for life. Deputies were chosen by indirect elections at least every four years. In 1831 Pedro II (1825–91), then a young child, had succeeded to the throne on the abdication of his father Pedro I (1798–1834). By 1850, now 25 years old, he no longer relied upon the narrow coterie of advisers which had guided his first steps as ruler, but he still exercised the powers vested in him by the constitution of 1824 with great caution, much more sensitive than his father to the realities of economic and political power in Brazil. He proved useful in adjudicating disputes among members of the dominant class. Despite a stream of instructions addressed to cabinet members generally advocating moderate reform, they only occasionally heeded his advice. He was never able – and rarely wished – to impose basic changes that would threaten the interests of the propertied who sustained his authority. He took pains never to discredit his office by acts of personal immorality or moments of levity. A sober, often sombre man, Pedro II attended to the minutiae of government, not because he wielded vast power, but because he exercised so little. By his constant meddling in details, however, he inadvertently drew the blame for Brazil's failure to undertake major change.

For the emperor's presence loomed visibly large. The nation invariably returned representatives to parliament who supported the cabinet in power. This was true despite the façade of liberal measures protecting the rights of political opponents, maintaining freedom of the press and attempting to ensure the honest counting of the vote. Only the emperor, by dismissing one prime minister and summoning a rival, could bring in another party to control the machinery of government. Since both political parties – Conservative and Liberal – drew support from virtually the same social and economic constituency – and in some cases alternating support from identical voters – Pedro II did not thus threaten any dominant social group or economic interest. Rather, he responded to the rhythms impelling or restraining modest shifts in the direction sought by the political and bureaucratic leaders closely in touch with regional concerns.

A Council of State, consisting of twelve senior politicians, appointed by the emperor for life, advised him on the exercise of his 'moderative power'. In choosing them the emperor, by custom, relied on nominations from the prime minister. The emperor turned to the Council, in turn, for advice in the exercise of his right to appoint and dismiss the ministers. Each cabinet had either to gain the confidence of the legislature as well, or to ask the emperor to dismiss parliament and call new elections which he would do after consultation with members of the Council of State. Legislation required the emperor's approval, and he would normally consult the council before granting it. Finally, the Council of State acted as a court to consider those cases involving disputes between branches of government and suits brought against the government, thus exercising a judicial review over the constitutionality of laws and decrees.

The prime minister, called President of the Council of Ministers, selected his cabinet members with a careful eye to balancing competing political ambitions, regional strengths and parliamentary skills and contacts.[11] The cabinet guided the policies of the government. It drew up the budget for submission to parliament, and, in practice, it prepared proposed legislation for debate. Most importantly, it named all other administrative officers, appointed, subject to some restrictions, all judges and bishops, and granted most military promotions.

The appointment of the presidents of each province stood out as most decisive. Although responsible for carrying out the directives issued by the cabinet and ensuring compliance with the laws of the empire, the provincial presidents' chief function, in fact, was to produce electoral returns favourable to the cabinet. For that task they relied on patronage as their most important instrument. Provincial presidents distributed positions as rewards for past – and future – political loyalty. The cabinet relied heavily upon the presidents for political information and sound judgement. Despite their crucial role, however, presidents had a very short term of office. They served at the pleasure of the prime minister, and in his constant re-shuffling of the national bureaucracy, he moved presidents from province to province, brought them to Rio to fill key positions, promoted them to cabinet posts, or shoved them into minor sinecures when he considered them inadequate. A significant number of presidents simultaneously served in parliament and therefore departed from their provincial capitals for Rio de Janeiro at the beginning of each

[11] José Murillo de Carvalho, 'Elite and state-building in imperial Brazil' (unpublished Ph.D. thesis, Stanford University, 1974), 190, shows that during the period 1853–71, 26 per cent of the cabinet ministers came from Bahia and Pernambuco, another 26 per cent came from the city and province of Rio de Janeiro, 18 per cent from Minas Gerais and São Paulo, 24 per cent from other provinces and 6 per cent from outside Brazil, presumably from Portugal.

session, leaving the day-to-day administration of the province in the hands of vice-presidents.

The provincial presidents' chief agents both in enforcing the law and gathering political intelligence were the provincial chiefs of police and their police commissioners (*delegados*), also appointed by the central government. Deputy commissioners (*subdelegados*) and block inspectors (*inspetores de quarteirão*) – twenty-five houses to a block – carried the authority of the central government, at least theoretically, into every small locality. Aside from the chief, however, police officials did not receive government salaries, but derived their personal income from their ordinary, private activities; in short, in the countryside most were landowners who cherished such positions in order to exert added authority, especially over local rivals. Henrique Marques Lins, the wealthy Pernambucan sugar planter, secured the position of police commissioner for one son-in-law and placed a brother-in-law as his deputy. Three other police officials in that county owned between them nine plantations. In the cities presidents preferred lawyers and judges but occasionally found it advantageous to name military officers to these positions. By relying on ordinary citizens to carry out its orders, the government kept open the lines of communication and recognized the power and importance of the locally prominent.

Just as from ancient times the Portuguese king ruled principally as judge, so distinctions between judicial authority and law enforcement or police functions were blurred. Since the passage of a controversial law in 1841, local police commissioners held judicial powers. They not only pressed charges, but also assembled evidence, heard witnesses and presented the county judge (*juiz municipal*) – also centrally appointed – with a written record of the inquiry from which the judge derived his verdict. Locally elected justices of the peace (*juízes de paz*) who had earlier held police authority now mattered only as organizers of electoral boards. For ordinary citizens, police commissioners now became the focus of authority. Mercy could temper the severity of the law, especially for the politically compliant; but no doubt remained that such benevolence could as easily be withheld.

In contrast to the police commissioners, judges, who shared a common education in either of Brazil's two law schools (often starting in one and finishing in the other), hoped for advancement within a professional hierarchy. Although they might own land, slaves, or businesses, they received a salary from the government and endured frequent removals from place to place. District Judges (*juízes de direito*) enjoyed tenure for life but normally remained at one location only for four years. At the end of that period they could either be re-assigned for another term or be 'promoted' to a court of higher rank but not always at a more attractive place. After a second term they faced, once again, the likelihood of a move. At any time, a district judge could lose his position by being named chief of police; after serving in such a position even for a short time, he would be returned to the bench but no longer necessarily at his old location. He could also be retained without a seat, receiving his salary while awaiting a vacancy. District judges were recruited from the ranks of county judges. The latter could be shifted around even more readily and, at election time, their placement resembled moves in an elaborate chess game.

All public servants who wished to keep their posts attended to winning elections for the party then in power in Rio de Janeiro. Elections were indirect and the suffrage limited. In addition to women and slaves whose exclusion from access to the ballot box was taken for granted, the law barred men under 25 years of age, beggars, vagrants, personal and domestic servants, as well as all those whose income from property did not reach 200 *reis* per year. Much debate concentrated on how income should be defined and proved, but anyone could vote if his name appeared on the list of qualified voters. This fact – as well as the decision whether a potential voter were really the person so named – depended entirely on the electoral boards. If challenged regarding income or identity, a prospective voter needed only to present the sworn statements of three witnesses to prove his case; contrary depositions, however, could as easily deny him the right to vote. If there were witnesses on both sides – as, of course, there usually were – the electoral board decided according to its best lights. From 1846, membership on the board depended upon the results of the previous elections. Voting was only for electors (except in the case of county councilmen who were directly elected). The electors then met in district electoral colleges to choose deputies to parliament, members of the provincial assemblies, and to nominate senators when a vacancy occurred. The most voted for elector in each parish became justice of the peace and presided over the electoral board at the next election; all the board's other members were also electors.

The electoral process provided ample opportunity for pressure both from the central government and from local oligarchs. Citizens did not vote secretly. Because most voters were illiterate, they deposited in the ballot box a list of candidates for electors received from a local patron. The police commissioner maintained order at election time; sometimes this meant keeping 'trouble-makers' – that is, opposition voters – away from the polls. The election, if challenged, could be thrown out either by the county judge or provincial president. The electors themselves, like the local potentates in general, had much to gain by supporting the government candidate and much to lose if he were defeated. Consequently, elections for parliament invariably returned a majority who favoured the cabinet then in power; sometimes the government's support in the Chamber of Deputies was nearly unanimous. In 1855 the creation of single-member instead of province-wide electoral districts enabled minority interests to gain some representation in parliament, since the government could not give its full attention to all areas, although even this opening narrowed again with changes in the electoral law in 1860 (see below).

A politician who aspired to national prominence, perhaps eventually to be prime minister, demonstrated his strength by rewarding supporters with local appointive offices. Since cabinet members or their direct appointees could fill virtually any local position – whether judicial, police, educational or tax-gathering – an elaborately articulated column of patronage formed the backbone of the political system.[12] Ultimately, patronage linked court and village to connect even the *agregados* to a national system of personal obligations. Through politics, local potentates defended a clientelistic and paternalistic social structure and projected it into the next generation. A slave-owner or his son participated in order to obtain bureaucratic appointments, sinecures, livings, or commissions for his family and for the vast network of dependents and clients each family member carried with him. The state, to be sure, was not simply the 'executive committee' of the economically powerful, first, because the latter were not themselves agreed upon particular ends and

---

12 Among the positions to be filled through political patronage were those of the Church. Following colonial precedent, the government proposed to the Vatican the names of those to fill the archbishopric of Bahia and the eight other bishoprics. Parish priests were similarly nominated to the bishops and promotions or transfers depended on political commitment. Although the Church could summon loyalties in its own right, it meshed with other institutions through the structure of patronage. The state collected and kept the tithe and paid only modest salaries to churchmen. Other ordained clergy sought employment as chaplains on *fazendas* or for wealthy lay brotherhoods in the cities. Patrons, whether private or public, expected deference from the clergy as from their other clients. Whereas in earlier times churchmen actively engaged in rebellions, by the middle of the century they preached order and obedience to constituted authority. Only in the 1870s did some churchmen question whether this authority resided in the emperor or the pope.

means and, secondly, because the safeguarding of the overall system sometimes required actions that offended the interests of powerful groups. But the state reinforced the hegemony of the propertied by reproducing within itself the paternalistic order of deference on the one hand and favours on the other.

In maintaining and consolidating national unity, the empire drew on the political and administrative skills of a relatively small group of men of similar backgrounds, education and experience. Recent research has shown that of those cabinet ministers whose social backgrounds could be identified from biographical dictionaries, 54 per cent were connected to landowning interests and another 14 to business. Seventy-two per cent had been trained in law, either in the case of the first generation at the University of Coimbra in Portugal or at the Brazilian law faculties in Recife and São Paulo.[13] To enter such faculties candidates needed both an expensive secondary education and connections to men of influence. Another path into the political elite lay through the military academy, more open to talented youth from modest backgrounds; but this route became less common after 1850. After graduation, the aspiring politician sought placement in ever more diverse geographic locations, broadening his contacts while also making him always more obligated to repay the patronage of older, more established figures. From district attorney to county and district judgeships and then on to provincial presidencies, the mobile candidate demonstrated his administrative abilities and political steadfastness. Election to the Chamber of Deputies and Senate finally put him into the pool from which cabinet ministers were chosen. As the landed, slave-owning class participated actively in politics at all levels, including the highest, it forged links across provincial and regional boundaries. Despite the sectional loyalties that arose from focusing on distinct export crops and the increasing orientation toward port cities which the railways encouraged, their fundamental political unity was strengthened in the middle decades of the nineteenth century. A common loyalty to the crown served as symbolic expression of this unity.

Yet within a narrow range disagreements surfaced of course. Although there was much truth in the saying that 'nothing more resembles a Conservative than a Liberal in power', some differences emerged, if for no other reason than that the Liberals were not as often in power. Some political leaders of the era – a majority – placed slightly greater emphasis on individual liberty than on public order and preferred

---

[13] Carvalho, 'Elite and state-building', 97–8, 132.

provincial or local autonomy to central authority. Yet even on these divisions, though they loomed at particular moments, the positions of individuals varied so much over time that one suspects they were merely rhetorical stands for momentary political advantage, rather than firm convictions. Certainly none of these divisions addressed the legitimacy of the system as a whole. Politicians in Rio Grande do Sul, São Paulo and Minas Gerais, and from the cities, more often tended to identify with the Liberal party than did those from the coffee-rich Paraíba valley, but numerous examples could be found to the contrary. Those who desired, for diverse reasons, to move towards an end of slavery typically sided with the Liberals, but the Conservatives actually passed a few emancipationist laws and Liberals proved easily divided on the issue, since their constituents, like those of the Conservatives, included slave-owners.

To speak of parties is somewhat misleading, for parliamentary agglomerations lacked unity and did not depend on disciplined electorates, nor represent ideologically defined movements. Several important leaders abandoned the Liberals to join the Conservatives and vice versa. Out in the districts party labels were adopted with little consistency, and much local-level struggle occurred within and not between the so-called parties. Village factions, entwined by family and the ancient ties of patrons and clients, vied for electoral victory in order to receive positions of local authority. No particular political philosophy distinguished one group from another. Their elected representatives, once in parliament, formed unstable alliances with each other. Contemporaries, however, continued to think of Liberals and Conservatives in terms of their nineteenth-century British counterparts.

A search for accommodation, a fear of party strife and an effort to head off extreme reformist demands characterized national politics from 1853 to 1868. The sequence of cabinets makes clear that, at most, a successful politician could advocate only gradual and measured change. Acceptable reforms must be bestowed by those above and never result from demands of those below. Based as it was on slavery, society appeared inherently unstable to contemporaries; paternalistic measures combined with firmness served to keep it stable.

Since 1837, as coffee emerged to give the nation a new economic centre of gravity, there had been a steady movement away from the liberalism of the previous decade and a reaction towards the restoration of the power of the central government. The institution in 1841 of centrally appointed police commissioners holding extensive judicial authority was the culmination of that process and remained the touch-stone for subsequent Liberal-Conservative differences. Unsuccessful Liberal revolts in 1842 and 1848 played into the hands of those who saw excessive provincial autonomy and individual liberty threatening social order with anarchy. The triumph of the Conservatives in the elections of 1849 – only one Liberal won a seat in parliament – provided the basis for strengthening still further the Conservative tenor of the cabinet named in September 1848 headed by the well-known Conservative and former regent, Pedro de Araújo Lima, visconde de Olinda (1793–1870). Paulino José Soares de Sousa, later visconde de Uruguai (1807–66) and his wife's brother-in-law Joaquim José Rodrigues Tôrres, later visconde de Itaboraí,[14] joined Eusébio de Queiroz Coutinho Matoso da Câmara (1812–68) in government. All three had close ties either directly or through marriage to slave-holding coffee-planters of Rio de Janeiro province. Known as the *Saquaremas* (from the locale of the *fazenda* where they often met) they believed in a strong central government, which they or their friends could count on dominating. The firm control exercised by this Conservative cabinet enabled it to pass and enforce a number of measures that had once been too controversial to tackle, notably the suppression of the international slave trade and the land law of 1850. The cabinet also pushed through parliament in 1850 a Commercial Code, which had been debated for fifteen years. By newly codifying commercial relations regarding partnerships, contracts and bankruptcies, as well as creating business-run courts to adjudicate commercial conflicts, the measure helped businesses within Brazil to mesh with the international economy. Not long after, parliament empowered the government to guarantee interest on the capital invested in railways, a measure which bolstered the efforts of the planters to link Brazil more closely to overseas markets. The creation of a semi-official Bank of Brazil expanded govern-ment control of the currency by replacing privately owned regional banks of issue. Itaboraí also initiated attempts towards lowering import duties. Finally, reform of the National Guard in 1850, by eliminating the election of its officers, placed it tightly under the command of the national government. This cabinet thus completed the process of central-izing authority in a government now firmly managed by the coffee-planters of Rio de Janeiro.

---

[14] For the sake of simplicity, upon second and subsequent reference to individuals titles will be used even if only acquired later.

Once central government had been solidly established it proved possible to conciliate warring political factions by granting space within the system to conforming Liberals. In 1853 the Conservative Honório Hermeto Carneiro Leão, visconde and later marquês de Paraná (1801–56), presided over a government of conciliation (*conciliação*) which included, for instance, both the distinguished *mineiro*, Antonio Paulino Limpo de Abreu, visconde de Abaeté (1798–1883), who had been a leader in the 1842 Liberal revolt in Minas Gerais and, as Minister of War from 1855, Luís Alves de Lima e Silva, marquês and future duque de Caxias (1803–80), who derived his prestige principally from his military exploits while suppressing regional revolts. Eusébio, Itaboraí and Uruguai found themselves excluded. The relatively young João Maurício Wanderley, future barão de Cotegipe (1815–89), who tried to modernize his Bahia sugar mills, similarly believed the way to preserve the old order generally was to modify it. José Maria Paranhos, future visconde de Rio Branco (1817–80), and Luis Pedreira do Couto Ferraz, visconde de Bom Retiro (1818–86), had both been Liberals but could now be counted as progressive Conservatives. José Tomás Nabuco de Araújo (1813–78), although considered a Conservative at this time, already leant toward the Liberal party which he would later direct: deeply committed to individual freedom, and somewhat anticlerical, he had doubts about the value of the monarchy and advocated the gradual emancipation of slaves, yet simultaneously felt that Brazil could be changed only slowly if it were to avoid the destructive disorder of social revolution.

One of the cabinet of *conciliação*'s most important measures, in the event, was the creation in 1855 of single-member electoral districts. By allowing the Liberals a chance to elect some members of parliament, despite Conservative control of the electoral system in general, it drew Liberals into peaceful participation and signalled the possibility of their once again attaining power. As a result of this law a sizeable minority of Liberals were elected in 1856. In response to their presence the new cabinet led by Olinda included as Treasury Minister the Liberal leader, Bernardo de Sousa Franco (1805–75). He finally pushed through the lower tariff first proposed by his Conservative predecessor in 1851, thus combining his ideological predispositions with support for the interests of export-oriented land owners. His pet project was the reform of the banking law, creating banks of issue and thus increasing the currency in circulation. On this issue planters divided as did merchants, depending on their particular circumstance as debtors or creditors. The measure proved short-lived, however. Eusébio, Itaboraí and Uruguai (the *Saquaremas*) all attacked it in the Senate. In a cabinet reshuffle in 1858, the journalist Francisco de Sales Tôrres Homen, later visconde de Inhomirim (1822–76), replaced Sousa Franco.

The appointment of Inhomirim signalled a renewed endorsement of conservatism. He had once been a Liberal, indeed a virulent critic of the emperor and had collaborated with the Liberal revolts of 1842, suffering exile as a result. He had since mellowed and been wooed back into the mainstream of national political life. Through a newspaper he edited he had ardently defended the moderately conservative policies of the *conciliação* cabinet. Sousa Franco's banking policy then provoked his ire and he became its most articulate critic, both in the press and in parliament. As Minister of Finance, Inhomirim proceeded to undo Sousa Franco's measures. He also opposed the efforts of Mauá to establish unregulated joint-stock companies. Finally, he began work on a severely restrictive company law which, when passed in 1860, forced all would-be companies first to obtain government approval. The next Conservative cabinet of 1859–61 not only pushed through that restrictive company law but reversed the direction of electoral reform by enlarging the area of electoral districts with three candidates instead of one chosen from each. Regional chieftains thus gained strength against local factions, and the representation of local interests and minority viewpoints became more difficult.

The elections of December 1860 halted the conservative drift. Middle-of-the-road (conciliation) Conservatives, disaffected by those retrograde measures, joined forces with the Liberals who, since their partial victories of 1856, had modest patronage to dispense. The campaign developed as a particularly heated one, especially in the city of Rio, hot-bed of dissident opinion and focus of national attention. One old Liberal leader, Teófilo Ottoni (1807–69), a veteran of the struggles in Minas Gerais of 1842, adopted a white handkerchief as his symbol when campaigning in Rio's parishes to the loud acclaim of the urban populace. The result of the election, while continuing the Conservative majority in parliament, also led to the seating of several fiery Liberals. Thirty years later Joaquim Nabuco, the first major historian of the empire, wrote that the 1860 election reversed the conservative trend begun in 1837 and marked the turn of the tide toward a reformism that would culminate in the overthrow of the monarchy in 1889. For the time being, however, accommodation continued to characterize cabinet-level politics.

The election of 1860 split both Conservative and Liberal 'parties'. The more progressive among the elected Conservatives joined with a number of Liberals to form a parliamentary league. The Progressive League, as it was sometimes called, intended to revoke the legislation of December 1841 and remove judicial powers from police authorities. The *saquaremas* still felt such a measure would threaten the order they had so carefully created, while at the other extreme some Liberals considered such measures far too moderate. They regarded such a reform as merely the first step toward a revision of the entire Constitution which would end, or at least restrict, the emperor's 'moderative power', require senators to stand for election at regular intervals, allow provincial presidents to be elected rather than appointed, and make elections for deputy direct. None of these far-reaching reforms could make headway in the 1860s.

These new divisions in parliament led to an early defeat for the Conservative cabinet named in 1861. League support for a motion of no-confidence proved crucial, but when a League member – former Conservative Zacarias de Góes e Vesconcelos (1815–77) – was named prime minister, proposing only modest changes in the 1841 law, the Liberals abandoned him, and he too was forced to resign. A compromise cabinet unwilling to move in any direction proved not much stronger, but managed to hang on for lack of an alternative until forced to call fresh elections in 1863.

The new parliament, meeting in January 1864, reflected two changes in the intervening period. The Progressive League had drafted a moderate programme of reform specifically excluding major alterations to the Constitution, but calling for the separation of judicial from police authority. Meanwhile, Conservative leaders had decided that the provisions of the 1841 laws were no longer a necessary condition for their own survival or for the stability of the empire. As these tendencies became clearer, the 'purer' Liberals found themselves isolated. The centre had again emerged victorious. Zacarias once more became prime minister.

From a wealthy family in Bahia, Zacarias had been elected to parliament in 1850 as a Conservative and soon joined the Itaboraí cabinet. As a student and then professor at the Recife law school, however, Zacarias had already been much influenced by his reading of John Stuart Mill and Jeremy Bentham: he increasingly believed the individual should be protected from state control, became an opponent of the 1841 law, and in 1860 published a stinging critique of the 'moderative power' of the emperor. Still, he did not question the larger framework of government, wished only cautious reforms and later, in fact, emerged as a staunch defender of Church prerogatives. A sharp-tongued speaker, he had a special gift for making enemies through his sarcasms and cruel jibes. Liberals from Rio Grande do Sul hastened to attack him when he appeared to lack forcefulness in pursuing Brazilian diplomatic goals in Uruguay. He fell from power after seven months as Brazil moved toward war, first with Uruguay and then with Paraguay.

The Paraguayan War, a major international conflict, had other effects besides preventing Zacarias from pushing through moderate reforms. It exposed the contradiction between the façade of polished discourse among political elites and the exploitative realities faced by most Brazilians. It also exacerbated tensions within the Brazilian military. Yet, by sharpening divisions within Brazil, it eventually advanced the cause of reform, especially with regard to slavery. Zacarias would be at the centre of that later storm, when he once again became prime minister in 1866. Initially, however, the War drew attention away from internal change.

First the Portuguese, then the Brazilians, had a long history of involvement in the affairs of the Banda Oriental of the Río de la Plata (Uruguay). The Portuguese had established themselves at Colônia do Sacramento in 1680 and only withdrew in 1776. Portuguese armies retook the region in 1816, and from 1821 until the creation of the independent state of Uruguay in 1828 the area had been a Brazilian province. Then, preoccupied with ensuring their own unity during the 1830s and 1840s, Brazilians had not been able to withstand the expanding influence in Uruguay of Juan Manuel de Rosas, the Argentine caudillo.[15] Meanwhile, the cattlemen of Rio Grande do Sul had extended their herds and lands on both sides of the border, frequently taking their young cattle to the better pastures of Uruguay and later driving them back to Rio Grande do Sul for slaughter. Having given up their ten-year struggle to create an independent state of their own in 1845, they looked to the central government to protect their interests in Uruguay. The Conservative and centralizing *saquarema* faction, in power in Rio from 1848, happily co-operated. As foreign minister, visconde de Uruguai also hoped eventually to open a secure passage for Brazilian ships to guarantee free navigation up the River Paraguay to the province of Mato Grosso. In pursuit of the goal of reasserting Brazilian influence to the south, Brazil allied itself in 1851 with a Uruguayan faction opposed to Rosas' influence and – with Justo José Urquiza, a restless caudillo in north-eastern

---

[15] The politics of the River Plate Republics and the origins of the Paraguayan War are discussed in detail in Lynch, *CHLA* III, chap. 15.

Argentina – committed Brazilian troops under the command of Caxias to the attempt (soon successful) to overthrow Rosas and install in his place in Buenos Aires a progressive, European-oriented, cosmopolitan government.

Uruguay continued, however, to be torn by internecine struggle. And whichever government was in power in Montevideo had to contend with at least 20,000 resident Brazilians who owned some 400 estates with lands totalling almost a third of the national territory. Constant civil war between *Blancos* and *Colorados*, the two 'parties' of Uruguay, meant many Brazilians nursed grievances and pressed monetary claims against successive Uruguayan governments. Furthermore, the Brazilians wished to move cattle from one estate to another or to drive them to market across the frontier into Rio Grande do Sul without paying taxes. All Uruguayan governments considered these revenues necessary to finance the costs of maintaining order. Mauá's firm had meanwhile virtually become Uruguay's official bank. Brazilian cattlemen in the area blamed Mauá for the taxes the government levied to pay off its debts to him, while he saw as excessive their claims for damages which threatened to force the government to default. Moreover, the Uruguayans, having abolished slavery in 1853, threatened to free the slaves Brazilians brought into the country. A clash was inevitable.

Some Brazilian Liberals who in the mid-1860s participated in the Progressive League owed political debts in Rio Grande do Sul. They were thus committed to pressing Brazilians' claims against Uruguay. One way of doing so was to back the faction then out of power – the *Colorados* – as they sought, with Argentine support, to overthrow the *Blanco* government in Montevideo. The *Blancos*, meanwhile, correctly perceiving the threat posed by both Brazil and Argentina, sought to ally themselves with Paraguay's dictator, Francisco Solano López.

López, to whom the guaraní-speaking Paraguayans were fiercely loyal, had inherited from his father leadership of a nation which had remained largely isolated from the rest of the world. He sensed the encroaching threat of Brazilian and Argentine power and feared the definitive loss of disputed territory claimed by Paraguay on both borders. He responded only too willingly to appeals for help from some Uruguayans, but did not announce his intentions clearly enough to make Brazilian and Argentine leaders understand that he considered any threat to Uruguay a threat to Paraguay and to himself. Nevertheless, when in June 1864 Argentine and Brazilian ministers met in Montevideo to work

out what they thought would be a settlement of the internal Uruguayan
struggle, they informally agreed on joint action should Paraguay come to
the rescue of the defeated *Blancos*.

The terms of this agreement proved a self-fulfilling prophecy. By their
action López felt confirmed in his conviction that Brazil and Argentina
planned to divide Paraguay between them. When the settlement in
Uruguay did not hold, Brazilian troops moved into Uruguay (September
1864) to enforce Brazil's claims to reparations for damages to Brazilian
citizens and to install the *Colorados* in power. Paraguay responded by
seizing Brazilian ships on the Río Paraguay and invading Brazilian
territory. Mistakenly counting on the support of Urquiza in north-
eastern Argentina, López ordered his troops to cross Argentine territory
and thus found himself at war with that country too. Secret clauses of the
treaty signed in May 1865 by Brazil, Argentina and Uruguay called,
among other things, for the transfer of disputed Paraguayan territory to
Argentina and Brazil, as well as for the opening of Paraguayan rivers to
international trade and the deposition of López. When these provisions
leaked to the press, an international outcry ensued, but the allies did not
abandon their aims.

The war has been presented by some historians as the result of the mad
schemes of a megalomaniac Paraguayan tyrant. In fact it resulted from
the step-by-step escalation of conflicting interests, complicated by a
series of mistaken but understandable judgements on all sides. López not
irrationally feared Paraguayan dismemberment and the end of his nation's existence, which he understood to depend on an equilibrium of
power in the region. He seriously miscalculated his own strength and the
support he could get from Urquiza, apparently doubting that the
Argentine caudillo had really made his peace with Buenos Aires in 1862.
Leaders in Buenos Aires quite reasonably feared the rise of Urquiza in the
north-east in an alliance with López and the *Blancos* of Uruguay. In
López's fear of Brazil he was encouraged by the belligerent statements of
some Brazilian parliamentarians and the contingency planning of Brazil's
diplomats. He believed he had made clear his views that Brazilian
intervention in Uruguay meant war. Brazil wanted the *Colorados* in
power in Uruguay so as to advance the interests of its citizens and to
assert its own power in the region. Brazilians did not believe López
would actually go to war, but were confident that, should he do so, Brazil
would easily win and thus rid itself of troublesome border questions
while guaranteeing the free navigation of the Río Paraguay.
Wrongheadedness on all sides had provoked war.

From the start the war went badly for the Paraguayans. Brazilian troops, having installed a compliant government in Montevideo, moved quickly to the Paraguayan front. By September 1865 the Brazilians had cleared foreign troops from Rio Grande do Sul. But Brazil, anxious to assert its hegemony in the region, then spurned Paraguayan efforts toward peace. The Paraguayans fought ever more steadfastly once the theatre of battle moved into their own territory. Allied troops suffered a major defeat at Curupaití in September 1866. The Argentine general and president Bartolomé Mitre, who had exercised a loose command over allied troops, now turned his attention to opposing dissidents in Argentina where the war had proved unpopular, especially among provincial caudillos. Brazil carried on alone, stubbornly insisting on overthrowing López himself, and the war dragged on for another four tragic years.

The war exposed several tensions within Brazilian society. Brazil's determination to pursue the war with Paraguay after Brazilian territory had been cleared of Paraguayan troops and to overthrow and kill López himself bespoke a deep national anxiety. Brazilian leaders justified their action on the grounds that they had to bring civilization to that barbaric country and to free the Paraguayans from tyranny. They frequently ridiculed the racial heritage of Paraguay and hinted at a concept of white supremacy. Perhaps Brazilian politicians doubted the degree of their own 'civilization' and feared disparaging comparisons with the European nations with which they so closely identified. Brazilians were surrounded by slaves, but felt an increasing sense of guilt regarding their enslavement. The ferocious pursuit of the war by Brazil seems to have been an opportunity to work out a gnawing self-doubt.

An opera first performed just as the Paraguayan War ended indirectly reveals some of those racial doubts. Antonio Carlos Gomes (1836–96) based his opera on a romantic novel by José de Alencar (1829–77) titled *O Guaraní*. Set in the sixteenth century, both novel and opera glorified the noble savage and racial mixture between Portuguese and Indians, but ignored the African background of the bulk of the Brazilian population. A search for a mythology encasing Brazilian themes within European forms – the opera had an Italian libretto and first played at La Scala – reflects not only the divorce between upper and lower classes but the alienation of the intelligentsia from a country in which 79 per cent of the adult free population did not know how to read or write. Even Antonio de Castro Alves (1847–71), usually remembered for the moving denunciation of the slave trade he included in his first book of poems in 1870, nevertheless endowed black protagonists with 'white' qualities, even

altering their physiognomy to make them acceptable as heroic characters. Slaves struggled not against flesh-and-blood masters but against
vague, sinister, impersonal forces. A Europeanized high culture in this
export economy revealed an understandable reluctance to confront the
shattering implications of a reality marked by personal oppression
witnessed daily on plantation or city street.

The Paraguayan War also brought to a head conflicts within the
Brazilian armed forces. The landed class had taken measures to ensure
their dominance over public instruments of force by creating in 1831 a
National Guard in which they were the officers. As a centralizing
measure, the Conservative cabinet in 1850 had made all positions as
officers in the National Guard appointive rather than elective, but these
appointments continued to go almost exclusively to large landowners.
Typical was the case of Henrique Marques Lins, the wealthy north-
eastern sugar planter, who commanded the county National Guard and
whose fifteen company captains included eight who between them
owned sixteen plantations.

The regular army officer corps, however, was also restructured and to
some extent professionalized in 1850. A career open to talent through the
military academies became possible for those who could neither afford
the costly secondary education needed to enter law school nor count
on the necessary contacts. The seeds were thus sown for the eventual
growth of a certain class hostility between military officers and civilian
politicians, although its flowering came only in the 1880s and later.
In the period before the Paraguayan War, the very highest military
officers still customarily came from or established close connections with
elite families. Caxias, for instance, was the brother of a leading financier
of the empire and was himself an active Conservative political leader who
had been elected to the Senate in 1845, serving in three cabinets, twice as
prime minister. As a political leader he defended the interests of the
dominant land- and slave-owning class. Younger, middle-ranking officers, however, especially those enjoying rapid promotion during the
war, did not share Caxias's easy familiarity with the powerful.

Since even the officers of the National Guard recognized they were
usually unsuited for leadership in actual combat, it was common at times
of national emergency to suspend such officers for indeterminate periods
and appoint army officers in their stead. During the Paraguayan War,
especially at the beginning, there were not enough army officers to go
around, and National Guard commanders whose experience had been

limited to parading in fancy uniforms on Sundays suddenly found themselves in charge of troops under fire. As the war dragged on however, the percentage of troops drawn from the National Guard fell from 74 per cent in 1866 to 44 per cent in 1869. The regular officer corps grew accordingly. Not surprisingly army officers had all their prejudices about their National Guard counterparts confirmed during the war. After the war the Rio Branco cabinet ended all compulsory service in the National Guard, made Guard officers purely honorific without command authority and denied them the right to recruit soldiers for the army or to exercise policing functions. Landowners acquiesced, partly because they welcomed the opportunity to turn over to others the task of fighting wars and partly because they correctly understood that their local authority remained secure and their national power did not depend on the direct command of military force.

Finally, the war with Paraguay exacerbated partisan political strife, provoked the return of the Conservatives to power (in 1868) and contributed to the break-up of the middle-of-the-road Progressive League. When Zacarias, the somewhat cautious Progressive reformer, fell from power in mid-1864 he had been replaced by Francisco José Furtado (1818–70), also a Progressive though more committed to reform than Zacarias. He was not, however, as able a politician. His appointment of the Conservative visconde do Rio Branco as emissary to Montevideo alienated the Liberal members of parliament. Then, when Paraguayan troops invaded Brazilian territory, the logical choice to lead Brazilian forces would have been Caxias. As a Conservative party stalwart and regular defender of the law of 1841, however, he appeared to Liberals as the personification of all they opposed. The Furtado government nevertheless approached him at this time of crisis. He replied that since he would rely principally on National Guard troops from Rio Grande do Sul, the provincial president there could not be the incumbent who had been appointed to carry out the political will of the Liberal-Progressives. The Minister of War agreed, but when Liberal members of parliament learned of this kow-towing to the Conservative leanings of Caxias, they raged, and Furtado hesitated. The Minister of War resigned and Furtado chose a well-known personal enemy of Caxias to hold that portfolio. Caxias, not surprisingly, now altogether refused to lead the Brazilian military effort. The controversy brought down the Furtado cabinet in May 1865, and its successor, still Progressive-Liberal in composition, determined to manage without Caxias.

Brazilian troops at first fared reasonably well without him and by October 1865 López seemed to be heading for an early defeat. Two generals and an admiral closely identified with the Liberals led the Brazilian troops. But the defeat at Curupaití (September 1866) changed everything. The need for a strongly unified Brazilian command became ever more evident. Meanwhile, the Progressive cabinet in Rio split over the old issue of repealing the 1841 law; as a result, in August 1866 Zacarias once again became prime minister.

At this time Zacarias demonstrated genuine political skill by winning over Caxias's support while not losing that of the Liberals. He offered the Liberals a stunningly radical proposal: major steps toward the emancipation of the slaves. In the Speech from the Throne which Zacarias drafted for delivery in May 1867 he had the emperor announce that measures towards this end would be taken up as soon as the fighting ended. Considerations other than political tactics led in the same direction. Some leaders feared British pressure for the abolition of slavery combined with a slave uprising.[16] Sectors of the new coffee elite, especially the planters of São Paulo, increasingly doubted whether slaves could continue to supply their labour needs. And there were some signs of growing urban middle class opposition to slavery. By moving toward emancipation, Zacarias won the firm support of many Liberals despite his appointment of Caxias as sole commander of Brazil's military efforts. Once Caxias finally got things in order on the war front and began winning battles in early 1868, however, the Conservatives felt they should be the main beneficiaries. They intrigued to bring about a rift between Caxias and the prime minister. Although their efforts proved unsuccessful at first, Zacarias did resign in the middle of the year over the emperor's choice, on the advice of the Council of State, of a by now notably anti-Liberal Inhomirim as senator. Both contemporaries and later commentators have disagreed, however, as to the motives behind

---

[16] The British minister to Brazil in the early 1860s, William Christie, had stridently called on Brazil to undertake a series of measures leading to the final end of slavery. In 1863 he ordered the seizure by British ships of several Brazilian vessels outside the port of Rio de Janeiro, ostensibly as reprisals for Brazil's failure to comply with some of his minor demands, but evidently to suggest British willingness to use force in the matter of slavery. The lesson was not lost on the Brazilian government. In 1867, for instance, José Antonio Pimenta Bueno, visconde de São Vicente, in submitting a proposal to the Council of State to free the children of slave mothers, indicated the need to thus avoid 'British pressure'. See Richard Graham, 'Os fundamentos da ruptura de relações diplomáticas entre o Brasil e a Grã-Bretanha em 1863: "A questão Christie"', *Revista de História*, 24: 49 and 50 (1962), 117–38, 379–402; and Richard Graham, 'Causes for the abolition of Negro slavery in Brazil: an interpretive essay,' *Hispanic American Historical Review*, 46/2 (1966), 123–37.

his resignation. For Joaquim Nabuco, the historian, the choice of Inhomirim as senator merely provided a pretext for the resignation of Zacarias; the real issue was Caxias's hostility to the cabinet. With the subsequent importance of civil-military relations in Brazil, this interpretation has gained wide currency. But there is much evidence, including the speeches of Zacarias himself, to support the view that Zacarias resigned because he believed conservative members of the Council of State opposed the speed with which he was moving toward the end of slavery.[17] Even the moderate Zacarias had gone too far too fast; the brakes must be applied. The choice for Zacarias's successor bears out this view.

Zacarias was replaced as prime minister in 1868 by Itaboraí, the arch-conservative *saquarema* coffee planter. Members of the new cabinet included Paulino José Soares de Souza Filho (1834–1901), a son of the visconde de Uruguai, as well as Cotegipe, emerging leader of the Bahian Conservatives, Rio Branco, and the novelist-politician, José de Alencar. The Council of State, having thus thrown its weight behind a Conservative reaction, backed Itaboraí's call for new elections when the Liberal chamber refused to endorse him. The government as usual had no difficulty in securing an overwhelming victory.

In response to these events Progressive-Liberals like Furtado and Zacarias joined their Liberal colleagues in parliament such as Nabuco de Araújo and even radical liberals like Teófilo Ottoni in organizing a Reform Club under the leadership of Nabuco. In May 1869 it issued a manifesto calling for thorough-going reform of the Constitution. They called for the repeal of the law of 1841 which gave the police judicial powers, greater autonomy for the judiciary, an end to the National Guard and to forced recruitment into the army, a limited tenure for senators, reduction of the power of the Council of State and the gradual emancipation of the slaves. Their manifesto nevertheless remained a cautious document despite the bravado of its last words, 'Reform or Revolution!'[18] In November of the same year another group issued a Radical Manifesto which, besides including these goals and others for which Liberals had long struggled, included direct elections and the extension of the suffrage, the election of provincial presidents and local police officials, the end of the emperor's moderative power and the

---

[17] Brazil. Congresso. Senado, *Annaes*, 15 and 18 July, 1870, 94–142.
[18] Américo Brasiliense de Almeida Mello (ed.), *Os programas dos partidos e o 2° império. Primeira parte: exposição de princípios* (São Paulo, 1878), 42.

Council of State, and the immediate abolition of slavery. Among the signatories of this document many went on in December of the following year to sign in Rio de Janeiro the Republican Manifesto calling for the end of the empire.

Once the war with Paraguay ended with the death of Solano López in March 1870 and in the face of mounting criticism of the Itboraí cabinet from a new reform-minded generation of young politicians, intellectuals, businessmen and progressive planters, the more enlightened leaders of the Conservative camp realized the time had come for major concessions in order to avert more serious dissidence. Even Itaboraí accepted a proposal to end public slave auctions. The fear that a Liberal cabinet would sometime use the 1841 law to elect a wholly Liberal parliament persuaded some Conservatives of the advantages of its repeal. The emperor, as always, put his weight behind the cause of reform. After a five-month interim cabinet, visconde do Rio Branco became prime minister in March 1871. His Liberal start in political life, his participation in the *conciliação* cabinet, his experience as a diplomat during the Paraguayan War, all augured well for moderate reform. Few, however, could have been prepared for the series of far-reaching measures which Rio Branco pushed through in quick succession with impressive political skill. He separated police and judicial functions, simultaneously strengthening the tenure of judges and removing from the police commissioners their judicial duties, thus finally undoing the law of 1841. He reduced the powers of the National Guard: henceforth professional police and, when insufficient, the army itself would be used to maintain public order. Most important of all, he persuaded the Council of State to do an about-face and back his effort to push through the Law of Free Birth (1871), granting freedom to all children subsequently born to slave women and setting up a fund for the emancipation of adults. While not dispossessing planters of their present property, he thus attempted to persuade slaves that continued obedience could win freedom. By these measures Rio Branco, a Conservative prime minister, against the opposition of the right-wing *saquarema* faction of his own party, satisfied the bulk of the Liberals. By his farsightedness and disinterested statesmanship, he disarmed the critics of the empire, postponing more far-reaching change to the end of the next decade. Once again Brazilian political leaders had searched for – and found – a middle position so essential to the maintenance of order in a hierarchical yet potentially unstable social system based on slavery.

Much of the intellectual energy of these two decades centred on the nature of the state and the correct exercise of political power. In a country where a successful career as lawyer or judge fulfilled the aspirations of so many literate men, the jurist headed the intellectual elite. Visconde de Uruguai himself, retiring from political and diplomatic activity in 1857, turned his attention to preparing two magisterial studies of Brazilian jurisprudence: *Ensaio sobre o direito administrativo* (1862) and *Estudos práticos sobre a administração das províncias no Brasil* (1865). His powerful defence of the conservative viewpoint doubtless influenced many subsequent generations of law-school students, bureaucrats and politicians. Somewhat more emphasis on individual freedom characterized the treatise on public law and the Brazilian constitution published in 1857 by José Antonio Pimenta Bueno, marquês de São Vicente (1803–78), but he also asserted the essential virtue of the Brazilian system of government. Both authors grasped the importance of the effort to construct a stable regime accomplished in Brazil by the middle of the century, and both merely advocated minor refinements. Much the same was true of *Escravidão no Brasil: ensaio histórico, jurídico, social*, Agostinho Marques Perdigão Malheiro's study of the laws of slavery, published in 1866 and 1867.

The creation of a new civil code to replace the one inherited from Portugal preoccupied a succession of jurists. Candido Mendes de Almeida (1818–81), who in 1870 published his massive and erudite edition of the existing Philippine Code (in force since 1603), provided the basis – principally through the footnotes referring to alterations worked by law and custom – for the elaboration of a new code. The Liberal Nabuco de Araújo set to work on a draft. Although not complete at the time of his death in 1879 his version remained the basis of discussion until the enactment of a new code in 1916.

The constitutional system also suffered a number of brilliant attacks, most effectively from the pen of Zacarias in 1860 in his pamphlet-book on the nature and limits of the moderative power. Rising above political party, the Liberal Aureliano Cândido Tavares Bastos (1839–75) addressed many major issues, above all regionalism; he laid the groundwork for the eventual emergence of federalism as a major force in Brazilian political life. Despite their reform efforts, however, Zacarias, Tavares Bastos and others like them continued to accept the essential structure of the imperial system even as they tried to modify it.

Essentially moderates, they sought a consensus within the ruling class in order to preserve a slave-based society.

The stability which so concerned both Conservatives and Liberals mainly sprang not from political institutions, however, but from social relationships based upon the exchange of loyal service for protection and favours. As surely as Pedro II enacted the part of father for the entire nation, so did *senhores de engenho*, coffee *fazendeiros*, or industrialists, for their workers. In turn, real fathers retained clear authority over wives and children, as they did over other relatives, servants, *agregados* and slaves. And in every case, benevolent care gloved outright force. In political life elaborate systems of patronage made it possible to grant benefits – especially authority over others – to those who steadfastly supported the existing structure. Favours not only won compliance from those expected to obey, but assuaged the sensibilities of those charged with enforcement. The expansion of foreign trade based on coffee exports in this period increased the resources available to the state and enabled it truly to fulfil a paternal role. Thus, the state simultaneously maintained its legitimacy and that of the hierarchical social order. For many Brazilians who still prize social hierarchy these two decades (1850–70) represent a golden age in which government was both liberal and stable.

4

1870–1889

In Brazil, as in many other Latin American countries, the 1870s and 1880s were a period of reform and commitment to change. Intellectuals, professional men, military officers – urban people though often with rural roots – joined associations for the abolition of slavery and organizations for the promotion of mass European immigration, campaigned in favour of federalism and provincial autonomy, argued for the separation of church and state, participated in campaigns for electoral reform, and supported the Republican party. Nor were representatives of the agrarian and mercantile dominant class, known for its conservatism, completely immune to progressive ideas. In the decade before 1870 staunch members of the Conservative party had broken away from their traditional loyalties and joined the Liberal party, while many devoted Liberals left their party to create the Republican party in 1870. Intellectuals also criticized traditional philosophy, condemned romantic literary conventions, and ridiculed the system of education; they cultivated positivist and evolutionist ideas, adopted new forms of expression, and proposed a new system of education more orientated towards science and technology; they repudiated what they perceived as empty liberal rhetoric, criticized the ruling classes, and made 'the people' their subject matter.

By the beginning of the 1890s, reformers could pride themselves on having achieved many of their aims. An electoral reform had been implemented in 1881. Parliament had abolished slavery in 1888. Large numbers of European immigrants had begun to enter the country. And in 1889, a military coup had overthrown the monarchy. The new republican regime adopted a federal system and extended the suffrage. The powers of the church and state were separated. Yet what was perceived as a success by some people seemed a failure to others. Many of those who had struggled to create a new political system soon expressed their disappointment. Rural oligarchies continued to control government, state and federal. And the great majority of the Brazilian population, free poor, ex-slave – and immigrant – continued to be exploited as it always had been. After two decades of reform the country did not seem fundamentally to have changed.

Some historians have attributed the reforms of the late nineteenth century to the influence of foreign ideas on Brazilian society. Abolitionism, social Darwinism, Spencerism, and positivism – they say – all led educated Brazilians to question existing institutions and to concern themselves with changing them. Other historians have seen the reforms as the product of a generational conflict, often described as a conflict between urban and rural groups, or between modern and traditional mores. Young men graduating from professional schools and accustomed to the urban style of living became critical of institutions created by the agrarian elites, from which many of them were descended.[1] The conflict between the rural oligarch (*o patriarca*) and his professional son (*o bacharel*) has even been interpreted in psychoanalytical terms.[2] But the interpretation that has found most favour in recent years relates the reforms to changes in Brazil's economic and social structure during the nineteenth century, and to the emergence of an urban bourgeoisie that allied itself with the most progressive segments of the rural oligarchies in order to fight the traditional elites.

These competing approaches, which have been seen as alternatives, are in fact quite compatible and even complementary. But they are not in themselves sufficient to account for the timing and content of reforms and they raise problems that they cannot solve. There is no doubt, for example, that Brazilian reformers quoted European authors to support their opinions. However, one cannot assume that they had those opinions *because* they had read European authors. In fact, the opposite might be true. It might be more correct to say that their desire to change society in certain ways predisposed them to prefer some European authors to others. Otherwise, how can we explain their preference for Comte over Marx or for Spencer over Fourier? And how can we account for the fact that abolitionist ideas became popular in Brazil only in the

---

[1] See, for example, Gilberto Freyre's classic *Sobrados e mucambos: decadência do patriarcado rural e desenvolvimento urbano* (2nd edn, 3 vols., Rio de Janeiro, 1951).
[2] Luís Martins, *O patriarca e o bacharel* (São Paulo, 1953).

second half of the century although slavery had been condemned in Europe since the Enlightenment?

If we cannot explain the reforms by mere reference to external influences, equally insufficient is the interpretation that opposes urban to rural groups or professional men to landowners, considering one the vanguard of progress and the other the bulwark of tradition. In fact, some of the most eloquent spokesmen for the rural oligarchies and leaders of the Conservative party were lawyers, bureaucrats, and medical doctors – men deeply rooted in the urban environment. And, if in most provinces the Republican party found followers mainly among professional groups, the core of the party in São Paulo was made up of coffee planters.

But even if we can demonstrate that most reformers were from the urban middle classes, we still have to explain why they became alienated from the regime. Similarly, if we can show that most of the militant reformers belonged to the generation born in the second half of the century and were in their thirties or early forties at the time of the proclamation of the Republic, we still have to explain why they, and not the generation before them, launched such a systematic attack against traditional institutions.

In general, we can say that reform in Brazil, as in other Latin American countries, was a response to the new economic and social realities that resulted from capitalist development not only as a world phenomenon but in its specifically Brazilian manifestations. Here, as elsewhere, economic development (urbanization, immigration, improvements in transportation, early manufacturing industry and capital accumulation) provoked social dislocations: the emergence of new social groups and the decline of traditional elites. To the new groups, the institutions created after Brazil's independence from Portugal in 1822 and the political hegemony of traditional landed and commercial oligarchies had become anachronistic obstacles to progress by the 1870s and 1880s.

However, to recognize that economic and social change led to demands for institutional change is not sufficient to explain why the traditional oligarchies were unable to co-opt the new groups or to satisfy their demands. To explain this failure and to understand the purpose and the rhetoric of the reformers, the nature of their demands, and their motives for opposing some institutions rather than others, we ought to look beyond economic change to the prevailing political and cultural institutions they attacked. Before we can explain why the political system created in 1822 became the target of criticism in the 1870s and 1880s, we need to know how the system actually functioned.

During the nineteenth century there were important demographic changes in Brazil. The population grew from 3.8 million in 1822 to a little over 10 million in 1872, and was more than 14 million at the time of the proclamation of the Republic in 1889. Demographic change was greater in some areas than in others, altering the initial distribution of population which had served as the basis for representation. Between 1822 and 1870 the population of the north-east grew at an annual rate of 2 per cent. During the same period, Pará, which benefited from the rubber boom, grew at an annual rate of 3 per cent and São Paulo at 3.5 per cent, mainly as a result of the expansion of coffee plantations. There were also changes in the slave population. Slaves, who constituted more than half of the population in 1822 and 15.8 per cent in 1872, represented a mere 5 per cent in 1888. The slave population diminished in the cities and became concentrated in plantation areas where the economy was expanding. In 1822 almost 70 per cent lived in the sugar-cane areas of the north-east and east. Sixty years later only 35 per cent of the total slave population lived there, while almost 65 per cent were in the coffee provinces of the south.

Immigrants also tended to settle in the south rather than in the north or north-east. Those who arrived between 1872 and 1889 were mainly located in rural areas of São Paulo, Santa Catarina, and Rio Grande do Sul. But many settled in urban centres. Rio de Janeiro had in 1872 a population of 275,000, of which 84,000 were foreign-born. At the same date immigrants represented 12 per cent of the population of Porto Alegre, 11 per cent of Curitiba, and 8 per cent of São Paulo. Their numbers continued to grow. The 1890 census showed that 22 per cent of São Paulo's total population was foreign-born. By that time there were 150,000 foreigners in the country, 70 per cent living in Rio de Janeiro, São Paulo and Minas Gerais, and another 17.6 per cent in Rio Grande do Sul.

A more important phenomenon, however, than either the growth of population or the arrival of immigrants, was capital accumulation due to the extraordinary growth of coffee exports, and to a lesser extent rubber and cacao exports, especially after 1860. Economic growth benefited some provinces more than others, altering their relative economic importance in the national scene. Coffee exports from the centre-south, and from São Paulo above all, increased 341 per cent and coffee prices 91 per cent in the second half of the nineteenth century, while sugar exports from the north-east rose only 33 per cent and sugar prices declined 11 per cent. Despite a steady rise of imports, Brazil had a considerable surplus on its balance of trade after 1861. But profit remittance, mainly to British companies which invested heavily in the most profitable sectors of the economy, interest payments on repeated British loans to finance government expenditure which tended to rise more rapidly than government revenue (in the late decades of the Empire interest payments on the foreign debt consumed on average 40 per cent of the surplus on the balance of trade), and manipulation of the rate of exchange by the British all limited local capital accumulation. Moreover, capital tended to accumulate in the hands of coffee planters and merchants connected with exports and imports. From these groups came part of the capital invested in railways, banks and industries. Only secondarily did capital accumulate in the hands of groups exclusively orientated towards the internal market. And in spite of its expansion the internal market continued to be limited. This peculiar way in which capital accumulation took place in Brazil – as a result not only of its position in the international market, its subordination to foreign markets and foreign capital, but also of decisions made by the Brazilian ruling classes – explains both the nature and the limitations of the changes that occurred in the society during the second half of the century, and to a certain point defines the limits of Brazilian reformism.

One of the consequences of this type of economic growth was that capital accumulation favoured mainly the urban centres and the rural areas related to the import–export sectors of the economy. The city of Rio almost doubled its population between 1872 and 1890. Between 1872 and 1886 the city of São Paulo grew at a rate of 5 per cent a year and from 1886 to 1890 its annual growth was 8 per cent. The population of the city of Salvador went from 129,000 in 1872 to 174,000 in 1890.

Concentration of capital, foreign and local, made it possible to improve urban facilities. Water, sewage, and gas companies, the paving of the streets, and new systems of urban transportation changed life in the big cities. Between 1868 and 1888 streetcars were introduced in Recife, Salvador, Rio de Janeiro, São Luís, São Paulo, and Campinas. In the 1870s a telegraph line linked Brazil to Europe, and in the following years most Brazilian cities were linked to each other. In 1861, 62,233 telegrams were sent. This number increased to 390,277 in 1885–6. In the 1880s, São Paulo, Salvador, Rio de Janeiro and Campinas had telephone services. In 1887 seven lines of streetcars carried a million and a half passengers in São Paulo.

The number of schools also increased in the cities, and illiteracy diminished. But it continued to be high in rural areas. In 1835 the literacy rate in the city of São Paulo was about 5 per cent. It was 42 per cent in 1882. At that time only 29 per cent of the rural population was literate. Journals and newspapers, artistic and cultural associations, inns, theatres, cafés and shops mushroomed, and the big cities acquired a more cosmopolitan atmosphere. In the rich quarters traditional houses built of *taipa* (lath and plaster) were gradually replaced by brick houses of European style. Inside, the heavy rosewood colonial furniture gave place to light English mahogany furniture. Slave quarters gradually disappeared. The free labourers who replaced slaves packed into tenement houses in the centre of the cities or lived in little houses on the outskirts. The streets were no longer the exclusive territory of men, slaves and the lower classes. Upper- and middle-class women were seen with more frequency in the central streets, and men and women were more often together in public places. There were more schools and jobs open to women than before. They could work as teachers, seamstresses, and clerks. In the last decades of the Empire mores were changing but, most important, there were new opportunities for investment, employment, social mobility and political mobilization.

All this, however, happened mainly in the port cities. In the interior only a few towns that functioned as important commercial centres – such as São Paulo, Campinas and Pelotas – developed. Plantation owners brought to the rural areas some progress. They modernized their plantation houses and gardens and promoted cultural and artistic associations in the towns of the backlands. But with those exceptions the contrast between the port cities and the rural areas continued to be striking. Being products more of the expansion of international trade than of the growth of an internal market, Brazilian cities, even more than cities in other parts of the continent, were primarily orientated towards Europe; they played a relatively unimportant role in the transformation of the interior of Brazil.

Railways, for the most part built with foreign capital, began to replace traditional systems of transportation on muleback, oxcarts and barges.

Between 1854 and 1872, 933.3 kilometres of tracks were built; between 1873 and 1889, 8,000 kilometres were added; and at the end of the Empire there were 15,000 kilometres under construction. In some regions railways did create better conditions for the integration of the internal market. However, they were built primarily to facilitate the flow of Brazilian products to the international market and for this reason tended to concentrate in the coffee and sugar areas and were orientated towards the port cities.

The improvement in the means of transportation, the growth of the internal market, capital accumulation, and most of all higher import taxes, which the government was forced to adopt to increase its revenues, all favoured the development of industries. Between 1875 and 1890 the number of factories grew from 175 to more than 600. In 1880 there were 18,100 people registered as industrial workers; ten years later there were about 50,000. Factories producing consumer goods – textiles, beer, cigarettes, soaps, candles, matches, hats – as well as tanneries, foundries, timber mills, and paper and glass factories were concentrated in the urban centres of Minas Gerais, Rio de Janeiro, São Paulo and Rio Grande do Sul, where the availability of labour and capital, an infrastructure of credit and transportation, and the existence of a relatively dependable market created favourable conditions. The Paraguayan War stimulated the manufacture of nautical, optical, and chemical products. By the 1880s the industrialists – although still a small number – felt strong enough to found the Industrial Association in Rio de Janeiro with the purpose of defending their interests. They were among many interest groups that had emerged on the political scene as a consequence of changes occurring in Brazil in the second half of the century. Economic and social change made it increasingly difficult for the political elites to run the nation according to traditional rules, and in the last decades of the century the imperial regime became the target of criticism from many groups in society.

Economic growth generated imbalances between economic and political power. Economic diversification created conflicts of interest between provinces whose economy was mainly orientated to the internal market and provinces mainly orientated to the external market, provinces still dependent on slave labour and provinces where slavery was not an issue any more. Provinces competed for government subsidies and credit. And the pressure to expand the infrastructure made provinces more aware of their dependence on the central government. The situation was complicated by conflicts within each province between planters who modernized their methods of production and those who continued to employ traditional methods. Sugar production underwent a fundamental transformation. In 1857, 66 per cent of the sugar mills in Pernambuco were still moved by animal power, 31 per cent by water, and only 2 per cent by steam. But after 1870 the number of steam mills grew rapidly, reaching 21.5 per cent in 1881. Vacuum pans, centrifugals, and other improvements in the furnaces were introduced. Coffee processing was also improved with the use of driers, hullers, and threshers. All this led to a great increase in productivity. Together with changes in the system of processing there were also changes in the system of labour, with the number of free labourers increasing in some areas while others continued to resort to slaves. Since not all plantation owners had capital enough to modernize their plantations, many had to hold on to traditional practices. They often clashed in the legislature with the representatives of the more productive areas in matters concerning land and labour policies, the routeing of railways, and government subsidies. Some wanted to replace slaves by coolies, others preferred European to Chinese immigrants. Some believed that the government should subsidize immigration and that immigrants should not have access to the land, so they would work on plantations. Others wanted to attract spontaneous immigration by giving them land.

Economic growth and diversification not only generated conflicts within agrarian groups, it created interest groups linked to the railways, industries, banks, insurance, immigration companies, and public utilities. These groups had their own claims, and their interests did not always coincide with the interests of those who controlled the central government. The industrialists, for example, demanded protectionist tariffs and government support, but at the same time they resented political interference and government control. The manifesto issued in 1881 by the newly created Industrial Association accused the government of ignoring the industrialists' efforts and of creating obstacles to their enterprises. It charged the government with favouring coffee planters by adopting a free trade policy that hampered industrial development. The manifesto also criticized the education the ruling classes received in the law schools, which made the leaders of the country men of letters rather than men of science. Finally, it complained about the lack of representation of the 'productive classes' in parliament.[3]

[3] 'Manifesto da Associação Industrial', *Temas*, 1 (1977), 91–100.

Industrialists had other reasons to be discontented. The frequent crises that struck the capitalist world in the nineteenth century hurt Brazilian businessmen. When banks in London and New York withdrew credit, and prices of export products fell in the international market, bankruptcies followed. In 1857, 1864, and 1873 important enterprises had to be liquidated, causing panic in the financial market and overall discontent, often translated into criticism against government economic policies.

Businessmen and entrepreneurs were not the only groups to resent the political elites, to criticize the ruling classes, and to hope for change. The urban poor suffered with the increase in prices of foodstuffs, and they often saw government policies as responsible for their misfortunes. The growing number of wage labourers in the cities raised new questions and created problems of social control, which an elite habituated to disciplined slaves still did not know how to deal with. The *revolta dos vintens* (penny riot), which caused the fall of a cabinet, was perhaps the most important of the period. It occurred on 1 January 1880 in Rio when the crowd, exasperated by an increase in the price of streetcar tickets, confronted the police, and after three days of rioting was violently repressed.

Artisans and workers who resented competition from foreign products often protested against government policies and demanded protection for national products. Their manifestos sometimes seemed to echo the demands of the industrialists. In 1885, for example, in a letter addressed to the emperor, the Corpo Coletivo União Operária demanded exemption from import taxes on industrial machinery, exemption from property taxes on factories, abolition of privileges and monopolies granted to certain trades, tariffs on foreign manufactures, and credit facilities.[4] But at the same time a rhetoric of class struggle started emerging with more frequency in newspapers addressed to the workers. The number of workers' organizations increased in the last decade of the Empire and the first socialist groups appeared. In the 1880s occasional workers' demonstrations changed the pace of life in the cities.

The new urban masses were not only a source of trouble and concern, they constituted a potential electorate. For the first time politicians addressed themselves to the masses in public places. The first group to do it systematically were the abolitionists. Men like Lopes Trovão (one of the few socialists of the time) left the conference rooms and the salons to talk

[4] In Edgard Carone, *Movimento operário no Brasil (1877–1944)* (São Paulo, 1979), 204–10.

to the people in the streets. Political mores were changing. An increasing number of women became involved in abolitionist associations. Women's journals multiplied and the first feminist press appeared, demanding access to professional schools for women.

Economic change in the countryside also caused profound social dislocations, which echoed in the political arena. With the expansion of the internal market and improvements in the means of transportation, populations traditionally devoted mainly to subsistence started producing more for the market. This transition was sometimes furthered by the imposition of taxes designed to provide the government with the resources necessary to develop the economic infrastructure. In the backlands, capital accumulation in the hands of merchants and a few artisans and small farmers accentuated social inequality, breaking traditional kinships and forms of accommodation and generating profound social malaise often expressed in popular rebellions.

A good example of this process was the muckers rebellion, which occurred in Rio Grande do Sul between 1868 and 1874. During these years, the traditionally peaceful German communities of São Leopoldo were agitated by a messianic movement that ended in a violent confrontation between the rebels and the local authorities. The rebels, known as muckers, condemned money and trade and rejected the new patterns of social mobility, prestige and class relations based on money. They accused the rich of obscurantism and tried to invert the social patterns by organizing a group ruled by principles of fraternity and equality. Muckers refused to vote and left schools and churches to create their own religion, a religion without a church, valuing direct communication with God. The movement was repressed by the authorities but made the political elites aware of the dangers of a popular rebellion.

About the same time the muckers were causing trouble in the south, the north-east backlands were swept by uprisings known as *quebra quilos* because the rebels protested against the metric system. But there was more to it than just the *quilos*. Poor farmers refused to accept the *quilos*, the draft, and the new taxes imposed by the government. Angry men and women invaded the city halls and notaries, destroyed tax and draft lists, ransacked stores, and terrorized foreign merchants. The government suspected that behind the rebels were the priests who opposed the government because of its protection of the freemasons, condemned by the Pope. But the slogan 'Down with the Masons' shouted by the rioters had more to do with their hostility to the ruling classes than with their loyalty toward the clergy. Both *quebra quilos* and muckers expressed the frustrations caused by increasing social inequalities and exploitation and the disruption of traditional ways of living.

THE POLITICAL SYSTEM OF THE EMPIRE

The political system created at the time of Independence reflected the needs of an elite of landowners and merchants and their clientele. They shared an interest in the maintenance of traditional structures of production based on slave labour and the export of colonial staples to the international market. Most of all, they intended to govern the country without taking any account of the mass of the population, whom they feared and despised. The system was extremely centralized, oligarchical, and unrepresentative. It was not flexible enough to adjust to the changes in the economic and social structure during the second half of the nineteenth century.

Under the constitution of 1824 the chief executive, the emperor, was responsible for the appointment and promotion of personnel in the civil and military bureaucracy. The emperor also implemented the legislation approved by the parliament, and had the final word on the distribution of resources among the different administrative branches. One of the most important responsibilities of the executive was to give or deny permission for the implementation of papal bulls in the country. The emperor also had the power to appoint bishops and to provide ecclesiastical benefices. In addition to his powers as the chief executive, the emperor enjoyed others as a consequence of the Moderating Power, an invention of the French publicist Benjamin Constant that had appealed to those who had drafted the constitution. Among these additional prerogatives he had the freedom to choose and dismiss his prime minister independent of the parliament, to adjourn, prorogue, or dismiss the Chamber of Deputies, and to call for new elections. This meant that if the Chamber denied confidence to a cabinet the emperor could keep the Cabinet and dismiss the Chamber, calling for new elections. He also had the right to appoint the members of the Council of State and to choose each senator from among the three candidates who received the most votes in any senatorial election. It would seem that the constitution had given almost absolute power to the emperor, and in fact this was a common opinion during the First and Second Empires. The constitution, however, had also limited his power by providing that his decisions be submitted first to the Council of State for discussion. One could argue that since the councillors were chosen by the emperor they would tend to agree with him, and even if they happened to disagree they did not have the power to veto his decisions. Yet gratitude was not necessarily a synonym for subservience. The councillors were appointed for life and to a point could be independent of the emperor.

When one looks beyond the words of the constitution to actual practice it becomes evident that, contrary to what his critics said, Pedro II – both by conviction and by temperament – never imposed his will on issues of national importance. In fact, pressured by the councillors, the emperor often acted against his own inclinations. The oligarchies, not the emperor, ruled the country. But the official position the emperor occupied in the political arena focused on him all hopes and resentments. If the leading senatorial candidate was passed over by the emperor in favour of a candidate who was second or third on the list, the unsuccessful candidate expressed his disappointment by attacking the Moderating Power. If the emperor chose a senator from the opposition, he was criticized by the party in power, and if he chose one from the party in power, he was attacked by the opposition. Thus the right to appoint senators and councillors, originally intended to increase his powers, weakened his position in the long run. The same is true of his right to intervene in parliament. Between 1840 and 1889 the emperor dissolved the Chamber eleven times. On eight of these occasions his intervention caused an inversion of the political situation: Liberals were replaced by Conservatives or vice versa. Each time, those forced to step out protested loudly against the abuses of the Moderating Power.

During the 1850s and early 1860s, the period known as the Conciliation, these crises did not have much impact because there was a relative degree of consensus among the elites, with Liberals and Conservatives included in the same Cabinets. But with the growing conflicts of interest resulting from economic and social changes the Conciliation was broken. Liberals and Conservatives competed for power on different platforms, and within each party members representing different and often conflicting interests disagreed on important political issues. As a consequence, not only were Cabinets unstable, but the emperor's intervention became particularly relevant and provoked stronger reactions. The frequent use of the royal prerogative of dissolving the Chamber and calling for elections undermined the prestige of both the emperor and the monarchical system.

The political process was vitiated by electoral fraud, which allowed a Cabinet to manipulate elections in favour of its own party. Since elections did not mean real consultation with the nation, the emperor's interventions were seen as arbitrary and illegitimate gestures intended to force political turnover. Electoral fraud was facilitated by the small size of the electorate. Income qualifications and the system of indirect elections reduced the number of electors to a small percentage of the total population. Only males over 25 (with the exception of military officers and married men over 21) with an annual income of 100 milréis could be voters and only those with an income of 200 milréis could be electors. All women, slaves, and servants (with a few exceptions such as accountants, farm administrators, and chief clerks) were excluded from the electorate. In 1872 the number of electors in the country was approximately 200,000 in a total population of 10,000,000. Such a small electorate could be easily manipulated.

During elections the Cabinets resorted to all sorts of manoeuvres to silence the opposition. They replaced provincial presidents and functionaries loyal to the opposition with others who gave their allegiance to the government. They created parishes where they had friends and abolished them where they had enemies. They harassed rank and file opposition voters, threatening them with conscription, and rewarded those who supported the Cabinet with jobs, promotions, and sinecures. Sometimes they went as far as to mobilize the National Guard to intimidate the opposition by forcing its voters to stay home on election day.

Reforms intended to eliminate electoral fraud and to guarantee representation of the opposition were implemented in 1842, 1855, and 1860, but they all failed. None of those reforms attacked the roots of the problem: the monopoly of land by a minority on which most of the rural population depended, the marginalization of large segments of the population from the productive sectors of the economy, and the lack of institutions that could guarantee the independence of the electors and mediate between them and the government. Most of all, the electoral reforms did not touch the sources of patronage that allowed a minority to control the nation.

This control of the electorate by a minority laid the foundation of a strong oligarchy, which perpetuated itself by blocking from access to power all those who were not willing to accommodate to the rules of patronage. The appointment of councillors of state and senators for life contributed to consolidating this oligarchy. A man who reached the Senate at the age of 40 (the minimum age required by law) could remain there for three or four decades. Some appointed in the middle of the century were still in the Senate when the monarchy was overthrown, almost 40 years later. These, of course, were exceptions. On the average the Senate was renewed every fifteen years. But for members of the Chamber who aspired to a position in the Senate this must have seemed a long time to wait.

Senators constituted a powerful group which monopolized important positions in the government. The permanent members of the Council of State were all recruited in the Senate. And with the exception of one, all cabinet presidents during the Empire were senators. Many senators became presidents of provinces and more than 40 per cent of the senators had titles of nobility.

The men who had created these tenured bodies had hoped that appointment for life – by placing senators and councillors above electoral struggles – would make them immune to political passions. What they had not predicted was that, with time, those bodies would lack the flexibility necessary to respond to changes occurring in society. This explains why abolition of tenure for senators and dissolution of the Council of State or reduction of its jurisdiction were frequent demands in the platforms of the reformers.

Another source of discontent was the lack of balance between economic and political power which became apparent in the final years of the Empire. Originally the number of representatives per province was more or less proportional to the total population (including slaves), and demographic concentration corresponded to economic importance and political power. Economic development and demographic growth broke this correspondence and at the end of the Empire the new economic elites, which were concentrated in a few thriving provinces, felt that their provinces were underrepresented. From the beginning Minas Gerais, the old gold mining area and the most populated of the provinces, had the largest delegation, with twenty representatives. São Paulo had nine, Ceará and Rio de Janeiro eight each. At the end of the Empire Minas continued to have the largest number of representatives and most of the provinces had increased their representation, with the exception of São Paulo, despite the fact that coffee production had made it the richest province in the country. Taking into account provincial resources, São Paulo, Pará, and Rio Grande do Sul were clearly underrepresented at the end of the Empire.

The political preponderance of some provinces was also apparent in the Senate and in the Council of State, where most members were from Rio de Janeiro, Bahia, Minas, and Pernambuco. Moreover, senators did not have to be native to a province or have residence there to represent it. Rio Branco, a native of Bahia, represented Mato Grosso in the Senate. Sales Tôrres Homem, a native of Rio de Janeiro, represented Rio Grande do Sul. Alfredo de Taunay, also from Rio, represented Santa Catarina. Four provinces had a representation in the Senate almost identical to all the other provinces together, and also monopolized Cabinet positions. Between 1847, when the position of president of the Cabinet, or prime minister, was created, and the end of the Empire there were 30 prime ministers; eleven were from Bahia, five from Minas Gerais, five from Pernambuco, four from Rio de Janeiro, two from São Paulo, two from Piauí, and one from Alagoas. From 1840 to 1889 the majority of the cabinet members were from Bahia (57), followed by Rio de Janeiro (47), Minas (35), and Pernambuco (29). These four provinces monopolized the central government, while other provinces that developed in the last decades of the Empire such as São Paulo, Pará, and Rio Grande do Sul had a relatively small representation in the government and grew increasingly dissatisfied with their lack of political power.

Representation was not a serious problem until economic development generated contradictory needs and different regional elites no longer agreed about such things as tariffs, labour and land policies, and government subsidies. The monopoly of power by an oligarchy that did not represent adequately the interests of the most developed areas of the country gave rise to bitter criticism.

The situation would not have become so critical if the provinces had enjoyed more autonomy and if the central government had not exerted so much control over the nation. But the centralization of the political system allowed a small group of politicians, many of whom were appointed for life, to intervene in several different aspects of the nation's life.

The provinces were economically dependent on the central government. Figures for 1868 show that this received 80 per cent of all revenues while the provinces received only 16.7 per cent and the municipalities 2.5 per cent. Provincial presidents were appointed by the central government. When a Liberal replaced a Conservative Cabinet, or vice versa, the new Cabinet immediately replaced all provincial presidents with others more compatible with the new political situation. This practice facilitated relations between the central and the provincial governments but could cause difficulties at the local level. A provincial president often came from outside the province. His term was usually not long enough to allow him to create strong ties, and he moved from one province to another. José Antônio Saraiva, for example, was successively president of the provinces of Piauí, Pernambuco, Alagoas, and São Paulo. João Lins de Sinimbu presided over Alagoas, Sergipe, and Rio Grande do Sul. The provincial presidents had great powers. Many important provincial bureaucrats, the police chiefs, the judges, the head officer of the National Guard, and the army commander depended on him for their appointments. This indirectly gave the central government great control over the provinces. As long as the interests of the politicians who controlled the central government and the regional elites coincided, the system functioned without serious tensions, but when economic and social change generated contradictory or competitive interests between provinces, the situation became strained. The dominant groups in Pará and Pernambuco as well as São Paulo and Rio Grande do Sul complained in the last years of the Empire that the central government did not do enough to satisfy their needs. One answer seemed to be greater provincial autonomy; many thus became sympathetic to federalism.

Another source of conflict in the last decades of the Empire was political interference in the army. The military resented their subordination to provincial presidents and demanded the creation of an independent military hierarchy directly subordinated to the ministry of war. They also resented the fact that promotions to and within the higher echelons of the military depended on the emperor and the Council of State. To those officers who did not have personal links with politicians – and their number was growing in the second half of the nineteenth century – promotion might have seemed an unrealistic dream. The politicians' use of conscription to threaten the opposition during elections was another source of complaint among army officers, as were the draft deferments politicians distributed to their clientele. While army officers were primarily recruited among the upper classes alienation from the system was not a serious problem, but with the democratization of the army, the number who felt victimized by the system in one way or the other increased and the situation became more tense.

After the wars against Argentina in the 1850s and Paraguay in the 1860s, the army became not only more democratic but more cohesive and developed an esprit de corps. Personal conflicts between officers and politicians were then translated into conflicts between the army and civilians. The wars also showed that the Brazilian army was ill-equipped and disorganized. Officers blamed the government for their failures, and when a group of officers decided in the 1870s and 1880s to improve the conditions of the army, they identified political influence as a main obstacle to their goals and became increasingly critical of the political institutions and of the political elites.

Priests committed to the new aggressive line adopted by Pius IX shared some of those feelings. The constitution of 1824 had made Catholicism a state religion, but at the same time the church remained under the control of the state. The government was entitled to intervene in minute details of church life such as the creation or closure of parishes, priests' salaries, and the adoption of textbooks in seminaries. Larger issues, such as the implementation of papal bulls or the recommendation of bishops to the Pope, had been also left to the discretion of the government. During the Empire all those decisions, which intimately affected the life of the church, were made by politicians, and often for political reasons. The church like other institutions was tied to the state and depended on political patronage. Reformist priests devoted to a stricter religious discipline resented the politicians' meddling in affairs of the church. This led to a conflict between church and state in the 1870s.

The central government not only interfered in the army and the church, it also played a major role in the economy. It legislated on import and export tariffs, supervised the distribution of unoccupied lands, formulated labour and immigration policies, and negotiated loans. It controlled banks, railways, and stock companies. No liability company could be created in the country without the permission of the Council of State. The government was not only the regulator but also the protector of national and foreign enterprises, authorizing or prohibiting, providing subsidies, guaranteeing interests, establishing priorities, granting tax exemptions. State patronage, or in other words the patronage of politicians, could determine the success or failure of many initiatives. To a significant degree entrepreneurs were at the mercy of politicians. This system could function without many problems as long as there were relatively few companies, and entrepreneurs either belonged to the elites or could easily find patrons through personal connections. But the system of patronage became more inefficient when business ventures multiplied. Thus it is not surprising that toward the end of the century there was growing condemnation of state intervention in the economy – and, by extension, oligarchical power and the institutions which supported it. In fact, most entrepreneurs, such as barão de Mauá, Brazil's most outstanding railway builder and industrialist of the nineteenth century, could not have survived without government support. Their success depended on tariffs, government contracts, government concessions, government credit and subsidies, and even sometimes on government diplomacy. Capitalism in Brazil developed within the web of patronage and the tension between the patronage system and the free enterprise ideas increasingly asserted by business did not disappear with the Empire.

Those in control of the central government were reluctant to give up the patronage system because it enabled them to dominate the regional elites and to keep a tight control over the army, the church, and economic enterprises. Patronage was their main source of power and political prestige. As a consequence of this practice politicians in Brazil were seen not only as representatives, but as benefactors, their political power depending on their capacity to distribute favours.

For the same reasons the oligarchies were unwilling to create a civil service system, which would have emancipated the bureaucracy from political patronage, as the emperor himself recommended. The creation of a permanent body of bureaucrats, appointed according to criteria of merit and talent, would take away from politicians one of their main sources of favours. The criteria that prevailed in the recruitment of the bureaucracy were personal friendship and party loyalty. Political party turnover always resulted in disruptive bureaucratic turnover. Bureaucrats lost their jobs overnight when their party suffered defeat. Persecution of the political adversary was the norm in the bureaucracy. One politician who was appointed provincial president records in his memoirs that local party leaders expected him to remove elementary school teachers to distant localities to punish their husbands for having supported the opposition.[5] It is easy to imagine the hostility and resentment of those who saw their careers suddenly interrupted by the intervention of powerful political leaders. Men totally dependent on political patronage would come in time to hate a system that made their lives so insecure and would dream of a system that would reward merit and competence.

But patronage, not talent, continued to be the prerequisite of success.

[5] Alfredo d'Escragnolle Taunay, *Memórias* (Rio de Janeiro, 1960), 416.

The free play of the market was not enough to guarantee social mobility. Behind every 'self-made man' there was always a sponsor. The proverb, still valid in Brazil today, that 'one who does not have a godfather dies a pagan' describes well the situation during the Empire. Politicians did not succeed in their careers, functionaries did not occupy public offices, writers did not become famous, generals were not promoted, bishops were not appointed, enterprises were not organized without the help of a patron.

The careers of most politicians of the Empire show that it was not his programme that recommended a candidate to the electorate but his kinship and his associations with powerful figures. The political career of a young man was a family decision. His political options were decided *a priori* by his family. And political struggle was, above all, struggle between factions under the leadership of prestigious families. Whether they came from the landowner elite, like the barão do Cotegipe, who owned a sugar plantation in Bahia, or from a family of professionals like Paulino José Soares de Sousa, the visconde de Uruguai, whose father was a medical doctor and who was himself a lawyer but who married into a family of politicians and landowners in Rio de Janeiro, politicians often represented in the Chamber, the Senate, or the Council of State the interests of plantation owners and merchants to whom they were tied by links of patronage and clientele.

This system of alliances and bargains and the manipulation of the electorate favoured the creation of dynasties of politicians: the Ferreira Franças, the Nabuco de Araújos, the Cavalcanti de Albuquerques, the Soares de Sousas. Fathers promoted their sons, uncles their nephews, and relatives and friends supported one another. Writing about the Cavalcantis, owners of a third of the sugar mills in the province of Pernambuco, Joaquim Nabuco said that they had the influence that a large, rich, and well-established family whose members always occupied prominent positions in government and in the legislature *ought* to have. Politicians like Nabuco, who himself sat in parliament because of family connections, tended to assume that the power of great families like the Cavalcantis derived 'from the nature of things'. Assumptions like this could only produce ambivalence in the minds of those who, like Nabuco, later turned to liberal reform and challenged the traditional oligarchy and the political institutions of the Empire.

This ambivalence would be shared by other people since, as we have seen, the system of patronage was not confined to the furthering of political careers. Bureaucrats, journalists, writers, artists, entrepreneurs, and merchants: everyone had to follow the rules of patronage. Characterizing the situation in the 1860s, the novelist José de Alencar commented: 'Industrial enterprises, commercial associations, banks, public works, financial operations, privileges . . . all these abundant sources of wealth issue from the heights of power. The bureaucracy distributes them to their favourites and denies them to those in disgrace. Everything depends on patronage, even the press, which needs state subsidies to survive.'[6]

The first generation of intellectuals who reached maturity at the time of Independence or immediately after were almost all absorbed by the political system. If the market for their books was limited in a country in which most of the population was illiterate, they could at least survive on patronage and have a career in politics and administration. They became representatives, councillors, senators, ambassadors, public officials. Many received titles of nobility. Domingos Gonçalves de Magalhães, considered the father of romanticism in Brazil, was a member of the Chamber, a diplomat in Europe, a member of the Council of State, and a personal friend of the emperor. He received many decorations and was made barão and visconde de Araguai. Antonio Gonçalves Dias, one of the most outstanding poets of this period, was appointed professor of Latin and History in the famous Colégio Pedro Segundo and later sent to Europe on an official mission. José de Alencar, the most important romantic novelist of the period, was a member of the Chamber, minister of justice, and councillor of state. And just as the politicians organized the nation after Independence according to European constitutional rules, this first generation of Brazilian writers, though intensely nationalist, imported European models and idealized Brazilian reality: a second-generation writer had a character complain, 'They portrayed forests without mosquitos and fevers.'[7] Gradually, however, opportunities for political careers diminished as most positions were filled, and only minor jobs in the bureaucracy or in the court system remained. With a few exceptions writers born in the 1830s, like Bernardo de Guimarães, Casimiro de Abreu, Manuel Alvares de Azevedo – because they died young or because they lacked the opportunities of the earlier generation – neither participated in politics nor had important posts in administra-

---

[6] José de Alencar, *Obras completas* (Rio de Janeiro, 1960), IV, 1097.
[7] Manuel Antônio Alvares de Azevedo, 'Macário', in *Obras completas de Alvares de Azevedo* (8th edn, 2 vols., São Paulo, 1942), II, 66.

tion. They also could not make a living as writers. It is thus not surprising that they felt they had reached a dead end. They postured as bohemians; Byron and Musset were their models. Alienated from the world around them – a world they felt incapable of changing – sunk in their personal torments, they scrutinized their souls endlessly, explored the grotesque, or mocked society.

The growth of the market for books – although modest – and the proliferation of newspapers and journals in the second half of the century opened new opportunities for a literary career. Social criticism and militant reformism offered an alternative to despair and solitude. While Alvares de Azevedo was haunted by personal ghosts, Castro Alves found in the struggle between men and society his source of inspiration and became the poet of the slaves. This third generation of writers condemned the rhetoric, the style and the themes of the previous generations, demanding a more 'objective' view of the world. Realism and naturalism rather than romanticism were their models. Young novelists and poets gave up the parliamentary rhetoric, the conventional prose of the salons, the intrigues of the well-to-do, the idealization of indianism, the lyrical despair of the earlier generations, to focus on the life of 'the people'. In the last years of the Empire and the early years of the First Republic Aluísio de Azevedo described the tribulations of life in a tenement house; Euclides da Cunha, the rebellion in the backlands. Sílvio Romero collected popular tales and songs and condemned 'the history books without science or passion, pages through which great and powerful men parade, but from which the eternal sufferer, the eternal rebel, the eternal hero: the people was absent'.[8] But the contradictions between the old and the new, 'aristocratic' and 'bourgeois' tendencies, remained. To a certain extent these contradictions reflected the position of the intellectual. Even then, when there was a new market for ideas, enough to feed the writers' fantasies of independence, the lives of Brazilian intellectuals continued to depend on patronage.

This dependence, which was, as we have seen, also a fact of life in the world of business, politics, and administration, allowed the ruling classes to control social mobility. Crossing lines of class and colour and harnessing the most talented members of the new emerging classes to the elite, patronage attenuated racial and class conflicts. But patronage had its own contradictions. It secured loyalties but generated resentments. It

---

[8] Sílvio Romero, *Novos estudos de literatura contemporânea* (Rio de Janeiro, 1898), 7.

could co-opt the enemy but alienate the ally, silence the critic of the system but transform a supporter into an opponent.

Some of the social climbers hardly concealed their ambivalence. Others endured silently the contradictions of their situation. Luís Gama, a mulatto, born of a slave mother and a white father, sold as a slave and later emancipated, became a practising lawyer, a militant abolitionist, and one of the founders of the Republican party in São Paulo. A satirical poet, Gama mocked in his verses a conceited elite that denied its African roots. Yet this did not prevent his becoming one of its members. Even though he was a leader of a political party that advocated the overthrow of the monarchy and an abolitionist in an area controlled by slave owners, Gama died honoured by the elite. His funeral was attended by a crowd ranging from ex-slaves he had helped to emancipate to prominent figures in politics and administration. If Gama expressed his uneasiness in satirical terms, Machado de Assis, another mulatto, hid his behind a veil of subtle irony while conscientiously performing the role attributed to him in the world of whites. As a novelist, he devoted most of his time to the study of whites and their personal anxieties, seldom referring to blacks or to slaves and keeping a reserved attitude towards abolition and politics. Although the experiences of men like Machado de Assis and Gama were quite exceptional they could be seen as evidence of the patronage system's efficiency, and their lives fed the myth of racial democracy and of the paternalism of the Brazilian elites.

Characterizing the alliance of the ruling classes with men of talent, José de Alencar wrote in 1865 that Brazilian elites were constituted of two sorts of people: 'men rich in talent but poor in assets and rich men deprived of enlightenment'. The former, moved by necessity and love of ostentation, sought important positions in administration; the latter offered their support in exchange for consideration and respect.[9]

This alliance of men of talent with men of power explains in part why, in the work of Machado de Assis and other novelists, the ethic of liberalism and the ethic of favour existed side by side. Their novels were written from two contradictory perspectives: on the one hand, from the perspective of a bourgeois ideology, which postulated the autonomy of the individual, the universality of the law, disinterested culture, commitment to thrift and labour; and on the other hand, from the point of view of the ethic of patronage, which stressed the individual's

---

[9] José de Alencar, *Obras completas*, IV, 1080.

dependence, cultivated the exception to the norm, praised leisure and ostentation, validated the 'culture engagé'. The ambivalent ideology resulting from this odd combination expressed the experience not only of the writers but of many other Brazilians. The coexistence of an ethic of patronage with a liberal ethic reproduced at the level of ideology and language the human experience of people living in a society in which capitalism grew within a network of patronage. The ambivalence of this ideology translated the contradictions of the *bourgeois gentilhomme*, who lived in Brazil but had Europe as his point of reference, who used slaves to produce for the international market, who 'had an eye on profit and another on gentility' – a contradiction that existed also in the precarious alliance of black and mulatto intellectuals with the ruling classes, of entrepreneurs with the rural oligarchies, of men of modest origins with the power elite. The ideology expressed contradictions permeating Brazilian society from top to bottom.

When the development of urban markets, the proliferation of schools and cultural institutions, and the growing number of readers opened new opportunities – even if still limited – to entrepreneurs, professional men, writers, artists, and politicians who dreamed of emancipating themselves from the constraints of patronage, these men found in liberalism the arguments they needed to fight the system. But even then their commitment to liberalism was not without ambivalence. They continued to judge patronage from the point of view of liberalism and to judge liberalism from the point of view of patronage.

While in Europe the criticism of liberalism was often made from the perspective of the working classes, in Brazil the lack of an industrial revolution and of a proletariat and the survival of traditional relations of production in many parts of the country made that type of criticism, if not impossible, at least exceptional. As a consequence while in Europe liberalism was on the defensive, it remained in Brazil – in the minds of many – a promise to be fulfilled. It was the hope that the promise *could* be fulfilled that, in the 1870s, was behind the criticism of imperial institutions – a criticism that expressed a naïve belief in the redeeming qualities of progress, science, and reform. However, parallel to this trend towards reform and sometimes within it there continued to run a conservative stream springing from the experience of patronage. The contradictory nature of this process was admirably captured by Machado de Assis's novels, in which both characters and language are constantly shifting between the ethic of patronage and the ethic of liberalism.

Brazilian architecture of this period suggests even more clearly the relations of 'old' and 'new' elements in Brazilian culture. The 'old' and the 'new' were juxtaposed in Brazilian architecture as they were in England but in an inverted way. In England the new technology was often disguised under respectable gothic or renaissance façades. In Brazil, on the contrary, buildings continued to be built according to traditional methods, but the thick walls were covered with paper and mirrors imported from Europe and the façades were decorated with glass windows that came to replace the traditional trellises. The modern was the detail, something to be shown, the genteel exterior that hid coarse structures in art as well as in politics.

If economic development and social change in the last decades of the Empire were not enough to destroy traditional structures, they were enough to generate increasing dissatisfaction – a dissatisfaction increasingly expressed by politicians and intellectuals. In the last decades of the Empire, old politicians who felt marginalized by their party cliques and young men who had to find their way to politics and wanted to replace 'the influence of people by the influence of ideas',[10] as a contemporary put it, found in a programme of reform the lever for a successful career. This was also true for many intellectuals. 'Today, there are two ways of moving upward', said Alencar in the 1860s: 'flattery and criticism, to carp or to beg'.[11] Once the relative unanimity of the elites was broken and new groups challenged the traditional oligarchies, dissent became as instrumental to personal advancement as complicity. To the new generation of politicians and intellectuals, reform offered both a theme and a constituency. When they committed themselves to reform they were not only expressing the interest of social groups from which they descended or with which they identified. They were also moved by their specific needs as politicians and intellectuals who aimed at creating constituencies. Economic and social change provided them with a constituency ready to welcome reformist proposals. And when politicians and intellectuals adopted a reformist rhetoric they helped stir up even more latent discontent and increased the number of those who saw reforms as a panacea for all social problems.

Reformers had their own vocabulary and their own themes. In their rhetoric 'the People' appeared together with other favourite words such as 'progress', 'reason', and 'science'. But in fact, no matter how

---

[10] Quoted in Sérgio Buarque de Holanda (ed.), *História geral da civilização brasileira, II: O Brasil monárquico*, vol. IV, *Declínio e queda do império* (São Paulo, 1971), 307.

[11] José de Alencar, *Obras completas*, IV, 1074.

sympathetic some of them might sound, they lacked any real connections with the people they preferred to protect rather than to represent and to represent rather than to allow them to speak for themselves.

In the eyes of the reformers Europe symbolized progress, and to be progressive meant to recreate the modes of European elites. Living in a country dependent on European markets they looked toward Europe for arguments and models, which not only served as guides but conferred prestige and authority. In spite of the proliferation of cultural institutions, newspapers, and journals and the constant increase in the number able to read, the conditions for the independent production of ideas were still far from ideal. Most of the population continued to be illiterate (78 per cent in 1872). There were few printing houses, and Brazilian writers often had to print their books in Europe. There were few bookshops (in São Paulo, at the end of the century, there were only five), and the internal distribution of books was difficult. It was easier to import books than to produce them locally. All this created obstacles for an internal debate of ideas conducive to the creation of a relatively autonomous culture. 'We are consumers, not producers of ideas', commented Tobias Barreto, a leading intellectual of the 1870s and 1880s.[12]

Reformers imported ideas, but this import continued to be selective, as it always had been. They chose what made sense to them. This explains why the Christian socialism of Lammenais, the utopian socialism of Saint-Simon, Proudhon, or Fourier, and the scientific socialism of Marx and Engels were merely matters of speculation for a few eccentric individuals. Men like Spencer and Comte, who had tried to reconcile order and progress and wanted to regenerate society through a moral revolution, had more appeal to Brazilian intellectuals and politicians than those who put their trust in class struggle or in the proletariat.

Placed between an oligarchy they wanted to combat and the masses they did not trust the reformers of the 1870s and 1880s found their inspiration in positivism. They abandoned Cousin and Jouffroy's eclecticism – which had served the elites of the Regency in the 1830s and the Conciliation of the 1850s and 1860s – to embrace Comte and Spencer. Those authors offered them a doctrine, a method of analysis, a political theory, and most of all the reassuring conviction that mankind was inevitably driven to progress and that change was possible without subverting the social order.

Since the 1830s, a few Brazilians who had studied in Paris had brought

---

12 Tobias Barreto, *Ensaios de sociologia* (Rio de Janeiro, 1962), 10.

home Comtian ideas, but it was only in the 1860s that those ideas became popular. In Comte, the generation of reformers found support for their programme aiming at reducing the state to a mere custodian of the social order. Comte's respect for civil liberties and his commitment to religious freedom, free association, freedom of speech, and free enterprise could not but appeal to those who resented the centralized political system and the oppressive patronage of the elites. This rather conservative group of reformers found equally appealing Comte's respect for social hierarchy and social inequalities and his conviction that freedom was a right but equality a myth. At a time when women were making their first steps toward higher education, his belief that the family was the basic social unit and that women should be subordinated to their husbands could only attract men raised in a patriarchal society who looked suspiciously at emancipated women. It was also pleasing to them that Comte argued in favour of an elite of technicians and men of science, distinguished by their virtues and knowledge – an elite he saw replacing the 'pedantocracy', the elite of literati, the reformers identified with the Brazilian oligarchies. And nothing could be more attractive to them than Comte's conviction that this new type of intellectual had an important role to play in changing the world. Comte's ideas spoke in particular to doctors, teachers, engineers, entrepreneurs, and students of the Military Academy, who resented the patronage of the traditional elites. Thus, with the exception of a few individuals such as Farias Brito, a follower of Hartman and Schopenhauer, Soriano de Sousa, who found inspiration in neo-thomism, and Tobias Barreto, who devoured everything he could read, especially German literature, most intellectuals of this period became positivists. Even those who, like Sílvio Romero, later moved to different positions had their positivist phase. A few preferred Spencer's evolutionism but the majority followed Littré's version of Comte. The interest in those new ideas grew side by side with the critique of the system and the demands for reform.

THE POLITICS OF REFORM

During the early 1860s a group of leading Conservative politicians, among them Pedro de Araújo Lima (marquês de Olinda), José Tomás Nabuco de Araújo, Zacarias de Góes e Vasconcelos, the marquês de Paranaguá, Sinimbu and Saraiva, convinced of the need to reform the political system, had left their party and joined the Liberal party, creating the Liga Progressista (Progressive League). The League's programme was presented in 1864. It demanded among other things decentralization, electoral reform, reform of the court system, a new Civil Code, and changes in the Commercial Code, especially in the sections concerning stock companies and bankruptcy. With the beginning of the Paraguayan War in 1865, however, the reformist campaign briefly receded. But the pressure for reforms continued to increase within the ranks of the Liberal party, where a more radical faction emerged. The conflict between the radicals and the moderates within the Liberal party led to the fall of the Liberal Cabinet in 1868. The emperor called on the Conservatives, who were to remain in power for the next ten years. The Liberals united themselves and proceeded to attack the government and the emperor. In May 1869 they issued a manifesto (apparently written by senator Nabuco de Araújo) which demanded decentralization, autonomy of the judiciary, creation of a system of education more independent from the state, transformation of the Council of State into an organ exclusively administrative, the abolition of tenure in the Senate, direct elections, creation of a Civil Register, secularization of the cemeteries, religious freedom, the extension of the right to vote to non-Catholics, and the gradual emancipation of slaves. The manifesto ended with a threat: 'Either Reform or Revolution', followed by a conciliatory remark: 'Reform and the country will be saved.'

In spite of its tone the Liberal manifesto did not satisfy the party radicals, and a few months later they issued their own. The new manifesto asked for the abolition of the Moderating Power, the National Guard, the Council of State, and slavery. It demanded elections for provincial presidents and police chiefs, universal suffrage, and direct elections. It also asked the government to restrict itself to administering justice, maintaining order, punishing crimes, and collecting taxes: the functions of a typical liberal state, which would secure freedom of initiative and guarantee civil rights. Everywhere radical clubs were formed. And with the end of the Paraguayan War in March 1870, the opposition intensified its campaign against the government. In December the Republican party was founded in Rio and issued a manifesto published in the first number of the newspaper *A República*. Of the men who signed the manifesto only one was a plantation owner. The others identified themselves as lawyers (fourteen), journalists (ten), medical doctors (nine), merchants (eight), engineers (five), bureaucrats (three), and teachers (two). A few had been militant in the Liberal party and had held important posts in politics and administration. In response to the manifesto several radical clubs declared themselves republicans and several republican clubs appeared. The Republican manifesto did not add much to the others. It made, however, one important suggestion: the creation of a National Convention with powers to change the regime.

In essence all three manifestos of 1868–70 – Liberal, radical and Republican – had the same goals, although they differed in the degree of their radicalism. They intended to curtail government interference in the private sector, to increase provincial autonomy, and to undermine the power of the traditional oligarchies. Their programme of reform appealed to a large spectrum of interests. They spoke to the bureaucrat, the judge, and the teacher tired of the uncertainties of patronage. They spoke to the businessman oppressed by government policies, and to the clergyman and military officer who condemned political interference in their institutions. They spoke to the immigrant who wished to regularize his situation, and to the urban and rural masses burdened by conscription and taxes. They appealed especially to the new young generation of politicians for whom the programme of reforms could win a growing electorate, and to the intellectual who found in reform new sources of inspiration and new constituencies. If the programme seemed to appeal to the emerging urban groups, it also attracted progressive planters and provincial elites dissatisfied with the central government's policies. But most of all the programme was used by the Liberal party politicians to attack the Conservatives between 1868 and 1878 when Liberals were politically ostracized.

The issues raised by the manifestos, however, transcended party boundaries. Among the members of the Liberal party there were some who would not endorse the demands of the most radical. And in the Conservative party there were those who could support a moderate programme of reform. They could win some of the most reluctant members of their party by presenting the reforms as a means of fighting the opposition. This strategy became a necessity when the emperor himself expressed his sympathy for some of the reforms. In the advice he gave to the Regent, Princess Isabel, before his trip to Europe in 1871, the emperor stressed the need to reform the electoral system, the judiciary, the National Guard, and the system of conscription and promotion in the army. He also suggested that immigration be encouraged and slaves gradually emancipated. On one issue he went even further than the Liberals or the Republicans. He suggested the creation of a civil service career that would remove bureaucracy from the manipulation of the political elites. But on other issues he adopted a more conservative line. He opposed the separation of state and church, the extinction of the Moderating Power, the abolition of tenure in the Senate and Council of State, and decentralization. He also disapproved of giving political rights to foreigners. The emperor's support for a moderate programme of reforms only increased their popularity. This explains why a Conservative Cabinet, headed by the barão do Rio Branco (1871–4), launched a series of reforms of which the most important was the emancipation of children born of slave mothers.

The issue of slave emancipation was not new. At the time of Independence a few politicians raised the question without success. Under pressure from the British, the Brazilian government outlawed the trade in 1831, but it continued illegally until 1850, when it was finally repressed. In the late 1840s and early 1850s, coffee planters, concerned with the problem of labour supply, tried to use immigrants on their plantations. The experiment ended in a harsh confrontation between workers and plantation owners. Foreign governments protested against the bad treatment of immigrants and some prohibited immigration to Brazil. After that, only a few stubborn planters continued to use immigrants on their plantations. The overwhelming majority resorted to slaves bought in the cities or in rural areas less dependent on slave labour. As a result, slaves were moved from areas of lower productivity to areas of higher productivity and from urban centres to rural areas. The slave population of the north-east declined while in the coffee areas it increased.

During the 1850s and 1860s several bills proposing gradual emancipation of slaves were presented to the Chamber but they were all rejected. Emancipation found more supporters after the American civil war, when Brazil became one of the few countries still to have slaves. In 1867, the emperor spoke in favour of gradual abolition. Parliament refused to discuss the question. But two years later it approved a law prohibiting slave auctions as well as separation of husband from wife and parents from children under fifteen years old. During the Paraguayan War slaves belonging to the state who served in the army were emancipated (November 1866), and in 1870 senator Nabuco de Araújo succeeded in getting the Senate to approve a budget amendment granting 1,000 contos for slave emancipation. All those measures, although small, were indicative of a growing abolitionist pressure. The inclusion of the issue of emancipation in the Liberal manifesto and the Emperor's approval of gradual emancipation made it impossible for the Conservatives to delay the parliamentary debate. Two Conservative Cabinets resigned before the issue could be brought to discussion. Called by the emperor to form a new Conservative Cabinet, Rio Branco decided in 1871 to present a bill to the Chamber proposing the emancipation of the newborn children of slave mothers. During the debates regional interests prevailed over party loyalties. The opposition came mainly from representatives of the coffee areas. They spoke of bankruptcy, social disorder, political chaos, the dangers of a slave rebellion. Some even argued that the bill was prejudicial to the slaves because it would split families and generate strife among them. And they did not forget to make the classic remarks about the benevolence of the masters and the slaves' good living conditions compared to those of the workers in industrial societies. But the most important argument against the bill was that it hurt the right of property. Some went as far as to say that the bill was a communist invention. The supporters of the bill resorted to a great variety of arguments. They not only condemned the institution on moral terms but also argued that slave labour was less productive than free labour. Some questioned whether the right of property could be applied to people. Far from being based on natural law, slavery, they said, was a 'monstrous violation'. Inside and outside the parliament the question was debated with great excitement. Petitions for and against flooded the parliament, where heated speeches in favour of the bill were applauded enthusiastically from the galleries. Finally, in spite of the sharp opposition, the bill was approved in the Chamber by 65 votes to 45. The law was enacted on 26 September 1871, after having been approved in the Senate by 33 to 7.

The law was a serious blow at the institution of slavery, although its effects would be felt only in the long run. According to the law the newborn children of slave mothers would be free, but the masters had to take care of them until they were eight years old. After that, slave owners could either give the children to the state, in exchange for financial compensation, or use their labour until they were 21.

After the approval of the law of free birth the government turned to other reforms, and in less than four years the Cabinet reformed the court system, the National Guard (1873), the system of conscription (1874), military schools, and pensions. It also approved an increase in military salaries, which had been frozen since the 1850s. The Cabinet also promoted the expansion of railways, doubling the track mileage, established telegraph lines linking Brazil to Europe and the provinces to each other, and subsidized immigration, raising the annual number of immigrants entering the country from 8,000 to 50,000. All those activities were favoured by a period of extraordinary economic prosperity. Soon, however, the 1873 world recession began to affect Brazil, putting an end to this euphoria and provoking the fall of the Cabinet – which had already been weakened by an intervening conflict between church and state.

The conflict had its roots in the policies of Pius IX for strengthening the authority of the Catholic church. The Pope's intolerant opinions in matters of religious discipline and faith and his aggressive religious campaign could only lead to confrontations between church and state, particularly in countries like Brazil where the church was subordinated to the state. The situation became tense after the Pope's encyclicals, *Quanta Cura* and *Syllabus* (1868), condemned many features of modern life, and a Vatican Council proclaimed the dogma of the Pope's infallibility (1870).

The Pope's new aggressive line was followed by many Brazilian priests, especially some young clergymen who had been trained in European seminaries and had returned to Brazil with a renewed sense of religious mission. This militant clergy found intolerable the subordination of the church to the state. They resented the laxity of the traditional clergy who had accommodated themselves to the rules of political patronage. The new priests struggled for more autonomy for the church and more religious discipline.

The issue that triggered the conflict was apparently minor. The Pope had condemned freemasonry and had forbidden Catholics to become masons. The bishop of Olinda, Dom Vital, acting independently, decided to prohibit masons from participating in religious brotherhoods. This could be seen only as an act of insubordination, since the constitution established that papal bulls had no validity without the emperor's approval. The conflict was aggravated by the fact that although the number of masons was small, many important politicians were masons, including the visconde do Rio Branco, the head of the Cabinet. Many priests were also masons. The masonic brotherhoods resisted the bishop's decision and appealed to the government. The bishop, ordered by the government to withdraw his demands, refused. This created a serious impasse. The government had either to bow to the bishop's ultramontane position or punish him for his disobedience. After failing to persuade the Pope to discourage him, the Cabinet decided to punish the bishop, who, after being arrested and tried, was sentenced to jail in 1874. The conflict might have ended there if other members of the clergy had not expressed their solidarity with the bishop. But the incident had widespread repercussions. In the cities and in the backlands there were demonstrations for and against the bishop while the press and parliament debated the issue. The arrest of another bishop, D. Antônio Macedo Costa, who had followed the example of D. Vital, and a second trial and condemnation, further aggravated the situation.

The Conservative Cabinet did not find unanimous support within its own ranks. Important Conservative leaders like Paulino José Soares de Sousa, Antônio Ferreira Viana, and Cândido Mendes condemned the arrests. Liberals were also divided. Many Republicans found themselves in the position of supporting the emperor and condemning the bishops. However, among them were some who used the incident to further the republican cause by arguing in favour of the separation of church and state.

The bishop's arrest caused profound malaise among Catholics and created a serious problem for the Cabinet. A conflict that had started as a small issue about the rights of freemasons had become a confrontation between church and state for which there was no good solution. For the government, the only alternative was to grant amnesty to the two bishops, but for that to happen the Rio Branco Cabinet had to go. In 1874 the Cabinet was replaced and the amnesty came in 1875; simultaneously the Pope ordered the suspension of the bans against the masons. This put an end to the conflict. There were no winners or losers, but the number of those who favoured the separation of the church from the state had increased on both sides, so in the long run the monarchy lost. Many years later, a few months after the proclamation of the Republic, D. Antônio Macedo Costa in a pastoral letter could say triumphantly: 'The throne has disappeared . . . And the altar? The altar still stands.'[13]

Traditional historiography has attributed to this conflict a great role in the fall of the Empire, ignoring the fact that the nation had been divided on the issue. Besides, the position adopted by the Council of State against the bishops represented the opinion of most elite groups. In fact, the Brazilian elites, with notable exceptions, had always cultivated an anti-clerical posture, and there were many who posed as free thinkers. This

[13] Joaquim Nabuco, *Um estadista du Império* (Rio de Janeiro, 1975), 830.

was also the attitude of the emperor, who disliked the bishop's ultramontanism. During the crisis even the church had been divided. Many priests had continued to support the rights of royal patronage. For these reasons the role of the so-called *questão religiosa* in the overthrow of the monarchy should not be overestimated.

If the state was harsh with the priests it was more generous with another discontented group, the military. Military complaints against the political system had a history going back to the 1850s. But at that time most of the military were more or less adjusted to the system of patronage. They joined political parties and were courted by politicians. A few famous generals participated in Cabinets. The Paraguayan War had exposed the weaknesses of the Brazilian army and many officers recognized the need to increase the army's efficiency. In 1874, a young officer, Sena Madureira, after travelling in Europe, presented to the minister of war some suggestions for the reorganization of the army. He proposed among other things a new system of recruitment and promotion based on merit and new types of training. His ideas were shared by many young officers. Reform-minded officers founded journals, ran for office, and publicized their complaints in the national press. Many realized that patronage was an obstacle to modernization of the army. In their struggle they developed a new esprit de corps that transcended traditional political party lines. They looked for support among other social groups equally interested in reforming the political system. More and more they came to see the traditional oligarchies as their enemy. Their resentment was expressed by their increasing interest in positivism and republican ideas.

In an attempt to satisfy their demands the government took several measures. It increased their salaries, changed the officers' system of training, making it more specialized, and approved a new conscription law in 1874. The government also altered the system of promotion in 1875, stipulating that war service count double for promotion or retirement. Most of those reforms, however, would never become reality. The recession of 1873 delayed the expected increase in wages for more than ten years. And in 1876 Sena Madureira uncovered schemes used by the elites to avoid conscription of members of their family or clientele. With the passing of time the gap between the oligarchies and the military widened. The appointment of the duque de Caxias, commander of the Brazilian army during the Paraguayan War, as prime minister in 1875, and the presence of two other popular generals (Osório and Pelotas) in the Liberal Cabinets that came after, postponed the crisis for a few years. But the conflict came to a head in the 1880s, with dramatic consequences for the monarchy.

In 1878, the Conservatives were finally ousted from power after ten years of rule. It was the debate over electoral reform that caused the fall of the Cabinet. An electoral reform intended to guarantee the opposition's representation and to curtail government intervention in elections had been approved in 1876. But the reform had been a failure. In the first election only 16 Liberals had been elected instead of the 25 stipulated by the law as the minimum. The Conservatives had won 85 per cent of the seats in the Chamber. The opposition immediately returned to the issue, proposing a system of direct elections.

At the end of ten years, the Liberals could argue that many of the reforms implemented by the Conservatives had been mere palliatives. But the reforms that seemed insufficient to the Liberal opposition were considered too radical by many Conservatives. In 1878 the Conservative party was divided over fundamental questions, just as the Liberals had been in 1868. These divisions reflected the changes occurring in society and the emergence of conflicting groups of interests that expressed themselves in both parties. Under these conditions it became increasingly difficult for any Cabinet to gain the unanimous support of its members in the Chamber. Thus, although some important Conservatives such as Paulino Soares de Sousa, Ferreira Viana, and Francisco Belisário were in favour of electoral reform, the emperor, aware of the split within the Conservatives, called the Liberals to organize the new Cabinet.

After ten years of political ostracism the Liberals were back in power with a programme that did not differ much from the programme of the Conservatives. They proposed to expand the railways and telegraph lines, to implement urban improvements in Rio de Janeiro, to subsidize immigration, to enlarge the elementary school network and to promote electoral reform. The new elections brought into the Chamber a group of young politicians – including Joaquim Nabuco, Rui Barbosa, Afonso Pena, and Rodolfo Dantas – who became important political figures in the last decades of the Empire and during the First Republic.

The debates about electoral reform showed profound rifts within the Liberal party between the moderates and the radicals. This division eventually led to the resignation of the Liberal Cabinet. The immediate cause, however, was the *revolta dos vintens* (penny riot) in Rio in January 1880 (see above). For the first time a popular movement brought down a government. It was the beginning of a new era. And it was not by chance that one of the most controversial issues during the debates over electoral reform was the vote for illiterates. The second question that triggered heated debates was the concession of political rights to non-Catholics, a measure politicians interested in pleasing immigrants were eager to see approved.

Once again, as during the debate about the bill to emancipate children born of slave mothers, or during the confrontation between church and state, there was no party cohesion. There were Conservatives for and against the electoral reform bill, and the same was true of the Liberals. The law which finally emerged was a compromise. It did not grant the suffrage to illiterates, but granted it to non-Catholics, freedmen, and naturalized foreigners. It abolished indirect elections, but it kept the income qualification. It enfranchised all males over 21 who had a net income of 200 milréis and were literate. One of the important innovations was the voter certificate, which eliminated certain kinds of manipulation in the registration process.

The reform had a curious result. By eliminating the two stages characteristic of the system of indirect elections, by fixing at 200 milréis the minimum income required, and by making literacy a prerequisite for voting it actually reduced the number of those who could vote. Before the reform 1,114,066 people were registered as voters and 240,000 as electors. With the institutionalization of direct elections the number of those who could vote went down to 145,296, about 1 per cent of the total population. At the same time political power shifted slightly from rural to urban areas, where literacy rates and income were higher.

The hope of those who had supported the reform seemed to be confirmed in 1881 when 75 Liberals and 47 Conservatives were elected. For the first time the opposition had a significant representation in the Chamber. In the years that followed, however, its positive effects became less clear. In 1884, 67 Liberals, 55 Conservatives, and 3 Republicans were elected. But in the elections that took place in 1885 under a Conservative Cabinet only 22 Liberals were elected out of a total of 125. By then, it had become clear that electoral reform had failed once again to correct electoral fraud. The encouraging results in the first elections after the reform were due to the integrity of the Cabinet that had supported it.

When the Conservatives took power they did not feel the same commitment to the reform and won the elections by an overwhelming majority. Once again, legislation had not attacked the roots of the problem and the vote continued to be controlled by money, prestige, and family connections. And when those failed, violence was still a successful strategy. Yet the politics of opinion continued to make slow progress in the wake of the debates about centralization, abolition of the Senate and the Council of State, immigration, financial policies, and abolition of slavery. Although it was still true that the support of the local leader counted for more than a candidate's platform, the emergence of a new urban constituency and the breaking down of elite consensus created the conditions for a new type of politics. In 1884 the abolitionist leader Joaquim Nabuco went from house to house in Recife competing with João Mariano for the voters' support.

The economic crisis of the 1880s brought new issues to the political debate and accentuated political conflict. The Liberals had inherited a difficult financial situation. The expansion of the railway network and telegraph lines, subsidies given to immigration, and centralized sugar mills and the assistance given to the population of the north-east, devastated by a series of droughts during the 1870s, had represented a tremendous financial burden for the state. Many loans had been made during this period and the foreign debt alone absorbed half of the total state revenues, and amortization of the debt was minimal. Government expenditures were higher than revenues in spite of the growing exports of coffee and rubber. The situation became more difficult in the early 1880s because of the falling prices of Brazilian products in the international market. The Liberal Cabinet that took power in 1881 was forced to postpone the programme of reforms to face a more urgent question: the growing deficit. It had simultaneously to attend to demands for more credit.

As was inevitable, recession brought conflicts of interest to light. Since groups tied to exports – overrepresented in the government – opposed land taxes and taxes on exports, the alternative was to raise taxes on imports. But this hurt importers and consumers. To reduce expenditure – the other alternative available – meant that important projects for the development of the economic infrastructure had to stop. The government was at a dead end. The easy way out in the short run was, as usual, to resort to loans or to issue currency. In either case this would only aggravate the deficit in the long run. Burdened by financial problems and undermined by conflicts between the radical and the conservative factions within the party, Liberal Cabinets lacked stability. Four Liberal Cabinets succeeded each other between 1882 and 1884, unable to assure a majority in the Chamber.

With the exception of electoral reform, most of the Liberal demands of 1869 were still to be met. Every new Cabinet had announced its purpose of guaranteeing the independence of the judiciary, decentralizing administration, giving more autonomy to the provinces, expanding state schools, and balancing the budget. But with the exception of the expansion of the elementary school system they failed to accomplish their programme.

This failure was due in part to the Liberals' reluctance to implement reforms that they had proposed when they were in the opposition but that could now undermine their own power. Once in power, Liberals, with the exception of the most radical, were not willing to go much further than the Conservatives. Martinho Campos, the head of the new Cabinet in 1882, said, correctly, that there was nothing more similar to a Liberal than a Conservative – or even a Republican.[14] They all had a family resemblance. Ideological differences were minor or irrelevant. His opinion was similar to the opinion of one of Machado de Assis's characters, who in an attempt to console a defeated politician tried to convince him that he could change sides. 'You were with them as one is in a ball, where it is not necessary to have the same ideas to dance the same square.'[15]

A careful analysis of the parties' composition revealed that agrarian groups (*fazendeiros*) corresponded to about half of either party while the other half was composed of bureaucrats and professionals, with bureaucrats predominating in the Conservative party and professionals in the Liberal party.[16] The predominance of bureaucrats in the Conservative party is not surprising since Conservatives were in power longer than Liberals and had more chance to control bureaucratic appointments. But considering the instability of the bureaucracy and its recruitment mostly of professionals, the two parties seem to have represented, and received support from basically the same social groups.

[14] Arquivo Nacional, *Organizações e programas ministeriais: regime parlamentar do império* (2nd edn, Rio de Janeiro, 1962), 196.   [15] Machado de Assis, *Esau e Jacó* (São Paulo, 1961), 181.
[16] José Murilo de Carvalho, 'A composição social dos partidos políticos imperiais', *Cadernos DCP* (1974), 15.

The differences between Liberals and Conservatives were essentially rhetorical. Once in power Conservatives could accomplish many of the reforms proposed by the Liberals, and Liberals in power did not go much beyond the limits accepted by most Conservatives. And in both parties there were internal strifes between moderates and radicals, as we have seen. The moderate factions tended to represent the interest of the traditional agrarian elites, the others spoke for the new emerging group of interests. After the fall of the Rio Branco Cabinet this internal division contributed to great political instability. Between 1880 and the fall of the Empire, ten Cabinets were formed and dismissed; the first seven (1880–5) were Liberal. Three times the Chamber was dismissed and the government called for elections. No legislature completed its legal term during this period.

As a result of political instability the emperor was often asked to intervene in the political arena. The constant intervention of the Moderating Power generated resentments and criticisms, which brought about a crisis in the political system. Even the traditional political elites started questioning the regime. Monarchical parties did not spare criticism of the monarchical regime they were supposed to defend. The Moderating Power was the main target of their criticism. The words of an experienced politician, Ferreira Viana, in the Senate on 31 July 1884 expressed the state of mind of many of his colleagues: 'I am tired of acting in this political comedy.'

Soon the politicians were to face a difficult test. Abolitionist pressure brought the question of abolition back to the parliament. The most conservative politicians had hoped that the 1871 law would solve the problem of the abolition of slavery, since it would now gradually come to an end. But as one ardent abolitionist argued, if nothing was done to accelerate the process Brazilians would still own slaves in the third or fourth decade of the twentieth century. This does not seem to have concerned the majority of those who sat in the Chamber of Deputies. Not even when the Liberals returned to power in 1878 did attempts to discuss the problem find support. A bill presented by Nabuco was rejected by 77 votes, with only 16 deputies supporting it. And in the following year, Nabuco, who could not count on the full support of his own party, was not re-elected. Meanwhile, outside parliament the abolitionist campaign gained new allies.

Several factors explain the progress of the abolitionist campaign and the reopening of the question in parliament. Not only were there fewer people dependent on slaves but those who were became increasingly aware of the need to look for alternatives. Planters could expand their coffee plantations only if they had an adequate labour supply, but the slave population fell from 1,566,416 in 1873 to 1,346,097 in 1883, and it continued to decline, to 1,133,228 in 1885 and 723,419 in 1887. The slave population decreased more rapidly in the north-east than in the south, where it tended to concentrate, but even there it declined in relative terms. In São Paulo, slaves represented 28.2 per cent of the total population in 1854 and 8.7 per cent in 1886. And because it could not renew itself, the slave population was ageing. The recognition that sooner or later there would be no more slaves forced the coffee planters to look for alternatives. In a meeting in 1878 a few suggested the use of Chinese immigrants. But the suggestion was not welcomed by most planters, who argued in favour of using either the Brazilian free rural population or Europeans. This was the solution that finally prevailed. In São Paulo the provincial assembly approved many bills subsidizing immigration, and between 1875 and 1885, 42,000 immigrants – predominantly Italians and Portuguese – entered the province. In the next two years another 114,000 arrived. Until the beginning of the 1880s, however, most coffee planters still depended almost exclusively on slaves. In the north-east the population that fled the droughts of the 1870s crowded into the sugar-cane areas, offering cheap labour to the planters.

Changes in the system of processing sugar and coffee and improvements in the means of transportation made it easier for the planters to use free labour. Labour productivity increased and the system of labour could be rationalized. In some circumstances free labour could be even more profitable than slave labour. The process of transition from slavery to free labour was also furthered by the opening of new opportunities for investment. Banks, railways, urban improvements, insurance companies, and manufacturers offered alternatives for capital investment. And even when they did not pay more than the investment on slaves, the planter could protect himself against the uncertainties of agriculture by investing simultaneously in railways, banks and other enterprises. The need to diversify investments became obvious in the beginning of the 1880s, when coffee prices suddenly fell. Free labour could now be more attractive than slave labour because it did not require immobilization of capital. Besides, the price of slaves and the cost of maintaining them had increased in the 1870s to a point where in some areas slave labour cost more than free labour. Nevertheless, although in the late nineteenth century everything seemed to point in the direction of free labour, most planters continued to oppose the abolition of slavery. After all, not only did slaves represent capital already invested but planters were still dependent on slave labour, and were sceptical about the possibilities of replacing slaves with free labourers. Immigrant riots in the main coffee-growing areas had shown that these were men who could not be driven as slaves.

While the planters agonized about the problem of labour, abolitionists made progress, especially among the urban population, and gradually became a political force. In 1884 slavery was in fact abolished in the provinces of Ceará and Amazonas. In São Paulo, a lawyer, Antônio Bento, organized an underground system based on the support of artisans and railway workers, mostly blacks and mulattos, to help runaway slaves. And slaves were fleeing in great numbers from plantations. Slaves had developed a new consciousness, as abolitionism provided them with a new ideology and a strategy. Abolitionists had also changed public opinion and acts of insubordination, which had existed since the beginnings of slavery, had acquired a new meaning. In the past, runaway slaves had been persecuted, but now they encountered increasing support. The urban population who in the past had persecuted runaway slaves now mocked the police. Judges and lawyers enforced with energy the laws that protected slaves and were lenient in the enforcement of repressive laws. The press, both abolitionist and anti-abolitionist – although for different reasons – propagated rumours of slave rebellion: the abolitionist to stress the violence of a system that led men to such despair, the anti-abolitionist to emphasize the need for more repression. Slave owners resorted to all means to fight the abolitionist campaign. They attacked abolitionist speakers, chased abolitionist leaders away from their communities, protested in the press against a government that was unable to control social disorder, and flooded the parliament with petitions. Visiting Rio and São Paulo in 1883 the French engineer Louis Couty had the impression that the country was on the eve of a social revolution.

It was in this atmosphere of excitement on the side of the abolitionists and distress on the side of the planters that Souza Dantas, a Liberal, was called to constitute a new Cabinet in 1884. In the programme he presented to the Chamber he defined his position in regard to slave emancipation: 'Neither to retreat, nor to halt, but not to precipitate . . .

to mark the line that prudence requires and civilization recommends.' He proposed a bill to emancipate, without compensation, slaves who reached the age of 60. The bill provoked a crisis of large proportions leading in the end to the fall of the Liberal Cabinet and its replacement by the Conservatives. Once again the issue transcended party loyalties and the Chamber saw Conservatives and Liberals on both sides. Seventeen Liberals, three from São Paulo, one from Rio, six from Minas and seven from other provinces, voted against the Cabinet. The final record showed 55 votes against the Cabinet and 52 in favour. The opposition to the bill had come predominantly from the coffee areas (of the 41 deputies from those areas, only 7 voted with the Cabinet). The Chamber was dissolved and the Cabinet called for elections.

Never had the country seen a more disputed electoral campaign. Businessmen, bankers, and planters gathered in Clubes de Lavoura e Comércio (Commerce and Agriculture Associations) and accused the abolitionists of being subversive elements threatening the country with economic disorganization and political chaos. 'The abolitionists are like those who in Russia belong to the nihilist party, in Germany are socialists, and in France, communists', remarked one deputy in the Chamber. The abolitionists on their part promoted public meetings and campaigned in the press, arguing that slavery inhibited industrial development and innovation in agricultural methods. It was responsible for the instability of fortunes and the disorganization of the family. It triggered racial hatred, demoralized labour, and helped to keep the free population ignorant and poor. But above all – and this was a decisive argument – it constituted an obstacle to progress.

The election brought to parliament 67 Liberals, 55 Conservatives, and 3 Republicans. Re-elected were 38 deputies who had favoured the bill and 18 who had opposed it. It seemed that the Cabinet had won. But in fact the election had brought in many others who were against the bill, and some, like Nabuco, who had battled for it, had difficulties in being re-elected. At the beginning of the new session a deputy from São Paulo proposed a motion of no confidence in the Cabinet, and the vote ended in a tie. Three weeks later it became clear that the Cabinet could not govern. A new motion of no confidence was voted on, and this time the Cabinet received almost unanimous opposition from the Conservatives (all but three voted against), while nine Liberals voted with the opposition. The emperor called another member of the Liberal party to constitute a new Cabinet in the hope that such a change would secure for the Liberal party the majority in the Chamber. But once again it became clear that the Liberals did not have enough support to rule. Finally, in 1885, the emperor called Cotegipe, a Conservative, to form a new Cabinet. With the Conservatives back in power a bill more moderate than the original was approved and converted into law in September 1885. Under the law of 1885 60-year-old slaves were liberated, but as a form of compensation to their masters they would perform unpaid labour for another three years or until they reached the age of 65.

During the four months of debates there had been a fundamental change in the position of one of the most outspoken Conservative leaders from the coffee areas. Antônio Prado, who had systematically opposed all emancipation legislation, gave his support to the bill. He told the Chamber that indemnification was not necessary if the masters were allowed to keep their slaves until they could replace them with free labourers. Paulistas were aware of the advantages of free labour and were taking steps to solve the problem, he added. This shift in opinion had to do not only with the increasing disorganization of labour, which resulted from slaves' running away from plantations, but also with new prospects for immigration.

While some planters turned to immigrants, others decided that, to keep their slaves from running away, they had to grant them conditional freedom. They emancipated their slaves with the condition that they stay on the plantation for a number of years. In 1887 the number of manumissions rose to 40,000 in São Paulo and the provincial assembly sent a petition to parliament asking for immediate abolition. Planters had come to realize that abolition was the only way to avoid social turmoil. This had become even more clear when the army sent a petition to the princess asking to be relieved of the task of persecuting runaway slaves.

When the legislature reopened in 1888 the new prime minister, João Alfredo Correia de Oliveira, announced his intention to abolish slavery without compensation, and the bill was approved without delay and converted into law on 13 May 1888. Only nine representatives voted against it; eight were from Rio de Janeiro – an area where the coffee plantations were in decline and the planters burdened by mortgages. Contrary to what the Cassandras had predicted, the economy did not suffer from the abolition of slave labour. It recovered quickly from the inevitable disruption of the first years, when several harvests were lost. A few planters whose plantations were already in critical condition faced bankruptcy – not the nation.

Abolition did not fundamentally change labour conditions on the plantation. In the coffee areas immigrants who came to replace slaves often found that life on a plantation was not as idyllic as they had thought and moved to the cities, or left Brazil. But the constant influx of immigrants kept the labour supply which planters needed to expand their plantations. Many ex-slaves stayed on plantations and continued to perform their usual tasks, for which they were paid meagre wages. Others who moved to the cities devoted themselves to minor tasks, remaining at the bottom of the society. Abolitionists seemed to have forgotten the blacks.

As had happened with other reforms promoted during this period – the electoral reform, the reform of conscription, the reform of the National Guard – the results of abolition corresponded neither to the fears of the Conservatives nor to the hopes of the reformers. They were enough, however, to generate frustration among the monarchists, who did not forgive the government for having abolished slavery without compensation. If abolition did not inflate the Republican party membership – as some historians have suggested – it helped to undermine the monarchical system. During the campaign the emperor had been criticized by all factions. For the radical abolitionists, like Silva Jardim, the emperor's sin was not to have intervened more drastically in favour of abolition. For the anti-abolitionists his sin was to have done too much.

Abolition came in 1888 after a tumultuous popular campaign. The year after, the Republic came silently, in the form of a military coup – a conspiracy that united members of the Republican party of São Paulo and Rio with certain army officers.

Since 1870 Republicans had made progress. At the beginning they were a small group. The original nucleus of the Republican party in Rio was about 30 people. The newspaper *A República* had in its first year a circulation of 2,000 copies, but by the end of the year it was already being sold in Rio, Alagoas, Pernambuco, Rio Grande do Sul, São Paulo, and Minas Gerais. The number of issues increased rapidly and two years later it boasted a circulation of 12,000 copies. Republican clubs appeared in several provinces although they were most numerous in Rio de Janeiro, São Paulo, Rio Grande do Sul, and Minas Gerais. In 1889 79 per cent of the newspapers and 89 per cent of the clubs were located in these areas.

Almost everywhere the Republican party had recruited its supporters among the urban population. Students and professionals and a few industrialists formed the bulk of the Republican party in Rio, Minas Gerais, and Rio Grande do Sul. In São Paulo, however, most of the Republicans were plantation owners. Although it has been shown that only 30 per cent of the members of the Republican party were plantation owners, while 55 per cent were professionals and 11 per cent merchants,[17] many plantation owners also had degrees from law, medical or engineering schools and could be listed either as professionals or as plantation owners. Of the 133 delegates who attended the first important Republican meeting in São Paulo in 1873, 76 declared agriculture as their profession. Others identified themselves as businessmen, lawyers, 'capitalists', 'artists', and 'proprietors'. Many had studied at the São Paulo Law School – a centre of abolitionism and republicanism. Some belonged to the second or third generation of plantation owners, others were professionals who had bought plantations or married into plantation owners' families. Manuel Moraes Barros was a lawyer and a plantation owner. Francisco Aguiar de Barros was a public functionary, had an import house, and was also a plantation owner. Muniz de Souza was a deputy in the provincial assembly and a coffee planter. Elías Pacheco Chaves was a coffee planter, an industrialist, a magistrate responsible for orphans, a police chief, and a provincial deputy.

Because of the support it received from men of standing and property, the Republican party in São Paulo became one of the most powerful in the country. As early as 1877 it succeeded in electing three deputies to the provincial assembly. However, two of the Republicans who were elected ran as candidates for the Liberal party – a strategy the Republicans followed many times. Although it was the most important Republican nucleus in the country the Partido Republicano Paulista (PRP) had only 900 registered members in 1880. In 1884, allying themselves with the Conservatives, they succeeded in sending two deputies to the Chamber: Prudente de Morais and Campos Sales, who later, after the proclamation of the Republic, became the first two civilian presidents of Brazil. At the end of the decade there were about 50 Republican clubs in São Paulo. According to estimates for 1889 one-quarter of the electorate in São Paulo was Republican (3,593 Republicans, 6,637 Liberals, 3,957 Conservatives). The party allied several times with the Liberals or the Conservatives – depending on who was in opposition – and adopted a

---

[17] Carvalho, 'A composição social dos partidos políticos imperiais', 15.

very flexible line in fundamental questions such as abolition or the conflict between church and state.

Republicans were also important in Minas Gerais, where many young politicians from traditional Conservative families, like Alvaro Botelho, or from Liberal families, like Afonso Celso, converted to republicanism. Some who had been important politicians in the monarchist parties became Republicans at the last minute. This was true of Antônio Carlos Ribeiro de Andrada, who in 1886 decided to join the Republicans, carrying with him many votes.

In general, however, Republicans received a very small number of votes in Minas and until 1887 the Mineiros had not created an organization that could unite all the clubs in the province. And in Minas as in other provinces many individuals who were Republicans did not qualify as electors. However, here as elsewhere Republican candidates often received the support of their monarchist friends and relatives. Family loyalties were often more important than political convictions. In 1888 when Republicans in Minas ran for a position in the Senate, they received one-third of the votes. It was only then that a Republican party was created in Minas. At this point they already had three deputies in the Chamber of Deputies and several in the provincial assembly. At the eve of the proclamation of the Republic, the Republican party in Minas had become as strong as the other two parties. Some politicians who had been in the Chamber for several years – João Penido, Felício dos Santos, Cesário Alvim – declared themselves Republicans. According to the polls, Republicans received 36 per cent of the votes. Oddly enough, in Rio, where the party had been originally created, the Republicans had less success. Rio was the centre of the monarchist bureaucracy and of big business. There, the Republicans recruited support mainly among the military and professionals. The rural areas were massively monarchist. Over and over again the Republican candidates who ran for elections in Rio were defeated, and Republican newspapers appeared and disappeared. One of the few Republican candidates to be elected for the provincial assembly was José do Patrocínio, a journalist and abolitionist leader, who had received the support of the Abolitionist Confederation. But in spite of its slow progress the party received one-seventh of the votes in the senatorial elections of 1887, and its candidates for the provincial assembly received one-fifth of the votes.

In Rio Grande do Sul the Republican party was organized in 1882. Here as in other provinces, Republicans founded clubs, created newspapers, and ran for election – without much success. In 1886 for the first time they succeeded in placing one candidate, Assis Brasil, in the provincial assembly. Many Republicans in Rio Grande do Sul were foreigners to whom the Republican programme had special appeal. Rio Grande do Sul's economy was mainly orientated to the internal market. The province was the main supplier of meat, jerked beef, leather, and foodstuffs. Immigrants had developed a thriving agriculture based on small properties. The peculiarity of Rio Grande do Sul's economic and social organization made its population particularly sensitive to the issues of decentralization, naturalization, and separation of church and state. This explains why in 1889 the Republicans received more votes than the Conservatives. They did not, however, stop the Liberals, who had always had great support in the province, from winning the elections by a large majority.

The similarity between the Liberal and the Republican programme constituted one of the Republicans' handicaps, not only in Rio Grande do Sul but everywhere. When the Liberals went back into power in 1878, many deserted the Republicans to join the Liberals. Even some of those who had left the Liberal party in 1868 to create the Republican party – Lafayette Rodrigues Pereira, Cristiano Ottoni, Salvador de Mendonça – soon returned to their original party, and Lafayette Rodrigues Pereira even accepted the post of prime minister. When the Liberals returned to power in 1878 the only alternative left to the Republican party was to attack their former allies. With that purpose they often supported the Conservatives, who were now in opposition. Between 1878 and 1884 – a period of Liberal hegemony – Republicans did not make much progress. It was only in 1885, when the Conservatives returned to power, that they took on a new life. But while Republicans made advances in the southern provinces, their situation in other parts did not improve much. Only in Pará where the rubber boom had fed an elite that resented centralization did they get more significant support, but even there Republicans constituted only a militant minority. In most of the other provinces there were just a few Republican clubs located in the most important urban centres, gathering a dozen or so idealist professionals.

Because they favoured a federation, the Republicans had initially refused to create a national organization, and clubs kept their autonomy. Republicans from different provinces often disagreed about emancipation, although most believed that the question should be decided by the provinces themselves, rather than be solved by the central government.

In 1884, during the debates over the bill that proposed the emancipation of 60-year-old slaves, Felício dos Santos, a Republican from Minas Gerais, refused to support any bill that did not recognize the right of compensation for the slave owner. But the two other Republicans in the Chamber, who represented São Paulo, Prudente de Morais and Campos Sales, supported the bill. Republicans diverged also about strategy. The great majority followed the opinion of Quintino Bocayuva, the leader of the party in Rio, who adopted a gradualist, legalistic, and democratic line. To enlarge the electoral basis of the party through political propaganda was his programme. Others like Silva Jardim adopted a revolutionary line, cultivating the idea of a popular revolution. There were also those who wanted Republicans to conspire with the military to overthrow the government. Republicans also disagreed about the ideal form of government. The majority defended the principles of sovereignty of the people and favoured a representative form of government; a few dreamed about an authoritarian republican regime like the one suggested by Comte.

Although there were many divergences among Republicans, most seemed to agree with the principles laid down in the constitution they drafted for the state of São Paulo in 1873: provincial autonomy, a bicameral system of government with the executive being an instrument of the legislature, universal suffrage, freedom of conscience, work, the press, and education, separation of the church from the state, abolition of the privileges and titles of nobility, guarantees of private property, and abolition of the system of conscription for the National Guard. Of all those issues the most important was federation. Resentment against centralization had grown so far that in São Paulo it gave rise to a small secessionist group. One of their leaders, Martim Francisco, lamented in the provincial assembly in 1879 the flow of provincial wealth to the imperial coffers, the interference of the central government in provincial affairs, and the inadequate representation of São Paulo in the central government. 'When we want to progress', he remarked bitterly, 'the central web envelops us, our political offices are filled with people alien to our way of life, to our interests, and to our customs.' Years later, after the electoral reform of 1881, he commented that each of São Paulo's nine deputies represented almost double the entire population of Espírito Santo, a province that elected two deputies, and nearly three times the population of Amazonas, which also elected two. He complained that São Paulo contributed 20 million milréis to the national treasury each year, one-sixth of the entire national revenue, but received a mere 3 million – a sum that corresponded to customs duties collected during three months in Santos, the principal port for coffee exports. These facts seemed to Martim Francisco sufficient to justify secession.[18]

His complaints were not unfounded. In 1883 São Paulo had four senators while Minas had ten, Bahia seven, and Pernambuco and Rio de Janeiro six each. While each Paulista senator represented 326,568 inhabitants, a senator from Pernambuco represented 185,138, and the senator from Amazonas represented 80,654. The same striking differences were noticed in the Chamber, where each Paulista deputy represented 145,141, while those from Pernambuco represented 85,448 and those from Amazonas 40,327. In 1889 only 3 out of 69 senators came from São Paulo, the richest province in the country (with a fourth seat vacant). Small provinces like Sergipe, Alagoas, and Paraíba had two while Rio had five, Bahia six, Pernambuco six and Minas Gerais ten. As we have seen, while São Paulo had only nine deputies, Ceará, one of the poorest provinces, had eight, Rio de Janeiro twelve, Pernambuco thirteen, Bahia fourteen and Minas Gerais twenty. It was rare to see a Paulista from the new coffee areas – the most progressive in the country – as a member of the Council of State, which was dominated by Minas Gerais, Bahia, Rio Grande do Sul, and Rio de Janeiro; most of the Paulistas who gained such positions represented plantation owners of the Paraíba valley, where coffee plantations had been in decline since 1870. To aggravate the situation São Paulo often had politicians from other provinces as provincial presidents.

Paulistas from the western parts of the province – the most productive – felt that they did not have a fair representation in the government and they began to see federation as the only adequate form of political organization. This opinion was shared by many people living in other provinces. The Paraenses, for example, also resented the central government, and criticism against centralization had become common in Rio Grande do Sul and Pernambuco. In an agricultural congress that took place in October 1878, the sugar plantation owners of Pernambuco complained bitterly about the government's emission bank which had loaned 25,000 contos to the south-central provinces of Rio de Janeiro, São Paulo, Espírito Santo, and Minas Gerais in the 1870s. To these

---

[18] Tácito de Almeida, *O movimento de 1887* (São Paulo, 1934); Emília Viotti da Costa, *Da monarquia à República. Momentos decisivos* (São Paulo, 1977), 313–16.

provinces, they said, went all the favours. 'While the planter in those provinces, protected by the government, with the advantage of credit, enjoys all comfort and displays an Asiatic luxury . . . the planters of the north are, with few exceptions, obliged to restrict themselves to their subsistence', said one of them.[19] Everywhere, for different reasons, there was an increasing awareness that centralization was a source of favouritism and an obstacle to development and progress. Federalism became the banner of all those who felt constrained by the government and resented the political oligarchies that perpetuated themselves in power through a system of patronage and clientele and through the monopoly of positions in the Senate and the Council of State. In 1885 a proposition signed by 39 Liberal deputies suggested that the electorate decide whether the constitution should be amended to give the country a federalist system. The proposed amendment never became law, and only with the proclamation of the Republic was a federal system adopted.

Federalism became one of the principal goals of the Republicans in their campaign against the monarchical system. From the moment the Conservatives took power in 1885 the Republicans intensified their campaign, trying to enlarge their bases and define new strategies. At a congress held in São Paulo in May 1888, revolutionary strategy was repudiated and the 'evolutionist' strategy was officially sanctioned through the appointment of Quintino Bocayuva as national leader of the party. This event generated a crisis within the party. Silva Jardim published a manifesto on 28 May violently attacking the moderate faction. But his protest had little effect. In the end the pacific faction prevailed. One year later, however, the monarchy was overthrown by a military coup.

By 1887 the leadership of the Republican party had begun to consider the possibility of asking the military for help. Rangel Pestana, a member of the Republican party in São Paulo, suggested to the Permanent Committee of the party that it join together with the military in order to carry out a coup. When he attended the national party congress in Rio he continued to express this point of view, and despite the disapproval of the committee, contacted certain individuals in the military, including Sena Madureira, Serzedelo Carreia, and the visconde de Pelotas. This tactic was favoured by Francisco Glicério, another Republican leader

[19] *Trabalhos do Congresso agrícola do Recife. Outubro do 1878. Sociedade Auxiliadora da Agricultura de Pernambuco. Edição facsimilar comemorativa do primeiro centenário 1878–1978* (Fundação Estadual de Planejamento Agrícola de Pernambuco, Recife, 1978), 17, 92, 114, 139, 147, 183.

from São Paulo, who in March 1888 wrote to Bocayuva insisting that he make contacts with the military. Américo Werneck, a leader of the party in Rio de Janeiro, also argued that the triumph of the Republican revolution would come about only through the use of military force. At the same time, the Republican high command in Rio Grande do Sul came out in favour of a militarist solution.

Once they agreed on the importance of obtaining military support, the Republicans started courting the army in several ways. Republican leaders contacted sympathetic officers, and the Republican press gave coverage to conflicts between the army and the government, never missing an opportunity to turn the military against the monarchy, while assuring them of Republican support.

Republicans found great receptivity in the army, where dissatisfaction was rampant. The officers' increasing alienation from the monarchical system coincided with their declining participation in the government. During the nine years of the First Empire (1822–31) twelve military men had seats in the Senate and five in the Council of State. Dom Pedro had appointed four officers to the Senate in the 1840s and two in the 1850s, but in the following 30 years of his reign he appointed only two. Military representation in the Council of State had also decreased. At the time of the proclamation of the Republic there was no military representation in the Council of State. Military representation in the cabinets and in the Chamber had also declined. More importantly, between 1881 and 1889 only civilians had been appointed as ministers of war.

During Cotegipe's Conservative Cabinet (1885–8) there had been several conflicts between military and civilians, conflicts which both Liberals and Republicans had exacerbated in their attempts to undermine the prestige of the Conservatives. Courted by politicians and by the press, the military had acquired an inflated sense of its importance. In 1886 when Cotegipe punished two officers (Cunha Matos and Sena Madureira) who, disregarding the government's prohibitions, had used the press to defend themselves against charges made by government officials, the incident had loud repercussions and many officers expressed solidarity with their colleagues. Marshal Deodoro da Fonseca, disobeying orders from the minister of war, refused to punish Sena Madureira who was under his command. Fonseca resigned from his post in Rio Grande do Sul and moved to Rio where he became the centre of attention. In the Senate, the visconde de Pelotas (Rio Grande do Sul), an experienced politician and a devoted and prestigious officer, warned the government of the imminent risk of a military uprising. The government, however, pursued its policies of disciplining disobedient officers, provoking even more discontent in the army. In 1887 the Military Club, which became the place of gathering of discontented officers, was created. The military became increasingly disillusioned with the political system. Expressing this disillusionment Floriano Peixoto, who later became president of the new Republic, writing to General Neiva in July 1887 commented: 'Our country is in an advanced state of moral corruption and needs a military dictatorship to cleanse it.'[20]

The conflict with the army contributed to the fall of Cotegipe who was replaced by João Alfredo, another Conservative, in March 1888. The new Cabinet, however, which abolished slavery in May, did not last long. And it was in an atmosphere of military unrest and Republican agitation that Ouro Preto, a Liberal, was called in June 1889 to form a Cabinet. Ouro Preto told the emperor that the only way to confront the Republican propaganda was to prove that the monarchical system could satisfy their demands and carry out their promises. In order to achieve this goal, the new minister devised a programme of political, economic and social reforms. But the programme he presented at the congressional session of 11 June was a slightly modified version of the programme presented twenty years earlier by the Liberal party. Ouro Preto proposed the limitation of the senator's term; the reduction of the Council of State to a mere administrative body; election of municipal authorities; nomination of provincial presidents and vice presidents from a list selected by the electors; and universal suffrage. He also suggested that freedom of worship be granted to all, and he proposed that the system of education be reformed to give private initiative more freedom. With regard to economic questions he recommended the reduction of export duties, the enactment of a law facilitating acquisition of land, the development of rapid means of transportation, the amortization of the foreign debt, the achievement of a balanced federal budget and the creation of credit institutions to issue paper currency. He did not include, however, any provision for adopting a federal system, which had been one of the crucial demands of the critics of the monarchy.

When the prime minister presented his proposal to the Chamber, Pedro Luís Soares de Sousa, a deputy from Rio de Janeiro, could not repress an exclamation which certainly expressed the feelings of most of

---

[20] J. F. Oliveira Vianna, *O ocaso do império* (São Paulo, 1925), 137.

those present: 'It is the beginning of the Republic', he said. Ouro Preto responded, 'No, it is the defeat of the Republic.' He was wrong – a few months later the monarchy was overthrown.

Ouro Preto's programme did not satisfy the radicals and irritated the Conservatives. The Conservatives proposed a motion of no confidence, which was approved by a vote of 79 to 20. A few days later, on 17 June, the Chamber was dissolved and the government called for elections. The situation became increasingly tense. Ouro Preto took measures that offended some important figures in the army. The nomination of Silveira Martins for the presidency of Rio Grande do Sul alienated Marshal Deodoro da Fonseca who had a history of personal conflicts with Martins. And the appointment of Cunha Matos to a post in Mato Grosso also provoked discontent. In late October there were growing rumours that the government might disband or exile insubordinate garrisons to remote areas of the country.

The Republicans took advantage of the irritation among military ranks. On 11 November, a few days before the Chamber was supposed to meet, Rui Barbosa, Benjamin Constant, Aristides Lobo, Bocayuva, Glicério and Colonel Solon met with Marshal Fonseca to convince him to take the initiative of overthrowing the monarchy. The old man still hesitated. He had always been loyal to the emperor and in spite of his irritation at the Cabinet he did not seem willing to support a military coup which would lead to the fall of the monarchy. On 15 November, however, when he left his house to force Ouro Preto to resign he met a stubborn minister decided to resist at all cost. The impasse did not last long. A few hours later a group of Republicans announced to the astonished nation the fall of the monarchy and the installation of the Republic. The royal family was sent into exile. No one rose to defend the monarchy.

The proclamation of the Republic had resulted from the concerted action of three groups: a military faction (representing at the most one-fifth of the army), plantation owners from the west of São Paulo, and members of the urban middle classes. They had been indirectly aided in the attainment of their goal by the declining prestige of the monarchy. Although the 'revolutionaries' were momentarily united by their republican ideal, profound disagreements among them would surface during their first attempts to organize the new regime. In the first years of the Republic, latent contradictions exploded into conflicts which contributed to the instability of the new regime.

CONCLUSION

1889 did not mark a significant break in Brazilian history. The country continued to depend as it always had on the export of agrarian products to the international market and on foreign investments. Power continued in the hands of planters and merchants and their allies. Universal suffrage did not increase the electorate much, since the literacy requirement deprived most of the Brazilian population of the right to vote. The system of patronage remained intact and oligarchical groups continued to control the nation to the exclusion of the masses. Universal suffrage, adoption of a federal system, abolition of tenure for senators, abolition of the Council of State and of the Moderating Power, separation of the church from the state – all those goals the reformers had battled for – did not have after all the miraculous effects they had expected. The main accomplishment of the Republic was to bring to power a new oligarchy of coffee planters and their clients who promoted only those institutional changes that were necessary to satisfy their own needs. For all the other social groups that had hoped that the Republic would represent a break with the past, 15 November was a *journée des dupes*.

Part Two

FIRST REPUBLIC (1889–1930)

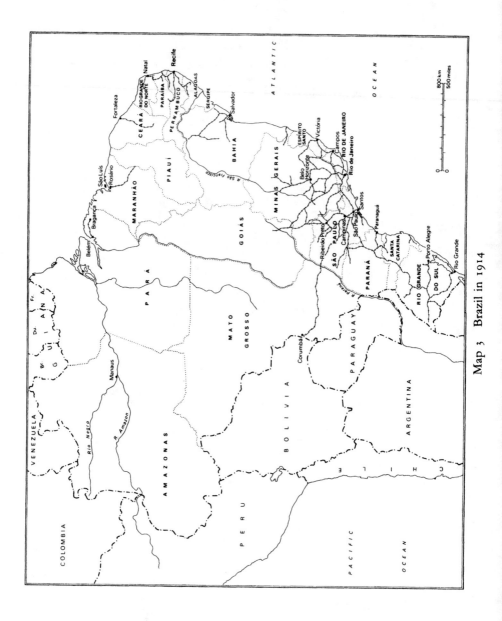

Map 3 Brazil in 1914

5

ECONOMY

The 60 years between 1870 and 1930 which comprise the last two decades of the empire and the whole of the First Republic represent the apogee of export orientation in Brazilian economic history. Resources were shifted by government and the private sector to export production, and exports rose from £1.31 to £2.83 per capita from the decade of the 1870s to that of the 1920s, a gain of about 1.6 per cent a year. Much of the social transformation and economic diversification experienced during the period, including European immigration, urbanization, improvements in communications and transportation and a modest level of industrialization, clearly derived from the expansion of exports. This expansion was also the principal attraction of foreign capital. The level of British and United States investments rose from £53 million in 1880 to £385 million by 1929. The world depression of the 1930s brought this era to a close. Exports ceased to exercise a dynamic influence on the economy and autarky and import-substitution had to be increasingly employed thereafter to try to stimulate further growth.

Exports appear to have been the principal stimulus to the onset of per capita economic growth, which seems not to have begun until shortly before 1900. There is no certainty concerning the rate of that growth, since national accounts have only been kept since 1947. An average rate of per capita growth of gross domestic product of almost 2.5 per cent a year has been calculated for the period 1900 to 1929, but downward correction may be necessary. Such a rate surpasses contemporary growth in the industrialized countries. Per capita gross national product at the end of the period 1925–9 may have amounted to US$110, in current dollars.[1]

---

[1] See C. Contador and C. Haddad, 'Produto real, moeda e preços: a experiência brasileira no periodo 1861–1970', *Revista Brasileira de Estatística* (1975); O. Dias Carneiro, 'Past trends in the economic evolution of Brazil, 1920–1965' (mimeo, Cambridge, Mass., 1966), Table 1B.

The centrality of export production during the period 1870–1930 represented in an important sense a continuity with the Brazilian past. From discovery in 1500 to independence in 1822 exports were the principal means by which the Portuguese crown and overseas merchants extracted monopoly profits from the colony; the promotion of exports had therefore been their central concern. They installed and elaborated a cane-sugar raising plantation system at points along the immense coastline, from Maranhão to São Vicente, and especially in Pernambuco and Bahia, employing Amerindian and African slave labour, locally managed by a colonial latifundist landowning class. Sugar remained Brazil's main cash crop throughout the colonial period, although from the late seventeenth century sugar exports fell in value. Towards the end of the eighteenth century, the crown stimulated the diversification of Brazilian plantation production, with some success. Exports of cotton, indigo, rice, cacao and other commodities grew significantly, and sugar revived, partly as a result of the interruptions in colonial trade in the Caribbean between 1776 and 1815. Most of Brazil's other exports were extractive. The coastal forests provided timber and other naval stores. In the interior regions of Minas Gerais, Goiás and Mato Grosso a century-long gold rush began shortly before 1700. Further inland itinerant traders advanced, collecting dyewood, cacao, pelts, feathers, parrots, essences, ipecac, sarsaparilla and the like to sell to exporters. The colony shipped tobacco and other goods to Portuguese African trading stations to pay for slaves and smuggled a variety of European products to the Río de la Plata region in return for the silver of Potosí. Portuguese mercantilist policy sought to provide cheap slave labour to the coastal plantations, limit access to the mining zones, prevent the local manufacture of goods which might profitably be sent from Lisbon, and staunch the leakage of gains into hands other than Portuguese overseas merchants and the crown.

Although population (little more than three million in 1800, including Indians outside Portuguese control, averaging about three persons per ten square kilometres) was concentrated on the coast, an unregulated settlement took place across a vast wilderness. The plantation and mining centres engendered an internal trade in slaves, mules and cattle which extended Portuguese control over a considerable inland area. Even beyond these zones a form of pioneering was practised by settlers, *mestiço* (offspring of Amerindians and Europeans) in technique as well as genes. Their slash-and-burn farming was itinerant, dependent on the wilds for game and fish, occupying the interstices and edges of the colonial economy. They provided the town markets with a few pigs, some tobacco, corn and beans and received in return little more than salt and gunpowder. This subsistence economy, surviving well into the twentieth century, cannot be regarded as the complement of a dual economy, a backward sector awaiting absorption by the modern. Its backwardness resulted from the denial of land titles to the poor and from the retention of revenues within the towns where the royal bureaucrats, overseas merchants, principal planters and mine concessionaires lived. Its continued backwardness was useful to the coastal colony, as a place to exile the non-conforming, as a buffer against attack by tribal peoples and convenient way to achieve their 'civilization', and as a cost-free means of clearing the omnipresent and axe-resistant forest. Pioneer settlement was even a crown project, along Brazil's vague and remote borders with Spanish territories, from Rio Grande do Sul to Mato Grosso.

After 1808, when the Portuguese court, fleeing Napoleon's army, transferred to Rio de Janeiro, Brazil's economic policy was no longer externally determined. Nevertheless colonial structures, and with them the centrality of the export trade (sugar, cotton and now coffee), largely remained intact. Conflicts between the landowning class and the Portuguese overseas merchants soon led to Brazil's political independence. Yet Independence, under a Portuguese prince who proclaimed himself emperor, produced few innovations. The new government was burdened with part of Portugal's London-contracted debt, many of the colonial functionaries were retained in office, the planter class confirmed its monopoly over land rights and its slave properties, and English merchants, privileged by an inequitable commercial treaty that was the price of recognition by Britain, replaced Portuguese export houses in the major ports. The new central government experienced difficulties in establishing its authority within the country. There were rebellions in the peripheral provinces, riots by urban artisans and slave uprisings which were at bottom reactions against the socially and economically disaggregative effects of neocolonialism. Political stability was not achieved until the late 1840s. By then, the debilitating post-Independence commercial treaties had expired, thereby liberating tariff policy. In 1850 a commercial code was written according to the English model, and a land law was passed. The African slave trade was abolished in the same year under pressure from the British government, embarrassing the imperial elite, but nevertheless forcing it to think more creatively about increasing the supply of labour.

ECONOMIC POLICY AND THE CREATION OF A NATIONAL MARKET

The Empire, which survived until 1889, did not pursue with any degree of consistency or energy economic ends that might be termed developmental. A few national projects were proposed, fewer still – most notably the census of 1872 and the beginning of a state-operated telegraph network – were executed. Instead, the interests of regionally dominant upper classes were supported with a modest level of funding or with profit guarantees. The landowners of the province of Rio de Janeiro tended to be the most likely to obtain backing, and they were in fact the political mainstay of the Empire. As coffee in particular experienced significant growth rates, export policy came to receive even greater attention from the central government's bureaucrats. Since the customs houses represented the nearly exclusive source of their revenues and certain imports were critical to the government's functioning, they had reasons of their own to support a policy of export orientation.

The 'business climate' of the Empire, however, was in general mildly hostile to capitalist entrepreneurship. The most energetic and innovative businessman of the 1850s and 1860s, Irineu Evangelista de Souza, though he received the title barão de Mauá, claimed that his career ended in failure partly because of faltering collaboration or distaste for his activities within the government. The money supply, apart from brief intervals, was controlled by a single government bank whose mandate was to contain rather than to promote private enterprise. Individual legislative authorization of joint-stock companies was retained until 1882. The emperor's Council of State insisted on the necessity of scrutinizing incorporations, alleging irresponsible tendencies in Brazilian businessmen. Government encouragement to business, when it was offered, normally took the form of exclusive concessions. The great landowners and merchants, themselves sensitive to the profit motive, preferred that the economy be steered within channels that preserved their control of resources and of the government. Their economy needed to grow only slowly and diversify hardly at all, since the gains were to accrue to a single, very small class. As one historian has remarked, 'Class interests were so disparate as to raise serious questions concerning the validity of using the nation as the unit of analysis.'[2]

The Republic, however, set loose the 'spirit of association' and transformed the nature of the economic debate. The provisional government made economic questions its central concern and aggressively promoted economic growth. Would-be capitalists and industrialists, along with certain politically active urban professionals and army officers, angered at the incompetence displayed in the Paraguayan War and by scanty postwar military budgets, promoted an interventionist economic programme. In the last months of the Empire the final abolition of slavery had been decreed and government bonds had been floated to aid planters suffering the uncompensated loss of their slaves. These funds were turned directly over to city creditors, fuelling a sudden boom. The provisional government then authorized the launching of banks of emission, joint stock companies and development schemes in a great speculative wave, dubbed the *encilhamento*, racetrack parlance for the saddling-up. Although numerous initiatives of this ebullient transitional period proved long-lasting, the nationalist coalition lost control by 1894, exhausted by its own excesses, obliged to put down a rebellion of the navy and another in Rio Grande do Sul, and overcome by inflation and the accumulation of foreign debt.

The governments that followed, apparently much less interventionist than those of the nationalists, can be seen to have put constraints on internal development. The first civilian government, for example, cancelled contracts that had been signed with Rio de Janeiro shipyards for the construction of destroyer-class warships. The planter-sponsored government, considering it more prudent to buy its naval vessels from English firms, so as to ensure the retention of British markets and an uninterrupted flow of British capital, let the half-built hulls rust into their ways. Circumstances and contradictions inherent in such policies, however, induced a sizeable number of developmental measures and impelled direct government intervention.[3] The planter's programmes were quite expensive and large in scale. Often it fell to the government to implement them when foreign concessionaires or native entrepreneurs wavered or proved too demanding of official subsidies.

It has often been noted that the planting and exporting interests

[2] N. Leff, *Underdevelopment and development in Brazil* (2 vols., London, 1982), I, 7.
[3] See S. Topik, 'The evolution of the economic role of the Brazilian state, 1889–1930', *Journal of Latin American Studies*, 11/2 (1979), 325–42.

desired monetary and fiscal policies that would induce a gradual inflation, thereby shifting real income to them. The overriding concern of civilian governments from 1894 was for their credit-worthiness in the eyes of foreign bankers. This outlook was essential because the same interests which installed these governments were unwilling to accompany their mandate with revenues adequate to cover expenditures. Even more than the Empire, the Republic produced deficits: 32 during its 41 years of existence, and in 13 of them the deficit exceeded 25 per cent of income. These deficits could not be resolved through internal loans. Local bond markets were unorganized, leading the government to the disreputable practice of paying some of its obligations with bonds that were hastily discounted by the recipients. Internal loans, furthermore, could not be applied to foreign debts already contracted and owed in gold. On the other hand, foreign loans were accompanied by conditions that reached into the directing organs of government and commandeered them. The London Rothschilds rescued the finances of the new civilian regime when it granted, in 1898, a funding loan of £10 million, permitting a delay of thirteen years in repayment of principal. But they demanded in return a surcharge on import duties, to be deposited in a reserve account in London, and a gradual retirement from circulation of paper milreis to an amount equivalent to the value of the loan. This deflationary programme remained the centrepiece of government policy, despite severe depressive impact upon production and employment, until 1905.

In spite of foreign loans, federal deficits continued to accumulate. According to the republican constitution, states and municipalities could also contract loans. And so they did: from 1900 to 1912 their foreign debts grew from £5 million to £50 million; the latter was a sum 37 per cent as large as the federal debt. The central government, pressed by its own creditors, disavowed any responsibility for the debts of the local governments. For the planting and exporting interests the deflationary exercise begun in 1898 was extremely painful, since it reduced their earnings in terms of milreis. They therefore achieved a compromise in 1905: the milreis was set at a new, somewhat higher par of 15 pence, but the government would act to prevent it from rising further by opening a Conversion Fund. The Fund would receive gold currencies that were deposited with it at that rate and it would simultaneously enlarge the money supply by issuing paper circulating notes in exchange.

The periodic funding of the Brazilian foreign debt could not be regularly achieved because of the cyclical nature of the export trade, exacerbated by the policies the bankers themselves instigated. Cyclical upswings in the industrial countries increased the demand for Brazil's commodity exports, thereby pushing up their prices. Rising commodity prices attracted an inflow of foreign capital, intensifying the recovery in Brazil and stimulating a disproportionate increase in imports as well as in domestic production. The downswing was equally steep, but more painful, as gold-backed currencies flowed out of the country and the customs houses were piled high with unpaid-for imports, and the foreign debt mounted higher than before. The foreign bankers would be dunned for another loan, but now their coffers were empty or their conditions were too offensive to national sovereignty to be accepted. The only recourse left to the Brazilian government at such a juncture, as in August 1914, was to suspend the rules of the game. It abolished gold conversion and emitted 250 million milreis in paper currency. Monetary orthodoxy, though embranced rhetorically, was only a relative good compared to the government's survival; inflation, though seemingly endemic, was usually undertaken only as a last resort.[4]

The implantation of a national developmentalist economic policy required the creation of a national market, but this was difficult to achieve. Brazil, geographically a subcontinent, was in demographic and economic terms an archipelago. With the important exception of Minas Gerais, the bulk of its population, a little less than ten million in 1870 and seventeen million in 1900, still lived along the extensive coast, clustered around port cities which were in most cases state capitals. Coastwise shipping lines maintained vessels that were over-age and poorly maintained, schedules that were rarely met, and rates that were double or treble those of overseas shippers. The smaller port cities without deepwater channels and dependent on coastal steamers sought funding to deepen their harbours so as to receive ocean-going vessels. These efforts the elites of the larger cities, such as Salvador and Recife, desirous of retaining their role as entrepôts, struggled to quash.

For shorter or longer distances into the hinterlands of the coastal cities stretched networks of rails, roads or trails. These networks were only casually tangential one to the next, and in some cases they were separated by hundreds of kilometres of utter wilderness. The coastal state of Espírito Santo, for example, was linked to adjoining Minas Gerais only

[4] See W. Fritsch, 'Aspectos da política econômica no Brasil, 1906–1914', in P. Neuhaus (ed.), *Economia brasileira: uma visão histórica* (Rio de Janeiro, 1980).

by an extremely difficult passage of the Rio Doce. Not until 1905 did construction begin on a railway paralleling the river, and not until the 1930s did it reach Belo Horizonte. Goiás and Minas Gerais were land-locked and isolated states, while Mato Grosso and Acre were accessible only by immense river detours. The cost of transport, it may be imagined, no matter how high external tariffs were set, represented a barrier to inter-regional trade of still more imposing dimension.

To these obstacles were added inter-state and even inter-municipal tariffs. The practice of taxing goods brought from other states and towns began during the Empire. Under the republican constitution, a federalist charter, import tariffs were exclusively levied by the central government, but export duties were granted exclusively to the states. The states which enjoyed large export revenues, principally São Paulo, evidently inspired this clause, which obliged the less fortunate states with no exports to tax to resort to these imposts. Often they were charged indiscriminately on imported goods as well as on goods originating in other states, so that they constituted a kind of tariff surcharge. The federal courts condemned these duties, which had no basis in the constitution, and yet they continued unabated. That this was possible is a clue to the manner in which the interests of the regional upper classes meshed with those who controlled the dominant, exporting states. Though the central government repeatedly intervened militarily in the smaller states to depose one faction or another of these lesser oligarchies, it never attempted to cut off this source of revenue in the interest of creating a national market.

Although nationalist republicans claimed that they desired the creation of such a market, this goal was probably beyond their intentions in another, more profound sense. Access to the factors of production depended in Brazil only to a slight degree upon the workings of a market. Political and social factors largely determined access to credit, entitlement of land, and conditions of employment. This reality came to be attenuated by European immigration and urbanization over the course of the period under study, but it was always the care of the property-owning classes that their rewards derive from their social ranking, that their ability to command resources exceed that to which their position in the market might have entitled them and that they be held immune from competition with persons of lower social status. In these circumstances, youthful ambitions were concentrated upon political goals, a surer path to upward social mobility than entrepreneurship; and risky entrepreneurship, even when successful, was obliged to make its peace with power.

The shift of internal resources to the growth of the export sector may be seen, from the point of view of domestic conditions, as the result of the preferences of the dominant social classes, who considered such a policy optimally profitable, convenient and adaptable to their desire for local autonomy and continued monopoly in the exercise of political power. These policies were nevertheless not without contradictions, arising from circumstances and factors inherent in the policies themselves. The linkages of these dominant classes with their external sources of funding were especially problematic and vulnerable to reactions from within the Brazilian polity. Even so, for most of the period under study the middle classes could be persuaded of their own stake in Brazil's growing incorporation into the world system of trade and finance through the stimulation of exports.

THE GROWTH OF EXPORT DEMAND

By 1870 world trade was entering a new phase, one in which commercial opportunities were to enlarge greatly. During the 1870s cargo-carrying steamships entered into regular service in the South Atlantic, halving the cost of transport, regularizing deliveries and much increasing the range and volume of goods that might be delivered. Industrialization in England had considerably expanded the variety and utility of those goods. In effect Brazil's export-orientation was also entering a new phase. The country was beginning to participate in the industrial revolution by exchanging its agricultural and extractive products for manufactured goods that embodied the new technologies. Undersea cables in the same decade connected Brazil's port cities with Europe, and indirectly with the United States, thereby reducing price and supply uncertainties and much facilitating the transfer of commercial credit. The spread of the industrial system to Germany, the United States and a few other countries intensified competition among manufacturers, thus enhancing the position of suppliers of raw materials and foodstuffs such as Brazil, which experienced improving terms of trade from the 1870s to the outbreak of the first world war.

The growth of exports was critical to Brazilian economic growth, yet for the period as a whole it was rather slow. Most of the increase in the value of Brazil's exports was sandwiched between financial panics and wars and depressions in Europe and the United States. It was also problematic. The number of staple products in world trade was small and geographic factors excluded Brazil from supplying any but a few of them. Prices fluctuated sharply and the threat of widening competition, of exclusion from markets, and the discovery of synthetics clouded prospects for entrepreneurs and policy makers alike. For Brazil, it might be said, the severest disadvantage of the policy of export orientation was the weakness of the stimulus of overseas demand. The difficulty may be observed in a review of the principal articles of trade during this period.

Coffee was by far Brazil's single most successful product in international trade. The plant had been introduced in the eighteenth century, but it achieved a significant place in the export list only in the decade of independence. The coffee bush was highly suitable to the climate and soils of south-eastern Brazil and coffee beans were easy to transport and store. No complex industrial processes were required to prepare them for market. In the 1870s various kinds of mechanical hullers were introduced and commercial roasting techniques were perfected. Late in the 1880s Brazil's Asiatic competitors were ravaged by a blight. With this promising conjuncture, Brazilian planters rapidly expanded their groves. Brazilian coffee was chiefly of low grade. In contrast to Colombia, Jamaica and other growing areas, where it was cultivated by smallholders, Brazil's coffee was unshaded and minimal care was devoted to its tending and harvesting. The resulting cheaper product, however, enjoyed the greater growth in demand from mid-century onwards because of the appearance of a mass market, principally in the United States. There consumption reached 5.5 kilograms per capita by 1921, as caffeine addiction spread among an urbanizing population.

Coffee exports had reached 60,000 tons per annum in the 1830s; by 1871 216,000 tons were shipped. In 1872 the great fertile plateau of São Paulo was opened by the arrival of the railway to Campinas. This state soon ranked first in sales. Stimulated by the inflow of foreign investments in the decade after 1885 and by the cheap money of the Republican provisional government, new planting in São Paulo doubled the Brazilian coffee groves. By 1901 exports reached 888,000 tons. The price of coffee went through three cycles between Independence and 1907, each time ending near US$0.15 per kilogram. The recurring tendency toward low prices discouraged potential competitors. Even though Brazil's market dominance was allowed to erode between 1870 and 1930, in the late 1920s it still possessed 2.1 billion of the world's 3.2 billion coffee bushes. For the period as a whole it supplied more than half the coffee sold in international trade. Unfortunately none of Brazil's other exports enjoyed similar sustained success in world trade, and as a result by 1925–9 coffee provided 75 per cent of foreign earnings. Thus the Brazilian economy was characterized by a very high dependence on the price of a single export product.

Natural rubber, by the late 1880s the second most important article of Brazil's international trade, went from boom to sudden collapse. The industrial applications of rubber multiplied rapidly in the last quarter of the nineteenth century, inducing an extraordinary surge in world demand. Its price, £45 a ton in 1840, rose to £182 in 1870, and to £512 by 1911. Rubber gatherers spread the length and breadth of the Amazon valley, which was the native habitat of several commercially valuable species of latex-bearing trees. Of these the most productive was *Hevea brasiliensis*. In 1870 6,591 tons of natural rubbers were exported; by 1911 shipments amounted to 38,547 tons. During the first decade of the twentieth century rubber provided more than a quarter of Brazil's foreign earnings. Immediately afterward a catastrophic decline in price set in. By the end of the first world war, Brazil had lost nearly all of its export market. *Hevea brasiliensis* had been introduced and acclimatized in Malaya and the Dutch East Indies and there plantations were formed which produced rubber at much lower cost. The Brazilian government projected, but did not execute, an expensive plan to develop the infrastructure of the Amazon region; in the short run it proved impossible to effect a shift to cultivation there. The rubber gathering network gradually came unravelled, and by 1930 exports had slumped to 6,000 tons.

Sugar, the most traditional of plantation crops, and the dynamo of Brazil's colonization, underwent a revival in the world market in the late nineteenth century. New, more efficient processing techniques turned sugar into an article of mass consumption, the cheapest of all carbohydrates, the ever-available caloric supplement to the workers' diet. Brazil participated in this revival through the early 1880s, but then suffered a decline in exports that became precipitous after 1900. Competition from beet sugar, protected in the industrial countries, and from cane sugar in newer producing areas overcame Brazilian planters. Cuba, Puerto Rico and the Philippines acquired preferential access to the United States sugar market after they were absorbed by the United States following the victory over Spain in 1898. Cuba, reduced to a protectorate, witnessed an infusion of US$1,000 million into its sugar sector during the succeeding decade. By then Brazilian cane-sugar exports were stagnant. The value of sugar exports from Pernambuco, the country's

most important sugar-growing state, was in 1898 only half what it had
been fifteen years before. Brazil's share of the world market, 10 per cent
in the 1850s, fell continuously; by the first decade of the twentieth
century it was less than 0.5 per cent.

Cotton had also been traditionally an important article of Brazil's
overseas trade. At the beginning of the nineteenth century native
arboreal long-fibred species supplied 10 per cent of the world market.
Although demand for raw cotton increased enormously during the
nineteenth century, the spinning mills of England came to be supplied by
the United States. During the American Civil war resulting from the
attempted secession of the southern states (1861–5) and for a few years
afterward, Brazilian cotton was again briefly competitive. In 1870 Brazil
exported 42,000 tons. But with the revival of the cotton trade in the
United States and increased cultivation in Egypt Brazil lost its British
market; by 1880 exports had fallen to half the volume of ten years before.

Brazil had sold cacao since colonial times, most of it gathered from
wild stands in the Amazon valley. It was planted on a large scale for the
first time in southern Bahia in the 1880s. World demand surged soon
afterwards from a little over 100,000 tons to almost 550,000 tons by 1928,
stimulated by new forms of consumption. Brazil's participation in this
market was, however, modest, supplying little more than a tenth of the
world market by the late 1920s. Most of the world's cacao came from
Britain's West African colonies. At the beginning of the first world war a
few meat packing plants were installed in Rio Grande do Sul and São
Paulo. Their early success in overseas sales, however, did not much
outlast the period of wartime shortages. Brazil also sold each year a few
thousand tons of hides, yerba maté, oil seeds, timber, manganese, pelts
and tobacco. None of these added much to export earnings although they
were significant stimuli within regional markets of the north-east and
south. Brazil, in addition, was a producer of immense quantities of
certain other staples such as maize, beans, bananas and manioc meal, but
only in unusual circumstances did it manage to sell any of them abroad.

It is remarkable that Brazil, a country of immense territory and varied
resources, participated in world trade essentially as a planter of a single
crop: coffee. External factors do not entirely explain the narrow range of
opportunities exploited nor the erosion of market shares that had been
achieved in earlier periods. To a degree the difficulties were beyond
remedy. Certain natural disadvantages were present that became more
severe or more obvious as world demand developed. For example, the

decisive advantage of the Cuban sugar growers was their flatter terrain, more suitable to the needs of the high-capacity grinding mills since it permitted the more rapid delivery of cane to the mill gates and speed of delivery was essential as cane juices quickly evaporate. Rubber cultivation was attempted on a large scale in the Amazon valley only in the 1920s, but then it was discovered that a blight exclusive to the genus *Hevea* destroyed rubber trees when they were planted in close stands. This fungus had not accompanied the rubber seeds that had been transferred to south-east Asia. In other cases the difficulties appear to have been remediable, but the remedies were incompletely applied. The loss of overseas cotton markets occurred even though short-staple cotton had been introduced to Brazilian plantations in the 1860s.

Brazil's overseas trade appears to have been limited to commodities in which overwhelming comparative advantages offset high costs of production and commercialization and high internal taxes. The capital resources necessary to improve methods of production and to organize more efficient marketing arrangements were indeed scarce, but not unavailable. In the absence of private initiatives, the central and state governments seemed willing to provide guarantees and even funding. But these schemes, when they were undertaken, often appear to have been tardy, ill-conceived or incompletely executed. Even in the coffee sector, which generated funds for improvement of productivity on a large scale, a lack of attention to competitiveness was displayed. Instead, the problem of declining market shares was viewed merely as a problem of declining prices. Emphasis therefore was placed almost exclusively upon price maintenance.

The Brazilian government undertook, on an immense scale, to stabilize the price of its principal commodity in world trade. Having greatly enlarged their plantings after 1885, in the late 1890s the Brazilian coffee growers confronted depressed world prices and the effects of the internal deflationary policy that was the condition of the funding loan of 1898. Brazilian delegates at the international coffee conference held in 1902 therefore pressed for a cartel, but they were rebuffed. The state of São Paulo declared a halt to new planting in that same year, later extended through 1912. By 1906 São Paulo had convinced the other principal coffee-producing states of Minas Gerais and Rio de Janeiro to participate in a scheme called 'valorization'. These states were to purchase coffee at a base price of US$0.15 per kilogram and store it against the time when prices might compensate the cost of the operation. Funding was secured from banks in Europe and the United States through the intercession of coffee importers. Thus 660,000 tons were removed from sale within six months. A surcharge was added to new coffee sales, to help defray the warehousing costs, and the federal government was finally persuaded to guarantee the loans. Coffee prices did begin to rise again, and by 1912 they had reached an average US$0.31 per kilogram. By the end of that year all the coffee stored in the United States had been hurriedly sold off in the face of mounting irritation there.

The valorization appears to have lessened the impact in Brazil of the world recession of 1907–8, it may have benefited the planters, and it was certainly profitable for the bankers and intermediaries who made sizeable commissions and increased their presence in the business within Brazil in consequence. The price of coffee might have risen in any case since world demand was still growing. The federal government was, however, won over to the procedure and sponsored a second valorization during the crisis of the First World War. This time 180,000 tons were bought and warehoused, prices climbed sharply, partly because of a severe frost in São Paulo, and the government made a profit. With the postwar slump in commodity prices a third valorization was initiated. By then, however, a levelling-off of world demand had set in and the resumption of new planting in São Paulo overwhelmed the venture. The federal government ended its participation, but São Paulo was hounded by its planters to take on the purchase of coffee single-handed. It declared a 'permanent defence' in 1925, and went on, until the crash of 1929, desperately buying up and storing a series of record harvests. The effect of this policy, which diverted resources from the other sectors of the economy and ignored the issue of productivity, was to encourage foreign competition to expand.

The erosion of market shares and the failure to develop potential markets may, in the case of other export products, also be attributed in part to public policy. The expansionary phase of each export was usually accompanied by parallel efforts on the part of established producers to hamper, through the agency of government, the creation of further producing units. This is easily observable in the coffee business, since coffee spread over state lines and involved inter-state rivalries. Indeed, the enthusiasm of São Paulo planters for republicanism after 1870 may be attributed in large measure to their annoyance at preferences shown by the Empire to the growers of Rio de Janeiro. This rivalry was also displayed by the north-eastern planters of sugar and cotton, who resisted the transfer of these crops to São Paulo, and it is manifest among the merchants who supervised the rubber gathering trade and abhorred the prospect of a domestic rubber plantation regime. Among the victories scored by established planters may be mentioned the extreme retardation of road, rail and port facilities in the interior of the cacao region of southern Bahia.

Heavy rates of taxation of exports reduced Brazil's competitiveness in world markets. Furthermore, to a considerable degree government expenditures were non-developmental. The federal and state governments devoted large sums to the beautification of their respective capitals and to other sumptuous ends, but even apparently developmental projects were often disguises for other purposes. Land colonization schemes whose first step was the purchase of an existing plantation, for example, were really rescue missions for failing planters, and when these estates subdivided the beneficiaries were more likely to be deserving party members who desired to speculate in land than sturdy husbandmen. The government spent much of its revenues, in fact, for the simple purpose of remaining in power. The erosion of competitiveness in world markets was a direct and cumulative outcome. This was politically not an entire disaster. Products which disappeared from the export list, such as sugar and cotton, received protection in the domestic market. Given the size and growth of that market, that was a moderately, even pleasingly, consolatory recompense. For example, Brazil itself consumed, by 1921–3, 77 per cent of its cotton harvests of 115,000 tons.

Brazil was less dependent on a single customer or supplier than most of the other non-industrialized countries of the day. Its coffee and rubber went chiefly to the United States, which levied no duties upon them; indeed, those two products, along with raw silk, were that country's most important tariff-exempt imports. It sought, in return, greater acceptance for its wheat and flour, kerosene, lumber and manufactured goods. Britain, however, was until after the first world war the principal supplier of manufactured goods – and of credit. Germany ranked second. Existing or potential trade complementarities with Africa or the rest of South America were little explored. Brazil's only sizeable exchange with Latin America was its purchase of Argentine wheat, a business in the hands of British intermediaries, in return for yerba maté, for which demand was stagnant. The possibility of tariff union with prosperous Argentina, Uruguay and Chile seems not to have been examined.

The world system of trade and investment upon which Brazil's export orientation was based suffered terrible reverses in the First World War. The war rescued Brazil's rubber, temporarily, from oblivion and provided improved opportunities for the sale of some of its less important exports – sugar, beef, beans, and manganese – to the desperate antagonists, but coffee was not high on the Allies' list of shipping priorities, nor were they much concerned whether the Brazilian economy might collapse for lack of spare parts and fuels. The value in pounds sterling of Brazil's exports fell during the five war years by 16 per cent, in comparison to the booming five previous years, while imports fell by 24 per cent. The cost of shipping climbed sharply, and so did the prices of imports. For example, imported textiles, which cost an average US$0.98 a kilogram in 1913, rose to US$3.46 a kilogram in 1918. Since more than half of Brazil's imports were foodstuffs and raw materials, the impact on the internal economy was severe. Internally prices doubled, buoyed by the emissions of paper currency necessitated by the repatriation of foreign currencies and gold. The federal government was saved at the last moment from default on its foreign loans in October 1914 by a £15 million funding loan raised in London. Rationing was not attempted; ceiling prices were imposed, but only in Rio de Janeiro and even there not effectually. Wages apparently did not keep pace with prices, causing terrible hardship among the urban population and provoking demonstrations and widespread strikes in Rio de Janeiro and São Paulo in 1917.

As a consequence of the Brazilian entrance into the war on the side of the Allies in October 1917, German banks and insurance companies were closed and firms with links to German capital were harassed or put out of business through the application of the British 'Black List'. The Brazilian government acquired, as spoils of war, 40-odd German vessels stranded in the country's ports, thereby doubling its merchant tonnage, but it lost a substantial amount of the value of bank accounts that had been opened in Belgium, with the proceeds of its sales of valorization stocks. More consequential than any of this were the long-term effects of the war, which weakened the economies of all of Brazil's trading partners (except the United States), reducing their capacity to advance credit and import from countries such as Brazil. The faltering British financial centre, critical to Brazilian export orientation, proved especially problematic in the 1920s.

FACTORS OF PRODUCTION

Land

Land, in the sense of dry terrestrial surface, was evidently abundant in Brazil, to the point approaching that of a free good. What rescued it from that category was the ephemeral quality of its soil fertility, at least as farming was practised in Brazil, and the extreme concentration of its land titles. The practice of agriculture in Brazil was limited to forest soils. The more accessible of these were located along the coast to a distance inland of 100 to 400 kilometres. Behind them stretched drier, poorer soils considered fit only for raising cattle. Lands newly cleared of primary forest were prized for spectacular yields. Coffee, it was believed, could only be successful on soils just cleared of virgin forest. Thus coffee planting encouraged a rapid expansion of the frontier in south-eastern Brazil. Coffee bushes were capable of bearing profitably for 40 years, but imprudence in locating the groves often reduced that span. Since most of the coastal strip of forested land derived its rainfall from its ruggedly mountainous topography, its humus quickly eroded.

Speculation in coffee lands introduced a feverish new form of enterprise. Formerly land increased in value as it was cleared and granted legal title; thereafter, as fertility gradually disappeared, so did value. The setting out of coffee seedlings became a business in itself which inflated land prices wondrously. Much of the coffee planting, it might be asserted, was carried out with no thought of growing coffee, but of speculating in mature new groves. The coffee frontier swept forward like a brush fire, obliterating thousands of square kilometres of timber and other forest resources. In the 1920 census, São Paulo's farms, comprising 8 per cent of the area of all Brazil's rural properties, accounted for more than 27 per cent of their value, the equivalent of US$2,600 million in current dollars. None of the gains of speculation reverted to the state. São Paulo, like almost all the other states, did not impose rural land taxes.

Concentration of landownership in Brazil was traditionally extreme. The Portuguese crown had believed that only landed aristocrats would produce for overseas markets, and therefore its grants were enormous, typically 40 square kilometres in extent. Under the Empire this tradition was maintained because the central government was too weak to make effective its law (1850) determining the sale of crown lands at auction. Instead locally powerful elites simply usurped public lands, employing fraud in land offices and evicting in the process smallholding squatters. Only in the southern states of Rio Grande do Sul and Santa Catarina did the Empire effectively promote smallholding. There, following the policy of the Portuguese crown in the peopling of border areas, it settled German and Italian immigrants in official colonies. Their descendants spread within those provinces and formed more colonies, but their influence on the national economy was limited. Nevertheless they presented an economic structure contrasting sharply with the great plantations and ranches.

The Republic granted, in effect, amnesty to the land grabbers, when it bestowed the remaining crown lands upon the states. The state governments then demonstrated the same incapacity to guard the public patrimony as had the Empire. A succession of state laws issued titles to all those whose social prominence had assured the local acquiescence to their private expropriations. During all this time no government had recognized land rights of tribal peoples or had set aside any but the most inconsequential reserves for their use. Although in 1910 the protection of tribal peoples came to be a federal responsibility under a service headed by General Cândido Rondon, the murder of entire tribes, as a preliminary to the private appropriation of state lands, continued to be practised. Landholding, as a consequence of these policies, or lack of them, remained highly concentrated. By 1920 no more than 3 per cent of rural dwellers possessed titles to the rural landholdings included in the census; of this tiny group of landowners, 10 per cent controlled three-quarters of those lands.

Labour

Brazil's population rose from 10.1 million to 30.6 million between 1872 and 1920. Its rate of growth accelerated from 1.85 to 2.15 per cent a year between these dates, and life expectancy rose from 27.4 years in 1872 (when slave life expectancy was about 21.0 years), to about 34.6 years in 1930. The urban population formed a small minority which tended to grow not much faster than the population as a whole. In 1872 persons living in towns of 20,000 or more inhabitants comprised a little less than 8 per cent of the total; by 1920 it was only 13 per cent. Much of this increase may be attributed to the influence of the export trade, since it was precisely those cities most engaged in it which grew the fastest. In 1920 more than half of the urban population resided in Rio de Janeiro and in São Paulo, which since 1870 had risen from tenth to second rank among

Brazilian cities. The labour force grew, between 1872 and 1920, at a rate of about 2 per cent a year. The economically active portion of the population is in fact difficult to calculate because the census of 1920 introduced more stringent definitions of employment, especially of females. Thus between 1872 and 1920 the percentage of females aged ten and over reported as economically active fell from 51 to 14 per cent. Since the ratio of economically active males also fell, from 77 to 75 per cent, it is possible that these lower figures were to some extent a sign of the reduced capacity of the economy to absorb the growing labour force.

Nevertheless, landowners and employers complained unceasingly of a shortage of labour. From 1870 onward the supply of slave labourers, who in 1872 constituted about 20 per cent of persons economically active and 70 per cent of plantation labour, was certainly precarious. From the late sixteenth century until the middle of the nineteenth century more Africans had been transported to Brazil than to any other area of the New World. With the effective suppression of the slave trade after 1850, however, the slave population began to decline. The cause of decline appears principally to have been high mortality, that is, an expropriation rate surpassing subsistence as well as reproduction costs, or simply incompetent and brutal labour management. Manumission and flight also occurred regularly, possibly as escape valves, rather cheaper to tolerate than further application of repressive force. Partly in response to increasing slave resistance, in 1871 a law was passed freeing children born thereafter to slave mothers. Chattel slavery was finished; lifetime slavery was to be gradually extinguished.

Since the free population could not be kept from squatting on unclaimed public lands, where their farming was as productive as that of the large estates, they could not be lured to work for wages that would have yielded a profit to the estate owners. Therefore in regions where unclaimed or unoccupied lands existed, the free population formed mainly a casual labour force, willing only to pay token rents in return for token labour. In zones well removed from the frontier, however, where all the land was already in private title and smallholders were hemmed in by the large estates, sharecropping and various forms of tenancy significantly increased the work force available to the plantations, even before the demise of slavery.

The decline in slave numbers was at first mitigated by an internal traffic which directed them from the stagnant north-east to the coffee-growing states of Rio de Janeiro and São Paulo, and from urban areas to the plantations. By the late 1870s this trade was inadequate, and many of the southern planters, whose earlier experiments in immigrant labour indentures had been failures, became quite despondent, predicting ruin for themselves and the bankruptcy of the central government. It has not been suggested that Brazilian slavery was at any time up to the last year or two before its abolition unprofitable. Indeed several studies have demonstrated the contrary. As long as slavery persisted it was at least as profitable as alternative investments. Nevertheless the General Legislative Assembly voted final abolition of slavery in 1888, in response to political pressure from planters in new zones of production who had no hope of securing a slave work force, the urban middle class, including army officers and civil servants impatient to bring about a more modern society, and ex-slaves and the slaves themselves, who were organizing violent opposition and large-scale abandonment of plantations.

The final transition from slave to free labour proved surprisingly easy, from the point of view of the large landowners. Although many freedmen fled to the cities, most accepted wage and sharecropping contracts on nearby or even the same estates. Pressure upon smallholdings because of population growth (Brazilian law divided inheritances equally among offspring), recurrent droughts in the interior of the north-east, and the continued political impotence of the lower class forced many free men to work on the plantations. In the north-east the effective costs of free labour to the planters were apparently lower than the former costs of maintaining slaves.[5] There was a great deal of migration to new zones of large-scale exploitation for export, such as southern Bahia (cacao) and the western Amazon (rubber). In the Amazon high wages exerted an effective attraction, but control of prices of subsistence goods by the rubber gatherers' outfitters and store keepers offset the expected advantages, and high mortality from disease turned the region into a population sink from which few escaped.

To the coffee region migrated an immense wave of Italian, Spanish and Portuguese workers. Net immigration to Brazil between 1872 and 1930 amounted to some 2.2 million. By 1920 immigrants represented 10 per cent of the male labour force. Much of this migration was subsidized by state and federal governments, thus socializing the planters' costs of labour reproduction. The immigrants were offered yearly contracts which combined money wages for tending and harvesting with the right to plant subsistence crops. Ex-slaves in the

---

[5] See D. Denslow, 'As origens da desigualdade regional no Brasil', *Estudos Económicos* (1973); P. Eisenberg. *The sugar industry in Pernambuco, 1840–1910* (Berkeley, 1974).

coffee regions who continued to work on the plantations were obliged to accept more precarious employments, at wage levels about half those of the Europeans, thereby making a contribution of their own to immigration subsidies. The flux of immigrants was kept as high as possible up to the first world war, and even through the 1920s the state of São Paulo continued to pay part of the costs of passage. This was necessary because the immigrants tended to withdraw to other employments after a few harvests or to re-migrate to their homelands. There was also a clear intent to keep wages low. It has been estimated by one historian that wages in the coffee industry did not rise between 1870 and 1914.[6]

Even though the abolition of slavery placed labour more or less within a market, improved its mobility and monetized to some extent its rewards, the period under study must be considered as transitional from that of a regime based on physical coercion. The social conditions of much of rural Brazil approximated that of servility. Even in the areas of European immigration, the great landowners demanded deference and employed the services of private gunmen to intimidate their workers. Wage earners, according to laws in force as late as 1890, were subject to imprisonment for non-fulfilment of contract. In 1902 Italy, acting upon the reports of its consuls, forbade further subsidization of emigration of its citizens to Brazil. In response the state of São Paulo created arbitration boards to hear complaints. Only in 1916 was equality of contract established in federal law. No other labour rights were effectively enforced before the 1930s.

Public education scarcely contributed to raising the general skill levels. The census of 1872 showed almost 90 per cent of females and 80 per cent of males were illiterate. By 1920 these rates had declined by only ten points each. The governing elite tended to regard the native-born lower classes as largely ineducable; indeed this was a major reason that it collaborated with the planters in schemes for European immigration. Immigrants were generally more literate than the native-born population; in São Paulo only 56 per cent were illiterate compared to 73 per cent of the general population, according to the census of 1920. Had the government spent on primary education the funds it allocated to subsidize immigration, it might have obtained similar economic results and discharged its responsibilities more humanely. Very little schooling

---

[6] Michael Hall, 'The origins of mass immigration in Brazil, 1871–1914' (unpublished PhD dissertation, Columbia University, 1969).

in productive skills was provided for the working class, or even the middle class. By 1920 total enrolment in secondary and technical schools, public and private, was only 62,500. Although early stages of machine production included successful innovations by Brazilians, notably in coffee and yerba maté processing equipment, the organizational and technical skills needed to install manufacturing and commercial enterprises were largely immigrant-supplied.

Capital

There are no estimates of gross capital formation before the 1920s. It has been calculated that it averaged 13.7 per cent of gross national product for that decade, or US$14 a year per capita, in current dollars. According to the same estimate, net capital flow from abroad during the 1920s averaged 8.8 per cent of gross capital formation and net capital stock reached US$260 per capita, in current dollars, by 1929.[7]

The mobilization of domestic capital was not highly institutionalized, at least in the first half of this period. Until well after 1900 most agricultural credit was informal and private: advances from brokers or importers, or loans from private money lenders, many of whom limited their dealings to kinsmen and neighbours. Interest rates began at 12 per cent and often rose to 24 per cent. Agricultural loans, almost up to the time of abolition, required slaves, not land, as collateral. Except for planters of export crops, credit of any kind was rarely available, and it was uncommon even for coffee planters to obtain mortgages.

In 1870 there were only six banks in Rio de Janeiro, two of them English, and there were only nine more in the rest of the country. These banks dealt almost exclusively in deposits and the discounting of short-term commercial paper. The foreign banks confined themselves largely to foreign exchange transactions and expended their best efforts on exchange speculation. The government-controlled Bank of Brazil began in the 1860s to make a few agricultural loans. A few land credit banks were founded after 1875, but they lacked a suitable mortgage law and were not successful. Only after 1900 did government-owned mortgage banks in the state of São Paulo and Minas Gerais provide a limited amount of funding. In 1909 a system of warrants finally became available in São Paulo, an innovation related to the valorization scheme, which

---

[7] Dias Carneiro, 'Past trends', Table 8A.

reduced interest charges to 9 per cent. The value of mortgages registered in land offices throughout Brazil grew tenfold between 1909 and 1929, when they reached the equivalent of US$181 million in current dollars. Much of this may have represented the financing of urban real estate transactions. By 1929 the great majority of these mortgages were at interest rates under 10 per cent, suggesting that the market had become more efficient. Yet the total sum was still quite modest, compared to the value of farm lands revealed in the 1920 census, showing that mortgages were still uncommon.

A low average productivity of investments derived from national savings has been calculated for the 1920s.[8] It seems unlikely that the productivity of capital in earlier decades had been any higher. Domestic enterprises experienced difficulty in growing to a scale that would enable them to apply new techniques and to encompass a national market. Share ownership beyond the limits of the family was almost unknown, except in the organization of banks and railways. Capital was derived from reinvestment of profits, sometimes involving monopolistic pricing, or was pieced together from commercial loans. There was no significant market for industrial bonds or shares. Briefly, during the boom of 1888 to 1893, a few of the banks that were granted the right of emission played the role of financiers to a few large industrial ventures, but these mostly failed. No other banks, not even the Bank of Brazil, undertook such a role thereafter. Thus those forces which had in other countries fused family firms into publicly held corporations were largely absent in Brazil. Occasionally there were formed consortia of two or more families, more or less stable, usually within ethnic groups, and sometimes eventuating in intermarriage. They appeared when newer and more complex technologies had to be installed; for example, in synthetic textiles, paper and cellulose, and chemical industries.

Foreign investment in Latin America increased in cyclical waves, notably 1888 to 1895, 1905 to 1913 and 1924 to 1929. In each of these periods Brazil received a sizeable share of European investments in Latin America, if not one proportionate to its share of Latin America's population. More than half of the foreign capital directed to Brazil financed the central and local governments. It also funded most of the banks, electric, telephone and gas systems, port facilities, railways, steamship lines, and, at the end of the period under study, airlines. Until

[8] *Ibid.*, Tables 27 and 29E.

the first world war this capital was overwhelmingly British. The London Rothschilds were the Empire's exclusive bond-raising agents, the leading exporters and importers were all British, and nearly all the railways were British-owned or financed. The largest British bank, the London and Brazilian, had considerably greater financial resources than the semi-official Bank of Brazil, and even in 1929 foreign banks were still carrying out half of all commercial banking transactions. On the other hand, foreign interests in land, natural resources and productive enterprises were quite limited, unlike the more 'penetrated' economies of Latin America and the then colonial world, and certain sectors – insurance, sugar milling, banking, and railways – began even during this period to be recuperated by Brazilian private capital or public interests. Furthermore, the average rate of return on capital, if the British return is typical, was a moderate 5 per cent. Nevertheless, remissions of interest and profits, which increased gradually during the period under study, represented a considerable charge upon the economy. By 1923 service on the federal and local government debt cost 22 per cent of export revenues.

The activities of British firms up to the first world war may be assessed as generally 'compradorist' in the sense that they concentrated their investments in the export sector. Local entrepreneurs who wanted to build factories to compete with imports were often not funded. There is the spectacular case of a sewing thread mill in Alagoas, bought up by a British firm that dismantled it and heaved the machinery into the São Francisco river. As for British banks, they prospered most when the exchange rates were volatile. They engaged themselves in manoeuvres to destabilize the milreis and resented efforts by the Bank of Brazil to interfere in these dealings. They were reluctant to lend to state-owned companies and even refused on occasion to accept banknotes emitted by the Bank of Brazil. The extreme deflationary measures imposed upon the federal government as the condition of the funding loan of 1898 caused a wave of bankruptcies that wiped out many commercial firms and domestically owned banks, reducing competition with British and other foreign enterprises.

British pre-eminence in the Brazilian economy was, however, subjected to strong challenges after 1900. Their vulnerability arose from their position as financiers and transshippers: since the demand for coffee was largely American and German, American coffee roasters and importers were able to take the place of British middlemen before the

first world war, and German export houses, supported by their government's trade offensive, gained strongly in the market for capital goods
and took interests in firms which bought their equipment. The
'Black List' revealed the degree to which German trading firms had
undercut their competition. In brewing, at one extreme, they controlled
the entire domestic output.

AGRICULTURE AND STOCK RAISING

The technological backwardness of Brazilian agriculture was extreme.
Slash-and-burn cultivation was mainly extractive, it implied the need for
immense forest reserves which supplied many of the farmer's necessities,
especially protein and raw materials. Forest lands newly cleared and
burned were extraordinarily, if temporarily, fertile. The ashes of the
forest provided abundant plant nutrients, often the only fertilizer ever
applied. Stumps and logs were left to rot and planting was nearly always
carried out uphill and down, encouraging erosion. Some 'cultivated'
crops, such as papaya, coconuts, bananas, pineapple and citrus, were
often merely allowed to grow wild. When the planted patch was invaded
by weeds and pests, it was abandoned, to grow back to secondary
woodland or grasses, as it would. When all the woodlands in a given
region were exhausted, farmers generally withdrew, and it was turned
over to cattle raising. The plough was irrelevant to this regime; indeed in
some regions it was entirely lacking. In 1920 less than 14 per cent of farm
properties included in the census employed them, and many of these
were probably wooden versions. Farm yields were thus nearly entirely a
function of the initial fertility of forest soils. Brazil's output of fertilizer
was tiny, and in the 1920s 90 per cent of it was exported. Rituals, amulets
and prayers were more commonly applied than animal manure, which,
according to folk agronomy, 'burned' the land.

Coffee plantations were better managed than the average farm, but
even coffee plantations were backward compared to contemporary
agricultural knowledge. Available organic fertilizers were only fitfully
applied, seed selection was not thought of, bees were not engaged as
pollinating agents, and ploughs were improperly utilized. The largest
plantations were generally in the hands of managers, since the owners
often possessed more than one estate and had multiple interests in the
cities. The form of labour contracts discouraged care in cultivating and
harvesting and provided excessive advantages to workers in new groves,

further stimulating expansion and waste of forest reserves and overplanting. On the sugar plantations of the north-east, where the superior lowland soils were already in use, expansion was carried out in the 1880s by cutting down hillside woodlands. These soils were less appropriate for sugar, required more labour and were subject to erosion. Since the trouble was not taken to remove stumps, the plough could not be employed on the hills. Sugar planters did not apply manure, but left their lands fallow for varying periods. However, the appearance of a fungal disease after 1879 encouraged the introduction of some new cane varieties, some local experimentation in cane breeding, and, briefly, some trials with imported fertilizers. Labour in the canefields remained highly seasonal and intensive, with planting, cultivating, and cutting done by hand. The most significant improvement in cane farming was the introduction in the 1870s of light railways, at first horse-drawn, then steam-powered, to carry the cane to the mills. Modernized steam-powered central sugar mills, heavily subsidized by the government, were installed mainly after the establishment of the Republic. These much improved productivity, and sugar yields about equal to the world average for the period were being achieved by 1910.

There were already two imperial agricultural schools in existence in 1873, and several more schools were founded in a number of the states shortly after the proclamation of the Republic, but they seem to have had little influence on farming practices, except perhaps in São Paulo. Quite a few of the state institutions were in fact practical schools for orphans, and it is not clear whether their graduates ever had the opportunity to apply their learning. During this period only São Paulo had a system of agricultural extension agents.

Food production for the domestic market in this period has been little studied, but it appears to have been a lagging sector. Up to the first world war prices of foodstuffs rose about three times as fast as prices of exports and imports. When coffee planting and rubber gathering surged forward in the 1890s, so did food prices – and food imports. Export growth evidently was based in part on capital resources diverted from the food-supplying sector. The supply of cities was carried out mostly by nearby small farmers, who sold surpluses when they had any. In the vicinity of São Paulo and Rio de Janeiro a few official colonies, opened to native as well as immigrant farm families, were organized to try to increase city food stocks. Cash-cropping small farmers, however, limited to lands abandoned by large-scale planters or to those of poor quality, were starved for credit and preyed on by intermediaries.

Nevertheless production for the domestic market was not stagnant. Although food prices rose steeply, they appear to have risen no faster than wages, in Rio de Janeiro at least, during the period under study, except for the crisis of the first world war. It can be observed, furthermore, that imports of foodstuffs were gradually reduced after 1900: per capita food imports fell from 142 to 34 kilograms between 1903 and 1929. The increasing life expectancy suggests that per capita food consumption was not declining and may have slightly increased. Besides the conversion of former export commodities such as sugar and cotton to the satisfaction of domestic demand, there was some diversification, mostly by smallholders, into wine, oils and fats and dairy products. Wheat, introduced into the diet by the immigrants, proved very difficult to cultivate in Brazil, but potatoes were successfully grown and cultivation of rice was much enlarged. In Rio Grande do Sul rice farming was undertaken on a considerable scale by large landowners for sale to national markets.

Cattle raising occupied vast areas of natural grassland and savanna and areas degraded by farming. Brazilians were much inclined to the consumption of beef. The southernmost state of Rio Grande do Sul, too distant to deliver live animals, industrialized its beef as jerked (pressed and sun-dried) meat. The Brazilian cattle population was somewhat more numerous than the human throughout the period under study. Much of it was crosses of zebu, imported from India in the 1880s and greatly appreciated for its resistance to disease and drought. Cattle raising, as practised in the interior, was extremely economical of labour and capital. Almost never were shelters, fences or watering stations built; animals, after branding, were left to forage and breed as they would. In 1920 the density of cattle on natural range land was about 18 per square kilometre. The only modification of the environment commonly carried out was the burning of fields, to induce the growth of new tender shoots. This had the tendency to promote fire-resistant, unpalatable grasses. Near railheads exotic grasses were planted in formerly forested land, to restore animals driven for long distances, and to fatten them for market.

ENERGY AND TRANSPORTATION

Brazil's coal deposits were low grade and exiguous; in 1929 output from the mines of Santa Catarina amounted to only 360,000 tons. For lack of this resource, wood and charcoal were burned, with further severe consequences for forest reserves, watersheds and topsoil. Per capita domestic use of fuel was estimated at two cubic metres a year. By 1930 Brazil was clearing 330,000 hectares of forest annually for this purpose alone. Since the regrowth of woodlots took about twenty years, this implied the need for a reserve of 66,000 square kilometres, but in fact almost no reserves were maintained. The difficulties in obtaining wood and charcoal limited the activities of railways, smelters and manufacturers. The planting of eucalyptus was resorted to by a few railways, though on an inadequate scale. Imported coal was employed in port terminals and in factories located in port cities, but in the interior wood-stoked boilers were the rule. Some of the early factories also employed hydraulic power, easily installed in a countryside of abundant rains and broken terrain.

Domestic petroleum sources were not discovered in commercial quantity until after the second world war. Imports of petroleum were necessarily restricted, limiting the application of internal combustion engines. Imports of motor vehicles nevertheless increased considerably in the second half of the 1920s. By 1929 more than 160,000 road vehicles were registered and more than 21,000 kilometres of roads had been improved. The first scheduled airline began to operate in 1927, and by 1930 there were four.

Thermal generation of electricity began in the 1880s. Constrained by the need to import coal, it had, however, by 1900 been passed in scale by hydro-generation. Brazil's total electrical capacity reached one megawatt in 1890, ten in 1900, and one hundred by 1908. The construction of large dams and improvement in generation and transmission were carried out in São Paulo and Rio de Janeiro in the 1920s, so that by the end of that decade nearly 780 megawatts were available. Although an impressive rate of growth had been achieved, this was just 22 watts per capita, one-fifteenth that of the United States at the time. Hydroelectric power was as fortuitous a technological advance for southern and south-eastern Brazil as coking coal had been in England two centuries before. It is not possible to imagine the development of industry on the limited base of charcoal, and the cost of importing coal and petroleum would have been as deleterious to industrial growth as it was in Argentina, where industrialization slowed after early rapid gains.

Steam power was early applied to harbour and river craft. By 1873 subsidized coastwise and riverine shipping spread over 36,300 kilometres of routes. Total coastwise shipping rose from a little less than 1 million tons in 1870 to 19 million tons in 1930 (shipping to foreign

ports rose during the same period from 2 million to 28 million tons).
Steam shipping made possible the extension of the rubber trade to the
upper Amazon and its tributaries and improved contact with Mato
Grosso via the Río de la Plata. The difficulties of navigation on interior
rivers was very great, however. Lack of funds for river and navigation
improvement made necessary portages and overnight anchorage.
Frieght charges between the upper Xingu river and Belém around 1912,
as an extreme example, amounted to nearly ten times those between
Belém and New York.

In 1873, there existed only 132 kilometres of canals more than 2
kilometres in length and only 607 kilometres of improved road.
Overland transport still depended almost entirely on mule pack trains.
By 1889, however, 9,000 kilometres of rails had been built, and by 1930
32,000 kilometres. The railways were entirely a response to the
opportunities of the export market, since all of their equipment, except
the cross-ties, had to be imported and therefore paid for in foreign
currency. Designed to drain the interior of exportable commodities, they
did not form a national network. Broad and narrow gauges were
employed, even within the same regional network. The largest system
was that of São Paulo, where half a dozen lines fanned out towards the
coffee-growing areas. A single line then descended the coastal escarpment from São Paulo to the port of Santos. São Paulo was also connected
to Rio de Janeiro and to the southern states by way of Sorocaba.

Railways were the principal expense of the central government from
the 1860s onward. The largest railway company, the Brazil Central, was
government-owned. Private companies, foreign and domestic, sometimes received direct government subsidies to extend their lines; more
often there were subsidies in the form of profit guarantees. The states
also granted profit guarantees on a more modest scale. The federal
government set freight rates, which were kept low, mainly to appease
landowners, so that only those lines intensively utilized to ship export
crops were able to earn profits. In the late 1890s the expense of covering
profit guarantees reached intolerable levels and, since they were owed in
gold, they pressed heavily on the balance of payments. The Republican
government therefore expropriated many of these lines, leasing most of
them out to concessionaires. The installation of railways stimulated
agricultural production for the domestic market, as well as serving to
bring exports to the docks. Suburban stations on the trunk lines and
narrow-gauge suburban lines permitted an augmented flow of foodstuffs

and wood for fuel. Rails laid beyond the plantation areas transported live cattle from interior range lands, thereby reducing weight loss suffered in driving, and lumber from the fast-disappearing virgin forests, thereby reducing the waste of hardwoods and cheapening construction costs. Railways were unquestionably a major instrument of Brazil's escape from economic stagnation, yet it must be noted that their stimulus came late and was limited to a few regions.

MANUFACTURING

The development of industry in Brazil may be seen as a process of substitution of handcraft production and of substitution of imports. Of the two, the second is more commonly remarked, since it more visibly affected urban populations and it may be traced in the import lists. But the first was, in the early stages at least, more important. The Brazilian market for non-agricultural goods was supplied in the main by handcrafts. The capacity of the economy to import was, after all, extremely limited, and much of what consumer goods were imported were luxuries for the affluent. Handcrafted goods were produced within the household for its own consumption and for sale or exchange and within artisanal workshops for sale in local markets. Cotton and wool textiles, for example, were widely produced by households before the installation of textile factories. Nearly every household and slave compound included someone who could spin and weave on a hand loom. The scale of domestic handcraft production is suggested by the disproportion in apparent consumption of sewing thread. In 1903 Brazil apparently consumed 1,045 tons of cotton sewing thread, all imported. Yet in the same year 21,900 tons of woven cloth, domestic and imported, were consumed. The ratio of 1:21 is anomalous, considering the modern ratio of about 1:60. It seems likely that at least half of the imported thread was employed in the confection of garments from homespun cloth and of embroidery. Besides this there were many kinds of domestic production – blankets, hammocks, ponchos, covers – that employed no thread. Even in 1966 a survey of rural families in Minas Gerais showed that half of those growing cotton still spun and wove their own cloth.[9]

The transition from handcraft to factory production was not usually abrupt or discontinuous. Handcrafts complemented local factory

[9] Maria de Lourdes Borges Ribeiro, *Inquérito sobre práticas e superstições agrícolas de Minas Gerais* (Rio de Janeiro, 1971), 37–8

production, for example, in the putting-out of cloth in the apparel trades. Much of the food processing industry grew out of domestic workshops which gradually acquired machine techniques. It is often difficult to discover the point at which repair shops began copying whole machines instead of spare parts, and the point at which they put production on a serial basis. Throughout this period many factories employed no steam or electric power at all. According to the census of 1920, the average worker applied just 1.1 horsepower to his job. Furthermore, 10 per cent of the factory work force was employed in firms with no more than four workers.

The German colonists of Rio Grande do Sul demonstrate the progressive incorporation of domestic production within regional and national markets. During the first generation of settlement, the pioneers integrated the material culture of their *mestiço* neighbours with their own. They grew and processed foodstuffs, and artisans among them produced a wide range of consumer and construction goods and agricultural implements. As steamboats were introduced in the 1860s, town merchants began transshipping settlers' products to Rio de Janeiro and other ports. By the 1870s funds from this trade were employed to build consumer goods factories in the major towns. Rural artisans, excluded from town markets, then specialized in a narrower range of processed goods, thereby providing demand for factory-made products.

In São Paulo and Rio de Janeiro, the other important incipient industrial centres, it was the export sector that provided demand and funding for early factories. In São Paulo the brief boom in cotton exports of the late 1860s enabled a few entrepreneurs, mostly planters, to construct small spinning and weaving mills. Eleven were in place by 1884, by which time they provided the only market available to local cotton planters. These mills sold cloth to the plantations for sacking and slave clothing. The planters of western São Paulo were by then willing to buy machine-made cloth for their slaves because slave labour costs were increasing faster than their other expenses.

Abolition created conditions for further development. The self-sufficiency of the slave plantation and its generally depressing effect on wages in the countryside and in towns had stunted demand beyond its gates. The market, in southern and south-eastern Brazil at least, was greatly expanded by the arrival of the immigrant farm workers. Not only were they paid wages and allowed to sell their produce, they aimed at maximizing their incomes, rather than at self-sufficiency. Therefore they purchased many of their necessities. This mass demand was satisfied for the most part by local manufacture. Brazilian labour costs were lower than those embodied in imports. Early manufactures were goods of low value by weight, easy to substitute when raw materials were locally available. Bricks and tiles, beer and beer bottles were early manufacturing successes. The immense cattle and swine herds made local production of soap, candles and leather goods competitive; tinned lard became a modest article of export. By the first world war, according to tax records, imports amounted to less than 5 per cent of the consumption of shoes and boots, less than 15 per cent of hats, and less than 20 per cent of textiles. The cotton textile industry, which boasted 1.3 million spindles by 1919, progressively substituted imports, beginning with coarse unbleached greys and proceeding through fabrics of finer grade.

Capital invested in Brazilian industry, up to 1920, was obtained in the main from importers of immigrant origin and from abroad, largely through émigré entrepreneurs. Planter capital, important in the earliest phase of industrialization in São Paulo, was more closely connected to exporting or the transformation of their own raw materials, and it tended to be gradually replaced by the capital of importers. Some importers turned to manufacturing in order to carry out finishing operations on goods they had imported. Usually dealers in a variety of goods, they were aware of the composition of the import list, of tariffs and domestic taxes and of local demand. They often acted as wholesalers to independent manufacturers and provided them with credit. Nearly all the more important industrialists continued to maintain importing agencies, to assure steady supplies of imported components and to keep abreast of diversifying demand.

In its early phase, Brazilian industry directly favoured the interests of the planters by serving as a market for planter-produced raw materials that lacked favourable export prospects. The planters, however, insisted on high tariffs for imports, such as jute, which competed with Brazilian cotton, and inveighed against the 'artificial' industries that utilized them. They saw to it that tariffs on agricultural implements were kept low. They detested factory jobs which lured away their work force. They often pronounced a phrase later to be repeated sardonically by the enthusiasts of development: 'Brazil is a country essentially agricultural.' Industrialists, on the other hand, did not directly challenge the planters. Instead they associated themselves politically with the plantation interest, partly on the assumption that their prosperity depended on the growth of exports, and partly because they enjoyed the prestige of that association and would have been repelled by the thought of an alliance with the urban middle classes or their own workers.

Despite the political pre-eminence of export-oriented interests, in particular coffee interests, measures favourable to industry were sometimes effectively advanced. High tariffs, as has been mentioned, were largely the inadvertent result of the government's impecuniousness. Domestic manufacturers also benefited from the planters' preference for a falling exchange rate, which made imports more expensive. Nevertheless industry enjoyed a certain amount of sympathy in Congress, some of whose members were partisans or survivors of the early Republican provisional government. The industrialists secured laws against government purchases of imports when domestic 'similars' were available, tariff exemptions for machinery, federal loans and interest guarantees for new lines of production, and benevolent interpretations of patent and copyright laws.

The First World War apparently represented an opportunity for Brazilian manufacture, since it reduced the volume of imports of finished goods while elevating their prices and it left the country awash in currency earned from exports and emitted by the government. The failure of wages to accompany the resulting inflation increased the profit rate. Although manufacturing plant could not be much renovated or enlarged because of the interruption of machine imports, factories in some lines of production were stimulated to run extra shifts and increase their output. Nevertheless, imports of raw materials and fuels were more sharply reduced than those of finished goods; scarcity and high costs of inputs, along with higher taxes, narrowed manufacturers' margins. The reported increase in manufactured output may have been exaggerated, since it was based on collections of taxes, which were more thoroughly exacted as import revenues fell. The output of cotton textiles rose from 70 million to 160 million metres between 1914 and 1917. To a considerable degree, however, this production seems to have been warehoused by the manufacturers, who were speculating on further price rises; they were marooned at the end of the war with warehouses full of unsold stock for which they asked government loan guarantees. Even so, the capacity of domestic manufactures to shore up the economy during the crisis increased their acceptance among consumers and earned them credit with the bureaucracy, which appreciated the new source of government revenue.

Until the 1920s industrial output was limited mainly to consumer goods. The census of 1920 counted more than 13,000 manufacturing firms, employing 275,000 workers, less than 3 per cent of the economically active population. (The population census of that year counted 1,264,000 in manufacturing and garment trades – a rough comparison between industrial and artisanal employment perhaps.) Textile factories represented 40 per cent of capital invested in these firms, and food processing, clothing, soap and candles represented another 45 per cent. Within a small intermediate goods sector nearly twice as much was invested in sawmills as in metalworking.

The origins of the iron and steel industry and of metalworking are nevertheless interesting to note, because of their high technical and capital requirements, their tendency to concentrate in cities and their linkages to mining and machine making. Iron smelting had been carried out in Brazil since the seventeenth century, and blast furnaces were built by the crown in the last days of the colony. Over the course of the nineteenth century small iron furnaces continued to operate fitfully in Minas Gerais, their output amounting to a few thousand tons of pig iron. Ironworking and implement making were meanwhile widespread, so that iron and steel imports mainly took the form of inputs to local industry such as wire, sheets, rail, rods and plates. Metalworking was devoted to equipping the export trade, since its own inputs, including skilled workers, were imported and technically advanced. Railway repair yards and shipyards were therefore the largest and best equipped of the metalworking shops.

Large-scale iron and steel manufacture, however, experienced only slight development until the last decade of the period under study. In the 1920s a Belgian firm added steel furnaces and a rolling mill to a newly installed charcoal-fired iron mill in Minas Gerais, and small electrical furnaces in São Paulo and Rio de Janeiro began recycling scrap. In 1910 a British consortium led by an American promoter named Farquhar had obtained rights to mines at Itabira, in Minas Gerais, and sought from the federal government an exclusive concession to export iron ore via the rail line which they planned to rebuild to the port of Vitória. At the same time they promised to construct an integrated mill which was to employ coking coal brought by the same vessels that were to bear off the ore. Negotiations stretched on. There was considerable nationalist opposition to the granting of so large and exclusive a concession, and there was also opposition from the owners of the charcoal and electric mills.

Eventually the world depression diminished world demand for steel, and the consortium abandoned the project. It is likely that they would have delayed as long as possible the delivery of the mill, to which the international iron and steel cartel of the era would have objected. Nevertheless the Farquhar proposal entirely engaged the attention of the government for twenty years and discouraged other potential steel producers. By 1929 Brazil's steel output was only 57,000 tons, 11 per cent of consumption.

THE CRISIS OF EXPORT ORIENTATION

The First World War, as we have seen, caused a sharp decline in the value of Brazil's exports. With the final collapse of the rubber boom at the end of the war Brazil was once more dependent on coffee alone for three-quarters of its foreign exchange earnings. And after a brief postwar commodities boom coffee prices slumped once again. As has been noted, the federal government responded with a third essay at valorization. The third valorization and the 'permanent defence' were perhaps effective in preventing a further fall of the price of coffee in dollars, but the levelling-off of demand and increased overseas competition kept Brazil from realizing an increased volume of sales. Coffee receipts reached 12 per cent of gross national product in 1923 and then began a long decline. Intervention had done little more than secure the income of the planters and encourage new investments in the coffee sector.

In 1924 the federal government, alarmed that the inflationary forces it had set loose were undermining its stability, undertook a policy of deflation. Then late in 1926 it tried again, as it had twenty years before, to adhere to the gold standard through the mechanism of a conversion fund. Again this measure helped to attract foreign capital, which was becoming essential to maintaining the level of imports in the face of rising demand. Brazil had need of a widening range of imports, such as telecommunications and aviation equipment, embodying novel technologies and necessary to improve its competitiveness in world markets. Banks in the United States were ready and eager to advance the funds. Their credits made possible a decline in the trade surplus from 22 to 11 per cent of export receipts between the first and second halves of the decade. The funded debt of Brazil's central and local governments nearly doubled between 1924 and 1930, rising to US$1,295 million. The internal debt grew at an even faster rate, stoked by record deficits in the first half of the 1920s. Oddly, the prewar tariff, eroded by inflation to about half its strength, was not subjected to a general revision. Internal taxation, mainly on transactions, was coming to play a larger role in federal government finances; by the end of the period under study it amounted to about 45 per cent of revenues.

Domestic industry suffered considerably from these vicissitudes. In addition, the prices of manufactured imports were declining while its own competitiveness had been weakened by the wartime interruption in the re-equipping of plant. The share of imports in domestic consumption of cotton textiles rose from 7 per cent in 1921–3 to 17 per cent in 1925–8, and the prices of domestic cotton goods fell by 25 per cent between 1925 and 1927. Cotton textiles represented the worst case, however, since that sector was beset by overproduction, yet even within it those manufacturers who had managed to buy new machinery were achieving profits. Other already established industries reported profits and by the second half of the decade those manufactures included on tax rolls were growing at a rate of about 5 per cent annually. Besides this, the 1920s witnessed considerable diversification of production: pharmaceuticals, chemicals, textile machinery, sugar-milling machinery, automobile parts, weighing devices, truck bodies, gas stoves, and agricultural tools. An indirect measure of the progress of these firms is the apparent consumption of flat steels, which rose from an average 59,000 tons a year in 1901–5 to an average 288,000 tons a year in 1926–30. Many of these new ventures grew out of repair shops which had learned to copy and adapt imported machines and had gone on to contract foreign technicians or to send their own workers abroad to acquire the necessary techniques.

The First World War increased the interest of American firms in the Brazilian market. American banks were established in Rio de Janeiro and São Paulo and scheduled steamships began to operate for the first time between United States ports and Brazil. American investment was more characteristically direct, a phenomenon encouraged by the transformation of business structure in that country after the merger movement. American companies became dominant in petroleum distribution and coffee exporting, where they by-passed the established system of brokers. Electrical and telephone equipment makers established offices to install their products in burgeoning urban power and communications networks. Other American and European multinationals began manufacturing rayon fibre, office machines, photographic papers, phonograph records, light bulbs and automobile tyres, and began assembling automobiles. Some of these ventures can be seen to have been stimulated by protective tariffs, as in the case of nickle plating and pharmaceuticals; others were carried out as the result of invitations by linked investors: the first foreign-owned cement plant was built in the expectation of supplying the Canadian-owned electric company of São Paulo, for example. In many cases, these investments were determined by international cartels, as was the match business by the Swedish trust and cigarettes by the British–American consortium. Many investments that might have been made by multinationals, on the other hand, were aborted by international agreements to which Brazil was not a party and of which it was not even cognizant.

The Brazilian market was not itself free of cartelization. Trade associations that probably engaged in price fixing and quotas existed in the 1920s in metallurgy, shoes, leather, hides, lumber and pharmaceuticals. There were also combinations in restraint of trade at one time or another in flour milling, paper, hats, jute sacking, beer and sugar refining. In most of the other mechanized lines of production firms were so few that they were free to operate oligopolistically within their regional markets. Only cotton textiles lacked price agreements, mainly because efficiency varied so greatly among mills that they lacked a common interest, but even in that industry wage rates were decided by agreement among owners. The government did not exercise sanctions against these practices. A policy of official cartelization was attempted in Rio Grande do Sul from 1928 to 1930 of distributors of jerked beef, wine, lard and lumber. These schemes, forerunners of corporativist planning by the federal government after 1930, were effective in stimulating re-equipment in the lard business, but in the other trades their main effect was to squeeze the margins of the producers.

The collapse of the advanced capitalist countries following the Wall Street crash in October 1929 had a profound impact on Brazilian trade and finances. Coffee, quoted at US$0.50 per kilogram in late 1929, sank to US$0.29 early the next year. The Brazilian government, desperately seeking to salvage its credit, released its entire gold reserve of US$150 million to its foreign bond holders. The state of São Paulo, burdened with 875,000 tons of unsaleable coffee, in 1929 valued at a sum equivalent to 10 per cent of the entire gross national product, cast about for funds to keep the valorization programme going and astonishingly managed to get another £20 million credit. The milreis, however, fell by nearly a quarter in value, money in circulation fell by a sixth and the conversion fund collapsed. The gross national product sank by 14 per cent between 1929 and 1931, the depth of the depression in Brazil, by which point coffee had declined to US$0.17 per kilogram. At the end of 1930, amid business failures, unemployment and social dislocation, the Republic was overthrown.

CONCLUSION

Celso Furtado characterized the 80-year period before 1930 as a transitional phase: the importation of capital, technology and skilled labour was necessary to bring about increased productivity, a monetized market and the beginning of capital accumulation. Viewing 1930 as a watershed, he saw a shift from an external to an internal stimulus to growth, a transformation brought about by the world crisis, but one which he clearly favoured. The more widespread view in Brazil, however, is that export orientation operated contradictorily as an obstacle to growth, that the interests associated with it did not aspire to further development, and that consequently industrialization proceeded in 'surges' only during moments when the international economy was disorganized, by war or depression. Underlying this interpretation is a suspicion that the international capitalist economy was merely imperialist in its workings. Some economic historians have tried to demonstrate that the Brazilian economy, on the contrary, grew and diversified rapidly, as a direct result of its integration into the world economy, that global conditions were at the time favourable to Brazil's development, and that the Brazilian government customarily acted shrewdly and in the national interest. Others, in an attempt at a partial synthesis, have asserted that the alternation of periods of growth and crisis in the world economy was in itself conducive to Brazil's industrialization.

The political and bureaucratic elite which fashioned the policies of export orientation may not have intended to deliver the national economy over to foreign interests, as important as foreign capital was to their strategy, yet they accepted an imported set of policy prescriptions and felt that deviations from them were aberrant, even pathological. Indeed, hidden within the programme of export orientation is an uneasy sense of inferiority that must have been deadly to initiative within the directing cadres and even within the mass of the population. The widespread practice of counterfeiting foreign labels suggests not merely a phase of learning through imitation, but also a contagion of self-doubt and alienation.

Export orientation was a strategy carried out by a bureaucratic elite to promote government stability and economic growth in the interests of a landowning class whose horizons did not extend far beyond short-run speculation. It was not really a national much less a redistributive policy. The gains derived from it were not widely shared. The recent research on the period has not taken up the question of income concentration, but it seems likely that it increased. Economic diversification and the fuller working of the market in towns and cities did make possible social mobility for a small minority in the south and south-east, among whom European immigrants were privileged – a petty bourgeoisie of shopkeepers and artisans, and a smallholding group which sold to city markets. The directing elite did not extend its concerns beyond this stratum. Trade unions they regarded as subversive, workers as indigent dependants, and the unemployed as lazy an potentially criminal. Labour relations in the cities, if practised at all, were considered a form of charity, and it was expected that workers should reciprocate with humility and gratitude. The fate of rural workers who were not under the eye of foreign consuls was not the concern of the federal or state governments. These attitudes clearly did not help to induce higher productivity or to promote development beyond extractive plantation agriculture.

The period under study witnessed the beginning of another form of income concentration: a gap in living standards between the south-eastern region and the rest of the country. By 1920, for example, the ratio of capital per worker in industry was already 59 per cent higher in São Paulo than in the north-east. This phenomenon has been variously explained, but it seems likely that in its inception it was the result of the fuller development in the south-east of markets and productive forces, under the stimulus of the export trade, and of the consequent initiation of a mass market. The federalism of the 1891 constitution, however, and an informal pact that the Republican party of São Paulo arranged with that of Minas Gerais, guaranteed these two states control of the economic policy of the central government. Even the rubber-exporting states of Pará and Amazonas, immense but slightly populated and rivals between themselves, were unable to retain federal revenues collected within their borders, nor to claim the resources of the Acre territory, which instead passed to the federal government. Only once were significant developmental expenditures invested outside the south-east: dam building was undertaken in the north-east as a countermeasure against drought during the presidency of the Epitácio Pessoa (1919–22), the only north-easterner ever to reach that office.

Brazil's participation in the great expansion of world trade and finance after 1870, modest as it was, had the important consequence of initiating economic growth and development. The transformations it worked upon society were, however, uneven, and they were muffled by a dominant class whose developmental goals fell considerably short of the available opportunities. The means of production and the organizational resources amassed during the phase of export orientation constituted nevertheless a valuable resource, to be marshalled in the succeeding crises of the world economy for purposes of development more ambitiously conceived.

6

SOCIETY AND POLITICS[*]

DEMOGRAPHIC AND SOCIAL CHANGE

At the time of the declaration of the Republic in 1889, Brazil was a country with a low population density, and there were vast areas in the north and the west which were virtually empty or only sparsely populated. Although these generalizations remain true for the entire period of the First Republic (1889–1930), there was nevertheless considerable demographic growth. Between 1890 and 1920 the population almost doubled, increasing from 14.3 million to 27.0 million. This was due to a process of natural growth, combined with mass European immigration in the centre-south. However, the age structure displays a feature characteristic of underdeveloped countries: a very broad base tapering sharply to a narrow peak, the result of high birth rate, coupled with high rates of general and especially infant mortality. The under twenties constituted 51 per cent and 56 per cent of the population in 1890 and 1920 respectively. The forty to fifty age group was almost three times larger than that of the over sixties in 1890, and over three times larger in 1920. The over sixties represented 4.7 per cent and 4 per cent of the population in these years. Estimates for the period between 1920 and 1940 suggest an average life expectancy of only 36–7 years; for the 1900–20 period it was even lower.[1]

In the centre-south where immigration played a major role in population growth and in the development of social stratification, São Paulo was the state which absorbed the majority of the immigrants: 51.9 per cent of the 304,054 immigrants who entered the country between

* Translated from the Portuguese by Dr David Brookshaw; translation revised by the Editor.
1 Aníbal Vilanova Villela and Wilson Suzigan, *Política do govêrno e crescimento da economia brasileira, 1889–1945* (Rio de Janeiro, 1973), 256.

1888 and 1890, 64.9 per cent of the 1,129,315 in the period from 1891 to 1900, and 58.3 per cent of the 1,469,095 in the period from 1901 to 1920. Immigration to the state of São Paulo was the result of government planning, the main objective of which was to supply labour to the coffee sector, the dynamic centre of economic growth in the decades immediately before and after the abolition of slavery (1888). After the failure of experiments with sharecropping the coffee bourgeoisie devised a system of production based on the *colonato*. The landowner would contract a family of *colonos* and pay them an annual salary for tending his coffee plantations. The harvest itself was paid for separately and could apply to any area of agricultural productivity on the estate. There was consequently no necessary link between the coffee plantation tended by a family and the harvesting of its crop. Apart from this, there was a certain amount of part-time work, usually to do with the upkeep of premises and transportation, which was paid on a daily basis and amounted to very little. The colonists were housed and provided with plots of land on which to grow subsistence crops, the excess from which they could sell in the local markets. Occasionally, they were allowed to keep one or two head of cattle, in deep valleys which were susceptible to frost and were therefore not suitable for coffee cultivation. The *colono* system combined a capitalist system of production with a non-capitalist system of renting land. This was particularly so in the case of the type of contractual agreement which was common practice on new coffee plantations, and which in fact was preferred by immigrants. The colonist and his family would plant the coffee and tend the plantation for a period of four to six years, as the coffee bushes usually began to yield a small crop in the fourth year. The *colonos* received practically no monetary payment, but were able to dedicate themselves to the production of food crops, especially corn and beans, between the rows of new coffee bushes. They also usually had a right to the first coffee crop. The production of food crops was not only for consumption by the family but also for sale locally, and indeed there is evidence that the latter was a particularly important factor.

The question of social mobility in rural São Paulo is still controversial. One study of the period between 1871 and 1914 takes the view that opportunities for *colonos* to become smallholders or owners of medium-sized properties were very limited. Access to land required influence, although the price of land was not high, and prospective buyers needed resources which were relatively inaccessible in order to make the land profitable. According to this study, in 1905 a mere 6 per cent at the most of rural landowners were Italian.[2] Another study of a longer period (1886–1934) arrives at a different conclusion, although it does not deny the difficulties and pressures experienced by immigrants. According to this study, a significant proportion of immigrant workers who settled in rural areas were socially mobile, and over the years came to constitute an important sector of small and medium landholders, particularly in western São Paulo, the most dynamic area of the state. This process would have resulted basically from the system of colonization which permitted colonists to save, and which even stimulated some landowners to sell off parts of their estate in order to make new investments elsewhere. The actual frequency of this phenomenon may be debatable but there is no doubt as to its significance. A survey carried out by the Secretariat for Agriculture of the state of São Paulo in 1923, covering the coffee producing municipalities, showed that 37.6 per cent of the rural properties counted belonged to Italians, Spaniards or Portuguese who together represented 87 per cent of the total number of immigrants arriving in São Paulo between 1886 and 1923. Natives of these three countries owned 24.2 per cent of the total number of coffee bushes inspected, with an average of 15,700 productive bushes per estate.[3] Clearly these were small landholders since over half the estates in São Paulo had more than 100,000 bushes and some, more than a million.

Inevitably, the question arises as to why the São Paulo agrarian-mercantile bourgeoisie preferred immigrant, especially Italian, workers to alternative sources of labour. As far as the ex-slaves are concerned, it should be remembered that labour relations had deteriorated during the last years of the slave regime. The growing frequency with which slaves had either fled or revolted presented considerable problems when it came to considering how to transform a slave labour force into wage earners. As immigrant workers arrived on the coffee plantations and problems with the slave population increased, landowners became more and more convinced of the superior quality of immigrant labour. The black population which remained in rural São Paulo after abolition generally speaking followed one of two courses: either it settled in isolated areas where it became involved in subsistence agriculture, or it was relegated on the coffee plantations to the most menial forms of labour not directly

2 Michael M. Hall, 'The origins of mass immigration in Brazil, 1871–1914' (PhD thesis, Columbia University, 1969).
3 Thomas H. Holloway, *Immigrants on the land. Coffee and society in São Paulo, 1886–1934* (Chapel Hill, NC, 1980).

linked to production. As for the poor free rural workers, they were already primarily engaged in subsistence agriculture and therefore able to maintain a relative degree of independence. To discipline this sector of the population to the labour requirements of the plantation was a problem which landowners preferred to avoid, given the availability of other forms of labour. Finally, various factors explain why immigrant, particularly Italian, workers were preferred over Brazilian labour drawn from other states: the prejudice of landowners against the native Brazilian work force, the existence of powerful interest groups in Italy prepared to provide cheap labour in reasonable quantity, the relatively low cost of international transport compared to inter-regional transport within Brazil, and the opposition of large interest groups to internal labour migration. It should also be stressed that, although in the north-east in particular there was labour to spare, it was not sufficient at the time to cater for the needs of the São Paulo coffee planters, who were interested in the speedy provision of labour on a large scale. Moreover, the rubber boom in the north between 1880 and 1912 absorbed much of the excess labour available in the north-east.

Variations in the level of immigration depended on international conditions, conditions in the country of origin, and above all on the state of the Brazilian coffee economy. The ten years from 1890 to 1900 constitute the period of heaviest immigration both in absolute and relative terms. The prolonged Italian economic crisis which lasted from the mid 1880s to the mid 1890s stimulated emigration, particularly from the north of the country. And while Argentina and the United States experienced a period of recession after 1890, Brazil entered a boom period thanks to coffee, at a time when it urgently needed to substitute its slave labour force and to increase its workforce generally. Immigrants were attracted for the most part by the Brazilian government's programme of assisted passages. Almost 80 per cent of the immigrants who entered the state of São Paulo between 1890 and 1900 had their transport paid in this way. The final years of the decade, on the other hand, witnessed a reversal of this trend. Brazil entered a period of overproduction and crisis in the coffee economy. In 1902 the government embarked on policies designed to limit the creation of new coffee plantations in São Paulo. At the same time, the Italian government, through the Prinetti Decree, prohibited further subsidized immigration to Brazil, in response to the continual complaints made by Italian citizens about living conditions on the plantations in São Paulo. The years 1903 and 1904 saw a negative balance in net immigration to the state of São Paulo. Immigration picked up once more when the Brazilian economy recovered and reached a peak in the years immediately before the first world war. In 1913, 116,640 foreigners entered the country as a whole, a figure equal to the best years of the 1890–1900 decade. However, the war interrupted the flow of immigrants and 1918 saw only 10,772 new arrivals. When immigration increased again during the 1920s it was no longer linked to the fluctuations of the coffee economy. Direct immigration to the large cities rapidly became the norm. In the rural areas of São Paulo and the south of the country, there were by now far more possibilities for small farmers dedicated to the production of food crops.

For the entire period from 1884 to 1933, Italians (1.4 million), Portuguese (1.1 million) and Spaniards (577,000) constituted the three main immigrant groups. As we have seen, the Italians made mainly for the state of São Paulo, and to a lesser extent for the areas of colonization in the south. Between 1884 and 1903, they were by far the largest foreign group to enter the country. From 1903, the number of Italian arrivals decreased considerably, falling to third place in all the subsequent decades. Portuguese immigration was the most stable during the period under consideration, occupying first place during the ten years from 1904 to 1913, and in subsequent periods. The Portuguese generally settled in the cities, where they occupied positions in commerce and in service industries. In 1920, 39.8 per cent of the total number of Portuguese in Brazil resided in Rio de Janeiro, where they constituted the largest foreign group. They were also predominant in the port of Santos, in contrast to their position in São Paulo. The Spaniards were more or less evenly distributed throughout the state of São Paulo. In the port of Santos they formed, after the Portuguese, the second largest foreign group.

After the Italians, Portuguese and Spanish, next in importance were the Germans and Japanese. German immigration was particularly significant in the south and was linked initially to the establishment of small farms. The Germans were not so easily assimilated as the Portuguese, Italians or Spaniards, and as late as the 1930s they formed a distinct cultural community – a factor which was to be a source of anxiety for the Vargas government. As for the Japanese, they began to arrive in Brazil in 1908, under an agreement between the state of São Paulo and Japanese immigration companies, which offered assisted passages and subsidies to immigrants. At first, they were brought in as agricultural workers, but from 1912 the state government began to provide them with land. Up until the mid 1920s Japanese immigration was relatively insignificant. However, in the period between 1924 and 1933, it became the second largest migratory current, totalling some 110,000 people. The Japanese settled mainly in the state of São Paulo where they became small and medium-sized landholders involved in food production.

The north and north-east of the country attracted few immigrants: there was little economic growth (apart from the rubber boom) and no shortage of labour. The ending of the slave system brought, for the most part, a reinforcement of the existing conditions. In the sugar plantation belt, the problem of wage labour was resolved by resorting to a practice which dated from the colonial period, and which involved the establishment of small landholders who were dependent on the large landed proprietor. Placed on small plots of land on which they cultivated subsistence crops, the workers were summoned for labour in the cane plantations whenever required. Labour was usually unremunerated or paid at a scandalously low rate. A similar system of relations was established between small landholders and cattle raisers. Although independent medium-sized estates existed in the north-east, especially in the sugar sector, the dominant system of social relations served to obstruct the formation of a free labour market and the development of a peasant economy.

In the far south, cattle raising on the *latifundia* situated in the south-western part of Rio Grande do Sul, producing jerked beef, which was consumed mainly by the low income groups in the urban centres of the centre-south and north-east, required only a small labour force and did not attract immigrants. Large numbers of Germans and Italians, however, settled in other parts of the state, drawn by the possibility of purchasing land. In the highland zone, they developed the cultivation of wheat and rice, under a combined regime of subsistence and commercial agriculture, most of their produce finding its market in the state of São Paulo. Rio Grande do Sul was therefore unique in that it developed an economy geared to the domestic market, and because it gave rise to a significant nucleus of independent, medium-sized, landed proprietors.

While large numbers of European immigrants were flooding into the centre-south during the last decades of the nineteenth century, there was an important internal migratory movement between the north-east and the north. The effect of this movement on the social structure was, however, relatively limited. From the 1870s, the growth of activities associated with the extraction of rubber in the Amazon basin attracted migrants from the north-east. The periods of drought which devastated the north-east during the 1870s and 1880s were also a major contributing factor in the displacement of the population. According to a rough estimate some 160,000 people were drawn to the Amazon between 1890 and 1900, and throughout the whole period from 1872 to 1920, Ceará, the north-eastern state closest to the Amazon region, presented a negative balance in terms of migration. Nevertheless, around 1912, faced with competition from rubber produced in the British and Dutch colonies in Asia, Brazilian production collapsed, and this had a rapid effect on internal migration. The rubber 'boom' stimulated the growth of some cities and favoured social mobility among certain urban groups. However, the migration of workers did not give rise to any significant social transformation in the region. The labour force, scattered throughout the rain forest area, was subject to extreme exploitation and trapped in various forms of debt bondage which prevented social change.

Internal migration to, and within, the centre-south during the late nineteenth century, and indeed before 1920, was limited. The urban areas and, in particular, the capital of the Republic (the Federal District) were important focal points for migration. And it is worth noting that Minas Gerais consistently presented a negative balance in terms of migration from 1890 onwards, a significant portion of the population making for the agricultural belt of São Paulo and for Rio de Janeiro. The 'spontaneous' displacement of the black population in the years immediately following the abolition of slavery is a subject which has caused some controversy. It seems likely that abolition caused a fairly large number of ex-slaves from the state of São Paulo to return to the north-east from where they had been sold during the years of the internal slave trade. Migration into the capital of the state of São Paulo was not particularly significant. On the other hand, the Federal District would seem to have received a large number of ex-slaves who had abandoned the coffee plantations of the interior of the state of Rio de Janeiro, then in open decline. Between 1890 and 1900, the net total of internal migrants of Brazilian origin entering the capital of the Republic reached a figure of 85,547, while during the same period the state of Rio presented a negative balance in terms of migration of 84,280.

From the early 1920s, the conditions which had limited internal migration in the centre-south during the phase of its economic expansion began to change. Migrants from Minas and the north-east entered the state of São Paulo in growing numbers. In 1928, internal migrants surpassed immigrants, and this was to be the case consistently from 1934. Although the rate of immigration was still considerable during the 1930s, the features of migratory movement would alter definitively, with migrants of Brazilian origin fulfilling a major role in the provision of labour for both the rural areas of the centre-south and industry then in a phase of expansion. This tendency was reinforced on the international level by the world crisis of 1929, and on the national level by measures taken to 'nationalize' the labour force and to establish a quota system for the entry of immigrants.

Many immigrants settled directly in the cities, or were later responsible to a considerable extent for the internal migration from the rural to the urban areas. This migratory current was motivated on the one hand by discontent with labour conditions in rural São Paulo, especially during periods of crisis in the coffee sector, and on the other hand by the opportunities for work in industrial and artisan activities which the cities provided. It was no coincidence that between 1890 and 1900, the decade which saw the greatest influx of foreigners, the state capital of São Paulo grew at a rate of 14 per cent per annum, its population increasing from 64,934 to 239,820 inhabitants. São Paulo became an 'Italian city', in which, by 1893, foreigners constituted 54.6 per cent of the total population. Though foreigners were few in the field of public administration and in the liberal professions, they accounted for 79 per cent of the total work force in the manufacturing industries and 71.6 per cent of those in commerce. In Rio de Janeiro, the federal capital, the immigrant contribution was also significant. In 1890 immigrants already accounted for 39 per cent of the industrial work force and 51 per cent of those involved in commerce.

Throughout the period of the First Republic, Brazil remained a predominantly rural country. In 1920, 69.7 per cent of the working population was involved in agriculture, 13.8 per cent in industry, and 16.5 per cent in the service sector. In the same year, there were 74 cities with more than 20,000 inhabitants, the total urban population constituting 16.6 per cent of the total population (some 4,500,000 people). Broken down by region, cities in 1920 accounted for 15.6 per cent of the population in the north, 10.1 per cent in the north-east, 14.5 per cent in the east, 29.2 per cent in the state of São Paulo, 14.6 per cent in the south,

and 2.8 per cent in the centre-west. On the other hand, the largest cities –
the state capitals – experienced consistent growth between 1890 and
1920. During the ten-year period from 1890 to 1900, São Paulo, which
was beginning its spectacular growth, and Belém, the centre for the
export of rubber, grew at a rate of 6.8 per cent per annum, and the overall
growth rate of state capitals reached 4.3 per cent. Between 1900 and 1920,
the rate of growth of state capitals dropped to 2.7 per cent, although São
Paulo continued to grow rapidly (albeit at a lower rate of 4.5 per cent) and
other cities like Porto Alegre (Rio Grande do Sul) increased in
importance.

From the beginning of the century, the urban network tended
consistently towards a process of concentration. Urbanization increased
in absolute terms, but the major cities expanded much more rapidly than
medium or small urban centres. This tendency would become more acute
in the period between 1920 and 1940. In 1920, however, Brazil had only
two major cities of more than 500,000 inhabitants: the Federal District
with a population of 1,150,000 and São Paulo with 570,000.

POLITICAL AND SOCIAL STRUCTURES

The establishment and consolidation of the Brazilian Empire in the first
half of the nineteenth century was the product of a coalition between
high-ranking bureaucrats, especially magistrates, sectors of the rural
landowning class, mainly in Rio de Janeiro but to a lesser extent in Bahia
and Pernambuco, and merchants in the principal cities who were anxious
to contain urban social and political agitation. In the conflict over
centralization and provincial autonomy, which characterized the early
decades of the Empire, there was a clear victory for increasing political
and administrative centralization. Supported by the coffee *fazendeiros* of
Rio de Janeiro, the bureaucrats, educated within the tradition of
Portuguese absolutism, were the main theoreticians and executors
of centralization.

Opposition to the centralized regime of the monarchy reappeared in
the later decades of the nineteenth century. The social classes which
emerged in new areas of economic expansion, particularly the coffee
bourgeoisie of São Paulo, began to argue in favour of a federal republic,
with a measure of provincial autonomy sufficient for them to be able to
levy taxes, formulate their own immigration programme, create their
own military force, and contract foreign loans. What united opponents

of the monarchy in the Republican party in São Paulo was the struggle for a federal structure, political and administrative decentralization; not, as has sometimes been argued, the issue of the abolition of slavery. After the triumph of the Republic, or more precisely of those regional class interests responsible for the formation of the Republic, the central government lost a considerable degree of power to the provinces, now called states, and their elected presidents.

As the dominant classes in each state became more articulate and those sectors, such as the judiciary, who were not linked to economic activity began to lose their influence in the machinery of state, there occurred a greater convergence between the dominant class and the political and administrative elite. The latter became more attached to their own regions, and as their geographical base shrank, they became more representative. In their turn, the interests of the dominant classes lay entirely within the state political framework as is shown quite clearly in the constitution of political parties which were originally conceived of as state organizations and so remained in their basic characteristic throughout the First Republic. The so-called national parties, such as the Federal Republican party or the Conservative Republican party, never became more than ephemeral attempts to organize a federation of state oligarchies. Even in the late 1920s, the attempt to launch a national Democratic party based on the opposition Democratic parties at state level was no exception to the rule.

Undoubtedly, the emphasis on political regionalization and decentralization served well-defined interests. The new institutional framework created the conditions which enabled the bourgeoisie of São Paulo to gain strength and consolidate its position within the state, and the nation. At the same time regionalism contained the seeds of its own destruction in that neither the state as a whole nor the ruling classes were able to legitimize themselves as representatives of the general interests of the nation.

Presented in simple terms, the political system of the First Republic in Brazil is usually described as being founded on three nuclei of power. At the base of the pyramid were the local potentates, the so-called *coronéis*, who controlled the rural population of a given area. At an intermediate level were the state oligarchies which were constituted to a greater or lesser extent by 'federations of *coronéis*', whose functions differed institutionally from those of the *coronéis* when taken in isolation. At the pinnacle of the power structure was the federal government, which was the product of an alliance between the oligarchies of the most important states, and was therefore the expression of a 'federation of oligarchies'. A feature of the whole system was the low level of political participation by the mass of the population. Furthermore, relations between social classes and groupings were expressed vertically, in accordance with the hierarchy implied by clientalistic relationships, and not horizontally as an expression of opposing class interests. Much attention has been given to the strategic role of the state oligarchies in oiling the wheels of government. While the *coronéis* basically furnished votes, they depended on the influence of the state oligarchies in government for obtaining a whole series of favours, including jobs and investments, which in turn were the basis of their power over the local population. On the other hand, the relationship between the state oligarchies and central government has been interpreted as being one of equality, with much emphasis being laid on the low degree of institutionalization at the national level. The political machinery at the state level determined the choice of the president of the Republic. In turn, the federal government did its utmost to assure the supremacy of the dominant factions at state level by not encouraging political dissidence.

There is no doubt a great deal of truth in this picture, but given the degree of generalization, it inevitably fails to take fully into account all the characteristics of the political system. The relationship between the *coronéis* and the population under their control, as well as that between *coronéis*, the state oligarchy and the federal government, varied considerably from region to region. The socio-economic characteristics of the country were by no means homogeneous. At one extreme was the state of São Paulo, at the other were the states of the north and north-east, not to mention the vast areas of sparse population. While São Paulo was entering a phase of capitalist development characterized by an intense level of immigration, the northern and north-eastern states, where precapitalistic relationships predominated, experienced a much lower level of growth, when not actually stagnating or even in recession. Paternalism coupled with violence, above all in relation to the rural population, existed throughout the country as two sides of the same coin, but the use of these two instruments of domination varied in style, frequency and degree of intensity.

Social and political life were dominated throughout the First Republic by clientalistic relationships, even in the major urban centres such as Rio de Janeiro and São Paulo. However, they were particularly strong in rural areas, for it was here that certain ideal conditions ensured the maintenance of social relationships based on the unequal exchange of favours between men situated at opposite ends of the social scale. Productive resources were controlled by a tiny minority; there was an almost total absence of public or private social welfare; and the generally precarious conditions for survival did not allow the dominated classes to pursue any course other than individually to seek the protection of the most powerful elements. Protection, in the form of land, financial assistance or employment, was exchanged for a guarantee of loyalty which, depending on individual cases, meant being prepared to defend the *coronel* physically, or obey his wishes at the ballot box.

A particularly effective instrument of power for the *coronéis* was the family structure known as the *parentela*, which was typical of the northeast. The *parentela* included the extended family, consisting of relatives by marriage, both vertical and collateral, as well as relations by kinship which were the result of ritual, such as godparents, or of adoption. However, not all family members were included in the *parentela* as this was based on loyalty to a patriarch.[4] For this reason, certain individuals linked to one another by blood or marriage were not part of a *parentela* although they were related. It is also worth noting that family norms did not necessarily operate when it came to choosing a new head of a *parentela*. Descendants in the vertical line of a patriarch could be ignored in favour of collateral relatives or relatives by marriage.

Institutionally, the Republic strengthened the power of the *coronéis*, in that the decentralization gave greater power to the *municípios* (counties), which were the smallest political and administrative units in each state. *Municípios* not only gained greater nominal autonomy, but also greater control over revenue. A comparison between the years 1868–9 and 1910 is revealing: in the former, the imperial government received 80.8 per cent of all revenue, the provinces 16.7 per cent and the municipalities 2.5 per cent; in the latter, the central government received 59.9 per cent of the total revenue, the states 21.5 per cent and the municipalities 18.6 per cent. Apart from this, the widening of the suffrage written into the constitution of 1891 strengthened the *coronéis* who, at the local level, gained greater bargaining power.[5] At the same time, however, the strengthening of the power of the states considerably limited the action

---

[4] See Linda Lewin, 'Some historical implications of kinship organization for family-based politics in the Brazilian northeast', *Comparative Studies in Society and History*, 21/2 (April 1979).

[5] Joseph L. Love, 'Political participation in Brazil, 1881–1969', *Luso-Brazilian Review*, 7/2 (1970), 7.

of the *coronéis*, or at least provided a focal point for tension between them and the state oligarchies.

At this point it is important to make some distinctions. In the states of the north and north-east, there were two main political patterns. In certain cases, a powerful family oligarchy would take over the machinery of government, thus minimizing the distinction between local *coronéis* and the state oligarchy. In others, groups representing urban interests, which included many professional politicians, or rural areas linked to the export trade, took power. Their position was, however, fragile and the so-called '*coronéis* of the interior' maintained a considerable degree of autonomy. This occurred throughout a vast region on both sides of the river São Francisco, where whole 'nations of *coronéis*' flourished. With the support of their own private armies, they became real warlords within their area of influence. Moreover, the development of internal trade in states like Bahia, Goiás, Pernambuco, Piauí, and Maranhão encouraged alliances between *coronéis* which crossed state boundaries. As a general rule, *coronéis* preferred to maintain maximum autonomy within their area, and did not object to the fact that the state capitals and coastal zones received a proportionately larger share of state revenue. Furthermore, they reacted against attempts to integrate them into parties or other organizations which might contribute towards the elimination of family feuds and banditry.

In these states, which did not form part of the powerful constellation centred on São Paulo, Minas Gerais and Rio Grande do Sul, the federal government's role was to a far greater extent one of arbitration, in which sometimes it lent its support to the local political oligarchy and sometimes negotiated directly with the *coronéis*. A case in point is the state of Bahia, which was characterized by the autonomy of the *coronéis* in the interior and by the weakness of the parties and of the political institutions of the oligarchy. Military backing from the federal government during the presidency of Marshal Hermes da Fonseca (1910–14) was decisive in the 1912 election for state president, which brought to power J. J. Seabra, a politician whose support came from the urban area of Salvador, the state capital. For several years, Seabra succeeded in controlling the power of the *coronéis* by means of a series of political reforms. Some years later in 1920 during a succeeding administration, the *coronéis* of the interior revolted against the state government, defeated its military forces in various clashes, and threatened to take Salvador itself. The president of the Republic arbitrated in the dispute, through the military commander of Bahia. Arbitration demonstrated the power of the *coronéis*.

The most famous of these, Horácio de Matos, obtained the right to keep his arms and munitions, as well as possession of twelve *municípios* which he held; authorities installed by him were recognized by the federal government. During the 1920s, in the case of Bahia, the traditional pattern by which the governor served as an intermediary between the *coronéis* and the president of the Republic ended once and for all. The latter became an arbitrator in local and regional politics. The *coronéis* of the interior gained greater autonomy vis-à-vis the state government and Bahia became fragmented into a number of states within a state. The result was a brand of federalism far removed from the model set out in the constitution of 1891.

In contrast, in the more developed states, the *coronéis* lacked autonomy, and associated themselves with wider structures such as the dominant political party and the state political machine. Here the dominant element in the whole network of client relationships was the state government, which distributed land, loans and public office. The difference was not without importance. On the surface, the state was merely a *coronel* on a grand scale, which propped up a system of domination similar to that in the north-east. However, the truth was that the relationship between society as a whole and the state was beginning to change. The state was increasingly coming to express class and not merely group interests, and to establish a sphere of autonomy vis-à-vis society. The best example of this process in São Paulo, where a homogeneous dominant class was formed and social differentiation was more intense. The local power of the *coronéis* persisted above all in frontier regions, but to a greater or lesser extent it was subordinate to the state government which controlled most of the resources which the *coronéis* relied on to maintain themselves in power. The state government also had at its disposal considerable military power which practically ensured its superiority when it came to armed conflict. Furthermore, the Paulista Republican party (PRP) had a considerable amount of organizational discipline and cohesion, and was clearly something more than an elaborate network of kinship and client relationships, although these aspects were important. The PRP, it has been argued, represented an intermediate stage between a grouping based on vertical 'client' relationships and a modern political party organized 'horizontally'.[6] Undoubtedly, the relations between state and society remained fundamentally clientalistic. However, given its role as executor of class interests, the state would from time to time take

---

[6] Joseph L. Love, *São Paulo in the Brazilian Federation, 1889–1937* (Stanford, 1980), 115.

measures whose purpose was the reduction of local power in sensitive areas. In 1906, for example, the president of the state of São Paulo, Jorge Tibiriça, not only delegated extraordinary powers to the state militia, but instituted a full-time civil police force. Although it is doubtful how independent the police in fact became, it nevertheless represented an attempt to transform the police from their traditional position as an appendage of the big landowners. Similarly, in 1921, the state president Washington Luís stimulated the professionalization of the judiciary, which became less dependent on local power. Among other measures, an entrance examination was established, promotions systematized and salaries increased.

Minas Gerais was a curious case. In terms of its economic structure it bore a certain resemblance to the state of Bahia.[7] However, the two states differed in the degree of their economic development and, above all, in the power of their governmental institutions. In Minas Gerais, the civil service constituted an effective tool for patronage, which was controlled by the party and by the state government. Although it was unequal in its treatment of different regions, the state government was able to offer loans, favours, and public works especially in the field of transport. While the *coronéis* of the interior of Bahia were commercially isolated from the capital up until 1930, in Minas those areas furthest from the urban centres, such as the north of the state, were ever hopeful of obtaining improved means of transport which might integrate them into the markets of the south. Furthermore, from the formation of the Minas Republican party (PRM) in 1897, the *coronéis* were politically subordinate to the state governor and the state political machinery. 'There is no salvation without the PRM' was a well-known slogan among the *coronéis* of Minas during the Old Republic. In Rio Grande do Sul, the figure of the 'bureaucrat *coronel*' was a clear demonstration of the greater power of the state government and of the state Republican party (PRR). If the 'bureaucrat *coronel*' derived his position from his economic power and social prestige in a particular area, he also had to be prepared to take orders from above. The post of *intendente* (county superintendent) which was in theory the domain of the *coronéis* was frequently occupied by people provisionally designated by the state government.[8]

The constitution of 1891 formalized the federal system while at the same time giving expression to the distinction of power between the most

---

[7] John D. Wirth, *Minas Gerais in the Brazilian Federation, 1889–1937* (Stanford, 1977), 118.

[8] See Joseph L. Love. *Rio Grande do Sul and Brazilian regionalism, 1882–1930* (Stanford, 1971), 79.

powerful and the weakest states. Against the opinion of some military leaders who wanted equal representation for all states, the Chamber of Deputies was established on the basis of proportional representation depending on the number of inhabitants in each state (on the basis of the 1890 census). State autonomy, which benefited the largest units, was guaranteed in the vital matters of distribution of revenue and military power. The levying of certain taxes, the most significant being that of the duty on exports, the second most important source of revenue during the Empire, was taken out of the hands of the central government. This was of considerable benefit to São Paulo which came to outstrip the central government itself in financial terms. The right of states to contract foreign loans enabled São Paulo to finance the expansion of its coffee economy and the improvement of its urban services. The smaller states with low export receipts and in practice lacking the power to impose taxes on the great rural estates tried in vain to obtain a portion of the duty on imports levied by the central government. The individual states had the right to organize their own military forces. Here again, thanks to their resources, the larger states took ample advantage of this right. The state militia of São Paulo in particular was well equipped and its active members were always greater in number than those regiments of the federal army stationed in the state. In 1925 and 1926 the state militia numbered as many as 14,000 men, trained since 1906 by a French military mission. Thus the more powerful states had the financial and military resources to limit interventionist pressures from the federal government.

The election of the president of the Republic reflected the degree of agreement or disagreement between the most powerful states. It is frequently affirmed that the so-called *café com leite* alliance between São Paulo and Minas Gerais effectively controlled the First Republic. This is certainly true to a great extent. However, it is important to bear in mind that there were areas of conflict within the alliance, particularly after 1910 when the entry of a third state on the political scene, Rio Grande do Sul, upset its balance. Ultimately, towards the end of the 1920s, the rupture between the oligarchies of São Paulo and Minas Gerais set off the chain of events which would lead to the Revolution of 1930. Nevertheless, it is true that, generally speaking, power lay with the São Paulo–Minas axis under the Old Republic. In eleven presidential contests, nine of the presidents elected came from these two states, six from São Paulo and three from Minas Gerais. Given the size of its population, the state of Minas was to play an influential role in the Chamber of Deputies, where it held 37 seats, followed by São Paulo and Bahia each with 22. Although it was by no means insignificant, the economy of Minas could not match that of São Paulo. Minas produced foodstuffs mainly derived from cattle raising. In addition, it was a producer of coffee. Fewer opportunities in the economic field encouraged the Minas political elite to expand and to seek posts in central government. During its apogee between 1898 and 1930, the Minas oligarchy was not only influential in the Chamber of Deputies, it was also the grouping which remained for the greatest number of years in charge of key ministries. The direct domination of federal politics by the São Paulo oligarchy which began almost with the birth of the Republic declined from about 1905. However, although this complicated the issue it cannot be said that the interests of São Paulo were no longer predominant at federal level. Given the characteristic features of the federal system, it was vital that São Paulo should control federal politics only in those areas where action at state level was impossible or inadequate: in the area of exchange regulations and financial policies, which guaranteed foreign loans contracted mainly to maintain the value of coffee, and in the matter of immigration laws and the distribution of revenue between the federal and state governments.

Obviously, the political power of each regional unit depended to a great extent on its economic power. However, the degree of cohesion within the state ruling classes and the regional parties was of fundamental importance. This point can be illustrated by a brief analysis of the political structures of São Paulo, Minas Gerais, and Rio Grande do Sul. In 1920 the three states were responsible for more than half of the total value of the country's agricultural and industrial production, excluding the Federal District. In São Paulo, the coffee bourgeoisie lent its political support to the PRP as a result of a long struggle dating from the 1870s in defence of the Republic and above all of federalism. No other party expressed so clearly class interests. Despite the rapid economic growth of São Paulo and the consequent social differentiation, the PRP managed to maintain its position as sole party of the ruling class until 1926, when the Democratic party (PD) was founded. The basic nucleus for economic expansion in the state of São Paulo was the coffee complex, on which all other economic activities as well as the administrative machinery of the state were directly or indirectly dependent. The internal differences within the coffee bourgeoisie between the main producers, bankers and *comissários* were never clearly expressed. In turn, the nascent industrial-ization did not give rise to a class which was radically opposed to the coffee entrepreneurs. Industry developed as an offshoot of the export economy which created a regional market and was responsible for the influx of capital necessary for the purchase of machinery. Industrial investment was often a parallel option to investment in the coffee complex, and adjusted to the conditions of the coffee economy. These circumstances facilitated the amalgamation of the landowner and the industrialist in one person, or at least one family group. Only in 1928 did there emerge in São Paulo a representative organ of the industrial bourgeoisie. Even then, Roberto Simonsen – the first great name among ideologists of industrialization in São Paulo – left no doubt as to the effectiveness of the initiative, when he agreed that the economic structure of Brazil should rest mainly on the cultivation of the soil. The PRP itself was therefore able to represent the limited and subordinate interests of the industrialists of São Paulo, as was seen for example in the struggle in the National Congress to impose tariff barriers for imported textile goods (1928).

In Minas Gerais, the economic activity of the ruling class was divided between coffee, cattle raising and to a lesser extent industry, in geographically distinct sub-regions. Internal political dispute was considerable, especially during the first years of the Republic. Nevertheless, despite frequent disagreements and factional rivalries, the Republican party of Minas (PRM) tended to gather strength and present a united front at the level of federal politics. Minas Gerais did not even witness the emergence of a sizeable opposition party in the 1920s, whereas in São Paulo social differentiation, above all the expansion of the urban middle class, eventually opened the possibility of a horizontal articulation of interests and the founding of the PD. In Minas, the close alliance between the PRM and the state through patronage was always the safest (indeed the only) way by which class interests might be expressed or by which the individual might make progress in the political arena.

In contrast, the unity of the regional ruling class in Rio Grande do Sul was always problematical. Here factional dispute was expressed predominantly through competing parties rather than through rivalries within a single party. It would be wrong, however, to establish a direct causal relation between different economic interests (cattle raising, wheat production, and so on) and this peculiar feature of *gaúcho* politics. From the beginning of the Republic, the Republican party of Rio Grande do Sul (PRR) took power at the regional level, although it had to face opposition from rival parties. Between 1893 and 1895, it was involved in a violent civil war with the Federal party, founded by the old liberals of the Empire and by dissidents from the PRR. In 1923, there was renewed armed conflict between the PRR and the opposition groups of the Liberal alliance. This political division undoubtedly contributed to reducing the influence of Rio Grande do Sul at the federal level, where for a long period it held the balance but was never a serious contender in the struggle for power. It was no coincidence, therefore, that during the presidential campaign of 1929–30 and the ensuing revolution which brought Getúlio Vargas to power, the political forces of the region finally managed to present a united front in the form of the Frente Única Gaúcha.

With regard to the north-eastern states, concerted action on their part could in theory give them a certain weight in federal politics, whether in the choice of president of the Republic, or in the Chamber of Deputies. In the Chamber, Bahia with 22 seats and Pernambuco with 17 constituted a sizeable grouping. For some time, between 1896 and 1911, the state of Pernambuco exercised a degree of influence at the federal level, through its leader Francisco Rosa e Silva. However, he only managed to produce a coalition of north-eastern states sporadically, as in 1906 when he attempted to prevent parliamentary approval of the coffee valorization scheme, which had been drawn up by the states of São Paulo, Minas Gerais and Rio de Janeiro. Indeed, any coalition between the north-eastern states was severely hampered, among other reasons, by problems arising from the characteristics of the federal system with regard to taxation. Given the sparse resources of the region, the various oligarchies competed for favours from the federal government and entered into lengthy disputes among themselves over the right to levy inter-state revenues in the case of goods circulating in more than one state.

A potential destabilizing factor during the First Republic was the failure of the oligarchic political system sufficiently to integrate the armed forces, especially the army. Until the 1880s the army had played only a minor part in national political decision making. The imperial government, although co-opting military figures, was fundamentally civilian and the politicians took pride in pointing out the advantages of the Brazilian system over that of its neighbouring Republics which were invariably subject to military rule. After the suppression of the last of the provincial rebellions in the middle of the nineteenth century, the role of the army was greatly reduced; it was primarily occupied in guarding the frontiers and the military colonies. It was the role of the National Guard to maintain civil order, at least until the beginning of the 1870s.[9] The National Guard mobilized practically the entire free adult male population, under the command of officers who were recruited from among the local landowners. After the Paraguayan War (1865–70) the army became more aware of its potential, and at the same time more conscious of its subordinate role. The bitterness of its struggle in the war also contrasted with the accusations of corruption, favouritism and political gerrymandering levelled at successive cabinets by the press. Gradually, certain officers came to see the army as a civic 'entity' which was independent of social class and of the Empire. They saw the army as an institution willing to make material sacrifices and destined to take power in order to regenerate the nation, for the armed forces embodied in themselves the notion of patriotism. Apart from this global vision, many officers complained of the discrimination suffered by the military, and openly demonstrated their opposition to the general policies of the government. They placed great emphasis on the importance of education, on industrial development, and on the abolition of slavery.

However, the officers were not a homogeneous group. On the one hand, there were those young officers who had attended the Military School at Praia Vermelha in Rio de Janeiro, which was more a centre for the study of mathematics, philosophy and letters than for military sciences. This group came under the influence of Comtean positivism, particularly after the arrival of Benjamin Constant as a teacher at the school in 1872. The Military School in fact was responsible for the training of a group of 'graduates in uniform' who, with a particular view of the world, began to compete with the traditional graduates from the schools of law and medicine. It was from this circle of officers that the concept of the 'soldier citizen' was born, as was criticism against the Empire in favour of modernization and against the slave regime. On the other hand, there were the *tarimbeiros*, a group of older officers, almost all veterans of the Paraguayan War. Many of these had not graduated from the Military School. Less concerned with issues of social reform, this group was nevertheless deeply conscious of the honour of the military

---

[9] This discussion on the armed forces is based on José Murilo de Carvalho, 'As forças armadas na Primeira República: o poder desestabilizador' and Fernando Henrique Cardoso, 'Dos governos militares, a Prudente-Campos Sales', in Boris Fausto (ed.), *História geral da civilização brasileira, III: O Brasil republicano*, vols. I and II (São Paulo, 1975–7).

community. In the 1880s the two groups united against the imperial government. In the *questão militar* the *tarimbeiros* took the initiative in defending the military against 'insults to its integrity'. However, it was the military graduates who prepared the coup of 15 November 1889 and dragged in the *tarimbeiros*, many of whom, including Marshal Deodoro da Fonseca who proclaimed the Republic, were not in fact republicans.

In spite of these formative differences, which corresponded in part to diverse social origins, it is possible to determine certain common characteristics within the military. Brazilian historians have frequently interpreted the military as being the spokesman of the middle class against the landowning oligarchy. This is, however, a somewhat narrow view. Many army officers were undoubtedly of broadly middle-class origin, but throughout the final decades of the Empire and during the whole of the First Republic, an army career also represented a limited but viable option for the sons of those branches of families within the oligarchy which were in economic decline, especially in the north and north-east. Apart from this it is important to recognize the process of socialization for which the army, as an institution with specific values and relatively independent of society at large, was responsible. Officers were also recruited from what became military families, especially in states like Rio Grande do Sul. The regional background of Brazilian military officers is revealed in the limited data available. Among the 52 officers who were members of the first Congress of the Republic, 24 were from the north-east and 9 from Rio Grande do Sul and the Federal District together, and only one came from São Paulo and Minas Gerais. Of the 30 divisional and brigade commanders in 1895, eight were from Rio Grande do Sul, none from Minas, and one from São Paulo; in 1930 eight were from Rio Grande do Sul, none from either Minas or São Paulo. Significant here was the importance of Rio Grande do Sul where there was a sizeable garrison responsible for the security of the frontier. The almost total absence of military leaders from São Paulo or Minas contributed to the weakening of relations between the army and the two most politically powerful states of the Republic.

Given their origins, army officers frequently gained within the military corporation a distinctive 'status', which was reinforced by the system of endogenous recruitment. It was a 'status' which could not easily be changed for another, and for this reason it was jealously guarded. At the same time, many officers were people of literate urban background, whose profession linked them directly with the centre of power. Given their military tradition, and the family connections many of them had with the oligarchy, the world of politics was not foreign to them. On the other hand, they did not identify themselves with the civilian oligarchies and much less with those of the dominant states. The officers conceived of themselves as protectors of the nation, the creators of an austere but progressive state, free from the political gerrymandering of the *legistas* (the graduates who constituted the political staff of the oligarchies) and the *casacas* (the *nouveaux riches* who accumulated fortunes on the money market). This state would integrate the people – an undifferentiated category inherent in the concept of the nation – and would strengthen national unity. This ideal was very different from the pragmatism of the most powerful oligarchies, such as that of São Paulo, for whom the Republic represented the protection of specific economic interests, the defence of state autonomy and the reinforcement of regional inequalities.

It cannot be said that the army was a persistent destabilizing factor in the oligarchic Republic. Its willingness to act depended on a variety of historical circumstances, and the most active elements changed continually. There was, however, a basic incompatibility between the oligarchies of the most powerful states and the military apparatus, although it was tempered by tactical and defensive alliances. In the end, the fall of the First Republic was due in part to the long-term disaffection, indeed insurrection, of middle-ranking army officers and, ultimately, intervention by the high command of the armed forces.

The political system of the First Republic was characterized by minimal popular participation. The constitution of the Republic (1891) formally expanded the base for political representation. In place of the suffrage based on property and income, as it had been throughout the Empire, the right to vote was extended to all *literate* male Brazilians over the age of 21. The widening of the electorate from the Empire to the Republic brought significant results. A comparison of the last parliamentary elections of the Empire (1886) with the first presidential election in which voters from all states took part (1898) shows an increase of almost 400 per cent in the number of voters. In 1886, 111,700 people voted out of a total population of 13.2 million, representing 0.89 per cent of the population. In 1898, there were 462,000 votes which corresponded to 2.7 per cent of the population of 17.1 million. However, the widening of the franchise does not alter the fact that the number of voters in relation to the total population of the country was extremely low throughout the whole period of the First Republic. In the three competitive elections for the presidency of the Republic (1910, 1922 and 1930), votes counted corresponded respectively to 2.8, 1.9 and 5.7 per cent of the population. Voting was optional; women did not have the vote; and illiterates were excluded in a country where 85.2 per cent of the population was illiterate in 1890 and 75.5 per cent in 1920.[10]

Perhaps more important than the low level of participation in elections was the dependence of the electorate on the local oligarchies. The subordination of the electorate was facilitated by the open vote, and it was therefore not surprising that the urban opposition campaigned for the adoption of the secret ballot throughout the whole period. When it became necessary to break the power of a particular faction or when the normal mechanisms of control ceased to function, it was always possible to resort to fraud, by, for example, including the vote of foreigners or the recently deceased, or falsifying ballot papers (a process which was made all the easier by the absence of an adequately structured state bureaucracy), and, if necessary, force. Obviously, any measures taken to increase the electorate, such as giving the vote to illiterates, would not have altered this situation. Indeed, it might have made it worse, at least initially. In a country with a low level of popular participation and where political citizenship was almost always used as currency for the unequal exchange of favours, the federal Republic, though in theory based on the ideal of democratic representation, was in practice no more than an instrument of the regional oligarchies.

In the rural areas where the mass of the population was dependent on the big landowners, the rural population was differentiated horizontally according to a hierarchy of minor privileges related to the conditions under which they settled and worked the land. Vertically, it was even more fragmented because of the need to maintain relations of loyalty to the big landowners and their kin. Nor did the small and medium-sized landed proprietors, mostly of foreign origin, who established themselves for example in Rio Grande do Sul, constitute an independent class from the political point of view, albeit for different reasons. They were less subject to the domination of the *coronéis*, but more so to that of the state with regard to tax obligations, land concessions and so on. Apart from this, as foreigners or first-generation Brazilians they were less culturally

---

[10] Love, 'Political participation in Brazil', 7.

and politically integrated; their basic objectives were primarily related to economic advance. All this explains why the dominant party in Rio Grande do Sul (PRR) managed to maintain proportionately greater control of those *municípios* where landowners of foreign origin predominated than in the rest of the state.[11]

As for the workers on the great coffee plantations of São Paulo, a number of circumstances hindered their social organization. The mass of immigrants entering a strange land were dispersed among isolated estates. This hampered the type of contact which might have led to a consciousness of their common situation and, thus, common action. Within the boundaries of his estate, the landowner held wide powers based on paternalism and coercion. The paternalistic approach was reinforced by certain features of the system of colonization; provision of housing and of strips of land for planting food crops was seen as a concession on the part of the employer rather than payment for services rendered. Coercion was the norm when the landowner held absolute power within his estate or when he dominated state institutions such as the police and the magistrature, and was able to place them at his service.

It would be mistaken, however, to assume that the system of domination in the rural areas produced no reaction among the mass of plantation workers. On the estates in São Paulo, there were constant clashes between landowners and colonists, particularly during the early years of mass immigration. Individual disputes, cases of whole families abandoning plantations, and complaints to consular representatives were common occurrences during the years. There is also evidence of strike threats, especially towards the end of April and beginning of May – the period of the harvest – when the landowners were more vulnerable to pressure. However, there was only one important cycle of strikes during this period. This occurred in 1913 in the area of Ribeirão Preto, near an urban centre, and involved some thousands of colonists from the large estates.

In other areas of the country, the disaffection of the rural population was expressed through movements of a religious type, of which the most important were the Canudos and the Contestado movements. Canudos was an abandoned estate in the north of the state of Bahia, where Antônio Vicente Mendes Maciel – better known as Antônio Conselheiro – and his followers established themselves in 1893. Deep in the *sertão* (backlands) a

---

[11] Love, *Rio Grande do Sul and Brazilian regionalism*, 134.

city grew up with a population which fluctuated between 20 and 30 thousand inhabitants. The people of Canudos defeated a number of military expeditions sent to crush them, in spite of the inequality of strength. Finally, in October 1897, after a struggle lasting many months, Canudos was destroyed. Its defenders, who numbered some 5,000 in the final phase of the war, were either killed in combat or captured and put to death.

The Contestado movement occurred in the south of the country in a frontier area disputed by the states of Paraná and Santa Catarina. It began in 1911 under the leadership of José Maria, who died in the first clashes and was heralded as a saint by the rebels of the Contestado. Unlike Canudos, the movement did not limit itself to one particular centre, but shifted to various points in the region, under pressure from military forces. The rebellion was put down in late 1915, when rebel strongholds were attacked and destroyed by 6,000 soldiers from the army and the police force, assisted by 1,000 civilians who joined in the process of repression.

In considering the principal social movements in the interior of Brazil during the First Republic, Joazeiro, a city in the south of the state of Ceará, which became the centre of activities of the priest Cícero Romão Batista between 1872 and 1924, also deserves mention. There are many common features between events in Joazeiro and the Canudos and Contestado movements. For example, from the point of view of the history of the transformation of the Catholic church in Brazil, particularly in the north-east – a theme which lies outside the scope of this chapter[12] – Canudos and Joazeiro were manifestations of similar developments. On the other hand, when considering social movements as manifestations of rebellion, Joazeiro has little in common with the other two movements. Although Padre Cícero clashed continuously with the ecclesiastical authorities, and at times with factions of the oligarchy, his movement for better or worse fell within the system of domination which prevailed during the First Republic. Put simply, the city of Joazeiro can be seen as an area controlled by a priest-*coronel*, who had a considerable degree of influence within the political oligarchy, particularly after 1909 when Padre Cícero began to involve himself directly in the political struggles.

The Canudos and Contestado movements were attempts to create an

---

12 For a discussion of the Catholic church in Brazil during this period, see Lynch, *CHLA* IV, ch. 12.

alternative way of life, and were considered sufficiently dangerous for both to be brutally crushed by military forces. This does not mean that they were totally opposed to the power structure of the *coronéis*. Before settling in Canudos, Antônio Conselheiro had been a practising member of the Catholic church, living an ascetic, nomadic life. He summoned the people together in order to build or rebuild churches. He built walls around cemeteries, and he showed concern for the small parish churches of the interior. There is evidence that at this stage he was well looked upon by certain *coronéis*, for whom his disciplined followers built roads and dams. The village of Canudos itself did not depart very much from the traditional pattern of settlement in the interior. There was a certain degree of social and economic differentiation, a considerable degree of trade with the surrounding area, and religious links with the priests of the neighbouring parishes. Canudos was also a source of votes and influence at election time.

The instigators of the Contesdado movement were the followers of a *coronel* who was a member of the opposition and seen as a friend of the poor. Others of varying origins joined this group, among them those who were the victims of the process of modernization in both urban and rural areas: rural workers driven off the land by the construction of a railway and a timber plant, people who had been recruited for railway construction from among the unemployed of large cities and then abandoned at the end of their contract, and criminals who were at large in the region. However, the village settlements which grew up during the Contestado, with their emphasis on equality and fraternity, clashed with established social values, and assumed characteristics which were clearly messianic. This can be seen, among other features, through the way many of the members of the Contestado remained loyal to the monarchy which, it has been argued, represented an eschatological kingdom more than a political institution.[13] The theme of the monarchy, whether because of the form it took or because of the period in which the Contestado movement occurred, was not exploited to any extent by the government. In contrast, the earlier monarchism of Antônio Conselheiro, with its attacks on the Republic, responsible for the introduction of civil marriage and for the taking of cemeteries away from the control of the church, took more concrete forms. As a result it was a mobilizing factor against Canudos in the urban centres, at a time when

[13] Duglas Teixeira Monteiro, *Os errantes do Novo Século: um estudo sobre o surto milenarista do Contestado* (São Paulo, 1974).

the possibility of the restoration of the monarchy was seen as a real threat.

Canudos, Contestado and Joazeiro were not episodes devoid of significance, nor were they isolated expressions by an ignorant rural population in contrast to the centres of civilization on the coast. In different degrees, these movements can be linked to changes in the Catholic church, to socio-economic changes in their respective areas, and to the political development of the nation itself. Their particular strength as a demonstration of popular religious belief cannot be ignored. Nevertheless, as attempts at independent organization on the part of the rural population, they effectively illustrate the severe limitations of such organization during the period of the First Republic.

Alongside these messianic social movements, social banditry has sometimes been considered as evidence of rebellion on the part of the rural population and of the small urban centres of the interior. We are referring here to the phenomenon of the *cangaço*, warlike bands of armed men which sprang up in the north-east of the country during the second half of the nineteenth century, and whose history spills over into the twentieth century, coming to an end only in the late 1930s. In the beginning the *cangaço* was closely connected to the ties of kinship and limited in its sphere of action to a small area. Gradually, new forms emerged, developing into professional bandit organizations whose sphere of action was much wider. This was the case of the famous group of bandits led by Virgulino Ferreira, known as Lampião. Lampião and his men were active over a long period from 1920 to 1938, and ranged over seven states of the north-east until their final confrontation with the police in which Lampião was killed.

As a general rule *cangaceiros* were white, from families of small landed proprietors or members of the elite who had been on the losing end in disputes over land, trade, or local political power. If this was the general background, some also had specific personal reasons for becoming bandits. Joining the *cangaço* often resulted from a series of events sparked off by the violent death of a close relative. Not having any reason to believe in the powers of the police or the judiciary, the future bandit set about satisfying family honour by his own hand, and ended up by gathering together a group of followers. Significantly, the death of a father in the circumstances described features in the biographies of Lampião and another famous *cangaceiro*, Antônio Silvino, who was active between 1897 and 1914. The bandit armies were recruited from among the poor, of dark skin, who formed the mass of the rural population. For these, banditry meant the possibility of greater individual independence coupled with attractive material incentives.

In the mythology of the poor of the Brazilian north-east, and in the films and songs of the 1960s, the *cangaceiros* are seen as social bandits or even as Brazilian equivalents of Robin Hood. The *cangaceiros* broke with established order by refusing to recognize the authority of the police and judiciary, as well as by the nature of their activities. These included the invasion of estates and the sacking of villages and towns, which were often connected with a desire to damage a particular group or individual within the ruling class. Nor can it be doubted either that many *cangaceiros* gained the co-operation of the poor, whose support was vital for the survival of the armed bands. Antônio Silvino, for example, gained considerable popular prestige by distributing money and part of the booty among the poor. However, it has been shown convincingly that between the *cangaço* and the power structure of the *coronéis*, there was always a relationship of interdependence, in which the *coronéis* represented the dominant sector.[14] For the *cangaceiros* the possibility of breaking the power of the *coronéis* went beyond their convenience and their mentality. The band of armed men counted on the sympathy of the poor, but it depended for its permanent security on the shelter and ammunition which only the powerful could provide. From the point of view of the local elites, the *cangaço* represented an important reserve force, in a situation where political power was segmented and violently contested by rival groups.

The disintegration and ultimate extinction of the *cangaço* resulted from a process by which the intervention of the state, with its growing ability to punish and to patronize, reduced the instability of the local elite, and transformed the *cangaceiros* into mere bandits, whose actions were no longer of any use to their erstwhile protectors. There remained the mythology rooted in the figure of the *cangaceiro*, who is the personification of a supreme physical violence which the poor, under the oppression of their local potentates, cannot hope to emulate.

The framework of social relations which prevailed in the urban centres was undoubtedly different. From the first years of the Republic, the importance of the cities far exceeded their economic significance and electoral weight. It was here that the social groups and classes who

[14] See Linda Lewin, 'The oligarchical limitations of social banditry in Brazil: the case of the "good" thief Antônio Silvino', *Past and Present*, 82 (February 1979).

formed the narrow caucus of public opinion were concentrated. These included representatives of the most enlightened sector of the ruling class, middle-class elements, and, in the case of the Federal District, the military. Also to be found there were the most potentially dangerous sectors: the working class, the low-paid white collar workers, and the urban unemployed and underemployed.

In both Rio de Janeiro and São Paulo, urban *coronéis* flourished, although their sphere of action was more limited than in the rural areas; domination by the oligarchy depended on more than manipulation of the vote. As the seat of the central government, the mayor of the Federal District was nominated by the president of the Republic. In 1928, the PRP managed to amend the constitution of the state of São Paulo to include a clause whereby the president of the state was given the power to choose the mayor of the capital. And the post of mayor of Recife, capital of Pernambuco, also ceased to be an elected post – by a decision of the legislature.

Indiscriminate references to the urban middle class have served to obscure its political role during the First Republic. More than any other, this sector was heterogeneous, divided in terms of income, social mobility, racial origin, and degree of dependence on the regional ruling class. Industrialists and merchants, mostly of immigrant origin, intent on economic and social advance, seem to have played little part in politics. The Brazilian-born middle class, with little economic power, but linked to the ruling class by family ties, was a different case. These were the so-called 'poor relations' of the oligarchy. For them, survival did not generally lie in economic activity, but in the state apparatus, on which they often depended as civil servants. Included in this 'national' middle class were those who moulded public opinion, such as journalists and prestigious figures within the liberal professions. These sectors were generally in conflict with the oligarchies in their struggle to establish a liberal democracy through measures such as the secret ballot and the creation of an electoral commission to curb fraud. However, middle-class participation in the campaigns for liberal democracy varied depending on the sector of the middle class involved, as well as on the influence of specific regional characteristics. Liberal ideology generally attracted the highest strata of the middle class, while the salaried masses of the service sector, such as bank and commercial employees and low-ranking civil servants, seem to have tended towards demands of a similar type to those of the working classes, that is, better salaries or improved housing. Nevertheless, this interpretation runs the risk of being too simplistic if one does not consider inter-class relationships in certain cities. Taking Rio de Janeiro and São Paulo as examples, it is possible to distinguish particular features in their social movements, which can be partially explained by the diversity within the structure of the middle class as well as by the hegemonic role played by the bourgeoisie of São Paulo.

In 1890 in Rio de Janeiro, then the only Brazilian city of any size and also the only one with a diversified social structure, the civil service, liberal professions, and the priesthood accounted for 8.6 per cent of the employed population (compared with 4.6 per cent in São Paulo in 1893). The capital of the Republic would become increasingly a city of services. In 1919, only 38.4 per cent of the economically active population was involved in actual physical production, while 61.6 per cent was involved in the provision of services, 15 per cent of these in domestic services. In Rio de Janeiro the middle class was less dependent on the agrarian bourgeoisie. It comprised the professional and bureaucratic middle class and, more especially, functional groups who were not linked to the coffee bourgeoisie, such as career military officers, students of the Military School at Praia Vermelha, and students in higher education. These sectors attempted to ally themselves to the working class, and provided a multi-class basis to various social movements in Rio de Janeiro such as the Jacobinist movement, which emerged in the last years of the nineteenth century. Jacobinism was rooted in the discontent which prevailed among wide sectors of the population of the capital, who were affected by inflation and bad living conditions, and was permeated with a vaguely patriotic ideology. For these sectors, the tangible cause of their difficulties lay in the fact that commerce was controlled by the Portuguese. In addition, Jacobinism, in attempting to prevent Prudente de Morais from assuming the presidency of the Republic in 1894, was a reaction against the rise to power of the Paulista coffee oligarchy.

In São Paulo, attempts by middle-class sectors to ally themselves with the lower classes were far more tenuous. The large immigrant sector lacked both the conditions and the reasons for presenting itself as a social force. The traditional middle class gravitated towards the coffee bourgeoisie, on which it was economically and culturally dependent. These characteristics, allied to the fact that there were no groups, such as military school students or officers of the armed forces, capable of forming an opposition, mean⁺ that social protest in São Paulo was limited to the working class. The liberal Democratic party (PD) was founded in 1926 for the purpose of strengthening 'the purity of republican institutions', and recruited members and voters from among the urban middle class. However, a year after the Revolution of 1930, the PD united with the PRP against the government of Getúlio Vargas.

The working class was concentrated mainly in the Federal District and in the larger cities of the state of São Paulo, particularly the capital. Quantitatively, the structure of industry was based to a large extent on small enterprises, operating with limited capital and technology. On the other hand, the larger units, particularly in the field of textile production, accounted for a considerable proportion of the working population. In 1919, companies with 500 or more workers accounted for 36.4 per cent of the work force in the state of São Paulo, and 35.7 per cent in the Federal District.

It was in the cities that the necessary conditions for the emergence of a labour movement existed. Social relations were less clientalistic and paternalistic; exploitation was more objective; easier contact and communication made possible the birth of a collective consciousness. Despite the fact that their activities were restricted, revolutionary ideologists and organizers established themselves in the urban environment. On the other hand, a number of factors limited the strength of the labour movement, which was never able to exert enough pressure to obtain greater participation in the political field. There was, in general, an abundance of manpower both in São Paulo and in Rio de Janeiro. In São Paulo, in view of its cyclical character, the coffee sector played an important part in the supply of urban labour. While in expansion, coffee encouraged a degree of immigration which exceeded its own needs, and this meant in turn that the surplus joined the urban labour force. At times of crisis in the rural areas, coffee plantation workers were left with no other option but to migrate to the urban centres or return to their countries of origin, as the other sectors of the agricultural export economy were incapable of absorbing them. In the case of Rio de Janeiro, internal migration to the largest urban centre in the country was a significant factor in the growth of the labour force. The size of the work force gave rise to ethnic friction – between Brazilian and foreign immigrants, Portuguese and Italians, and even between Italians from different parts of Italy. At the same time, because industrial expansion was not regular, employment in manufacturing industries was only intermittent, and this meant that improvements in labour conditions were slow. Finally, by emphasizing spontaneous class movements, and by refusing to organize, anarchism could be said to have fed those structural features of the social system which militated against working-class cohesion. Given its ideological perspectives, it also contributed to the failure of the organized working class to adopt a programme of reforms favourable to the broadening of the base of the political system. At the same time, although industry was only of secondary importance to the economy, the leading industrialists were able to exert a considerable degree of influence on the centre of power and could count on the repressive force of the government. The semi-legality of the unions, the violence unleashed on strikers, and the expulsion of foreign labour leaders all contributed to the disunity of the working class.

Strikes had occurred in the urban areas of Brazil since the end of the nineteenth century. However, the phase of major growth in the labour movement within the period under consideration occurred between 1917 and 1920, under the influence of wartime inflation and within the general pattern of labour unrest which followed the end of the first world war. Its high point was the general strike in São Paulo in July 1917, which was joined by 50,000 workers. This period witnessed not only a large number of strikes, but also, in some cases, increased union membership. At the end of 1918, the textile union of Rio de Janeiro, for example, had as many as 20,000 members, no small figure if one considers that a large proportion of the labour force in that particular sector was made up of women and children who did not join the union.

Until the beginning of the 1920s, anarcho-syndicalist ideas predominated among the small groups of organized workers in the city of São Paulo. In Rio de Janeiro, anarcho-syndicalism was less influential. The climate of opinion tended to favour 'apolitical syndicalism', which was geared solely towards improvements in working conditions and wages. This tendency was particularly strong among railway and port workers. The socialists never managed to create more than small partisan sects, which is not surprising in a country where the transformation of society through political participation seemed no more than a utopian dream.

The great strikes of 1917–20 did not bring about any improvement in the conditions of the Brazilian workers in terms of organizational stability. Throughout the 1920s, the labour movement stagnated. Following the failure of the strikes, and in the wake of the Russian Revolution, anarchism went through a period of crisis. A group of former anarchists most closely linked to the workers' struggle, together with a few socialists, founded the Brazilian Communist party (PCB) in 1922. Indeed, one of the characteristics of the PCB was that its main caucus originated in anarcho-syndicalism and not socialism. New concepts were formulated on a wide variety of themes, such as the role of the unions and the party, class alliances, anti-imperialism, and agrarian reform. However, the party did not expand to any great extent during the 1920s, its active membership fluctuating between 73 in 1922 and 1,000 in 1929.

Nevertheless the clear warning given by the strikes of 1917–20, coupled with the steady growth in the size of the working class, produced the first signs within the ruling class of new attitude to the 'social problem', one which was not bent solely on repression. Some social rights were recognized, above all in the service sector, which was a strategically important area for the agricultural export economy. When the labour movement gained new impetus following the 1929 crisis and the 1930 Revolution, attempts to create autonomous working-class organizations would have to compete, on an unequal footing, with government measures aimed at organizing, and controlling, the urban working class.

THE POLITICAL PROCESS

The most sensitive critical features of the oligarchic system of the First Republic lay in the difficulties in adjustment between the different regional oligarchies, in the pressures exerted by the urban middle class for political participation, and in the presence of the armed forces as a destabilizing factor within the state apparatus. In the long term, the domination of the oligarchy was affected by the gradual alteration of the structural basis on which the system of clientalism in social relations rested. This, in turn, was the result of internal migration and urban growth, greater class differentiation and, ultimately, industrial growth. A brief analysis of the political process during the First Republic will show in more concrete terms how the oligarchic system consolidated itself after 1889, and how its crisis developed in the period up to the Revolution of 1930.

The overthrow of the monarchy on 15 November 1889 was the result of a military coup which had been planned by a group of young army officers in Rio de Janeiro. The most well-organized civilian republican group, representing the São Paulo coffee bourgeoisie, had few contacts with the military and doubted the convenience of involving the army in their campaign. The military took power, and provided republican Brazil with its first two presidents, Deodoro da Fonseca (November 1889 – November 1891) and Floriano Peixoto (November 1891 – November 1894). During the first years of the Republic, half of the states were governed by members of the armed forces. On the other hand, the great oligarchies were the dominant social power, and the constitution of 1891, as we have seen, protected the interests of the largest states, especially São Paulo. The armed forces did not act as a homogeneous group in the face of a social class whose party, the PRP, was clearly aware of the interests which it represented, despite a certain amount of dissension. Rivalry within the armed forces occurred between the army and the navy, and between supporters of Deodoro and those of Floriano. While the former symbolized the interests of the *tarimbeiros*, the latter derived support from the graduates of the Military School at Praia Vermelha, the soldier citizens who were active in the Jacobinist movement in Rio de Janeiro. In the end, real or imaginary threats to the consolidation of the Republican regime brought about a *rapprochement* between the coffee bourgeoisie and the military sector. Floriano Peixoto, for example, was supported by wealthy financiers from São Paulo and by its powerful state militia during the Federalist Revolution and the Naval Revolt. While consolidating the Republic, he also, somewhat against his will, opened the way for the new ruling classes of Brazil to enter the political arena. His minister of finance, Rodrigues Alves, represented the political interests of São Paulo, in a strategically planned cabinet. The presidencies of the Chamber and Senate were held by leading figures in the PRP. Hesitation on the part of the military between resentment against the oligarchy and respect for the legality of the republican regime which it had helped to create made it easier for the oligarchy of the principal states, above all São Paulo, to achieve victory. On 15 November 1894, the first civilian president of the Republic assumed power – the Paulista, Prudente de Morais. Opposition was limited to the popular sectors, and to young officers and cadets from the Praia Vermelha School in Rio de Janeiro. Ten years later, in 1904, demonstrations against the government's decision in favour of compulsory vaccination to combat yellow fever again brought together two currents of opposition: popular elements, whose protest was directed largely against the high cost of living and the evacuation of those living in houses condemned as unhygienic, and military officers and cadets from the Military School who, while protesting against vaccination, were also levelling their sights at a higher target, namely that of the 'republic of landowners'. However, the military hierarchy itself gradually withdrew from national politics. The Military Club – which had co-ordinated political activity – was closed between 1896 and 1901.

Now that there was no longer any threat from the military, it remained to institutionalize the oligarchic system. The second civilian president, another Paulista, Campos Sales (1898–1902), set himself this task with three main objectives in mind: to put an end to the hostility which existed between the executive and the legislature, to minimize as much as possible the impact of dissidence within individual states, and to achieve a basic consensus between central and state governments. Thus was born the concept of 'the politics of the governors', a 'doctrine' which was largely lacking in substance, but which was nevertheless sufficient to establish the basis of the oligarchic system. In principle, it sought reciprocal agreement. The central government would support the dominant political groups in the states, while these, in turn, would support the policies of the president of the Republic. In this way, Campos Sales sought to neutralize opposition at the regional level.

To tame Congress, whose function came to be very different from how the constitutional division of powers had envisaged it, among other measures the process by which members were elected to the Chamber of Deputies was modified. On the occasion of elections to the Chamber, candidates accepted as having been elected in their states received a diploma, and the first meetings of the new legislature were thus held with deputies duly bearing their diplomas. However, these diplomas were often challenged, and their validity depended on the decision of a credentials committee, which was chosen by plenary vote from among the members of the new Chamber. The president of the newly elected Chamber played a decisive role in influencing the choice of members of the credentials committee. Until the reform instigated by Campos Sales, the ruling stated that *pro tempore* presidency of the Chamber would fall to the oldest of the diploma-bearing deputies. As a result of the reform, the deputy who had served as president in the previous legislature, always assuming that he had been elected to the new legislature, which was normally the case, continued to serve. Choosing the oldest deputy introduced an element of uncertainty, while the president of the Chamber in the previous legislature was inevitably someone who had supported the president of the Republic. In this way, the executive gained greater control of the candidates who would be officially confirmed as deputies.

The oligarchy of São Paulo and the PRP dominated the political scene at the beginning of the Republic, but could count on the support of Minas Gerais at vital moments, such as the vote on the constitution (1891), and the election of Prudente de Morais (1894). The first three civilian presidents of the Republic were all Paulistas: Prudente de Morais, Campos Sales and Rodrigues Alves (1902–6). Until 1897, when the PRM was founded, the oligarchy of Minas Gerais was divided into various factions (mainly corresponding to sectors of the state economy: coffee, cereals, livestock), a factor which reduced its influence at the federal level. From 1898 when it supported Campos Sales for the presidency and the fiscal and monetary policies which resulted from the agreement signed with Rothschilds for the consolidation of the Brazilian national debt, Minas brought its full weight to bear in federal politics. The fourth civilian president of the Republic, Afonso Pena, who was elected in 1906 and who died in office in 1909, was a Mineiro.

After the scars of civil war had healed, and the PRR had consolidated itself, Rio Grande do Sul began to emerge as a third major star in the oligarchic constellation. At the federal level, the influence of senator Pinheiro Machado illustrated this increasing power. Under his leadership, the *gaúchos* lent their consistent support to Paulista presidents, and to the proposals emanating from São Paulo designed to gain central government approval for foreign loans to support the coffee economy. However, Pinheiro Machado was not exactly a 'client' of São Paulo. Assuming a strategic position in the Senate, he managed to create a new network of alliances. By controlling the Senate credentials committee, and exercising his influence on that of the Chamber, Pinheiro managed to dominate the representatives of the weaker states. This resulted in an alliance between Rio Grande do Sul and some satellite states of the north-east, which to a certain extent would be institutionalized in November 1910 with the founding of the Conservative Republican party (PRC), an attempt to create a national party of the oligarchy. The first opportunity for Rio Grande do Sul to use its influence in a presidential succession came in 1909, when internal dissension within the Minas oligarchy facilitated the candidature of Marshal Hermes da Fonseca to the presidency of the Republic. Hermes was the nephew of Deodoro, and minister of war from 1906 to 1910. Minas and Rio Grande do Sul both rallied to his support. The candidate put forward by São Paulo, with the support of Bahia (which since the Empire had been reduced to a position of secondary importance) was Rui Barbosa, whose political career dated from the Empire, and who was a representative of the tiny enlightened elite of the period. For the first time, the *café com leite* alliance ran into difficulties.

Significantly, the *gaúchos* emerged as a force in federal politics by backing a military candidate. The affinity between the *gaúcho* oligarchy and the army can be attributed to several factors. The importance of the garrison stationed in Rio Grande do Sul (and later in 1919 the creation there of the Third Military Region) seems to have encouraged *gaúchos* of a certain social level to follow a military career. Intermittent fighting in the region also favoured contact between army officers and the political parties. The establishment of links between various officers and the PRR resulted from the Federalist Revolution. Certain ideological features and political peculiarities also contributed to this convergence. Rio Grande do Sul, under Júlio de Castilhos and later the important state leader, Borges de Medeiros, was a region where the influence of positivism was particularly strong, an ideology which also spread through the ranks of the army. Apart from this, the economic and financial policies defended by the *gaúchos* for economic and ideological reasons tended to coincide in many ways with the ideals of the military. Rio Grande do Sul, whose economy was essentially geared to the domestic market, was a centre of opposition to the agrarian export interests, for which the army had little sympathy, and with which it maintained few links. The *gaúchos* defended price stabilization along with conservative fiscal policies, essentially because inflation would cause problems for the jerked beef market in particular. Jerked beef was consumed mainly by the lower classes of the north-east and the Federal District. Any reduction in the purchasing power of these classes resulted in a fall in demand. A conservative financial policy always met with the approval of the military, and not only among the higher ranking personnel. The *tenentista* rebellions of the 1920s were to point to inflation and budgetary imbalance as evils as serious as fraud and regional inequalities.

The candidature of Hermes da Fonseca can be placed in a different context to that of the struggles which followed the proclamation of the Republic. The army was accepted as a political partner in order to end the impasse caused by dissension within the oligarchies. It did not present itself as an autonomous force. It was Rui Barbosa who criticized the intervention of the army into politics during the electoral campaign of 1909–10. He attacked the officer corps and pitted the state militias against the army. Although Rui's political base was essentially the oligarchy of São Paulo, his ideological platform was that of the struggle of the intelligentsia for civil liberties, culture and liberal traditions, against the Brazil which was ignorant, oligarchic and authoritarian. Rui sought to attract the urban vote. He supported democratic principles and the secret ballot. He referred to the need for strong central power, to be achieved by unifying the judiciary, punishing those states which violated the federal constitution, intervening more frequently in the economic and fiscal conflicts within states, controlling the right of individual states to contract foreign loans, and ensuring federal protection of the coffee economy. His programme illustrates that São Paulo was not so much interested in extreme state autonomy as in being the dominant power in a more or less integrated country. The programme of Hermes da Fonseca supported budgetary equilibrium, the impermeability of the constitution, ample state autonomy, and laid particular emphasis on the views and interests of Rio Grande do Sul. It is important to remember, however, that the issue of autonomy was particularly important to the politicians of Rio Grande do Sul, but not in general to the military. The armed forces always supported programmes designed to reinforce the centralization of power. In addition, Hermes deliberately referred to the rights and grievances of workers. And during his administration, he lent his support to the holding of a national workers' congress, in which moderate elements participated under the auspices of the government.

The administration of Hermes da Fonseca (1910–14) witnessed the fragmentation of the decision-making process, which became divided among three sectors: the civilian oligarchies of Minas and, especially, Rio Grande do Sul, the president himself, and a group of army officers, particularly the colonels, who wished to carry out modifications in the control of power within the states. The army officers formed a pressure group around the president, and were largely responsible for the 'salvationist' movement, whose aims were to 'preserve' the purity of republican institutions.

The 'salvationists', anticipating the *tenentes* in the north-east after the Revolution of 1930, intervened in Pernambuco, Alagoas, Bahia and Ceará to bring down oligarchic leaders who, in most cases, counted on the support of the PRC. There were cases of personal ambition behind many such military encroachments, but these reflected more complex issues at play within the army. Entrenched in the central government the 'salvationists' sought to curb the political power of the oligarchies, while at the same time reducing the more blatant aspects of social inequality. They had a relative if transitory success in the north-east, given the weakness of the local elites, but failed in their attempts to name a military candidate for the presidency of Rio Grande do Sul, and to intervene in São Paulo.

The dangerous upheavals which occurred during the Hermes administration served as a warning to the political elites of São Paulo and Minas Gerais, who patched up the *café com leite* alliance in 1914, and elected Wenceslau Brás from Minas Gerais to the presidency (1914–18). Severely damaged by the 'salvationist' movement, the PRC entered a period of crisis, which came to a head in 1915 with the assassination of Pinheiro Machado.

The outbreak of the first world war marked the end of the *belle époque* of the oligarchy. The economic difficulties resulting from the international situation stimulated the emergence of labour agitation between 1917 and 1920, as we have seen. The wave of strikes died down relatively quickly, but other social forces were to threaten the stability of the Old Republic. The pressures of the urban middle class, which sought to widen the base of the oligarchic system, and the attacks of middle-ranking army officers were to alter the political framework. Although these sectors lacked autonomy, they would lend an added dimension to the rifts between and within the regional oligarchies.

In the presidential election of 1919 the growing political participation of the urban population was clearly visible. The election was held in exceptional circumstances because of the death of president-elect Rodrigues Alves (a Paulista, who had been president in 1902–6 and who was re-elected in 1918). It was won by the 'official' compromise candidate, Epitácio Pessoa from Paraíba, the first – and only – north-easterner to serve as president (1919–22) during the First Republic. However, Rui Barbosa, who had been defeated in 1910 and 1914, presented himself as an independent candidate, campaigned on a moderate reformist ticket which included labour legislation, and secured approximately one-third of the votes. He was the outright winner in the Federal District.

The election of 1922 revealed the growing regional tensions within the ruling class; it was the only election in which there was a clear rift between the two major states on the one hand, and a bloc of intermediate states on the other. Moreover the army, prompted by some episodes which involved its honour, intervened on the side of the opposition. The São Paulo–Minas alliance put forward as its candidate during the first months of 1921 the Mineiro politician, Artur Bernardes. Rio Grande do Sul contested his candidature, and denounced the political arrangement as being a way of guaranteeing resources for coffee valorization, at a time when the country was in need of financial stabilization. The politicians of Rio Grande do Sul also feared a possible revision of the constitution which might limit the autonomy of the states, as was, in fact, carried out by Bernardes in 1926. Rio Grande do Sul was joined by Bahia, Pernambuco, and the state of Rio de Janeiro, which ranked fourth, fifth and sixth in terms of electoral importance, and under the banner of the 'Republican Reaction' they put forward Nilo Peçanha as their candidate. Nilo had occupied the presidency for some months after the death in office of Afonso Pena in 1909, and had guaranteed Hermes da Fonseca's subsequent electoral triumph. A man of humble background, he had been a supporter of Floriano Peixoto, and had his political base in the oligarchy of his native state of Rio. The programme of the 'Republican Reaction', which was directly inspired by the politicians of Rio Grande do Sul, concentrated on measures against inflation and in favour of currency convertibility and budgetary stability. The more powerful states were accused of imperialism, and protective measures were requested for all Brazil's export products, not just coffee. Nilo was not opposed to the current policy of coffee valorization, which also benefited the state of Rio de Janeiro, but he was critical of the special treatment given to coffee. This was a theme which was especially dear to the representatives of Rio Grande do Sul. The military's intervention in the succession problem was made all the easier because of its links with the politicians of Rio Grande do Sul and the candidate himself. On the surface, however, it sought to preserve the values and honour of the military establishment, which had been the target for virulent attack through letters published in the Rio newspaper *Correio da Manhã* in October 1921, bearing the false signature of Bernardes.

Bernardes, the 'official' candidate, won the election of March 1922. It only remained for Congress to confirm the result. From the point of view of the regional oligarchies, as soon as one of the candidates was deemed to have won, the defeated parties had to come to an agreement in order to preserve the system. In 1922, the rule was almost broken. Because of the tense situation vis-à-vis the military, consideration was even given to the withdrawal of the president-elect, and the choice of a third candidate. There were also some revolutionary utterances among the army hierarchy. In the event, however, the leader of the Rio Grande oligarchy, Borges de Medeiros, refused to support further opposition. The struggle between the government and the opposition gradually died down. Dissidents within the defeated regional oligarchies and the military hierarchy were gradually neutralized, although the Bernardes administration had repeatedly to resort to declarations of a state of seige.

At another level, the crisis in the oligarchic system was revealed in the breaking of the political monopoly of the PRP in São Paulo, where the Democratic party (PD) was founded in 1926. The creation of the PD resulted from the effects of social differentiation in São Paulo, from the pressures of new generations in favour of a widening of career opportunities and access to the political system, and from ideological disagreements. Among its leading figures were the young sons of coffee planters and of traditional Brazilian families, some industrialists, and above all middle-class professionals, such as lawyers, journalists, and professors from the law faculty. The PD appeared on the political scene as a liberal democratic party. Its aims were to separate republican institutions from republican practice by means of a secret ballot, minority representation, the separation of executive, legislative and judicial powers, and the assumption of electoral supervision by the judiciary. It made vague gestures in the direction of social reforms, while on the economic and financial front its differences with the PRP were superficial. The official newspaper of the PD conveyed a message which was particularly relevant to the aspirations of the traditional urban middle class during the 1920s. Its favourite targets for attack were 'artificial industrialization', which was associated with powerful industrialists of foreign origin, the mass of immigrants controlled by the PRP, and the foreign companies responsible for basic services in the city of São Paulo. Events following the Revolution of 1930 were to show that the PD would not sacrifice its regional interests in order to align with other opposition groups. Nevertheless, during the late 1920s, its activity contributed to the weakening of the political power of the São Paulo oligarchy at the national level.

In the meantime the middle ranks of the army (*tenentes*) had broken with the 'republican order' in a series of *tenentista* rebellions. In July 1922, there was an uprising at the Copacabana fortress in Rio de Janeiro. In

July 1924, the rebels actually got as far as controlling the city of São Paulo for more than two weeks. In October 1924, and in 1926, there were revolts in various cities in Rio Grande do Sul. However, the *tenentista* movement created its great myth through the activities of the Prestes Column, a military force which joined together the revolutionaries from São Paulo and Rio Grande do Sul. Led by Miguel Costa and Luís Carlos Prestes, the future leader of the Brazilian Communist party, the Column undertook a 'long march' through the interior of the country, travelling some 24,000 kilometres between April 1925 and February 1927, when its remnants eventually crossed the border into Bolivia.

The insurrections of the 1920s continued the tradition of rebellion among young army officers, which dated from the beginning of the Republic. There were, however, important differences, which were the result of changes in the military apparatus, in the relationship established over the years between the army and the oligarchic system, and in the political system itself.

The *tenentes* had been educated during a period when both the military and society were going through a process of transition. The officer corps had begun to change with the creation of the Military School at Realengo in 1911, which replaced the old school at Praia Vermelha, closed for good in 1904, after its last revolt. The ideology behind the new school was very different from that of its predecessor. By providing markedly military teaching and discipline, it sought to produce a professional soldier, removed from politics, and directed towards specifically military purposes. Although products of Realengo, the *tenentes* adopted one of the principles of the doctrine of the soldier citizen, namely that of the right of the military to intervene in politics, even against the wishes of the civilian and military authorities. However, the positivist ideologists of Praia Vermelha had tended to lay greater stress on the citizen as opposed to the soldier. In its most extreme form, according to the thinking of Benjamin Constant, positivism held that the 'industrial regime' would ultimately render armies useless; 'the armies hitherto used as tools of destruction [would be] confined to the museum of history'. This corollary to the doctrine of the soldier citizen was unknown to the *tenentes*. Their ideology was not based on the interdependence of the civilian and military worlds, but on the general function of the armed forces as protectors of the people. This military consciousness was helped by the growing organization of the army, and by the concept of the soldier as being a person removed from civilian life. Like the former *tarimbeiros*, the *tenentes* were supremely conscious of the special values of the 'caste' to which they belonged. The initial stimulus to their actions derived in part from the insults directed at the army in the so-called forged letters of October 1921.

At the same time, the *tenentista* movement produced a rift within the military establishment, between middle-ranking officers and their commanders. Despite the fact that they always sought to associate themselves with certain high-ranking personnel, in order to lend some prestige to their rebellions, the rebels never succeeded in attracting the military hierarchy apart from the occasional support of individual figures. Because of this, they became more entrenched in their resolve to cleanse not only society at large, but the very institution to which they belonged. One of the revolutionary leaders, Juarez Távora, for example, openly attacked the minister of war, accusing him of indulging in 'mean and low' (*tacanho e porco*) militarism, which was tailor-made to accord with the whims and weaknesses of President Bernardes.

This division between a section of the officer corps and the army hierarchy can be attributed to various factors. The cohesion of the officer corps as a whole had never been strong in the army, and the situation tended to become more acute as a result of the cautious attitude adopted by high-ranking officers toward the oligarchic system. Within the military framework itself, the system of slow promotion created a large body of men in intermediate positions, whose prospects for achieving higher rank were few. For its part, the hierarchy enjoyed privileges, but was unable to impose complete control of the whole organization. The situation was very different from that prevailing in the navy, which, ever since the days of the Empire, had been considered a stronghold of the aristocracy, where the basic division was between the officer corps and the ratings. It was no coincidence that the main rank and file movement within the armed forces during the First Republic, the Sailors' Revolt of 1910, should have occurred in the navy – in protest against the system of corporal punishment. The navy was relatively immune from *tenentista* influence, the only evidence of rebelliousness being the revolt on the destroyer *São Paulo* in 1924.

With regard to social and political objectives of *tenentismo*, there was an important change of direction with the Revolution of October 1930 and the entry of the *tenentes*, along with other factions, into government. (Prestes had broken with the movement in May, issuing a manifesto in which he proclaimed his adherence to revolutionary socialism.) During the 1920s, however, the *tenentes* were effectively outside the machinery of government, and involved in a struggle against the power structure. They made their presence felt through military action, and their internal differences had not yet been clearly debated. Despite this, however, two tendencies appeared in embryonic form within the movement itself. One of these, formed by Prestes, Siqueira Campos and Miguel Costa, associated the overthrow of the oligarchies with a vaguely popular nationalistic programme. The other, whose most representative figure was Juarez Távora, was not concerned with popular mobilization; it saw military intervention as a means of destroying the oligarchic system, while at the same time curbing 'the excesses of indiscipline among the masses'.

Tenentismo can be seen as a movement which was born at a particularly sensitive point in the state apparatus. It exposed the crisis in the oligarchic system, and offered in its place the prospect of a structure along corporatist lines. The type of political reform advocated by the *tenentes* was based on the need to widen the central government's sphere of action, and included in its ideology elements of anti-liberalism in vogue at the time. This was the essential tone of the movement during the 1920s, preaching as it did a rather naïve brand of social reform, coupled with an equally vague brand of nationalism. Its statements of theory during the 1920s were far more impregnated with 'nationalistic feeling' than with objectives directly attributable to the interests of a social class. The strengthening of the power of the state required uniformity of institutions, the expansion of education, and the consolidation of the government at the national level. Economic issues, including industrialization, were either ignored or given only scant consideration. In so far as their objectives were not clearly defined, while their unselfish idealism was unequivocally stated, the *tenentes* were able to count on the sympathy of those social sectors opposed to the prevailing order, including the working class. On the other hand, as far as the most representative dissident sectors within the oligarchy were concerned, the *tenentes* represented a reserve force which they could manipulate, while avoiding any permanent commitments. Nevertheless the resort to radical methods, namely violence, even though for limited ends, broke with normal political procedures, and created rifts which were only healed as a result of the special circumstances of 1929–30.

By the late 1920s the *tenentes* had been marginalized or were in exile, and the urban middle class was clearly limited in its ability to mobilize itself.

The deepening of the crisis in the oligarchic system was therefore due more to the reappearance of inter-state conflict and problems of adjustment within the oligarchic pact, though now in a new context. In 1926, the Paulista candidate, Washington Luís, assumed the presidency without any problems, and with the support of both Minas Gerais and Rio Grande do Sul. (In order to implement his programme of financial stabilization, which was welcomed by Rio Grande do Sul, Washington Luís nominated to the treasury a *gaúcho* politician who was gaining ascendency within the political oligarchy of his state, Getúlio Vargas.) The difficulty in reaching a unanimous agreement on the presidential succession in 1929 can be blamed on the political initiative of the president himself. During 1928, it had become clear that the dominant political group in São Paulo, encouraged by Washington Luís, did not intend to loosen its grip on the central government. The name of Júlio Prestes – president of the state of São Paulo – emerged as a candidate for the presidency. This broke all the rules of the game. Ever since 1914, the presidency had rotated between São Paulo and Minas, with the exception of 1919, following the death of president-elect Rodrigues Alves. The return of a Mineiro president to power in 1930 would have normally been expected. The intransigence of Washington Luís can be attributed to personal characteristics and to reasons of a more general nature. Taking for granted the inflexibility of the oligarchic system, which made it very difficult for the opposition to achieve any measure of success, the president set about trying to ensure the continuity of his policy of financial stabilization, through the choice of a successor whom he could trust. There was at least one historical precedent in his favour: in 1902, Campos Sales had guaranteed the pursuit of a deflationary financial policy through the (first) election of Rodrigues Alves, which resulted in a Paulista succeeding a Paulista in the presidency. The attitude of Washington Luís should also be seen in the light of a situation in which the São Paulo elite had been gradually losing the most important administrative posts to men from Rio Grande do Sul and Minas Gerais, a tendency which was to increase substantially after 1930.

By imposing the candidature of Júlio Prestes, Washingon believed he could neutralize any serious dissension which might eventually emerge, given that relations between the federal government and Rio Grande do Sul were good. At most, it seemed that Minas Gerais would enter the struggle in isolation, not only without much chance of success, but also without producing any serious repercussions. Sure enough, it was the president of Minas, Antônio Carlos Ribeiro de Andrada, who began to negotiate for an opposition candidate. In order to propel Rio Grande do Sul into a contest which would mean breaking its agreement with the federal government, and losing the advantages which this implied, it was necessary to offer the presidency to that state. In June 1929, after much negotiation, Minas Gerais and Rio Grande do Sul agreed to launch the reticent Getúlio Vargas, now governor of Rio Grande do Sul, as candidate. They obtained the adherence of the tiny north-eastern state of Paraíba, which was to put forward João Pessoa as vice-presidential candidate. The chances of this group achieving victory in the election were slight, for the central government had the support not only of the oligarchy of São Paulo but of seventeen states in all.

The Liberal Alliance was formed as a regional front, which included the vast majority of the political representatives of Rio Grande do Sul and Minas Gerais, and was also joined by the Democratic party of São Paulo. As for Paraíba, in-fighting within the oligarchy caused one fairly influential sector to support the government. It appeared that a new regional rift was emerging, which was of greater importance than any previous rift, but which nevertheless belonged to the traditional pattern of succession disputes typical of the First Republic. The Alliance made great efforts to remain within the limits of the system, to which most of its leaders were committed. Even Vargas openly stated this intention in a letter to Washington Luís in July 1929, and João Neves da Fontoura – leader of Rio Grande do Sul in the Federal Chamber – declared that the opposition was disposed to give its sympathetic consideration to other candidates from São Paulo.

The programme of the Liberal Alliance reflected the aspirations of those regional ruling classes not directly linked to coffee. Its objective was also to gain the sympathy of the middle class – and to some extent the working class. It defended the need to stimulate national output generally, and not just that of coffee. It also opposed the various schemes for coffee valorization in the name of financial orthodoxy, and for this reason it did not disagree on this particular point with the policy of Washington Luís. It proposed certain measures for protecting workers, such as the right to pensions, special regulations regarding the employment of women and children, and the right to paid holidays. (In the major urban centres, where Vargas was obliged to campaign somewhat against his will, he was received enthusiastically – even in São Paulo where the anti-Paulista character of the Liberal Alliance would have been easy to exploit.) As a clear reply to the president who had asserted that the social problem in Brazil was 'a police problem', the opposition platform stated that it could not be ignored, and that it constituted 'one of the problems which would have to be seriously considered by the administrative power'. It laid greatest emphasis on the defence of the rights of the individual, amnesty (in order to gain the sympathy of the *tenentes*), and political reform to guarantee genuinely representative elections. With regard to the theme of industrialization, its programme made the old distinction between natural and artificial industries, namely, those which operated with raw materials available in the country, and those for which materials had to be imported. It condemned the protectionism afforded to the latter, under the allegation that it pushed up the cost of living, while benefiting one or two privileged enterprises. The protection of the rights of the worker was, in turn, set out in terms designed to contrast with the privileges enjoyed by the industrialists. The associations representing most industries in São Paulo supported Júlio Prestes, the official candidate. This attitude can be explained by the firm relations which had been established among the different sectors of the ruling class in São Paulo, and by the fact that the opposition did not present itself as being attractive to the industrial bourgeoisie.

It was in the middle of the electoral campaign, in October 1929, that the world economic crisis began. The opposition leaders began to use the crisis as a new argument with which to demonstrate the ineptitude of the government. The immediate outcome was hardly noticeable. However, the crisis led to disagreement between the coffee sector and the central government. It had come at a time when the problems of overproduction were becoming increasingly serious. The coffee sector requested from Washington Luís financial concessions and a moratorium on its debts. These concessions would be payable through the Bank of Brazil in view of the difficulties which the bank of the state of São Paulo was experiencing. The president, who was particularly anxious to preserve his plan for stability in currency exchange, which would certainly have collapsed if these concessions had been made, refused to attend to the pleas of a sector which he in theory represented. This provoked a wave of discontent in São Paulo. The Congresso dos Fazendeiros, organized not only by supporters of the PD but also by all those rural associations whose leaders in the main supported the PRP, and held at the end of December 1929 and the beginning of January 1930, was a clear manifestation of these grievances. In spite of this, the situation did not reach breaking point. After the Congress, the mobilization of coffee growers decreased and the benefit to the PD in terms of votes was relatively insignificant. The coffee sector, despite its discontent, had no reason to believe that a victory for the Liberal Alliance would result in any greater attention being paid to its interests. Indeed, the regional composition of the opposition and one or two carefully worded pronouncements seemed to indicate the contrary.

The elections of 1 March 1930 were carried out in accordance with the traditions of the Old Republic. Both government and opposition resorted to fraud on a large scale. It is sufficient to remember that Getúlio Vargas obtained 298,677 votes against 982 in his own state. The victory of Júlio Prestes, conceded publicly by Borges de Medeiros, seemed to mark the end of regional division. However, at this point, differences of opinion within the Liberal Alliance began to be voiced. These can be explained in terms of a generation gap rather than ideological disagreement. Alongside the traditional politicians in Minas Gerais and Rio Grande do Sul, there was a group of educated younger Mineiros and *gaúchos* who were busy climbing the political ladder within the shadow of the old oligarchy. In Rio Grande do Sul, men like Vargas himself, Flores da Cunha, Osvaldo Aranha, Lindolfo Collor, João Neves and Maurício Cardoso formed a group known as 'the generation of 1907', which was the year when they had completed their schooling. In Minas Gerais, too, younger political figures emerged, such as Virgílio de Melo Franco and Francisco Campos, both from traditional regional families. Until the late 1920s, these men had not openly denounced the political system of the First Republic. In 1930, however, this sector of the political elite chose to follow the road which until then only the *tenentes* had taken.

Although defeated, the *tenentista* movement was still a force to be reckoned with because of its military experience and its prestige within the army. The conditions were now ripe for a *rapprochement* between younger politicians and rebellious army officers. Even during the electoral campaign, some steps had been taken in this direction. However, the *tenentes* proceeded with the utmost caution. The balance of their relations with the legal opposition was fairly negative. They had been used for the benefit of the opposition without receiving anything in return. Apart from this, the Liberal Alliance contained some of their worst enemies: for example, ex-president Bernardes, who had pursued the Prestes Column and who was seen to synthesize all the vices of the Republic, and João Pessoa, who had been responsible for the prosecution of more than a few military rebels. Among the younger politicians there were several – for example, Osvaldo Aranha – who had played a part in putting down the insurrection in Rio Grande do Sul. In spite of these barriers – and the suspicions were mutual – an agreement was reached. However, significantly, the military leadership of the revolutionary movement was given to a man who represented 'the most responsible sectors of the armed forces', and who had the complete trust of the *gaúcho* leaders. This was Góes Monteiro, then a lieutenant-colonel, who was a native of Alagoas but whose career was closely linked to Rio Grande do Sul. Góes had not been a member of the revolutionary faction during the 1920s. On the contrary, he had fought against the Prestes Column in the north-eastern states.

The conspiracy planned between March and October 1930 went through a series of twists and turns, helped along by an occasional dramatic event, such as the assassination in August of João Pessoa over local political issues. Finally, the rebellion began on 3 October in Rio Grande do Sul, and on the following day in the north-east. In the rebel states the state militias declared their loyalty to the Revolution. The adherence of the army was only immediate in the south, while in Minas Gerais and some north-eastern states there was a degree of resistance. Washington Luís remained in power in Rio de Janeiro. His government's main base of support was São Paulo, where both the state militia and the army prepared to resist troops advancing from the south. The prevailing climate in São Paulo was, however, far from euphoric. The Paulista ruling class, which was in a state of disagreement with its representatives in central government, had not got as far as switching its allegiance to the opposition. However, it had no intention of throwing itself into armed conflict by mobilizing the population under its control. Apart from this, a large sector of the middle class rallied behind the Democratic party which, although it had scarcely participated in the plans for revolution, supported the revolutionaries. These factors contributed to create a climate of expectancy in São Paulo, where an attempt by the central government to call up reservists failed miserably.

Any serious military confrontation in São Paulo was, in the event, avoided by the intervention of the hierarchy of the armed forces in Rio de Janeiro. For the first time, the high commands of the army and the navy united in order to carry out a 'moderating intervention', which deposed Washington Luís on 24 October. The military hierarchy tried to remain in power, and even formed a governing *junta*. On the other hand, pressure from the revolutionary forces advancing from the south, and popular demonstrations in Rio de Janeiro, guaranteed Getúlio Vargas's claim to the presidency. He duly took office on 3 November 1930 as the head of a provisional government. Few could have foreseen that Vargas would remain in power for the next fifteen years.

The Revolution of 1930 was the product of various social groupings whose values and objectives differed widely: dissident regional oligarchies, sectors of the urban middle class, and intermediate ranks in the army. With some exceptions, the urban workers remained outside the movement. The revolutionaries, however, benefited from their sympathy as a result of the prestige of the *tenentes* and the vaguely reformist rhetoric of the Liberal Alliance. (The tiny Communist party had produced its own candidate for the elections and denounced the Alliance as being 'fascist' in character. It is worth remembering, however, that until the eve of the elections at least, the leaders of the party were taking delivery of arms and establishing contact with *tenentista* elements who were plotting in São Paulo.) When considering the 1920s as a whole, the role of the younger generation in voicing political opposition or in revolutionary activity is particularly noteworthy. The PD of São Paulo contrasted clearly with the PRP in the relative youth of its leaders. *Tenentismo* was a movement of junior officers in the army. Within the dissident sectors of the oligarchy, it was the younger elements who adopted revolutionary attitudes. From this viewpoint, the crisis in the oligarchic system can be seen as a consequence of the inability of the system to respond to the demands placed on it, which in return were the result of social differentiation and both upward and downward social mobility.

The demise of the Old Republic in 1930 brought an end to the system of oligarchic rule which had guaranteed the hegemony of the coffee bourgeoisie of São Paulo. However, it did not mark the end of *coronelismo*, particularly in the rural areas. New *coronéis* emerged to replace the old, and the system of patronage remained and adapted slowly to the corporative pact which was gradually elaborated between civil society and the state. The continuation of clientalism, albeit in modified form, was largely due to the fact that the Revolution of 1930 did nothing to change the system of production in the rural areas, although agrarian reform had become relevant to the political debate by this time. Developments after 1930 combined two elements which historically are impossible to separate: the victory of a heterogeneous revolutionary movement and the effects of the world economic crisis. The latter transformed long-standing problems into urgent issues and inevitably speeded up the slow process of change. Given the historical conditions in which the industrial bourgeoisie had been formed, it required a world crisis and the breaking of the hegemony of the São Paulo coffee bourgeoisie for the process of industrialization, for example, to be given renewed impetus. The expansion and centralization of the power of the state was the main feature of institutional change during the years after the Revolution of 1930. It was a move which was dictated by the requirements of the new economic and financial order, but it also corresponded to the interests and concepts of some of those forces, not least the military forces, which had been responsible for the Revolution. The central bureaucracy was expanded and virtually transformed into a new social category with its own interests, apart from carrying out its function as the mouthpiece of the interests of the dominant class. Moreover, the relationship between civil society and the state changed in the sense that the different sectors of the dominant class, the urban middle class and at least one section of the working class now confronted each other and reached agreement largely under the shadow of an increasingly powerful state.

BIBLIOGRAPHICAL ESSAYS

ABBREVIATIONS

CHLA   *Cambridge History of Latin America*

HAHR   *Hispanic American Historical Review*

JGSWGL   *Jahrbuch für Geschichte von Staat, Wirtschaft und Gesellschaft Lateinamerikas*

JLAS   *Journal of Latin American Studies*

LARR   *Latin American Research Review*

1. THE INDEPENDENCE OF BRAZIL

The first chronicle of the events of the entire period 1808–31, though concentrating on the years 1821–31, is John Armitage, *History of Brazil from the arrival of the Braganza family in 1808 to the abdication of Dom Pedro the first in 1831*, published in London in 1836 when the author, who had gone to Rio de Janeiro as a young merchant in 1828, was still only 29. Intended as a sequel to Robert Southey's monumental *History of Brazil* (1810–19), the first general history of Brazil during the colonial period, Armitage's *History* has been used and justly praised by every historian of the independence period in Brazil. Of the many contemporary accounts perhaps the best known and most valuable is Maria Graham, *Journal of a Voyage to Brazil and Residence there during part of the years 1821, 1822, 1823* (London, 1824). The author was resident in Brazil from September 1821 to March 1822 and again from March to October 1823, that is to say, immediately before and immediately after independence. Indispensable for the period of Dom João's residence in Brazil (1808–21) is Luiz Gonçalves dos Santos [1767–1844], *Memórias para servir à história do Reino do Brasil* [1825] (2 vols., Rio de Janeiro, 1943).

The traditional historiography of Brazilian independence is dominated by four great works, all essentially detailed accounts of political events: Francisco Adolfo de Varnhagen, *História da Independência do Brasil* (Rio de Janeiro, 1917); Manoel de Oliveira Lima, *Dom João VI no Brasil 1808–21* (1909; 2nd edn, 3 vols., Rio de Janeiro, 1945), the classic study of the Portuguese court in Rio, and *O Movimento da Independência* (São Paulo, 1922); and Tobias do Rego Monteiro, *História do império. A elaboraçao da independência* (Rio de Janeiro, 1927). And for the story of the independence of Bahia, Braz do Amaral, *História da independência na Bahia* (Salvador, 1923).

Caio Prado Júnior was the first historian to analyse the internal tensions and contradictions in the process leading to Brazilian independence. See, in particular, *Evolução política do Brasil* (São Paulo, 1933 and many later editions); *Formação do Brasil contemporâneo: Colônia* (São Paulo, 1963) which has been translated as *The colonial background of modern Brazil* (Berkeley, 1967); and the introduction to the facsimile edition of *O Tamoio* (São Paulo, 1944). Octávio Tarquínio de Souza, *José Bonifácio* (Rio de Janeiro, 1960) and *A vida do Dom Pedro I* (3 vols., 2nd edn, Rio de Janeiro, 1954), are important biographies.

Among more recent general works on Brazilian independence, especially worthy of note are Sérgio Buarque de Holanda (ed.), *História geral da civilização Brasileira*, Tomo II, *O Brasil Monárquico*, vol.1 *O Processo de emancipação* (São Paulo, 1962); Carlos Guilherme Mota (ed.), *1822: Dimensões* (São Paulo, 1972); and, above all, José Honório Rodrigues, *Independência: revolução e contrarevolução* (5 vols., Rio de Janeiro, 1975): I, *A evolução política*; II, *Economia e sociedade*; III, *As forças armadas*; IV, *A liderança nacional*; V, *A política internacional*. By far the most important and provocative single essay on Brazilian independence is Emília Viotti da Costa, 'Introdução ao estudo da emancipação política do Brasil' in Carlos Guilherme Mota (ed.), *Brasil em Perspectiva* (São Paulo, 1968); revised English version 'The political emancipation of Brazil' in A. J. R. Russell-Wood (ed.), *From colony to nation. Essays on the independence of Brazil* (Baltimore, 1975). See also an essay by Emília Viotti da Costa, 'José Bonifácio de Andrada e Silva: a Brazilian Founding Father' in *The Brazilian Empire: myths and histories* (Chicago, 1985). On the independence movement in Rio de Janeiro the essay by Francisco C. Falcón and Ilmar Rohloff de Mattos, 'O processo de independência no Rio de Janeiro' in Mota (ed.), *1822* is particularly interesting. And on the movement in Bahia, see Luís Henrique Dias Tavares, *A independência do*

Brasil na Bahia (Rio de Janeiro, 1977), and F. W. O. Morton, 'The conservative revolution of independence: economy, society and politics in Bahia, 1700–1840' (unpublished D.Phil, thesis, Oxford, 1974).

On relations between Portugal and Brazil and the development of Brazil in the late eighteenth century, see Mansuy-Diniz Silva, *CHLA* I, chap. 13 and Alden, *CHLA* II, chap. 15. The outstanding recent work on the late colonial period, in particular on economic policy-making and on the trade between Brazil, Portugal and England, is Fernando A. Novais, *Portugal e Brasil na crise do antigo sistema colonial (1777–1808)* (São Paulo, 1979). On the balance of trade, see also José Jobson de A. Arruda, *O Brasil no comércio colonial* (São Paulo, 1981). The influence of the Enlightenment on colonial Brazil is examined in Maria Odila da Silva, 'Aspectos da ilustração no Brasil', *Revista do Instituto Histórico e Geográfico Brasileiro* 278 (1968), 105–70. Also see Carlos Guilherme Mota, *Atitudes de inovção no Brasil (1789–1801)* (Lisbon, 1970) and E. Bradford Burns, 'The intellectuals as agents of change and the independence of Brazil, 1724–1822' in Russell-Wood (ed.), *From colony to nation*. The best study of the *Inconfidência mineira* (1788–9) is to be found in Kenneth R. Maxwell, *Conflicts and conspiracies. Brazil and Portugal 1750–1808* (Cambridge, 1973). See also his essay 'The generation of the 1790s and the idea of Luso-Brazilian empire' in Dauril Alden (ed.), *Colonial roots of modern Brazil* (Berkeley, 1973). There are several studies of the *Inconfidência baiana* (1798): Luis Henrique Dias Tavares, *História da sedição intentada na Bahia em 1798: a 'conspiração do alfaiates'* (São Paulo, 1975); Alfonso Ruy, *A primeira revolução social brasileira, 1798* (2nd edn., Salvador, 1951); Kátia Maria de Queirós Mattoso, *A presença francesa no movimento democrático baiano de 1798* (Salvador, 1969); and chapter IV of Morton, 'Conservative revolution'. There is a modern edition of the *Obras económicas* of José Joaquim da Cunha de Azeredo Coutinho with an introduction by Sérgio Buarque de Holanda (São Paulo, 1966). For a commentary, see E. Bradford Burns, 'The role of Azeredo Coutinho in the enlightenment of Brazil', *HAHR* 44/2 (1964), 145–60.

The transfer of the Portuguese court from Lisbon to Rio de Janeiro (1807–8) has been thoroughly studied by Alan K. Manchester, *British preeminence in Brazil. Its rise and decline* (Durham, N.C., 1933), chap. III; 'The transfer of the Portuguese court to Rio de Janeiro', in Henry H. Keith and S. F. Edwards (eds.), *Conflict and continuity in Brazilian society* (Columbia, S.C., 1969); and 'The growth of bureaucracy in Brazil, 1808–1821', *JLAS*, 4/1 (1972). On the opening of Brazilian ports to foreign trade (1808), besides Manchester, *British preeminence*, see Manuel Pinto de Aguiar, *A abertura dos portos. Cairú e os ingleses* (Salvador, 1960) and José

Wanderley de Araújo Pinho, 'A abertura dos portos – Cairú', *Revista do Instituto Histórico e Geográfico Brasileiro*, 243 (April–June 1959). Manchester, *British preeminence* remains the best study of the Anglo-Portuguese treaties of 1810 and of Portuguese expansionism in the Banda Oriental. Early attempts at encouraging industrial growth in Brazil are examined in Nícia Vilela Luz, *A luta pela industrialização do Brasil, 1808–1930* (São Paulo, 1961) and Alice P. Canabrava, 'Manufacturas e indústrias no período de D. João VI no Brasil' in Luis Pilla, *et al.*, *Uma experiência pioneira de intercambio cultural* (Porto Alegre, 1963). The French artistic mission is the subject of Affonso d'Escragnolle Taunay, *A missão artística de 1816* (Rio de Janeiro, 1956; Brasília, 1983). There has been only one modern study of the revolution of 1817 in Pernambuco: Carlos Guilherme Mota, *Nordeste, 1817. Estruturas e argumentos* (São Paulo, 1972), which concentrates on the ideological aspects of the struggle. Still useful is the account by one of the leading participants: Francisco Muniz Tavares, *História da revolução de Pernambuco em 1817* (3rd edn, Recife, 1917). On the armed forces during this period, besides volume III of Rodrigues, *Independência*, there is an interesting case study of Bahia, F. W. O. Morton, 'Military and society in Bahia, 1800–21', *JLAS*, 7/2 (1975). The Portuguese Côrtes, and especially the role of the Brazilian representatives, is the subject of two essays: George C. A. Boehrer, 'The flight of the Brazilian deputies from the Côrtes Gerais in Lisbon, 1822', *HAHR*, 40/4 (1960), 497–512, and Fernando Tomaz, 'Brasileiros nas Côrtes Constituintes de 1821–1822' in Mota (ed.), *1822*. The most recent work on the constituent Assembly is José Honório Rodrigues, *A Constituinte de 1823* (Petrópolis, 1974). The question of the continuation of the slave trade and Brazilian independence has been studied by Leslie Bethell, *The abolition of the Brazilian slave trade* (Cambridge, 1970), chapters 1 and 2. See also his article, 'The independence of Brazil and the abolition of the Brazilian slave trade: Anglo-Brazilian relations 1822–1826', *JLAS*, 1/2 (1969). On Anglo-Brazilian relations in general, and British recognition of Brazilian independence, Manchester, *British preeminence* remains the best study. But see also Caio de Freitas, *George Canning e o Brasil* (2 vols., São Paulo, 1960).

2. 1822–1850

Two volumes of the *História geral da civilização brasileira* (ed. Sérgio Buarque de Holanda) cover the period 1822–48: Tomo II, *O Brasil monárquico*: Vol. 1, *O processo de emancipação* (São Paulo, 1962) and vol. 2, *Dispersão e Unidade* (São Paulo, 1964). The only general history in

English, sensible and well organized, but somewhat superficial and now out of date, is C. H. Haring, *Empire in Brazil. A New World experiment with monarchy* (Cambridge, Mass., 1958). Still valuable is Stanley J. Stein, 'The historiography of Brazil, 1808–1889', *HAHR*, 40/2 (1960), 234–78. For the period 1822–31 Tobias do Rego Monteiro, *História do império: O primeiro reinado* (Rio de Janeiro, 1939), remains the most detailed account of political events. An indispensable contemporary account is John Armitage, *History of Brazil from the arrival of the Braganza family in 1808 to the abdication of Dom Pedro the first in 1831* (2 vols., London, 1836). Other important nineteenth-century accounts include João Manuel Pereira da Silva, *História do Brasil de 1831 a 1840* (Rio de Janeiro, 1878), Manuel Duarte Moreira de Azevedo, *História Pátria: O Brasil de 1831 a 1840* (Rio de Janeiro, 1884) and Heinrich Handelmann, *Geschichte von Brasilien* (Berlin, 1860; Portuguese translation, *História do Brasil*, Rio de Janeiro, 1931).

Nícia Vilela Luz, 'Brazil' in Stanley J. Stein and Roberto Cortés Conde (eds.), *Latin America. A guide to economic history, 1830–1930* (Berkeley, 1977), 163–272 is a useful guide to the secondary literature on Brazilian economic history. There are two general economic histories of Brazil, both now classics, which touch on this period: Caio Prado Júnior, *História econômica do Brasil* (6th edn, São Paulo, 1959), and Celso Furtado, *Formação econômica do Brasil* (Rio de Janeiro, 1959): English translation, *The economic growth of Brazil. A survey from colonial to modern times* (Berkeley, 1963). The most comprehensive (and provocative) recent study of Brazil's economic history after independence is Nathaniel H. Leff, *Underdevelopment and development in Brazil*, Vol. I, *Economic structures and change 1822–1947*; Vol. II, *Reassessing the obstacles to economic development* (London, 1982). On the beginnings of the coffee boom, see Stanley J. Stein, *Vassouras. A Brazilian coffee county, 1850–1900* (Cambridge, Mass., 1957), Warren Dean, *Rio Claro. A Brazilian plantation system, 1820–1920* (Stanford, 1976), and, still useful, Affonso d'Escragnolle Taunay, *História do café* (15 vols., Rio de Janeiro, 1939–43). On sugar, see Maria Teresa Schorer Petrone, *A Lavoura Canavieira em São Paulo: expansão e declínio, 1765–1861* (São Paulo, 1968), and Peter L. Eisenberg, *The sugar industry in Pernambuco: modernisation without change, 1840–1910* (Berkeley, 1974). For two different views on the impact made by British imperial preference, especially the sugar duties, on Brazilian economic development or underdevelopment, see Paulo Nogueira Batista, Jr, 'Política tarifária britânica e evolução das exportações brasileiras na primeira metade do século XIX', *Revista Brasileira de Economia* (34/2 (1980),

203–39, and Roberta M. Delson, 'Sugar production for the nineteenth century British market: rethinking the roles of Brazil and the British West Indies', in A. Graves and B. Albert (eds.), *Crisis and change in the international sugar economy, 1860–1914* (Norwich 1984). The outstanding work on Anglo-Brazilian commercial and financial (as well as diplomatic and political) relations in the first half of the nineteenth century is Alan K. Manchester, *British preeminence in Brazil. Its rise and decline* (Durham, N.C., 1933). Brazil's failure to industrialize in the period after independence is examined in the early chapters of Nícia Vilela Luz, *A luta pela industrialização no Brasil* (São Paulo, 1961). On the financial history of the period, see Carlos Manuel Pelaez and Wilson Suzigan, *História monetária do Brasil* (Rio de Janeiro, 1976). On government income and expenditure in particular, Liberato de Castro Carreira, *O orçamento do império desde a sua fundação* (Rio de Janeiro, 1883), and *História financeira e orçamentária do império do Brasil* (Rio de Janeiro, 1889) remains indispensable. See also Amaro Cavalcanti, *Resenha financeira do ex-império do Brasil em 1889* (Rio de Janeiro, 1890). A recent monograph which breaks new ground by examining internal trade, and in particular the organization of Rio de Janeiro's food supply, is Alcir Lenharo, *As tropas da moderação (O abastecimento da Corte na formação política do Brasil, 1808–1842)* (São Paulo, 1979).

The most wide-ranging study of the political system of the empire is José Murilo de Carvalho's Ph.D. thesis, 'Elite and state building in imperial Brazil' (Stanford University, 1974), parts of which have been published in *A construção da ordem* (Rio de Janeiro, 1980) and *Teatro de Sombras* (São Paulo, 1988). See also his article, 'Political elites and state building: the case of nineteenth century Brazil', *Comparative Studies in Society and History*, 24/3 (1982). Two other important recent contributions are Fernando Uricoechea, *The patrimonial foundations of the Brazilian bureaucratic state* (Berkeley, 1980) which examines in particular the National Guard, and Thomas Flory, *Judge and jury in imperial Brazil, 1808–1871. Social control and political stability in the new state* (Austin, Texas, 1981), which examines the political and administrative role of the judges. On the National Guard, see also Jeanne Berrance de Castro, *A milícia cidadã: a Guarda Nacional de 1831 a 1850* (São Paulo, 1977). There is no study of the army in this period, but see the early chapters of John H. Schulz, 'The Brazilian army in politics, 1850–1894', (unpublished Ph.D. thesis, Princeton University, 1973). João Camilo de Oliveira Torres, *A democracia coroada (teoria política do império do Brasil)* (Rio de Janeiro, 1957) remains valuable for the political history of the empire. Indispensable as a reference work is *Organizações e programas ministeriais. Regime parlamentar no império* (2nd edn, Arquivo Nacional, Rio de Janeiro, 1962). The electoral legislation of the period can be found in Francisco Belisário Soares de Souza, *O sistema eleitoral no império* (1892: Brasília, Senado Federal, 1979). Also useful are José Honório Rodrigues (ed.), *O Parlamento e a evolução nacional* (8 vols., Senado Federal, Brasília, 1972), which covers the period 1826–40, José Honório Rodrigues (ed.), *Atas do Conselho de Estado* (14 vols., Senado Federal, Brasília, 1973) and Tavares de Lyra, *Instituições políticas do Império* (Senado Federal, Brasília, 1979).

There are a number of biographies of leading politicians in this period, notably those written by Octávio Tarquínio de Sousa: *José Bonifácio* (Rio de Janeiro, 1945), *A vida de D. Pedro I* (3 vols., Rio de Janeiro, 1952), *Bernardo Pereira de Vasconcelos e seu tempo* (Rio de Janeiro, 1937), *Evaristo da Veiga* (São Paulo, 1939) and *Diogo Antônio Feijó (1784–1843)* (Rio de Janeiro, 1942), republished as vols. 1–7 of *História dos fundadores do Império do Brasil* (10 vols., Rio de Janeiro, 1957–8).

An excellent well-documented recent study of the political mobilization at the beginning of the regency is Augustin Wernet, *Sociedades políticas (1831–1832)* (São Paulo, 1978).

On the provincial revolts of the 1830s and 1840s, besides the various regional histories in the *História geral da civilização brasileira*, II, 2, and chapters 3 and 4 of Caio Prado Júnior, *Evolução política do Brasil* (São Paulo, 1933), a number of works deserve mention. The best available study of the War of the Cabanos is Manuel Correira de Andrade, *A Guerra dos Cabanos* (Rio de Janeiro, 1965) which is partly summarized in 'The social and ethnic significance of the War of the Cabanos', in Ronald H. Chilcote (ed.), *Protest and resistance in Angola and Brazil: comparative studies* (Berkeley, 1972). A recent study by Dirceu Lindoso, *A utópia armada. Rebeliões de pobres nas Matas do Tombo Real* (Rio de Janeiro, 1983), emphasizes the ideological and cultural aspects of the war. See also, Manuel Correia de Andrade, *Movimentos Nativistas em Pernambuco: Setembrizada e Novembrada* (Recife, 1971), for the smaller rebellions in Pernambuco during the regency. Astolfo Serra, *A Balaiada* (Rio de Janeiro, 1946), and Luiz Vianna Filho, *A Sabinada (A República Bahiana de 1837)* (Rio de Janeiro, 1938), remain the best studies of these movements. On the Sabinada, see also F. W. O. Morton, 'The Conservative revolution of independence: economy, society and politics in Bahia, 1790–1840' (unpublished D.Phil. thesis, Oxford, 1974, ch. XI). Although very disorganized, Domingos Antonio Rayol, *Motins políticos ou história dos principais acontecimentos políticos da Província do Pará desde o ano de 1821 até 1835* (3 vols., Belém, 1970), is still the best study of the Cabanagem. The best-documented study of the Farroupilha is Alfredo Varela, *História da Grande Revolução* (6 vols., Porto Alegre, 1925). Walter Spalding, *A revolução Farroupilha. História popular do Grande Decênio* (São Paulo, 1939), is also valuable. A recent study which emphasizes the economic roots of the rebellion is Spencer L. Leitman, 'Socio-economic roots of the Ragamuffin War: a chapter in early Brazilian history' (unpublished Ph.D. thesis, University of Texas at Austin, 1972), published as *Raízes sócio-econômicas da Guerra dos Farrapos* (Rio de Janeiro, 1979). The only recent work on the liberal revolts in Minas Gerais and São Paulo is Victor M. Filler, 'Liberalism in imperial Brazil: the regional rebellions of 1842' (unpublished Ph.D. thesis, Stanford University, 1976). For the view of a participant, see José Antônio Marinho, *História do movimento político que no ano de 1842 teve lugar na província de Minas Gerais* (Conselheiro Lafaiete, 1939). Apart from the Farroupilha, the Praieira is the best studied rebellion of the period. There are two important recent studies: Izabel Andrade Marson, *Movimento Praieiro, 1842–1849; imprensa, ideologia e poder político* (São Paulo, 1980), which stresses ideology, and Nancy Priscilla Naro, 'The 1848 Praieira revolt in Brazil' (unpublished Ph.D. thesis, University of Chicago, 1981), which examines the political and economic aspects of the revolt.

Useful information on the population of Brazil (as well as on slavery and immigration) in the decades after independence can be found in T. W. Merrick and D. Graham, *Population and economic development in Brazil, 1808 to the present* (Baltimore, 1979). See also Maria Luiza Marcílio, 'Evolução da população brasileira através dos censos até 1872', *Anais de História* 6 (1974), 115–37. The best study of immigration before the beginnings of mass European immigration is George P. Browne, 'Government immigration policy in imperial Brazil 1822–1870' (unpublished Ph.D. thesis, Catholic University of America, 1972). A critical view of Senator Vergueiro's free labour policies by a German-Swiss *colono*, which tells us much about rural São Paulo in the middle of the nineteenth century, is Thomas Davatz, *Memórias de um colono no Brasil (1850)*, edited with an introduction by Sérgio Buarque de Holanda (São Paulo, 1941). Land policy, and especially the origins of the law of 1850, is examined in Warren Dean, 'Latifundia and land policy in nineteenth century Brazil', *HAHR* 51/4 (1971), 606–25; José Murilo de Carvalho, 'A modernização frustrada: a política de terras no Império', *Revista Brasileira de História*, 1/1 (1981), and Emília Viotti da Costa, 'Política de Terras no Brasil e nos

Estados Unidos' in *Da Monarquia à república: momentos decisivos* (São Paulo, 1977). More generally, Ruy Cirne Lima, *Pequena História Territorial do Brasil. Sesmarias e Terras Devolutas* (Porto Alegre, 1954), remains useful. On urban growth in this period, see the works by Richard Morse, Emília Viotti da Costa, Eulália Maria Lahmeyer Lobo and Kátia M. de Queirós Mattoso cited in bibliographical essay 3. The bibliography on slavery in nineteenth-century Brazil is also discussed in bibliographical essay 3. In addition, on urban slavery in Rio de Janeiro during the first half of the century, see Mary C. Karasch, *Slave life in Rio de Janeiro, 1808–50* (Princeton, 1987). Also important are João José Reis, 'Slave rebellion in Brazil. The African Muslim uprising in Bahia, 1835' (unpublished Ph.D thesis, Minnesota, 1983) and *Rebelião Escrava no Brasil* (São Paulo, 1986). The slave trade question in Anglo-Brazilian relations and the final abolition of the slave trade in 1850–1 are thoroughly examined in Leslie Bethell, *The abolition of the Brazilian slave trade. Britain, Brazil and the slave trade question, 1807–1869* (Cambridge, 1970). The best diplomatic history of the period is still João Pandiá Calógeras, *A política externa do império* (3 vols., São Paulo, 1927–33), vol. II, *O primeiro reinado*, vol. III, *Da regência à queda de Rosas*.

An important source for the social history of Brazil in the period after independence are the accounts of the many European travellers, scientists and artists who visited the country: for example, Maria Graham, Auguste de Saint-Hilaire, Jean Baptiste Debret, Johann-Moritz Rugendas, Alcide d'Orbigny. They are listed in Bernard Naylor, *Accounts of nineteenth century South America* (London, 1969). See also Gilberto Freyre, *Sobrados e mucambos. Decadência do patriarcado rural e desenvolvimento do urbano* (2nd edn, 3 vols., Rio de Janeiro, 1951; English translation *The mansions and the shanties: the making of modern Brazil* (New York, 1963)), a continuation into the nineteenth century of his more famous *The masters and the slaves*; and his 'Social life in Brazil in the middle of the nineteenth century', *HAHR*, 5/4 (1922), 597–630. A pioneer work which makes good use of judicial records is Patricia Ann Aufderheide, 'Order and violence: Social deviance and social control in Brazil, 1780–1840' (unpublished Ph.D. thesis, University of Minnesota, 1976).

3. 1850–1870

Rubens Borba de Moraes and William Berrien (eds.), *Manual bibliográfico de estudos brasileiros* (Rio de Janeiro, 1949) is essential; although uneven in its coverage, its annotated entries and historiographical essays provide a base from which the historian can build using the *Handbook of Latin American Studies*. Still useful is Stanley J. Stein, 'The historiography of Brazil, 1808–1889', *HAHR*, 40/2 (1960), 234–78. Among aids for the researcher on mid-nineteenth-century Brazil, Cândido Mendes de Almeida's splendid *Atlas do império do Brasil* (Rio de Janeiro, 1868) deserves special mention.

Two broad interpretive studies of Brazilian history that give prominent attention to the social and political circumstances of mid-century are Raymundo Faoro, *Os donos do poder* (2nd edn, Porto Alegre and São Paulo, 1975), and Florestan Fernandes, *A revolução burguesa no Brasil* (Rio de Janeiro, 1975). Both are concerned to trace the connection between social structure and political institutions and events. Both are heavily influenced by Weberian typologies, although Fernandes also includes a certain amount of Marxist thought in his scheme. Less ambitious and more mechanically Marxist is Nelson Werneck Sodré, *História da burguesia brasileira* (Rio de Janeiro, 1964). Caio Prado Júnior's *História econômica do Brasil* (5th edn, São Paulo, 1959), is not so rigid as is Sodré in the economic interpretation of society and politics.

The first historian of the empire, who still exerts great influence on our understanding of the period, was Joaquim Nabuco whose biography of his father, *Um estadista do império* (2 vols., 2nd edn, São Paulo and Rio de Janeiro, 1936), first published in 1897–1900, dealt chronologically with politicians and political events without neglecting the larger social setting within which they acted. Nabuco's conservative, pro-imperial point of view can be contrasted with the critical stance adopted in 1909 by Euclides da Cunha in *À margem da história* (2nd edn, Oporto, 1913); da Cunha felt much more clearly than Nabuco the empire's failure to change. A defence of the empire that plays down the role of the emperor and stresses the responsiveness of the system to the shifting tempers of social and economic elites is José Maria dos Santos, *A política geral do Brasil* (São Paulo, 1930).

Another political history, this one built around the theme of legislation regarding slavery and the slave trade, is Paula Beiguelman's *Formação política do Brasil, 1: Teoria e ação no pensamento abolicionista* (São Paulo, 1967). C. H. Haring prepared the only chronological account of the entire period in English, *Empire in Brazil* (Cambridge, Mass., 1958). Based as it was on his reading of standard works up to that time, it can be used to measure the changes in the understanding of the empire during the next ten to fifteen years, when contrasted with the various essays in Sérgio Buarque de Holanda (ed.), *História geral da civilização brasileira*,

Tomo II: *O Brasil monárquico*, vols. 3, 4 and 5 (São Paulo, 1967–1972).

Two Brazilian scholars – one a political scientist, the other a sociologist – have produced impressively detailed studies of political life in nineteenth-century Brazil: José Murilo de Carvalho has constructed a composite picture of the political elite in his *A construção da ordem* (Rio de Janeiro, 1980) and *Teatro de sombras: a política imperial* (São Paulo, 1988), which are largely based on his unpublished doctoral thesis, 'Elite and state building in imperial Brazil' (Stanford University, 1974); Fernando Uricoechea went to the manuscript sources to explore the values and social relationships displayed in the life of the National Guard in his *The patrimonial foundations of the Brazilian bureaucratic state* (Berkeley, 1980). A less sophisticated, but nevertheless still useful, description of political institutions during the empire is João Camilo de Oliveira Torres, *A democracia coroada* (Rio de Janeiro, 1957). His conservative, pro-monarchical point of view is also found in Affonso d'Escragnolle Taunay's two studies of members of the houses of parliament: *O senado do império* (São Paulo, 1942) and 'A Câmara dos Deputados sob o império', *Anais do Museu Paulista*, 14 (1950), 1–252. The Council of State – part legislature, part court – has been ably studied by José Honório Rodrigues in *O Conselho de Estado: o quinto poder?* Brasília, 1978). Although most of Thomas Flory's *Judge and jury in imperial Brazil* (Austin, 1981) deals with the period before 1850, the final chapter (pp. 181–200) is a fine discussion of changes in the place of magistrates within the social, political and ideological system of Brazil to 1871. Also provocative is Eul-Soo Pang and Ron L. Seckinger's 'The Mandarins of Imperial Brazil', *Comparative Studies in Society and History*, 14/2 (1972), 215–44. There has been no significant study of the provincial presidents who so importantly shaped the course of the empire's political history, and the only study of elections was first published in 1872: Francisco Belisário Soares de Souza, *O sistema eleitoral no império* (2nd edn, Brasília, 1979). A study of how the Conservative leadership was forged by mid-century is Ilmar Rohloff de Mattos, *O tempo saquarema* (São Paulo, 1987). Also important is the series of perceptive essays on the politics and ideology of the period in Emília Viotti da Costa, *The Brazilian Empire: myths and histories* (Chicago, 1985).

Of the many biographies of the Emperor Pedro II the best remains Heitor Lyra's *História de Dom Pedro II, 1825–1891* (2nd rev. edn, 3 vols., Belo Horizonte and São Paulo, 1977). Mary W. Williams presented a romanticized account in her *Dom Pedro the Magnanimous* (Chapel Hill,

1937). Of the triumvirate – Eusébio, Itaboraí and Uruguai – who defined what we could call the far right at mid-century, only the last has received a worthy biography: José Antônio Soares de Souza, *A vida do visconde do Uruguai (1807–1866) (Paulino José Soares de Souza)* (São Paulo, 1944). The more creative conservatives at the centre-right – Rio Branco and Cotegipe – have been more fortunate: see, for example, José Wanderley Pinho, *Cotegipe e seu tempo: primeira phase, 1815–1867* (São Paulo, 1937), which was unfortunately not continued by the author; José Maria da Silva Paranhos, 2nd baron Rio Branco, *O visconde do Rio Branco* (2nd edn, Rio de Janeiro, 1943); and, more interestingly interpretive, Lídia Besouchet, *José Ma. Paranhos, visconde do Rio Branco. Ensaio histórico-biográfico* (Rio de Janeiro, 1945). At the centre-left stood Nabuco de Araújo, whose biography by his son Joaquim Nabuco was mentioned earlier. Teófilo Ottoni defended the most reformist measures of the period; see Paulo Pinheiro Chagas, *Teófilo Ottoni, ministro do povo* (2nd rev. edn, Rio de Janeiro, 1956).

Alongside the debates in parliament, pamphlets formed the central pieces of political discourse in the nineteenth century. Many of these have been reprinted. See, for example, Raymundo Magalhães Júnior, *Três panfletários do segundo reinado: Francisco de Sales Torres Homem e o 'Líbelo do povo'; Justiniano José da Rocha e 'Ação, reação, transação'; Antonio Ferreira Vianna e 'A conferência dos divinos'* (São Paulo, 1956).

On the Paraguayan War the literature is still unsatisfactory except on its military aspects. John Hoyt Williams, *The rise and fall of the Paraguayan Republic, 1800–1870* (Austin, 1979), provides the necessary background, while Pelham Horton Box, *The origins of the Paraguayan War* (Urbana, 1930) examines its immediate causes. The point of view of Paraguay is ably presented by Efraím Cardozo, *El imperio del Brasil y el Río de la Plata* (Buenos Aires, 1961). The best military history of the war is Augusto Tasso Fragoso, *História da guerra entre a Tríplice Aliança e o Paraguai* (5 vols., Rio de Janeiro, 1956–60). The Brazilian military itself is provocatively discussed in Nelson Werneck Sodré, *História militar do Brasil* (Rio de Janeiro, 1965).

A study of Brazil's economic history for the period must begin with the chapter on Brazil by Nícia Villela Luz in Stanley J. Stein and Roberto Cortés Conde (eds.), *Latin America: a guide to economic history, 1830–1930* (Berkeley, 1977), 163–272. Celso Furtado presents a general interpretive survey in *The economic growth of Brazil: a survey from colonial to modern times*, translated by Ricardo W. de Aguiar and Eric Charles Drysdale (Berkeley, 1963). Furtado's knowledge of Keynesian economic theory enlightens rather than beclouds his treatment. A contrasting Marxist perspective can be found in Caio Prado Júnior's account, already mentioned. Older, but still useful is J. F. Normano, *Brazil, a study of economic types* (Chapel Hill, N.C., 1935). Nathaniel H. Leff, *Underdevelopment and development in Brazil* (2 vols., London, 1982) is somewhat tendentious, but full of useful data.

Particular sectors of the economy have not been studied in sufficient detail. Notable on the sugar economy is Peter L. Eisenberg, *The sugar industry in Pernambuco: modernization without change, 1840–1910* (Berkeley, 1974), although Eul-Soo Pang argues an alternative point of view in 'Modernization and slavocracy in nineteenth century Brazil', *Journal of Interdisciplinary History*, 9/4 (1979), 667–88. The classic account regarding coffee, which includes the transcription of many documents, is the *História do café* prepared in fifteen volumes by Affonso d'Escragnolle Taunay (Rio de Janeiro, 1939–43). It is said that the author was paid by the word and wrote as many of these as he could; fortunately, he also prepared a summary entitled *Pequena história do café no Brasil (1727–1937)* (Rio de Janeiro, 1945). A more lively and still briefer account can be found in Odilon Nogueira de Matos, *Café e ferrovias: a evolução ferroviária de São Paulo e o desenvolvimento da cultura cafeeira* (2nd edn, São Paulo, 1974). On coffee, see also the books by Richard Graham, Stanley J. Stein, Warren Dean and Emília Viotti da Costa cited below. The coffee trade is examined by Joseph Sweigart, *Coffee factorage and the emergence of a Brazilian capital market, 1850–1888* (New York, 1987). In contrast to the many studies on coffee and sugar, there are relatively few on the production of other crops or on the cattle economy. Still useful, after more than a century, however, is the work of Brazil's first statistician, Sebastião Ferreira Soares, especially his *Notas estatísticas sobre a produção agrícola e a carestia dos gêneros alimentícios no Império do Brasil* (2nd edn, Rio de Janeiro, 1977). Also see a chapter on the economy of Rio Grande do Sul in José Hildebrando Decanal and Sergius Gonzaga (eds.), *RS: Economia & política* (Porto Alegre, 1979), and the first part of Barbara Weinstein's *The Amazon rubber boom, 1850–1920* (Stanford, 1983). Also see Alice Cannabrava's discussion of the brief period of cotton production in São Paulo province, *Desenvolvimento da cultura do algodão na província de São Paulo* (São Paulo, 1951).

There are a number of works on transport in nineteenth-century Brazil. Almost folkloric, but with some useful data on muletrains is José Alípio Goulart, *Tropas e tropeiros na formação do Brasil* (Rio de Janeiro, 1961). Much more detailed, and at times even erudite, is José B. Sousa's book on ox-carts, *Ciclo do carro de bois no Brasil* (São Paulo, 1958). The early history of railways in Brazil is discussed in Richard Graham, *Britain and the onset of modernization in Brazil, 1850–1914* (Cambridge, England, 1968). Subsequent works include the book by Odillon Nogueira de Matos, already mentioned, and Robert H. Mattoon, Jr, 'Railroads, coffee, and the growth of big business in São Paulo, Brazil', *HAHR*, 57/2 (1977), 273–95.

Richard Graham, *Britain and the onset of modernization* also explores foreign control of the export and import business. Ana Célia Castro, *As empresas estrangeiras no Brasil, 1860–1913* (Rio de Janeiro, 1979), provides a brief summary of foreign investments. To place this trade and investment in a larger context, consult D. C. M. Platt, *Latin America and British trade, 1806–1914* (New York, 1972), as well as Irving Stone's two articles: 'British long-term investment in Latin America, 1865–1913', *Business History Review*, 42/3 (1968), 311–39 and 'British Direct and Portfolio Investment in Latin America before 1914', *Journal of Economic History* 37/3 (1977), 690–722. These works suggest the need for revisions in J. Fred Rippy, *British investments in Latin America, 1822–1949* (Minneapolis, 1959).

First steps toward modern manufacturing in Brazil are closely tied to the figure of Mauá. Unfortunately, no satisfactory account of his life has yet been written. Anyda Marchant's *Viscount Mauá and the empire of Brazil* (Berkeley, 1965) does not seek to explain entrepreneurial success or failure, attributing Mauá's problems – as he did – to the personal enmity of others. Her omission of all footnotes advances scholarship no further than did Alberto de Faria, *Mauá: Ireneo Evangelista de Souza, barão e visconde de Mauá* (3rd edn, São Paulo, 1946). The best study of textile mills, really a collection of provocative essays, is Stanley J. Stein's *The Brazilian cotton manufacture: textile enterprise in an underdeveloped area, 1850–1950* (Cambridge, Mass., 1957).

Slavery shaped Brazilian life both in the cities and the countryside. It has consequently been the subject of a large number of studies. Robert Conrad, *Brazilian slavery* (Boston, Mass., 1977) is a useful bibliography. Leslie Bethell has written the major study of the end of the slave trade: *The abolition of the Brazilian slave trade* (Cambridge, 1970). For the abolition of slavery itself, see Robert Conrad, *The destruction of Brazilian slavery, 1850–1888* (Berkeley, 1972), Robert Brent Toplin, *The abolition of slavery in Brazil* (New York, 1972) and, above all, Emília Viotti da Costa, *Da senzala à colônia* (São Paulo, 1966), the major work on slavery and abolition in São Paulo. All works on Brazilian slavery respond in one way or another to the views of Gilberto Freyre on the plantation system as expressed, for instance, in his *The mansions and the shanties*, translated by Harriet de Onís (New York, 1963). In sharp contrast to his favourable view of the paternalistic relationship between master and slave stands Stanley J. Stein's brilliant *Vassouras. A Brazilian coffee county, 1850–1900* (Cambridge, Mass., 1957). A similar approach focused on a region that turned to coffee only later is Warren Dean, *Rio Claro. A Brazilian plantation system, 1820–1920* (Stanford, 1976). See also Amilcar Martins Filho and Roberto B. Martins, 'Slavery in a non-export economy: Nineteenth century Minas Gerais revisited', *HAHR*, 63/3 (1983), 537–68, and the comments upon it, pp. 569–90. For a survey of the different approaches to the subject, see Richard Graham, 'Brazilian slavery re-examined: a review article', *Journal of Social History*, 3/4 (1970), 431–53. Maria Sylvia de Carvalho Franco notes the importance of free men to slave society in her *Homens livres na ordem escravocrata* (2nd edn, São Paulo, 1974). An impressively detailed quantitative analysis is Robert W. Slenes, 'The demography and economics of Brazilian slavery, 1850–1888' (unpublished Ph.D. thesis, Stanford University, 1975).

The issues of population, urban life and land-tenure have not received the attention they deserve. Maria Luiza Marcílio notes the various estimates for Brazil's population at mid-century in 'Evolução da população brasileira através dos censos até 1872', *Anais de História*, 6 (1974), 115–37. Richard Morse makes stimulating suggestions regarding the relationship of villages, rural estates and cities in his 'Cities and society in nineteenth-century Latin America: the illustrative case of Brazil', in Richard Schaedel, Jorge Hardoy and Nora Scott Kinzer (eds.), *Urbanization in the Americas from its beginnings to the present day* (The Hague, 1978). See also Emília Viotti da Costa, 'Urbanização no Brasil no século XIX', in *Da monarquia à república: momentos decisivos* (São Paulo, 1977). Rich statistical information on the city of Rio de Janeiro is included in Eulália Maria Lahmeyer Lobo, *História do Rio de Janeiro (do capital comercial ao capital industrial e financeiro)* (2 vols., Rio de Janeiro, 1978). Sandra Lauderdale Graham explores the urban setting and cultural values of domestic servants in *House and street: The domestic world of servants and masters in nineteenth-century Rio de Janeiro* (Cambridge, 1988). Kátia M. de Queirós Mattoso discusses the social and economic life of Salvador (Bahia) in *Bahia: a cidade do Salvador e seu mercado no século XIX* (São Paulo, 1978). Urban women are the subject of June E. Hahner's *A mulher brasileira e suas lutas sociais e políticas, 1850–1937*, translated by Maria

Theresa P. de Almeida and Heitor Ferreira da Costa (São Paulo, 1981). On the 1850 land law, see the essays by Warren Dean, José Murilo de Carvalho and Emília Viotti da Costa cited in bibliographical essay no. 2. The literary history of the period is ably surveyed in the relevant sections of Antônio Cândido de Mello e Souza, *Formação da literatura brasileira* (2 vols., São Paulo, 1959). He is careful to suggest the connections between the larger society and trends in literature. More attentive to stylistic criticism is José Guilherme Merquior, *De Anchieta a Euclides: breve história da literatura brasileira, I* (Rio de Janeiro, 1977). A quick reference work is Alfredo Bosi's *História concisa da literatura brasileira* (São Paulo, 1970), while much greater detail can be found in Afrânio Coutinho (ed.), *A literatura no Brasil*, Vol. 1, Tomo 2: *Romantismo* (2nd edn, Rio de Janeiro, 1968). José de Alencar, Brazil's most famous mid-century novelist – also a politician – has been the subject of several biographies; see, for instance, Raimundo Magalhães Júnior, *José de Alencar e sua época* (2nd edn, Rio de Janeiro, 1977).

Philosophy and music are other topics that provide an insight into the nineteenth-century ethos. João Cruz Costa, *A history of ideas in Brazil*, translated by Suzette Macedo (Berkeley, 1964), like the work of Antônio Cândido, relates intellectual life to social and economic change. The ideas of political thinkers are explored in Nelson Saldanha, *O pensamento político no Brasil* (Rio de Janeiro, 1979). Finally, Gerard Béhague, *Music in Latin America, an introduction* (Englewood Cliffs, New Jersey, 1979), makes important observations on Antônio Carlos Gomes, the composer whose *Il Guarany* excited the opera world in 1870.

4. 1870–1889

Rubens Borba de Moraes and William Berrien, *Manual de estudos brasileiros* (Rio de Janeiro, 1949), although outdated, is still the most important bibliographical guide. Specifically about the Empire but now also somewhat outdated are Stanley Stein, 'The historiography of Brazil, 1808–1889', *HAHR*, 40/2 (1960), 234–78; George Boehrer, 'Brazilian historical bibliography: some lacunae and suggestions', *Inter-American Review of Bibliography*, 11/2 (1961), 137–49, and 'The Brazilian Republican Revolution, old and new views', *Luso-Brazilian Review*, 3/2 (1966), 43–57. A more recent analysis of the historiography of the last two decades of the Empire is Emília Viotti da Costa, 'Sobre as orígens da República' in *Da monarquia à república: momentos decisivos* (São Paulo, 1977), 243–90.

See also the essays in Emília Viotti da Costa, *The Brazilian Empire; myths and histories* (Chicago, 1985).

A variety of interesting data can be found in the travellers' accounts published in the nineteenth century. Particularly informative and containing many useful tables is Santa-Anna Nery, *Le Brésil en 1889* (Paris, 1889). Also relevant for the study of the last decade of the Empire is Louis Couty, *Le Brésil en 1884* (Rio de Janeiro, 1884); C. F. Van Delden Laerne, *Le Brésil et Java. Rapport sur la culture du café en Amérique, Asie, et Afrique (avec chartes, planches et diagrammes)* (The Hague, 1885); Max Leclerc, *Cartas do Brasil* (São Paulo, 1942) and Alfred Marc, *Le Brésil, excursion à travers de ses 20 provinces* (Paris, 1890).

The years between 1870 and 1889 have been seen as years of crisis for the monarchical institutions. The first versions of the fall of the Empire were written either by monarchists or by republicans. The monarchists overestimated the role of the military in the 1889 coup while the republicans stressed the failure of monarchical institutions and the success of the republican campaign. Written from a republican perspective is José Maria Bello, *História da República, 1889–1954* (4th edn, São Paulo, 1959), Eng. trans. by James L. Taylor, *A history of modern Brazil 1889–1954* (Stanford, 1966); from a monarchist perspective, J. F. Oliveira Vianna, *O ocaso do Império* (São Paulo, 1925) and Heitor Lyra, *História da queda do Império* (2 vols., São Paulo, 1964). During the 1940s and 1950s Marxist historians offered a new interpretation: see, for example, Caio Prado Jr, *Evolução política do Brasil* (São Paulo, 1933) and Nelson Werneck Sodré, *Formação histórica do Brasil* (Rio de Janeiro, 1944). Practically ignored has been the psychoanalytical study of the fall of the Empire by Luís Martins, *O patriarca e o bacharel* (São Paulo, 1953), which relied on Gilberto Freyre's generational model described in *The mansions and the shanties*, trans. by Harriet do Onis (New York, 1963). In the 1960s and 1970s academic historiography made important contributions to the revision of traditional interpretations. The best synthesis of this period appears in a collective work published under the direction of Sérgio Buarque de Holanda, *História geral da civilização brasileira, II: O Brasil monárquico* (5 vols., São Paulo, 1962–72), especially vol. IV, *Declínio e queda do império* and vol. V, *Do império à república*. Although the quality of the essays is uneven and the connections between economic, social, political and ideological changes is often left to the reader, this is the most complete synthesis available. Well informed but somewhat chaotic is João Camillo de Oliveira Torres, *A democracia coroada* (Rio de Janeiro,

1957), a book written from a conservative perspective. For a liberal perspective see Raymondo Faoro, *Os donos do poder, Formação do patronato político brasileiro* (2 vols., São Paulo, 1975). Richard Graham, *Britain and the onset of modernization in Brazil (1850–1914)* (Cambridge, 1968) describes several important changes occurring in Brazilian politics and society during this period and is the best synthesis available in English.

For a long time the history of Brazil was seen as the history of masters and slaves. Historians neglected the population of small farmers, tenants and sharecroppers that constituted the great majority of the population in the nineteenth century. More recently these groups have been the subject of several studies. Some of the most important problems confronting the free population were discussed in Maria Sylvia Carvalho Franco, *Homens livres na ordem escravocrata* (São Paulo, 1969). Particularly interesting is G. I Joffley, 'O quebraquilos, a revolta dos matutos contra os doutores', *Revista de História*, 34 (1978), 69–145. See also Roderick Barman, 'The Brazilian peasantry reexamined. The implications of the Quebra-Quilos revolt (1874–1875)', *HAHR*, 57/3 (1977), 401–25. Armando Souto Maior, *Quebra-Quilos. Lutas sociais no outono do Império* (São Paulo, 1978) considers the *quebra-quilos* as an expression of class tensions and social dislocations in the Brazilian north-east caused by the impact of capitalist development in the backlands. Analogous is Janaina Amado's conclusion in her study on the muckers: *Conflito social no Brasil. A revolta dos Muckers. Rio Grande do Sul (1868–1878)* (São Paulo, 1978). On social banditry, see bibliographical essay 6.

Labour history is relatively new in Brazil. For a long time the study of the workers was in the hands of political militants or sociologists more interested in the twentieth-century labour movement. As a consequence the emerging working class of the nineteenth century has received little attention. Edgard Carone, *Movimento operário no Brasil (1877–1944)* (São Paulo, 1979) is a collection of documents. We are still waiting for studies on workers' conditions of living, forms of organization and their participation in the political system. The same lacunae can be found in the study of urban demonstrations and urban riots that multiplied towards the end of the nineteenth century. Sandra Lauderdale Graham, 'The vintem riot and political culture. Rio de Janeiro, 1880', *HAHR* 60/ 2 (1980), 431–50 shows the many possibilities that the study of these urban crowds offer. Another group waiting for a historian are the *capoeiras* – free blacks and mulattos, and perhaps some slaves, who threatened the Rio de Janeiro urban population and who seem to have played an important role in the political life of the last years of the Empire, particularly in the abolitionist campaign. Women also have not received much attention. In a pioneering article, June Hahner has identified several organizations created by middle- and upper-class women in the last decades of the Empire: 'Feminism, women's rights and the suffrage movement in Brazil', *LARR*, 16/1 (1980), 41–64.

The best study of urbanization is Paul Singer, *Desenvolvimento económico e evolução urbana* (São Paulo, 1968). See also Richard Morse, 'Cities and societies in nineteenth century Latin America. The illustrative case of Brazil' in R. Schaedel, J. Hardoy and N. S. Kinzer (eds.), *Urbanization in the Americas from its beginnings to the present* (The Hague, 1978). For a different perspective, see Emília Viotti da Costa, 'Urbanização no Brasil no século XIX' in *Da monarquia à república*, 179–208. On immigration, see bibliographical essay 6.

A detailed description of the political institutions can be found in Oliveira Torres, *A democracia coroada*; Buarque de Holanda, *História geral da civilização brasileira, II: O Brasil Monárquico*, IV and V; Faoro, *Os donos do poder*; and Nestor Duarte, *A ordem privada e a organização política nacional* (São Paulo, 1938). Many institutions have been the object of specific studies. The Senate is described in Beatriz Westin Cerqueira Leite, *O Senado nos anos finais do Império, 1870–1889* (Brasília, 1978) which supersedes A. E. Taunay, *O senado do Império* (São Paulo, 1941). For the Chamber, A. E. Taunay, *A Câmara dos Deputados* (São Paulo, 1950) remains valuable. The Council of State is examined in Fernando Machado, *O Conselho de Estado e sua história no Brasil* (São Paulo, 1972).

The best study on political parties and political elites is José Murilo de Carvalho, 'Elite and state building in imperial Brazil' (unpublished PhD thesis, Stanford University, 1974). The first part, revised and expanded, has been published in *A construção da ordem. A elite política imperial* (Rio de Janeiro, 1980). See also his 'A composição social dos partidos políticos Imperiais', *Cadernos do Departmento de Ciencias Políticas da Faculdade de Filosofia e Ciências Humanas da Universidade Federal de Minas Gerais*, 2 (1974), 1–34, and 'Political elites and state building: the case of nineteenth century Brazil', *Comparative Studies in Society and History*, 24/3 (1982). Carvalho revises many traditional notions that have prevailed in the literature. For the study of the imperial elites, see also Olavo Brasil de Lima Jr, and Lucia Maria de Klein, 'Atores políticos do Império', *Dados*, 7 (1970), 62–88, and Ron L. Seckinger and Eul-Soo Pang, 'The mandarins of imperial Brazil', *Comparative Studies in Society and History*, 9/

2 (1972). For a study of the political party system from a juridical point Afonso Arinos de Melo Franco, *História e teoria do partido político no direito constitucional Brasileiro* (Rio de Janeiro, 1948) remains valuable.

Although there are no monographic studies of the two main parties there are several studies of the Republican party. Goerge Boehrer, *Da monarquia à república. História do Partido Republicano no Brasil, 1870–1889* (Rio de Janeiro, 1954), is the main source for the study of the party at the national level. For the study of the party in São Paulo, see Emília da Costa Nogueira, 'O movimento republicano em Itu. Os fazendeiros do oeste paulista e os prodromos do movimento republicano', *Revista de História*, 20 (1954), 379–405, and José Maria dos Santos, *Bernardino de Campos e o partido republicano paulista, subsídios para a História da República* (Rio de Janeiro, 1960). The ambiguous position of the Paulista Republican party toward abolition was described by José Maria dos Santos, *Os republicanos paulistas e a abolição* (São Paulo, 1942). Nícia Vilela Luz, 'O papel das classes médias brasileiras no movimento republicano', *Revista de História* 28/57 (1964), 213–28, calls attention to the important role played by the sons of traditional elites who had lost status. Two studies have examined political participation during the last decades of the Empire: Joseph Love, 'Political participation in Brazil, 1881–1969', *Luso-Brazilian Review*, 7/2 (1970), 3–24, and Maria Antonieta de A. G. Parahyba, 'Abertura social e participação política no Brasil, 1870–1920', *Dados* 7 (1970), 89–102.

Much more needs to be investigated before we can begin to understand the sociology of electoral behaviour during the Empire. Meanwhile several studies have been published about the system of patronage. The most complete study is stil Faoro, *Os donos do poder*. It can be supplemented by Simon Schwartzman, 'Regional cleavages and political patriarchalism in Brazil' (unpublished PhD thesis, University of California, Berkeley, 1973). A colourful description of the system of clientele and patronage is found in Maria Isaura Pereira de Queiroz, *O mandonismo local na vida política brasileira* (São Paulo, 1969), reprinted from the original essay published in *Anhembi*, 24–6 (São Paulo, 1956–7). Administration at the local level in one province is examined in Francisco Iglésias, *Política económica do governo provincial Mineiro, 1835–1889* (Rio de Janeiro, 1958).

More research on the formal and informal connections between businessmen and politicians needs to be done. The articles published by Eugene W. Ridings point in the right direction. Particularly interesting are 'Elite conflicts and cooperation in the Brazilian Empire. The case of Bahian businessmen and planters', *Luso-Brazilian Review*, 12/1 (1975), 80–99; 'The merchant elite and the development of Brazil during the Empire', *Journal of Inter-American Studies and World Affairs*, 15 (1973); 'Class sector unity in an export economy. The case of nineteenth century Brazil', *HAHR* 58/3 (1978), 432–50; 'Internal groups and development. The case of Brazil in the nineteenth century', *JLAS*, 9/2 (1977), 225–50. And we still have much to learn about the political role of economic groups, family links and the importance of patronage in determining party affiliation and party performance. A reading of the biographies of important political figures provides interesting information. Particularly useful are Joaquim Nabuco, *Um estadista do Império: Nabuco de Araújo, sua vida, suas opiniões e sua época* (3 vols, São Paulo, 1936); Luis Viana Filho, *A vida de Rui Barbosa* (São Paulo, 1965); Hermes Vieira, *Ouro Preto, o homem e a época* (São Paulo, 1948); Wanderley Pinho, *Cotegipe e seu tempo* (São Paulo, 1937); Craveiro Costa, *O visconde de Sinimbú, sua vida e sua atuação na política nacional 1840–1889* (São Paulo, 1937); Luis Viana Filho, *A vida de Joaquim Nabuco* (São Paulo, 1944); José Antônio Soares de Souza, *A vida do Visconde de Uruguai, 1807–1866* (São Paulo, 1944); Luis Viana Filho, *A vida do Barão do Rio Branco* (Rio de Janeiro, 1959). The best biography of Pedro II is Heitor Lyra, *História do Imperador Pedro II* (3 vols., São Paulo, 1938–40). In English, see Mary Wilhelmine Williams, *Dom Pedro the Magnanimous* (Chapel Hill, NC, 1937).

A few politicians of the Empire published their memoirs. Particularly interesting are Afonso Celso, *Oito anos de parlamento* (São Paulo, n.d.); Alfredo d'Escragnolle Taunay, *Memórias* (Rio de Janeiro, 1960), *Homens e coisas do império* (São Paulo, 1924), and *Cartas políticas* (Rio de Janeiro, 1889); Albino José Barbosa de Oliveira, *Memórias de um magistrado do império* (São Paulo, 1943); Júlio Belo, *Memórias de um Cavalcanti. Trechos de um livro de assentos de Felix Cavalcanti de Albuquerque e Melo (1821–1901)* (São Paulo, 1940); Visconde de Mauá, *Autobiografia (Exposição aos credores e ao público seguida de o meio circulante no Brasil)* (Rio de Janeiro, 1942). Equally interesting is the correspondence exchanged between political or intellectual figures. Particularly relevant for this period are Raymundo de Menezes (ed.), *Cartas e diário de José de Alencar* (São Paulo, 1967); José Honóro Rodrigues (ed.), *Correspondência de Capistrano de Abreu* (3 vols., Rio de Janeiro, 1954–6); *Correspondência de Machado e Joaquim Nabuco* (São Paulo, 1933); Raymundo de Magalhães (ed.), *D. Pedro II e a Condessa do Barral* (Rio de Janeiro, 1956); José Wanderley de

Araújo Pinho (ed.), *Cartas do Imperador D. Pedro II ao Barão de Cotegipe* (São Paulo, 1933); *Correspondência entre D. Pedro II e o Barão do Rio Branco (1889–1891)* (São Paulo, 1957). These last two publications constitute important sources for the study of the emperor's view of the Brazilian system. Even more relevant in this respect is D. Pedro II, *Conselhos à Regente*, introduction and notes by J. C. de Oliveira Torres (Rio de Janeiro, 1958).

The abolition of slavery has attracted the attention of many scholars. The most complete bibliography available is Robert Conrad, *Brazilian slavery: an annotated research bibliography* (Boston, 1977). Conrad is also the author of the most complete study available in English, *The destruction of Brazilian slavery 1850–1889* (Berkeley, 1971). For a different approach, see Robert Toplin, *The abolition of slavery in Brazil* (New York, 1972) and Richard Graham, 'Causes of the abolition of Negro slavery in Brazil. An interpretive essay', *HAHR*, 46/2 (1966), 123–37. For a more comprehensive study of the process of transition from slavery to free labour including its economic, social, political and ideological aspects, see Emília Viotti da Costa, *Da senzala à colônia* (São Paulo, 1966; 2nd edn, 1982). On the profitability of Brazilian slavery in its final stage, see bibliographical essay 5. In spite of the many studies on abolition we still lack information about the grass roots of abolitionism. Evaristo de Morais, *A campanha abolicionista (1879–1888)* (Rio de Janeiro, 1924) is still useful in this respect. Recently the *caifazes*, an abolitionist organization operating in São Paulo, was examined by Alice Barros Fontes, 'A prática abolicionista em São Paulo. Os caifazes, 1882–1888' (unpublished MA thesis, University of São Paulo, 1976). Paula Beiguelman, *Teoria e ação no pensamento abolicionista* (São Paulo, 1962) called attention to the importance of political mechanisms in the abolition of slavery. Richard Graham in 'Landowners and the overthrow of the Brazilian monarchy', *Luso-Brazilian Review*, 7/2 (1970), 44–56 analyses the impact of abolitionism and abolition on planters. See also Eul-Soo Pang, 'Modernization and slavocracy in nineteenth century Brazil', *Journal of Interdisciplinary History*, 4/4 (1979).

Relations between church and state are examined in George Boehrer, 'The church in the second reign, 1840–1889', in Henry Keith and S. F. Edwards (eds.), *Conflict and continuity in Brazilian society* (Columbia, SC, 1963), 113–40; George Boehrer, 'The church and the overthrow of the Brazilian monarch', *HAHR*, 48/3 (1968), 380–401; and Mary C. Thornton, *The church and freemasonry in Brazil, 1872–75* (Washington, DC,

1948). See also, David Queirós Vieira, 'Protestantism and the religious question in Brazil 1855–1875' (unpublished PhD thesis, American University, Washington DC, 1972); António Carlos Villaca, *A história da questão religiosa no Brasil* (Rio de Janeiro, 1974); Nilo Pereira, *Conflicto entre Igreja e Estado* (Recife, 1976); and António Carlos Villaca, *O pensamento católico no Brasil* (Rio de Janeiro, 1975). For an understanding of the elite's behaviour during the conflict, there is interesting information in Joaquim Nabuco, *Um estadista do Império*.

There are four important essays on the role of the Brazilian military in the proclamation of the Republic: John Schulz, 'O exército e o império' in Buarque de Holanda (ed.), *Historia geral da civilização brasileira*, IV, 235–49; W. S. Dudley, 'Institutional sources of officer discontent in the Brazilian army, 1870–1889', *HAHR*, 55/1 (1975), 44–65, and 'Professionalisation and politicisation as motivational factors in the Brazilian army coup of 15 November 1889', *JLAS*, 8/1 (1976), 101–25; and June Hahner, 'The Brazilian armed forces and the overthrow of the monarchy. Another perspective', *The Americas*, 26/2 (1969), 171–82. For a more theoretical analysis see Frederick Nunn, 'Military professionalism and professional militarism in Brazil, 1870–1970. Historical perspectives and political implications', *JLAS*, 4/6 (1972), 29–54. A more detailed study of the army during the Empire is John Schulz, 'The Brazilian army in politics 1850–1894' (unpublished PhD thesis, Princeton, 1973). Nelson Werneck Sodré, *História militar do Brasil* (Rio de Janeiro, 1968) is also informative. Some biographical studies focusing on important figures in the army add interesting details: for example, Raymundo de Magalhães, *Deodoro e a espada contra o império* (Rio de Janeiro, 1957), a biography of the general who led the coup in November 1889. There is a biographical study of Deodoro in English: Charles Willis Simmons, *Marshal Deodoro and the fall of Dom Pedro II* (Durham, NC, 1966). The intriguing personality of Benjamin Constant and his role as a republican and as a positivist is examined by Raymundo Teixeira Mendes, *Benjamin Constant* (2nd edn, Rio de Janeiro, 1913). The hostility with which some loyal monarchists evaluated the military and its role in the overthrow of the Empire is well documented in Visconde de Ouro Preto, *Advento da ditadura militar no Brasil* (Paris, 1891) and Eduardo Prado, *Fastos da ditadura militar no Brasil* (São Paulo, 1902). This unsympathetic view was kept alive in the works of historians like Oliveira Vianna, who did not hide their identification with the monarchy and monarchical institutions. For an opposite point of view one should consult A.

Ximeno de Villeroy, *Benjamin Constant e a política republicana* (Rio de Janeiro, 1928). And for a more balanced discussion, see Emília Viotti da Costa, 'A proclamação da república', in *Da monarquia à república*.

Antônio Cândido de Melo e Souza, *Formação da literatura brasileira* (2nd edn, 2 vols., São Paulo, 1964) has in an appendix a short biography of the most important writers of this period. Also useful is José Aderaldo Castello, *Presença da literatura brasileira. História e antologia* (3 vols., São Paulo, 1964). For an overview of the history of ideas the best source is João Cruz Costa, *História das ideias no Brasil* (Rio de Janeiro, 1956), Eng. trans. by Suzette Macedo, *A history of ideas in Brazil* (Berkeley, 1964). Several books have been published about positivism in Brazil. Most of them associate the middle classes and positivism. Typical is Robert Nachman, 'Positivism, modernization and the Brazilian middle-class', *HAHR*, 57/1 (1977), 1–23. The most reliable source published in Portuguese is Ivan Lins, *História do positivismo no Brasil* (São Paulo, 1964). See also João Camillo de Oliveira Torres, *O positivismo no Brasil* (Petrópolis, 1952). For a critical examination of liberalism, see Maria Stella Martins Bresciani, 'Liberalismo, ideologia e controle social' (2 vols., unpublished PhD thesis, University of São Paulo, 1976).

The problem of cultural dependency and the contradictions generated by the import of European ideas, first discussed by Nelson Werneck Sodré in *Ideologia do colonialismo. Seus reflexos no pensamento brasileiro* (Rio de Janeiro, 1961), became the subject of an important controversy with the publication of Roberto Schwarz's essay 'As ideias fora do lugar' in *Estudos Cebrap*, 3 (1973), 151–61, later reproduced and expanded in his study of Machado de Assis *Ao vencedor as batatas* (São Paulo, 1977). Applying to the study of ideas the 'dependency theory' model, Schwarz noticed a contradiction between the ideology of patronage characteristic of Brazilian society and European liberalism. This contradiction was denied in Maria Sylvia Carvalho Franco, 'As ideias estão no lugar', *Debates* (1976).

Brazilian racial ideology is examined in Thomas Skidmore, *Black into white. Race and nationality in Brazilian thought* (New York, 1974) which includes an extensive bibliography about different aspects of Brazilian society during the Empire and First Republic. For a different interpretation, see Emília Viotti da Costa, 'The Myth of Racial Democracy: a legacy of the Empire' in *The Brazilian Empire: myths and histories* (Chicago, 1985).

Few studies have been published about cultural institutions. For an overview see Fernando de Azevedo, *Brazilian culture, an introduction to the study of culture in Brazil*, trans. William Rex Crawford (New York, 1950). More specific is Robert Havighurst and Roberto Moreira, *Society and education in Brazil* (Pittsburgh, 1965). The São Paulo law school which was the incubator of most of the professional politicians of the Empire was the subject of two important books: Almeida Nogueira, *A Academia de São Paulo. Tradições e reminiscências* (9 vols., São Paulo, 1906–9) and Spencer Vampre, *Memórias para a história da Academia de São Paulo* (2 vols., São Paulo, 1924). Maria de Lourdes Marioto Haidar examines the secondary school system in her book *O ensino secundário no império brasileiro* (São Paulo, 1972). Valuable information about the debate over the creation of the university in the nineteenth century can be found in Roque Spencer Maciel de Barros, *A ilustração brasileira e a ideia de universidade* (São Paulo, 1959).

5. ECONOMY

The historiography of this period may be approached through Nícia Vilela Luz, 'Brazil', in Roberto Cortés Conde and Stanley Stein (eds.), *Latin America: a guide to economic history, 1830–1930* (Berkeley, 1977), which contains several hundred annotated entries of primary and secondary sources, as well as a valuable interpretive article. Important collections of recent scholarship include Colloque Internationale sur l'Histoire Quantitative du Brésil, *L'Histoire quantitative du Brésil de 1800 à 1930* (Paris, 1971); Flávio Rabelo Versiani and J. R. M. de Barros (eds.), *Formação econômica do Brasil; a experiência da industrialização* (São Paulo, 1978); Paulo Neuhaus (ed.), *Economia brasileira: uma visão histórica* (Rio de Janeiro, 1980); Carlos Manuel Pelaez and Mircea Buescu (eds.), *A moderna história econômica* (Rio de Janeiro, 1976); and Werner Baer, *et al.*, *Dimensões do desenvolvimento brasileiro* (Rio de Janeiro, 1978). Among general studies of the Brazilian economy in historical perspective the following deserve mention: Werner Baer, *The Brazilian economy, its growth and development* (Columbus, Ohio, 1979); Mircea Buescu, *História econômica do Brasil, pesquisa e análise* (Rio de Janeiro, 1970); and Carlos Manuel Pelaez, *História econômica do Brasil* (São Paulo, 1979).

The study of Brazilian economic history owes much to three central figures, whose works have been much debated and who represent significant tendencies in policy debates. Roberto Simonsen was an industrialist and political figure whose many essays were designed to show the feasibility of industrialization. Some of these have been collected in *Evolução industrial do Brasil e outros ensaios* (São Paulo, 1973). Caio Prado Júnior, a Marxist historian, wrote mainly on the colonial period, but his *História econômica do Brasil* (São Paulo, 1949) and *História e desenvolvimento* (São Paulo, 1972) deserve mention. Celso Furtado sought specifically to defend a structuralist position in his *A economia brasileira* (Rio de Janeiro, 1954) and in his influential *Formação económica do Brasil* (Rio de Janeiro, 1959); Eng. trans. *The economic growth of Brazil* (Berkeley, 1963). Two other early studies of importance are J. F. Normano, *Brazil, a study of economic types* (New York, 1935; 1968) and Roy Nash, *The conquest of Brazil* (New York, 1926; 1968).

Until quite recently the economic historiography of Brazil has been institutional, in fact more sociological than economic. Nevertheless a number of monographs which deal in part with economic processes deserve mention. On the plantation system, see Stanley J. Stein, *Vassouras: a Brazilian coffee county* (Cambridge, Mass., 1957); Peter Eisenberg, *The sugar industry in Pernambuco, 1840–1910* (Berkeley, 1974): Jaime Reis, 'From *bangüé* to *usina*', in K. Duncan and I. Rutledge (eds.), *Land and labour in Latin America* (Cambridge, 1977); J. H. Galloway, 'The sugar industry of Pernambuco during the nineteenth century', *Annals of the Association of American Geographers* (1968); Thomas Holloway, *Immigrants on the land: coffee and society in São Paulo, 1886–1934* (Chapel Hill, NC, 1980); Warren Dean, *Rio Claro: a Brazilian plantation system* (Stanford, 1976); and the various essays in II Congresso de História de São Paulo, *O café* (São Paulo, 1975). Richard Graham assesses the impact of Britain on Brazilian development in *Britain and the onset of modernization in Brazil* (Cambridge, 1968). Two excellent regional studies are Pierre Monbeig, *Pionniers et planteurs de São Paulo* (Paris, 1952) and Jean Roche, *A colonização alemã e o Rio Grande do Sul* (2 vols., Porto Alegre, 1969). The regional studies by Joseph Love on Rio Grande do Sul and São Paulo, John Wirth on Minas Gerais and Robert Levine on Pernambuco (see *CHLA* v, bibliographical essay 21) though primarily political, contain useful information on regional economies. Important recent studies of the Amazon region are Roberto Santos, *História econômica da Amazônia 1800–1920* (São Paulo, 1980) and Barbara Weinstein, *The Amazon rubber boom, 1850–1920* (Stanford, 1983).

Economic policy in this period has been much studied. A general institutional approach is Edgard Carone, *A república velha* (São Paulo, 1970). Steven Topik demonstrates government interventionism in 'The evolution of the economic role of the Brazilian state, 1889–1930', *JLAS*, 11/2 (1979), and 'State interventionism in a liberal regime, 1889–1930', *HAHR*, 60/4 (1980). Aníbal Vilanova Villela and Wilson Suzigan, *Política do governo e crescimento da economia brasileira, 1889–1945* (Rio de Janeiro, 1973), Eng. trans. *Government policy and economic growth of Brazil 1889–1945* (Rio de Janeiro, 1977) is an important study that emphasizes the distortions introduced by coffee valorization. Nícia Vilela Luz, *A luta pela industrialização no Brasil* (São Paulo, 1961) analyses pro-developmental debates. See also the collected works of two major figures, Leopoldo Bulhões, *Discursos parlementares* (Brasília, 1979), and Serzedelo Correia, *A problema econômica do Brasil* (Brasília, 1980). Two useful regional studies are Gabriel Bittencourt, *Esforço industrial na república do café: o caso do Espírito Santo, 1889–1930* (Vitória, 1982); and Janice Teodoro da Silva, *Raízes da ideologia do planejamento: Nordeste, 1889–1930* (São Paulo, 1978). Thomas Holloway, *The Brazilian coffee valorization of 1906* (Madison, 1975), and Carlos Manuel Pelaez's essay in *Ensaios sobre café e desenvolvimento econômico* (Rio, 1973), deal with the coffee support scheme. On cartels, see Joan Bak, 'Cartels, cooperatives and corporativism: Getúlio Vargas in Rio Grande do Sul on the eve of Brazil's 1930 revolution', *HAHR*, 63/2 (1983). Government policy in agriculture and railways is discussed by Eulália Lahmeyer Lobo in *História político-administrativa da agricultura brasileira, 1808–1889* (Rio de Janeiro, 1980). An analysis of the impact of tariffs can be found in Maria Teresa R. O. Versiani, 'Proteção tarifária e crescimento industrial nos anos 1906–12: o caso de cerveja', *Pesquisa e Planejamento Econômico*, 12/2 (Rio de Janeiro, 1982). Eulália Lahmeyer Lobo, *História do Rio de Janeiro, do capital comercial ao capital industrial e financeiro* (2 vols., Rio de Janeiro, 1978) is a major study of the economic aspects of urbanization, with important price and wage data. Regional diversity is treated in Antonio Barros de Castro, *Sete ensaios sobre a economia brasileira* (2 vols., Rio de Janeiro, 1971), David Denslow, 'As orígens da desigualdade regional no Brasil', *Estudos Econômicos* (1973), and Nathaniel Leff, *Underdevelopment and development in Brazil* (2 vols., London, 1982).

Macroeconomic studies began with O. Dias Carneiro, 'Past trends in the economic evolution of Brazil, 1920–1965' (mimeo, Cambridge, Mass., 1966). Important estimates of national product are to be found in C. Contador and C. Haddad, 'Produto real, moeda e preços: a experiência brasileira no período 1861–1970', *Revista Brasileira de Estatística* (1975), Claudio Haddad, 'Crescimento do produto real brasileiro, 1900/1947',

Revista Brasileira de Economia, 29 (1975) and, most recently, Leff, *Underdevelopment and development*, which incorporates material from his various essays on this subject: 'Long term Brazilian economic development', *Journal of Economic History* 29/3 (1969); 'Economic retardation in nineteenth century Brazil', *Economic History Review*, 2nd ser., 25 (1972); 'Tropical trade and development in the nineteenth century: the Brazilian experience', *Journal of Political Economy*, 81 (1973). On terms of trade, see R. Gonçalves and A. Coelho, 'Tendências dos termos-de-troca: a tese de Prebisch e a economia brasileira, 1850–1979', *Pesquisa e Planejamento Econômico*, 12/2 (1982). On inflation, see Oscar Onody, *A inflação brasileira, 1820–1958* (Rio de Janeiro, 1960), a pioneering study; Mircea Buescu, *300 anos de inflação* (Rio de Janeiro, 1973); and Paulo Neuhaus, 'A inflação brasileira em perspectiva histórica', *Revista Brasileira de Economia* 32 (1978). On monetary policy, J. Pandiá Calógeras, *A política monetária do Brasil* (São Paulo, 1960) has been superseded by Paulo Neuhaus, *História monetária do Brasil* (Rio de Janeiro, 1975) and Carlos Manuel Pelaez and Wilson Suzigan, *História monetária do Brasil* (Rio de Janeiro, 1976); the latter is based on monetarist theory.

The profitability of slavery in its final stage is studied in Leff, *Underdevelopment and development*, H. O. Protocarrero, 'Viabilidade económica de escravidão no Brasil, 1880–1888', *Revista Brasileira de Economia*, 27/1 (1973), and Jaime Reis, 'Abolition and the economics of slavery in northeastern Brazil', *Boletín de Estudios Latinoamericanos y del Caribe*, 17 (1974). See also Robert Slenes, 'The demography and economics of Brazilian slavery: 1850–1888' (unpublished PhD thesis, Stanford University, 1975); Pedro Carvalho de Melo, 'Estimativa de longevidade de escravos no Brasil', *Estudos Económicos* (1983) and Kit Taylor, 'The economics of sugar and slavery in northeastern Brazil', *Agricultural History*, 44/3 (1970). A. Martins Filho and R. B. Martins, 'Slavery in a non-export economy: nineteenth-century Minas Gerais revisited', *HAHR* 63/3 (1983) is an interesting recent contribution.

Another aspect of labour supply that has been much analysed is immigration and internal migration. The essential study is T. W. Merrick and D. Graham, *Population and economic development in Brazil, 1808 to the present* (Baltimore, 1979). See also IV Simpósio Nacional dos Professores Universitários de História, *Anais: colonização e migração* (São Paulo, 1969) and Chiara Vangelista, 'Immigrazione, struttura produttiva e mercato de lavoro in Argentina e in Brasile', *Annali della Fundazione Luigi Einaudi* (1975). In addition to his *Immigrants on the land*, Thomas Holloway has contributed essays on this subject in D. Alden and W. Dean (eds.), *Essays in the socioeconomic history of Brazil and Portuguese India* (Gainesville, 1979) and Duncan and Rutledge (eds.), *Land and labour.* See also his 'Condições de mercado de trabalho e organização de trabalho nas plantações na economia cafeeira de São Paulo, 1885–1915', *Estudos Económicos* (1972). Also important is Michael Hall, 'The origins of mass immigration in Brazil 1871–1914' (unpublished PhD thesis, Columbia University, 1969).

On foreign investment during this period, see Leff, *Underdevelopment and development*; Graham, *Britain and the onset of modernization*; Ana Célia Castro, *As empresas estrangeiras no Brasil, 1860–1913* (Rio de Janeiro, 1979); Victor Valla, *A penetração norte-americana na economia brasileira* (Rio de Janeiro, 1978), and David Joslin, *A century of banking in Latin America* (London, 1963). See also B. R. Magalhães, 'Investimentos ingleses no Brasil e o Banco Londrino e Brasileiro', *Revista Brasileiro de Estudos Políticos*, 49 (1979) and R. Fendt, 'Investimentos ingleses no Brasil, 1870–1913, uma avaliação da política brasileira', *Revista Brasileira de Economia*, 31 (1977). R. Greenhill, 'The Brazilian coffee trade' in D. C. M. Platt (ed.), *Business imperialism 1840–1930* (Oxford, 1978), contests the thesis of neo-imperialism. Emily Rosenberg, 'Anglo-American economic rivalry in Brazil during World War I', *Diplomatic History*, 2 (1978), provides insight into the rise of American influence. Richard Graham, 'A British industry in Brazil: Rio Flour Mills, 1886–1920', *Business History*, 17/1 (1966) examines the largest British manufacturing investment and demonstrates the difficulties of control of overseas firms before the first world war.

The central problem in recent historiography has been that of the development effect of export orientation. Antonio Delfim Netto has argued that the market, up to 1906, permitted Brazil to gain from the trade in coffee: see *O problema do café no Brasil* (São Paulo, 1958). Thereafter, coffee profits were artificially maintained, and the issue has arisen whether the coffee trade or cyclical crises in the trade stimulated further development. Warren Dean, *The industrialization of São Paulo, 1880–1945* (Austin, Texas, 1969); W. Baer and A. Villela, 'Industrial growth and industrialization: revisions in the stages of Brazil's economic development', *Journal of Developing Areas*, 7/1 (1973); and C. M. Pelaez, *História da industrialização brasileira* (Rio de Janeiro, 1972) view export orientation as favouring industrialization, while a contrary view is expressed by Sérgio Silva, *Expansão cafeeira e orígens da indústria no Brasil* (São Paulo, 1976); José de Souza Martins, 'O café e a gênese da industrialização em São Paulo', *Contexto*, 3 (1977); and Wilson Cano, *Raizes da concentração industrial em São Paulo* (São Paulo, 1977). Albert Fishlow's valuable synthesis 'Origins and consequences of import substitution in Brazil' can be found in L. di Marco (ed.), *International economics and development* (New York, 1971). On industrialization, see also Wilson Suzigan, 'Industrialization and economic policy in historical perspective', *Brazilian Economic Studies*, 2 (1976), and F. R. Versiani, 'Industrial investment in an export economy; the Brazilian experience before 1914', *University of London, ILAS Working Papers* 2 (1979), and 'Before the depression: Brazilian industry in the 1920s', in Rosemary Thorp (ed.), *Latin America in the 1930s* (London, 1984).

Other notable studies of industrialization include Armen Mamagonian, 'Notas sobre o processo de industrialização no Brasil', *Boletim do Departamento de Geografía do FFCL de Presidente Prudente*, 2 (1969); Edgard Carone (ed.), *O pensamento industrial no Brasil, 1880–1945* (São Paulo, 1977), a documentary collection, and a historiographical study by E. Salvadori de Decca, 'O tema da industrialização: política e história', *Tudo é História: Cadernos de Pesquisa*, 2 (1978). An important sectoral study is Stanley J. Stein, *The Brazilian cotton manufacture* (Cambridge, Mass., 1957). Alisson Mascarenhas Vaz, 'A indústria textil em Minas Gerais', *Revista de História*, 56/3 (1977) and W. Dean, 'A fábrica São Luiz de Itú: um estudo de arqueologia industrial', *Anais de História*, 8 (1976) concentrate on single firms.

Another recent concern in Brazilian historiography is that of tracing the origin of capital applied in the export sector. Alcir Lenharo, *As tropas da moderação* (São Paulo, 1979) shows the transfer from internal trade into coffee in the early stages of the coffee cycle. Urban food supply is dealt with in Maria Yedda Leite Linhares, *História do abastecimento, uma problemática em questão, 1530–1918* (Brasília, 1979) and M. Y. Leite Linhares and F. C. Teixeira da Silva, *História política do abastecimento* (Brasília, 1979).

6. SOCIETY AND POLITICS

The bibliography of Brazilian society and politics during the period from 1889 to 1930 is examined in Thomas E. Skidmore, 'The historiography of Brazil, 1889–1964', *HAHR*, 55/4 (1975), 716–48, and 56/1 (1976), 81–109. An analysis of the modern trends in Brazilian historiography, in which there are references to works written on the period from 1889 to

1930, can be found in José Roberto do Amaral Lapa, *A história em questão* (Petrópolis, 1976).

A general history of the period is Boris Fausto (ed.), *História geral da civilização brasileira, III: Brasil republicano*, vols. I and II (São Paulo, 1977). See also three valuable books by Edgard Carone: *A República Velha: instituições e classes sociais* (São Paulo, 1970), *A República Velha: evolução política* (São Paulo, 1971) and a collection of documents, *A Primeira República, 1889–1930: texto e contexto* (São Paulo, 1969). Among older studies, worthy of particular note are José Maria Bello, *História da República, 1889–1954* (4th edn, São Paulo, 1959), Eng. trans. by James L. Taylor, *A history of modern Brazil, 1889–1954* (Stanford, 1966); and Leôncio Basbaum, *História sincera da República* (4 vols., São Paulo, 1962–68).

Few scholars have attempted a global analysis of the system and the political process of the period. Most noteworthy is Maria do Carmo Campello de Souza, 'O processo político-partidário na Primeira República', in Carlos Guilherme Mota (ed.), *Brasil em perspectiva* (São Paulo, 1968), 181–252. See also Joseph L. Love, 'Political participation in Brazil, 1881–1969', *Luso-Brazilian Review*, 7/2 (1970), 3–24; and Maria Antonieta de A. G. Parahyba, 'Abertura social e participação política no Brasil, 1870–1920', *Dados*, 7 (1970), 89–102. The most important studies on the individual states and their role in national politics are Joseph L. Love, *Rio Grande do Sul and Brazilian regionalism, 1882–1930* (Stanford, 1971) and *São Paulo in the Brazilian Federation, 1889–1937* (Stanford, 1980); John D. Wirth, *Minas Gerais in the Brazilian Federation, 1889–1937* (Stanford, 1977); Robert M. Levine, *Pernambuco in the Brazilian Federation, 1889–1937* (Stanford, 1978); and Eul-Soo Pang, *Bahia in the First Brazilian Republic: coronelismo and oligarchies, 1889–1934* (Gainesville, 1979). On Minas Gerais, see also Paul Cammack, 'The political economy of the "politics of the states": Minas Gerais and the Brazilian Federation, 1889–1900', *Bulletin of Latin American Research* 2/1 (1982), 51–65.

June Edith Hahner, *Civilian-military relations in Brazil 1889–1898* (Columbia, SC, 1969) is one of the best studies on the years which followed the proclamation of the Republic up until the time when the oligarchic system was firmly established. An analysis of political changes through government expenditure can be found in Richard Graham, 'Government expenditure and political change in Brazil, 1880–1899: who got what', *Journal of Inter-American Studies and World Affairs*, 19/3 (1977), 339–67. See also Eduardo Kugelmas, 'A Primeira República no período de 1891 a 1909', in Paula Beiguelman (ed.), *Pequenos estudos de ciência política* (2nd edn, São Paulo, 1973). An important biography is Afonso Arinos de Melo Franco, *Rodrigues Alves: apogeu e declínio do presidencialismo* (2 vols., Rio de Janeiro, 1973). Very little has been written on the years following the presidential succession crisis of 1909 or on the political effects of the first world war, apart from texts of an apologetic or superficial type. On the other hand, the crisis of the 1920s and the Revolution of 1930 have been the subject of more serious consideration. A general study on the 1920s is Paulo Sérgio Pinheiro, *Política e trabalho no Brasil* (Rio de Janeiro, 1975). There are several works on the *tenentista* movement. A starting point is Virgínio Santa Rosa, *O sentido do tenentismo* (Rio de Janeiro, 1933). A general analysis can be found in John D. Wirth, 'Tenentismo in the Brazilian Revolution of 1930', *HAHR*, 44/2 (1964), 229–42. With regard to episodes in the *tenentista* movement, see Hélio Silva, *1922: sangue na areia de Copacabana* (Rio de Janeiro, 1964) and *A grande marcha* (Rio de Janeiro, 1965); and Neill Macaulay, *The Prestes column: revolution in Brazil* (New York, 1974). A collection of documents has been published by Edgard Carone, *O tenentismo: acontecimentos – personagens – programas* (São Paulo, 1975). One of the most important contemporary studies on the Revolution of 1930 is Alexandre Barbosa Lima Sobrinho, *A verdade sobre a Revolução de Outubro* (São Paulo, 1933). A historiographical analysis can be found in Boris Fausto, *A Revolução de 1930: Historiografia e história*. See also Celina do Amaral Peixoto Moreira Franco *et al.*, 'O contexto político da Revolução de Trinta', *Dados*, 7 (1970), 118–36; and Boris Fausto, 'A Revolução de 1930', in *Brasil em perspectiva*, 253–84.

Although a great deal has been written on the *tenentista* movement, specific studies on the armed forces are few. Worthy of note is José Murilo de Carvalho, 'As forças armadas na Primeira República: o poder desestabilizador', in Boris Fausto (ed.), *História geral da civilização Brasileira, III: O Brasil republicano*, II, 183–234. In addition to Hahner, *Civilian-military relations*, a valuable analysis which takes in the first years of the Republic is John Schulz, 'The Brazilian army in politics, 1850–1894' (unpublished PhD thesis, Princeton University, 1973). Enlightening data on the socialization process of the military can be found in Nelson Werneck Sodré, *História militar do Brasil* (Rio de Janeiro, 1965). Compulsory military service is the theme of the work by Frank D. McCann, 'The nation in arms: obligatory military service during the Old Republic', in Dauril Alden and Warren Dean (eds.), *Essays concerning the socioeconomic history of Brazil and Portuguese India* (Gainesville, 1977), 211–43. There are one or two useful volumes of memoirs and biographies of military figures. Among these are the books by Estévão Leitão de Carvalho, *Dever militar e política partidária* (São Paulo, 1959) and *Memórias de um soldado legalista* (3 vols., Rio de Janeiro, 1961–); Pantaleão Pessoa, *Reminiscências e imposições de uma vida, 1885–1965* (Rio de Janeiro, 1972); Tristão de Alencar Araripe, *Tasso Fragoso: um pouco da história de nosso exército* (Rio de Janeiro, 1960). Almost nothing has been written on the state militias. One of the few works of quality is Heloísa Fernandes, *Política e segurança. Força Pública do estado de São Paulo; fundamentos histórico-sociais* (São Paulo, 1974).

The classic study on clientalistic relations within the power structure is Victor Nunes Leal, *Coronelismo, enxada e voto: o município e o regime representativo no Brasil* (Rio de Janeiro, 1948), Eng. trans. by June Henfrey, *Coronelismo: the municipality and representative government in Brazil* (Cambridge, 1977). An important analysis of clientalism in the north and north-east of Brazil, particularly in the state of Ceará, can be found in Ralph Della Cava's study on Padre Cícero, *Miracle at Joazeiro* (New York, 1970). With regard to the state of Bahia, see Eul-Soo Pang, *Bahia in the First Brazilian Republic.* The links between kinship, family organization and client relations in a north-eastern state are explored in Linda Lewin, *Politics and Parentela in Paraiba: a case study of family based oligarchy in Brazil* (Princeton, 1987). See also Maria Isaura Pereira de Queiroz, *O mandonismo local na vida política brasileira* (São Paulo, 1969).

On plantation society and on immigration, see bibliographical essay 5. Among the social movements in rural areas of Brazil, the Canudos episode is dealt with in Euclides da Cunha's classic account, *Os sertões* (Rio de Janeiro, 1902), Eng. trans. by Samuel Putnam, *Rebellion in the backlands* (Chicago, 1944). The so-called War of the Contestado is the subject of Maurício Vinhas de Queiroz, *Messianismo e conflito social: a guerra sertaneja do Contestado, 1912–1916* (Rio de Janeiro, 1966) and Duglas Teixeira Monteiro, *Os errantes do Novo Século: um estudo sobre o surto milenarista do Contestado* (São Paulo, 1974). The relationship between messianic movements and national politics has been studied by Ralph Della Cava, 'Brazilian messianism and national institutions: a reappraisal of Canudos and Joaseiro', *HAHR*, 48/3 (1968), 402–20. On the phenomenon of banditry in Brazil, see Maria Isaura Pereira da Queiroz, *Os cangaceiros* (São Paulo, 1979), Linda Lewin, 'The oligarchical limitations of social banditry in Brazil: the case of the "good" thief Antônio Silvino',

Past and Present, 82 (1979); Amaury de Souza, 'The cangaço and the politics of violence in northeast Brazil', in Ronald H. Chilcote (ed.), *Protest and resistance in Angola and Brazil: comparative studies* (Berkeley, 1972), 109–31, and Billy Jaynes Chandler, *The bandit king: Lampião of Brazil* (College Station, Texas, 1978).

There are few historical studies devoted to urbanization in this period. The most wide-ranging study is Paul Singer, *Desenvolvimento econômico e evolução urbana; análise da evolução econômica de São Paulo, Blumenau, Porto Alegre e Recife* (São Paulo, 1968). On the city of São Paulo, see Richard M. Morse, *From community to metropolis: a biography of São Paulo, Brazil* (New York, 1974). For the history of Rio de Janeiro, see Eulália Maria Lahmeyer Lobo, *História do Rio de Janeiro. Do capital comercial ao capital industrial e financeiro* (2 vols., Rio de Janeiro, 1978). Michael L. Conniff, *Urban Politics in Brazil. The Rise of Populism, 1928–1945* (Pittsburgh, 1981), although referring more to the post-1930 period, nevertheless contains a good analysis of the politics of the oligarchy of the city of Rio de Janeiro during the 1920s.

Studies on the urban social movements have been mainly limited to the working class. Notable exceptions are Décio Saes, *Classe média e política na Primeira República brasileira* (Petrópolis, 1975) and June E. Hahner, 'Jacobinos versus Galegos', *Journal of Inter-American Studies and World Affairs*, 18/2 (1976), 125–54, which deals with the nationalist and multi-class movement in Rio de Janeiro at the end of the nineteenth century. Among studies on the working-class movement and organization from a predominantly sociological point of view, the most outstanding are Azis Simão, *Sindicato e estado: suas relações na formação do proletariado de São Paulo* (São Paulo, 1966); José Albertino Rodrigues, *Sindicato e desenvolvimento no Brasil* (São Paulo, 1968); Leôncio Martins Rodrigues, *Conflito industrial e sindicalismo no Brasil* (São Paulo, 1966). From the point of view of social history, see Sheldon L. Maram, *Anarquistas, imigrantes e o movimento operário brasileiro, 1890–1920* (Rio de Janeiro, 1979) and Boris Fausto, *Trabalho urbano e conflito social* (São Paulo, 1976). Michael M. Hall, 'Immigration and the early São Paulo working class', *JGSWGL*, 12 (1975) provides a convincing criticism of the theory that the foreign immigrant in São Paulo was predisposed to radical ideology. A detailed description of the anarchist and communist organizations can be found in John W. F. Dulles, *Anarchists and communists in Brazil, 1900–1935* (Austin, Texas, 1973). On the formation of the Brazilian Communist party, see Ronald H. Chilcote, *The Brazilian*

Communist party: conflict and integration, 1922–1972 (New York, 1974) and Astrogildo Pereira, *Formação do PCB, 1922–1928. Notas e documentos* (Rio de Janeiro, 1962). Documents on the labour movement during the period have been published in Paulo Sérgio Pinheiro and Michael M. Hall, *A classe operária no Brasil, 1889–1930: Documentos*, vol. I, *O movimento operário* (São Paulo, 1979), vol. II, *Condições de vida e de trabalho, relações com os empresários e o estado* (São Paulo, 1981); and in Edgard Carone, *Movimento operário no Brasil, 1877–1944* (São Paulo, 1979).

On relations between blacks and whites in Brazil, see Florestan Fernandes, *A integração do negro à sociedade de classes* (Rio de Janeiro, 1964), translated and abridged under the title *The negro in Brazilian society* (New York, 1969), and Thomas E. Skidmore, *Black into white: race and nationality in Brazilian thought* (New York, 1974). A bibliography on women, including a general history of women, family organization and the feminist movement, was published by the Carlos Chagas Foundation in São Paulo: *Mulher brasileira. Bibliografia anotada* (São Paulo, 1979). See, in addition, June E. Hahner, 'Women and work in Brazil, 1850–1920: a preliminary investigation', in Alden and Dean (eds.), *Essays concerning the socioeconomic history of Brazil and Portuguese India*, 87–117, and 'Feminism, women's rights and the suffrage movement in Brazil, 1850–1932', *LARR*, 15/1 (1980), 65–111; Branca Moreira Alves, *Ideologia e feminismo: a luta da mulher pelo voto no Brasil* (Petrópolis, 1980). For the history of the Catholic church, the most important work is Margaret Patrice Todaro, 'Pastors, prophets and politicians: a study of the Brazilian Catholic church, 1916–1945' (unpublished PhD thesis, Columbia University, 1971). See also Ralph Della Cava, 'Catholicism and society in twentieth-century Brazil', *LARR*, 11/2 (1976), 7–50. The best studies on the role of the intellectuals and education are respectively Sérgio Miceli, *Intelectuais e classe dirigente no Brasil, 1920–1945* (São Paulo, 1979) and Jorge Nagle, *Educação e sociedade na Primeira República* (São Paulo, 1974). An important recent work on the cultural life of Rio de Janeiro during the Old Republic is Nicolau Sevcenko, *Literatura como missão. Tensões sociais e criação cultural na Primeira República* (Rio de Janeiro, 1983). On Brazilian art and architecture, music and literature in this period, see also *CHLA* IV, bibliographical essay 11. Finally, a pioneer work on the violence of the state against the popular classes is Paulo Sérgio Pinheiro, 'Violencia do estado e classes populares', *Dados*, 22 (1979), 5–24.

INDEX

Printed in the United States
71450LV00004B/1-30

9 780521 368377